RAF Police Dogs
on Patrol

An Illustrated History of the Deployment of
Dogs in the Royal Air Force 1942-2004

STEPHEN R. DAVIES

Woodfield

RAF POLICE DOGS ON PATROL

Keith,

Enjoy

Newton &
Judy

July 2015

First published in 2005 by

WOODFIELD PUBLISHING
Bognor Regis, West Sussex, England
www.woodfieldpublishing.com

© Stephen R. Davies, 2005

The right of Stephen R. Davies
to be identified as Author of this work
has been asserted in accordance with
the Copyright, Designs and Patents Act 1988

ISBN 1- 84683-000-1

Contents

List of Photographs

The Author

Stephen R Davies was a member of the Royal Air Force Police for 25 years. In 1975 he joined the Royal Air Force as a policeman and during his service completed tours of duty in the United Kingdom and numerous countries around the globe. He qualified as a specialist in Royal Air Force Police Special Investigation and Counter-Intelligence matters and successfully completed the Home Office Detective Training program and Drug Enforcement courses with the UK civil police and United States Air Force Office of Special Investigations. In 1991 he qualified as an instructor and lectured at the Airmans' Command School and the RAF Police School. In April 1997, he published his first book, 'Fiat Justitia – A History of the Royal Air Force Police'.

In the Spring of 2000, he retired from the Royal Air Force and together with his wife, moved out to Portugal where they now live. The author's research into the Royal Air Force Police continues and he is currently working on a new book to commemorate the first 100 years (1918 – 2018) of this unique branch of the Royal Air Force.

Steve Davies (photo taken in New Zealand whilst on exchange in 1987).

Foreword

By Squadron Leader P C Somerville RAF (Retired)
Formerly Officer Commanding RAF Police Dog Training Squadron
and Joint Service Dog Training Wings at Newton and Melton Mowbray

RAF Police dog handlers have served in a wide variety of climates during their 60 years of service to the Royal Air Force. From the damp chills of Scotland's west coast to the burning heat of Aden, and from icy German winters to the humidity of the Malayan jungle, the RAF Police and their dogs have patrolled in all conditions. There is nothing cut and dried about being a dog handler; patrolling with a dog can be tedious, boring and monotonous, besides being very uncomfortable at times. There are many good moments as well of course, and seeing a dog progress in its ability as a police dog always gives enormous satisfaction to a dog handler. Trials work is challenging and extremely rewarding, and for those handlers with a degree of showmanship there was always the chance of a tour with the excellent RAF Police Dog Demonstration Team.

Unlike his or her counterpart in the civilian police, or indeed in other areas of the Armed Forces, the RAF Police dog handler always invariably works longer shifts, with a greater degree of responsibility. Six hour patrols are normal, with additional patrol time during times of tension or when a major exercise is sprung on the station at short notice. Additionally, the RAF Police dog handler is expected to take decisive action at times when immediate support is not readily available, and when time is of the essence. I recall patrolling the perimeter fence of RAF Khormaksar in Aden in 1964, when the airfield was under constant threat of intrusion. The outer perimeter was covered by the Parachute Regiment at the time, whose fighting patrols were armed to the teeth. They were astounded to come across the dog handlers, working on their own, and armed with a few rounds of ammunition and a .38 Smith & Wesson revolver. I, like my colleagues, was not in the least concerned; after all we had our dogs.

I must also pay tribute to other very special people, who have worked alongside us. First of all we were always well supported by the kennel maids, who could sometimes put us all to shame by their efficient handling of difficult and awkward dogs. Secondly, we were well served in our training by many exceptional civilian instructors, who gave many years of loyal and very professional service to our trade. People sometimes remark that the dog trade is very close knit, and very much a family; a description I believe to be true. As far as I'm concerned, the RAF Police dog handler was and is the best of the best, and I am immensely proud of my long association with the dog handlers, civilian instructors and kennel maids who formed our part of the RAF Police trade group.

Stephen R Davies has given us a wide and interesting view of the RAF Police dog handler, in a book spanning the 60 years we have served the Service. I am sure it will be of enormous interest to all our colleagues, past and present, who have worked with the best military working dog in the world bar none.

Peter Somerville

Introduction

On a large military airfield in some far off part of the world a RAF Police dog handler and his German Shepherd dog are on patrol protecting the aircraft that are standing on the dispersal area prepared and ready for their next mission. It's a moonless night filled with the sounds of the local wildlife and a gentle breeze offers some relief from the oppressive sticky heat. In the darkness the dog suddenly picks up on an unfamiliar scent and as his hackles begin to rise, he strains at his leash. The handler, attuned to his dog's reactions knows that something is amiss. He immediately sends a discreet radio message to alert the staff in the RAF Police Control Room as the dog leads him towards the source of the scent. Suddenly, a figure breaks cover from behind a nearby building and starts to run off into the darkness where he thinks it will be safe. The handler immediately shouts out the warning, 'Halt or I'll release my Dog', but the man foolishly ignores the warning and continues to run, hoping to make good his escape. At that point the handler releases his dog and the chase begins. In a matter of seconds the dog has caught up with his quarry and brought him down to earth. The dog stands guard over the terrified man until the handler arrives to take charge. The dog is called off and the man is ordered to stand up with his hands in the air. While the dog continues to guard the intruder, the handler uses his radio again to request urgent assistance at his location. A RAF Police mobile patrol is despatched to the scene and as the intruder is searched and taken away, questions urgently need to be addressed; who is the man, what was he doing in the area, where had he been and what had he taken or left behind? At the end of the shift another incident was recorded and another attempt to interfere with the country's defences was foiled by the vigilance of the RAF Police corporal and his dog...

The domesticated dog (*Canis familiaris*) has coexisted with human beings as a working partner and household pet in all eras and cultures since the days of the cave dwellers. It is generally believed that the direct ancestor of the domestic dog is the wolf, originally found throughout Europe, Asia, and North America. The first dogs that joined forces with the early cave dwellers were used for their keen hunting instincts and abilities, as a means of procuring food to eat and skins for clothing, and for protection against predators. Subsequent civilisations that developed in both the eastern and western hemispheres depended greatly on dogs and their cunning in the struggle for survival. Asians, Egyptians, Assyrians, Greeks, and Romans all used dogs as guards, companions, and hunters and in times of war. Archaeological discoveries, cave drawings, paintings, ancient artefacts and written records all verify the role of dogs in early cultures in all parts of the world. The dog mainly used by the RAF is of course the Alsatian or German Shepherd dog. The dog we know today had its origins around the end of the 19th Century in Germany. Several breeders, who also happened to be shepherds, began to inter-breed the then existing strains of the Wurtenberg sheep dog with sheep dogs from Thuringia. The two strains each had their particular advantages for sheep folding, and the object was to combine the good qualities of both strains into one single breed. Both dogs had previously possessed splendid qualities of alertness, reliability as guard dogs, were keenly intelligent, and responsive to training with very strong attachments to their masters. However, too many had been of a clumsy aspect, small in size, with a thick head and pointed nose. The majority carried ears and tails anyhow, with coats of all kinds and colour. The efforts of the pioneer breeders were eminently successful, and attracted the attention of several noted experts. Thus was laid the foundation of the society of the German Shepherd dog.

The Royal Air Force Police was formed on the 1st April 1918, at the birth of the RAF, and has developed a colourful history along the way to becoming the large and highly professional organisation of today. At its height at the end of World War II, the Royal Air Force Police had some 21,000 men and women serving within its ranks. The relationship forged between the Royal Air Force Police and its dogs, has over the years, been a very special one. Consequently, up until only recently, if you told anyone that you were a member of the Royal Air Force Police, they would invariably want to know all about your police dog, assuming that every member of the branch was automatically issued with a dog when appointed. Such was the high esteem that the service and the public held of that special relationship, which began during the dark years of World War II.

I will now tell you the remarkable story of just how the Royal Air Force Police came to be involved with their dogs, and more importantly, how they became a world-class professional organisation in the training and use of police dogs in a wide scope of duties which included general patrolling, anti-terrorist operations, tracking, searching for dangerous drugs, searching for arms and explosives, and of course public relations exercises.

I served with the RAF Police for just over twenty-five years and although I was never a dog-handler myself, I was on a number of occasions responsible, as the senior NCO in charge of the RAF Police, for the overall management of the dog section under my control. Therefore, I think I am well qualified to state that the RAF Police (men and women) dog handlers are indeed a very special group of people within the branch.

Although to the ill-informed, both within the RAF and outside of it, dog handling duties seem to be an easy and glamorous life, in reality however, nothing could be further from the truth. The job of a dog handler demands a lot. The men and women who volunteer for such duties do so because they love the challenge of working with dogs. In doing so, a considerable amount of their time is dedicated to the training, care and welfare of their charges. Likewise, the kennel-maids who joined the RAF to look after the dogs in kennels did so because they loved working with dogs, even though their chances of promotion were slim. As for the job itself; well those who served with the Royal Air Force Police Dog Demonstration Team were indeed constantly in the public eye and were without doubt *the front line ambassadors* of the branch. Alternatively, those employed on specialist drug and explosive detection duties were always proving their worth in very difficult and often dangerous situations. Yet the majority of dog handlers employed on normal patrol duties rarely ever-encountered real intruders as they quietly patrolled their aircraft dispersal areas, special storage areas or technical sites, although there were notable exceptions. Indeed, their presence was in itself a very real deterrent to any would-be intruder or criminal.

Having personally watched many of the dogs in action during numerous training periods I can quite understand why their presence has provided such a deterrent over the years. I, for one would certainly not like to be within the sights of a RAF Police dog that had been released by its handler, after giving that famous command, *'Halt, or I'll release my Dog'.*

Once again however, I make no apologies for the fact that many of the remarkable success stories connected with Royal Air Force Police dogs are not mentioned within this book, but that is probably because many of those events were taken at the time as being just a routine part of the job. Consequently, they were not considered to be important enough to be recorded anywhere that has survived the test of time. Having said that, I am sure that what has been recorded over the past sixty years will stand proud to highlight a most successful and exciting period in the history of the Royal Air Force Police and indeed, the Royal Air Force as a whole.

It was somewhat ironic that on the 24th November 2004, sixty years after the RAF Police started officially using dogs, a memorial was dedicated by The Princess Royal in Park Lane Mayfair, to honour the sacrifices made by all creatures, great and small, during times of conflict to assist British Forces around the globe. Carrying the simple inscription *'They had no Choice'*, the huge memorial, designed by David Backhouse, comprises a carved Portland stone wall alongside bronze sculptures of a stallion, a dog and two mules carrying battle equipment.

In preparing this book, I would like to thank the many people who took the time to write to me with their stories or to provide photographs or other snippets of information. However, I feel that special thanks must be offered to Peter Somerville who kindly agreed to write the foreword to the book, and to Michael O'Neill, Clive Gilmore and Stewart McArdle, who besides helping directly with this complicated project, channelled a great deal of valuable information my way from various other sources.

Finally, during its existence as a single service training establishment, the Motto of all RAF Police Dog Training Schools established at home and abroad was simply; *"Don't punish your dog – train it!"*

Stephen R Davies
October 2005

1.   1942 – 1951

Great Britain declared war on Nazi Germany on 3rd September 1939 following
their invasion of Poland two days earlier. When Great Britain declared war,
British military commanders felt that it would be a war of machines and mecha-
nisation and that there would be no room for the animal contingent so
prominent in the Great War of 1914-18. Because of that belief and the prospect
of severe food rationing, well over 200,000 dogs alone were sent to their deaths
during the first four months of the conflict. Reports however, slowly trickled
through that Germany was using a huge number of trained dogs to assist their
military forces in a variety of defensive areas. Indeed, Germany boasted in its
newspapers that Airedales, Boxers, German Shepherds and Doberman Pincers
had been enlisted to help its armies win the war. Despite these reports British
military commanders were not at all impressed until Colonel E H Richardson
and Lieutenant Colonel J Y Baldwin DSO took up the argument. A later demonstration using trained dogs convinced the government of the day to change its
mind and as a result British dogs started to help the war effort instead of being
marched off to their deaths. Unfortunately, because so many dogs had been
destroyed so early in the war there was, in fact a shortage of healthy and suitable
dogs and of the 10,000 dogs offered for military service only about 3,500 were
found to be acceptable. As a result, the Royal Society for the Protection of Animals, the Animal Protection Societies of Scotland and Ireland and The Canine
Defence League agreed to help with the recruitment of suitable dogs. Initially,
Lieutenant Colonel Baldwin, an Army officer on reserve service, began training
dogs for security duties with the *Rotal Air Screws Aircraft Company.*

Although a British Expeditionary Force had been sent over to France soon
after war was declared, they were evacuated to Britain in May and early June
1940, just before a massive German force swept into Belgium and Northern
France. At that point with Nazi Germany occupying most of Western Europe, it
seemed that Great Britain stood alone to face the imminent threat of a German
invasion. Winston Churchill had become the British Prime Minister and had
quickly rallied the British people in preparing to resist an invasion by all means.
Factories worked flat out to produce weapons and other items required for the
war effort; the people worked long hours to produce those items and the food
needed to sustain a nation under siege, and the British armed forces were
strengthened. In respect of the RAF, hundreds of new recruits joined the ranks

each week and new airfields were established along the east coast and in the southern counties. New aircraft were produced and sent out to the new airfields and the newly recruited pilots and aircrew trained non-stop to enhance their fighting skills. During that summer the German Luftwaffe had attacked RAF airfields and other military installations around the country in an effort to destroy Britain's air force before launching their seaborne invasion from France. However, the RAF had risen to the challenge during the *'Battle of Britain'* and had shown the Germans that they were made of better things. As such, the German high command had been forced to change tactics and instead of attacking RAF airfields and military installations, the Luftwaffe began attacking British town, cities and factories. During this period, the establishment of the RAF Police, under the control of the Provost Marshal, Group Captain F G Stammers, had grown considerably in line with the growth of the RAF.

Although a number of RAF stations and units throughout the country had during the early part of World War II, been using locally obtained dogs to guard airfields and the aircraft on them, our story officially begins in November 1942 when Flight Lieutenant Hugh Bathurst-Brown, the Station Adjutant at RAF Staverton, located just outside Gloucester, received a telephone call from Lieutenant Colonel Baldwin. After a brief introduction, Baldwin asked Bathurst-Brown if he would like the appointment of commanding one of the two newly formed Ministry of Aircraft Production Guard Dog Schools. Bathurst-Brown was quite fond of dogs and had fortunately become rather bored with his routine life at Staverton and so he immediately accepted the offer, even though he had no real experience of training or even dealing with dogs. Lieutenant Colonel 'Jimmy' Baldwin on the other hand, had plenty of experience on the subject. He had served in the trenches of Picardy in France, during the Great War of 1914 – 18 and had been highly impressed by the way the German Army had used their war dogs to good effect. Not only did they utilise them in the guarding role but they also used them to locate their wounded men and to pull their ammunition supplies around the battlefield. The dogs, being used by the German troops were called *Deutsche Scheaferhunde*, or German Shepherd dogs and they possessed a keen nose, speed, endurance, aggressiveness and above all, courage. In addition, they seemed able to adapt to all types of weather conditions. The breed was eventually introduced into England in 1919 and because 'all things German' were highly unpopular at that time it was first registered with the Kennel Club of Great Britain, as the *Alsatian wolf dog*. Baldwin was so impressed by what he had seen of the war dogs, that he later discussed the matter with a close friend, Captain Moore Brabazon, who had commanded the first air photography unit in France and who was at the time, serving with the Royal Flying Corps. After the war ended, Baldwin left the Army and pursued his interest in that particular breed of dog and eventually established his own breeding kennels, which he called 'Picardy Kennels' after the area where he first saw them in action. In addition, he became something of an expert when it came to the subject of the Alsatian breed.

Baldwin maintained his close links with Moore Brabazon, who, after leaving the Royal Flying Corps, went into politics. When war broke out again in 1939, Brabazon was appointed as the Minister of Aircraft Production and found that he was responsible for thousands of expensive aircraft, a large number of air-fields and various storage depots around the country. Of course, with the increasing threat of German espionage and sabotage looming, he was deeply troubled with the problem of providing adequate security protection for his valuable assets. Remembering the conversation he had shared with his friend Jimmy Baldwin some years earlier on the subject of dogs, he turned to him for advice and assistance on the matter. Consequently, Baldwin was able to persuade him that dogs were indeed the most effective and economical method of guard-ing his interests. After all, dogs had been used successfully to protect and defend armies and their assets going back over many centuries. Convinced that dogs were the only economical way ahead, Brabazon put his proposals to the govern-ment and shortly after obtained the necessary authority to form the Ministry of Aircraft Production Guard Dog School. As a consequence, Lieutenant Colonel Baldwin was duly offered and readily accepted the appointment of Dog Advisor and Chief Training Officer. However, the actual administration of the school was to be carried out by the RAF, although the RAF Police at that stage were not involved in the scheme. At the time, Lieutenant Colonel Baldwin was described as a 'Grand old chap' who used to wear his lieutenant colonel's uniform from the Great War and who used to salute with either hand, as was the tradition during the Great War depending on which side you were passing the person to be saluted.

Some time later, Flight Lieutenant Bathurst-Brown, having received his post-ing notice from the Air Ministry, left his office in Staverton and reported to Woodfold, the site of one of the new schools, situated only five miles down the road. The other school had been established at Beoley near Redditch. While Woodfold turned out to be a very comfortable requisitioned country manor house, set in its own pleasant grounds, the facilities made available to the school turned out to be rather sparse indeed. Bathurst-Brown as he was shown around his new command, noted that the school comprised a garage, which was to be used as their headquarters and administrative centre, and several stables around a courtyard, which were to be used to kennel the dogs. At around the same time a

RAF sergeant was posted in to Woodfold to assist Bathurst-Brown in setting everything up, but it turned out to be several more weeks before any further staff or indeed any dogs arrived to join them. Baldwin however, carefully gathered around him the willing assistance of true 'Alsatianists' and enthusiastic trainers from around the country such as Mrs Margaret Griffin, who was later awarded the British Empire Medal for her work with rescue dogs, Miss Holman, Mr Fricker and Mr Burrow to name just a few. Indeed, one of Mrs Griffin's own breeding bitches, 'Crumstone Irma', would later be awarded the Dickens Medal for gallantry; the canine equivalent to the Victoria Cross. The dogs that were initially trained at Woodfold were all donated by members of the public or recovered from dogs' homes and consisted of a wide variety of breeds.

In December Group Captain F G Stammers retired as Provost Marshal and was replaced by Air Commodore O W de Putron, a veteran of the Great War, who had served in the Durham Light Infantry and the Royal Flying Corps before transferring into the RAF in 1918.

Aircraftsman R F Young became one of the first RAF dog handlers to be trained at Woodfold in 1942. Although he and his fellow trainee dog handlers were accommodated at Staverton, they had to march between Staverton and the kennels at Woodfold several times a day during the course of their training. The training facilities were very basic and he recalls that there were two civilian instructors to train them. Shortly after his arrival there, he was teamed up with a three-year old German Shepherd bitch by the name of Flick. Flick's owners, who lived in Scotland, had lent their dog to the RAF to assist with the war effort, and because of that, Aircraftsman Young had to write personally, once a month, to the dog's owners informing them of how the dog was getting on. In addition, each donated dog was issued with a numbered bronze disk and enrolled in the PDSA (People's Dispensary for Sick Animals) Allied Forces Mascot Club; Flick being issued the serial number 158. As soon as the dog training program got under way it attracted student dog handlers from both the RAF and the United States 9th American Air Force, who were keen to undertake their initial six-week train-ing course. Although at that stage, the RAF Police had still not shown any interest in working with dogs in the United Kingdom.

The Allies, realising that the Germans had used gliders successfully during previous operations, urgently stepped up the production of the Horsa, a rather ungainly beast made of plywood, which had a wing span of eighty-eight feet. Although it had to be towed into the air by a conventional aircraft it was capable of carrying thirty men together with their personal combat equipment. At the time, production of seaborne 'landing craft' capable of taking assault troops onto the beaches of France was also in full swing and the Horsa gliders were in essence the 'landing' craft from the skies; a most efficient and cost effective way of doubling the air transport fleet required for any planned invasion.

In early 1944 at RAF Brize Norton in Oxfordshire at least two Horsa gliders with their towing aircraft would be in the air at any given time constantly practicing manoeuvres for the big event. With the build-up continuing towards D-Day, security at the base was high and a RAF guard dog section had been established to patrol the base. Leading Aircraftsman R H Gregory was one of the dog handlers assigned to the important duty of helping to protect the base from the threat of sabotage and espionage. He had been called up for RAF service in the early part of the summer in 1942 when he was just eighteen. Originally he had opted to become a wireless operator and after being kitted out with his uniform at RAF Padgate he had been sent up to Blackpool for his initial training. He had been accommodated in civilian billets in the town and the daily routine of learning to march, weapons drill and how to use the bayonet had been carried out on the promenade. After completing his recruit training he was sent over to the wireless training school, which had been set up in rooms located above the town's branch of Woolworths. Unfortunately, he soon realised that the role of a wireless operator was not for him and subsequently volunteered to become a dog handler. While he was waiting to join a dog training course he had been sent to RAF Eynsham, located between Whitney and Oxford. The unit was a huge bomb storage facility lying under miles and miles of camouflage netting to hide it from patrolling enemy aircraft. Security at the unit was strict and undertaken by personnel from the Military Field Security Police. During his time at Eynsham he joined a 'decontamination squad' and had been sent off to Barnard Castle in the North-east on a train that had two freight trucks loaded with containers of lethal mustard gas. Avoiding main line routes and air raids, the journey was slow and uncomfortable, but the train arrived safely at its destination two days later. Shortly after returning to Eynsham, he received his orders to report to RAF Staverton to begin his training as a dog handler. During his time at Staverton he recalled seeing Lieutenant Colonel Baldwin often, but the day-to-day training program was in the hands of Mr Norman Braithwaite, a civilian dog trainer, and one of Baldwin's hand picked team. After successfully completing his training, Aircraftsman Gregory and his dog were posted to No 6MU (Maintenance Unit) at RAF Brize Norton. During the months that followed, he and a few of the other dog handlers paid a number of welfare visits with their dogs to the John Radcliffe Hospital in Oxford where they proved to be very popular with many of the patients but especially with the children. Members of the dog section together with their dogs also took part in several 'Wings for Victory' parades that were organised in the locality. As such, it seems that these events were the forerunners of the later organised public dog displays around the country. Additionally, the members of the dog section formed part of the guard of honour for their HRH the Duke and Duchess of Gloucester who paid an official visit to the unit. While speaking to Aircraftsman Gregory, the Duke was keen to know if the handlers took their dogs with them when they were granted leave.

Since the beginning of the war a considerable amount of manpower had been taken up by the RAF in providing physical security measures to protect its stations, aircraft and equipment from the threat of sabotage, espionage and pilfering to supply the demands of the 'black market'. Not only was the practice expensive but it also diverted a large number of essential personnel from other more important tasks connected with the war effort. As a result, a number of solutions were discussed at the Provost Marshal's Office, in Princes Gate, London, in an effort to try and alleviate the problem. As various solutions were introduced, the use of properly trained guard dogs and dog handlers was suggested by Squadron Leader S Barnes and Squadron Leader E Dangerfield; both Assistant Provost Marshals (APM), employed as staff officers to Air Commodore de Putron, the Provost Marshal. With the security threat of any German invasion disappearing, it seemed that there was a real possibility that the Ministry of Aircraft Production Guard Dog Training School would be disbanded towards the end of the war. Accordingly, Squadron Leader Barnes arranged for the Provost Marshal to meet Lieutenant Colonel Baldwin, and more importantly arranged for him to view a demonstration of what the dogs and their handlers could do. The Provost Marshal was extremely impressed with what he saw and when he returned to London he suggested that the Ministry of Aircraft Production Guard Dog Training School, if disbanded, should be taken over by the RAF Police. He argued with senior officers that the future use of dogs by the RAF Police would be a very cost effective and efficient way of protecting airfields and their valuable assets. After a considerable battle within the Air Ministry, approval was finally granted from the Air Minister and the Chief of Air Staff, for the dog school to become part of the RAF Police organisation. It was an important turning point in the history of the RAF Police and at Woodfold on the 24th March 1944, the first batch of RAF Police NCOs commenced their training to become professional dog handlers. By then, arrangements were underway for the Ministry of Aircraft Production's Guard Dog School to be taken over by the RAF Police and re-titled as the 'RAF Police Dog Training School'. As the limited facilities at Woodfold became far too small, the dog school was duly transferred from its cramped accommodation at Woodfold to larger premises at RAF Staverton, which was able to provide large areas for training (The area used by the school at that time today runs alongside the current M5 motorway in Gloucestershire). Although

Lieutenant Colonel Baldwin remained as the Chief Training Officer, Flight Lieutenant Bathurst-Brown had retired and for the first time the school was commanded by a RAF provost officer, Flight Lieutenant R D Cooper, a lively Australian with the nickname 'Digger', who apparently lived life to the full and very much enjoyed driving fast cars and gambling, especially when it came to horse racing.

Shortly after the RAF Police took over the Ministry of Aircraft Production Dog School (MAPGDS), many of the airmen who had been temporarily assigned as RAF dog handlers were transferred over to the RAF Police. Acting Corporal R F Young and his dog Flick, who were by then stationed at a satellite unit of RAF Kinloss near the town of Forres in Scotland, were amongst those affected by the takeover. It was at that unit that the dog handlers were tasked with ensuring that the WAAF cooks were woken up at a quarter to five in the morning so that they could prepare breakfast for the troops. Corporal Young recalls that the duty dog handler would fasten his dog up outside the cook's accommodation before going inside to quietly wake up those detailed to prepare breakfast. The procedure continued without problems until a fierce looking WAAF corporal was posted into the unit one day and brought an instant end to the dog handlers entering the WAAF accommodation. As luck had it, Corporal Young was on duty the night following the issue of the new order and the new WAAF corporal was one of those detailed for an early call. Consequently, Corporal Young approached the WAAF accommodation just before the dedicated time and using the butt of his Sten-gun, banged rather loudly on the wooden wall of the hut close to the bed space occupied by the WAAF corporal. Needless to say, that everyone sleeping in the whole hut was woken rather abruptly by the 'not-so discreet wake up call'. Strangely though, later the same day the WAAF corporal swiftly rescinded her earlier order, and common sense prevailed once more at the unit.

In March, as the RAF Police were taking over the MAPGDS, Aircraftsman Gregory was sent to RAF Weeton to undertake an initial police course; No 376, and was subsequently promoted to acting corporal on his return to RAF Brize Norton. The dog patrols at RAF Brize Norton were maintained around the clock, but for safety reasons they operated on the very edge of the 'active' airfield. After being pulled into the air by the towing aircraft, the heavy cables would be released from between the aircraft and the airborne glider and would silently snake down to earth causing serious injury or even death to anyone below who might be unfortunate enough to be struck by one. On the 24th of May, the station commander received detailed orders to seal the station; special security passes were issued; unauthorised visitors were denied entry; no one could leave without special permission; telephone calls of a non-operational nature could not be made off the camp; the post boxes were sealed and all outgoing mail was censored. As part of the security ring thrown around the station, the patrols by the dog handlers were intensified with personnel taking their meals at the No 6MU canteen in between going out on patrol. Outside the base the local roads were patrolled by the Air Ministry Constabulary and RAF Police from the local mobile unit. Whilst on patrol one night at one of the many aircraft dispersal areas, Corporal Gregory's dog became quite agitated and indicated towards one of the gliders, the side door of which was open. Upon investigating, he discovered a young couple inside who were passionately embracing each other and somewhat oblivious to his presence. His dog barked which abruptly interrupted their activities and they were instructed to come outside where he identified them as a sergeant pilot and a WAAF corporal. Although they were in a prohibited area, the deeply embarrassed couple, who had no doubt received the fright of their lives, were allowed to return to the domestic area without formal action being taken against them.

At the height of the German V1 rocket campaign against London and the southern counties, certain key figures at the Air Ministry asked if it was possible to train dogs to detect the presence of human victims buried under rubble and debris. The question was subsequently put to Lieutenant Colonel Baldwin who thought it was indeed possible. Consequently, a number of dogs were taken from the RAF Police School, to Birmingham, where they took part in an exercise to find a number of men who had been carefully 'buried' under about four feet of debris. The exercise was highly successful and the dogs located all the victims very effectively. As a result of their success, the dogs were sent soon after to London to help the hard-pressed emergency services in locating victims buried as a result of the rocket attacks. Lieutenant Colonel Baldwin accompanied the dogs to London, one of which was Air Dog Gundo under the control of his handler Corporal A Thompson. During their first night in the capital, a number of rockets had hit various buildings and the RAF Police Dog teams were summoned to assist in searching for the victims, however, the conditions at the various sites were appalling. The quiet ruins in Birmingham, where the trials had been so successful, were a far cry from the chaos and devastation of London at the height of the German rocket attacks. Water and gas mains had burst and earth had showered up into the air and was thrown everywhere. The smell was foul and the overall conditions were about as bad as they could ever be. It seemed hopeless amongst all the chaos and the confusion but Lieutenant Colonel Baldwin and his team went ahead with searching an area that had been declared free of victims. After about fifteen minutes, a handler reported that his dog had made a positive indication. The spot was marked and the dog was taken away. A second dog was brought into the area and it also indicated on the same spot. The search continued and a further two indications were given by the dogs and three bodies were subsequently recovered by the rescue parties. After that occasion, the dogs were used to good effect and worked well with the other rescuers. Depending on the site being searched, different techniques were used; for instance if the building had been completely demolished then the dog would run free over the area trying to pick up the scent or sounds of buried victims. If located, the dog would bark and start scratching at the surface debris. If however, the building concerned was partly demolished and directly inaccessible to the rescue squad or the dog handler then the dog would be placed on a long lead before being sent inside to search for victims. If the dog indicated that someone was trapped inside then the rescue squad would start pulling debris away to affect the rescue. On one occasion, Corporal Thompson was a little concerned when Gundo refused to enter one partially demolished house on the long lead. It seemed that whatever Corporal Thompson tried to do to get the dog going, the dog just simply refused to enter. The dog was taken away and when rescue workers entered the house they quickly discovered a gas leak and rapidly evacuated the area. It seems that Gundo's keen sense of smell had detected the gas from outside the building and that is why he refused to enter it. During their two-week detachment to the capital, Gundo and Corporal Thompson were responsible for finding eighteen trapped victims. However, in the first four months, RAF Police dogs managed to locate over five hundred victims buried in the rubble.

Corporal Thompson, who had been a farm worker in civilian life, had joined the RAF in early 1941 and after completing his training was mustered into the trade of Aircrafthand. However, when volunteers were required for dog handling duties he immediately volunteered and was accepted almost straight away. Ten days after arriving at RAF Staverton / Woodfold, he had been teamed up with his dog, a German Shepherd named Gundo, who he recalled looked rather fierce. Gundo, like so many of the dogs being trained by the MAPGDS, had been donated for war service by his civilian owners. After successfully completing the training course, Aircraftsman Thompson and Gundo were posted to a RAF maintenance unit where together they carried out nightly security patrols to deter any would be thief or saboteur.

At some point before D-Day, members of the dog section, including Corporal Gregory, were tasked to guard a Luftwaffe Heinkel He280 jet powered aircraft that had crashed nearby. The recently developed jet aircraft had quickly been recovered to No 6MU at RAF Brize Norton, where it was kept under tight security whilst being examined by a team of experts. During daylight hours the hangar containing the aircraft was guarded by officers of the Air Ministry Constabulary but at night security was enhanced around the area by the deployment of RAF dog teams. Rumours circulating around the base were rife until the morning of the 5th June, when the 'Air Armada' took to the skies from RAF Brize Norton and the nearby airfields at RAF Upper Heyford and RAF Fairford. Eventually news arrived back that the Allied Expeditionary Force had launched an invasion onto the beaches of Normandy in France as the starting point to liberate Western Europe and bring about the defeat of Nazi Germany. As part of that force, the Headquarters 2 Tactical Air Force (2TAF) had been formed to provide the necessary air cover and offensive air operations to the invasion force as it moved from France towards Germany. From that point on, the base was extremely busy with a steady stream of aircraft, flying in and then straight back out again loaded with equipment that would be parachuted down to the troops who were fighting it out in Normandy.

A few weeks after the D-Day landings in France, the dog-section at RAF Brize Norton was no longer required and was therefore disbanded. The dogs were sent across to the RAF Police Dog School at Staverton and the RAF dog handlers were posted to various RAF stations around the country. Those who had completed their police training were posted as RAF Police NCOs while those who had not were posted as 'RAF Policemen under-training'. After a short spell at RAF Shepherds Grove, near Bury St Edmunds, Corporal Gregory returned to the RAF Police School at Weeton, where together with two colleagues from RAF Brize Norton, he completed a further police training course before being posted to RAF Fazakerly in Liverpool, where he was employed on station duties within the guardroom. The guardroom at Fazakerly was a busy place and the cells were always occupied by prisoners arrested for a wide spectrum of offences. While Corporal Gregory was stationed at Fazakerly he was detailed on two separate occasions to escort prisoners to the *'Glass-House'*, or to give it its correct name, the Military Detention Barracks at Chorley, which was run by strict disciplinarians from the Military Provost Staff Corps. One prisoner had been found guilty of selling RAF radio equipment to a shop in Liverpool and the other had threatened a RAF Police flight sergeant with a knife.

A group of German officers and civilians concluded in July that getting rid of Adolf Hitler offered the last remaining chance to end the war before it swept onto German soil from the west and the east. On the 20th July they tried to kill their leader during a conference by placing a bomb in his Rastenburg headquarters in East Prussia. Although four of his staff officers were killed and a number of other officers were seriously wounded, Hitler miraculously sustained only minor injuries and lived to inflict swift revenge on those who had plotted against him.

Paris was liberated on the 25th August by the Americans and Free French Forces and shortly afterwards Squadron Leader Swanwick and six RAF Police NCOs established a RAF Police office within the city. Similar offices were also established later on in Brussels and Antwerp as the Allied push towards Germany gathered pace. In addition, during their move through Belgium, Security Sections of the RAF Police were authorised to form and establish an auxiliary security force in Brussels known as the Belgian Auxiliary Air Police Service (BAAPS) which was used to guard important stores and installations at various points throughout the country, which in turn released combat troops for the push towards Germany. The system turned out to be a very successful venture and a number of locally obtained dogs were used by the force to assist in their important guarding role. As the RAF moved through into Holland a similar type of force was formed there to carry out the same type of work.

In December, an order was released by the Air Ministry regarding the brassard, or armband, worn by the RAF Police. At the time, the station police, including the newly absorbed group of dog handlers, were wearing a dark blue armband with the red letters 'RAF SP' on it to signify, RAF Service Police. While those employed outside stations in the 'regional system' and under the direct control of the Provost Marshal wore a black brassard with a central red band around it onto which the letters RAFP were displayed in black. After a change in policy, the order stated that from that date onwards the term 'RAF Service Police' was to be scrapped and that all NCOs employed on police duties within the RAF would be known by the term 'RAF Police'. As a consequence, the order informed all former RAF Service Police NCOs to un-sew and remove the letter 'S' from their brassard and sew the remaining letter 'P' against the letters 'RAF' to form 'RAFP', as a temporary measure until the black and red brassard could be issued to all personnel.

In April 1945, Corporal A Thompson, who had recently joined the trade of RAF Police, and Air Dog Gundo were posted to 2TAF and found themselves moving with the Allied Expeditionary Force through France, Belgium and towards Germany guarding the makeshift airfields that were being used by RAF fighters and bombers to bring Germany to its knees. The invasion of course made it possible for the RAF Police to use their dogs for the first time on the European mainland.

On the 8th May, hostilities in Europe ended. Adolf Hitler, leader of Nazi Germany, had committed suicide in his Berlin bunker as Russian forces entered the devastated German capital. At that point, the remnants of the German High Command surrendered to the Allies.

With the war in Europe over, the Air Ministry was confronted with the problem of re-deploying thousands of redundant aircrew, all of whom were highly trained, motivated and courageous young men. Indeed, the vast majority had been highly decorated for their bravery, having flown countless dangerous missions against the enemy during the war. At the time it was impossible to discharge them quickly from the service but unfortunately there was no further call for their skills in the air. Some were reluctant to leave especially those who had enjoyed the exciting way of life and therefore many expressed a desire to remain in the RAF even if it meant that they could no longer fly. Accordingly, many were offered the chance to re-muster into six other branches of the service, with the RAF Police being one of those choices.

Sergeant W Gausden had been an air gunner serving on Liberator Bombers during the war and had flown a great many missions against the Germans with No 70 Squadron. However, at the end of the conflict, whilst still in Italy, he handed in his flying kit and at the age of only nineteen, volunteered to transfer into the RAF Police. After reporting to the RAF Police Headquarters located in Naples and after being interviewed by Wing Commander S N Kettle, the Deputy Provost Marshal (DPM), he was duly accepted as a trainee RAF Police NCO. A short time later he reported to Portici, on the outskirts of Naples, where he began his training as a RAF Police dog handler under the watchful eye of Sergeant B Lee, himself a very experienced dog trainer. The dog section at that time however, was under the firm control of Sergeant J Mungo, who prior to being called up for war service, had been a fourth year veterinary student studying in Northern England. At the time, there were twenty dogs and their handlers on the strength of the section, assisted by two Italian soldiers who were responsible for feeding the dogs and for cleaning out the kennels. A variety of breeds were being used at that time and included; Labradors, German Shepherd dogs, Airedales, German Shepherd / Airedale cross breeds, Great Danes, Collies and even a Blood Hound, which was used for tracking. The RAF Police dog section at Portici provided the important security coverage to a number of outlying RAF Units, the largest being a maintenance depot located at Otaviano on the lower slopes of the volcano Mount Vesuvius. Each evening a heavy truck, converted to carry a number of transit kennels, would leave Portici, accompanied by five dog teams. During their tour of duty they were required to make a number of random surprise calls at all the outlying units where the handlers and their dogs would mount high-profile patrols to deter and in some instances detect the presence of intruders within the various sites. Like elsewhere in warn-torn Europe, everything was in short supply to the civilian population and as a consequence pilfering from military stores to supply the 'black market' demand was rife.

As previously stated, during the war members of the public had lent a large number of dogs to the MAPGDS, the Army and the RAF to assist with the war effort. Indeed, with severe rationing on almost everything and the increased pace of wartime life it was impossible for the vast majority of working people to retain pets, and an appeal for dogs to help guard defence assets had been well received by the general public. However, with the war over, the majority of those who had donated their pets wanted them back and so a program was quickly implemented to 'discharge' the dogs concerned from the service. Each dog, prior to being returned to its owner, was medically checked to ensure that it was fit and a certificate, signed by the Provost Marshal himself, stated that the certificate had been issued 'in grateful recognition of tireless effort and constant devotion to duty willingly rendered to Britain and all the free peoples of the world in time of war'. As some of the dogs used by the RAF had served overseas a special quarantine kennel was acquired and set up at Brockworth on the outskirts of Gloucester to ensure that all animals were free from rabies and other problems prior to being returned to their owners. Some owners however, decided to let the RAF keep their former pets, mainly because they were unable to feed them properly with the severe rationing that was still in force. Others were afraid of taking back dogs that had been trained to attack would-be intruders and Flick, the dog handled by Corporal R F Young was one of those cases. Apparently, Flick had been trained so well as a police dog that his owners were not quite confident enough to take him back. As a consequence, the owners wrote to the RAF agreeing that Corporal Young could purchase Flick for the sum of five pounds at the end of his war service, and the RAF agreed. Shortly after, Corporal Young and Flick were separated for the first time in four years when he was posted to RAF Filton near Bristol for a few months before being posted out to Egypt onto the strength of the mobile dog section at RAF Kasfareet. The RAF agreed to retain Flick on active service while Corporal Young was away and Flick was sent over to Northern Ireland, where he was teamed up with another dog handler.

During the operation to locate and return donated dogs home to their original owners, Corporal J Watkins who was stationed at No 104 RAF Police Flight in Hamburg, was detailed to accompany a RAF warrant officer and a dog handler to collect dogs from the Russian Army and the American forces that had been donated by the British public for war-work. As neither the warrant officer nor the dog handler had a licence to drive the heavy truck that they had been assigned, Corporal Watkins assumed the role of driver. Their first port of call was to liaise with the Russians at Helmstedt on the 'border' between the British and Russian zones where the handover of dogs took place. From Helmstedt, the three RAF men made their way to Frankfurt where they met up with their American Allies. In all, a dozen dogs were collected and placed in crates inside the truck for security. However, they all had to be exercised, fed and watered each day while they were travelling. Suitable overnight accommodation was usually provided at various British Army barracks along the route and the parade ground provided an ideal place to exercise their charges who were being sent back home. After completing the task Corporal Watkins often wondered what the original owners would make of their pets on their return home as most of the dogs were a real handful, even for an experienced dog handler.

Soon after arriving in Egypt, Corporal Young was teamed up with a large German Shepherd cross-breed with the unusual name of Oubass. At the time, the mobile dog section was being used to provide night-time dog patrols to all the RAF units in the Canal Zone area on a random basis. As such, in order to deter and to arrest any 'would-be' thieves at large in restricted areas, the dog teams would simply turn up at a particular unit unannounced after dark and would 'sweep' the areas most at risk for anyone who had no reason to be there. Then just before daylight the dog teams would be withdrawn and returned to their unit. The system was most effective in making maximum use of limited re-sources in controlling the activities of the local Egyptian thieves, who had a reputation of stealing anything that was not guarded. Although armed military guards were on duty at all British military bases in Egypt, the dogs with their acute sense of smell could detect the presence of intruders in the darkest of nights, unlike the human guards who were for all intents and purposes blind. At that time the vehicle being used to drop off the dog handlers at their various posts was an old three-ton truck that had eight wire cages and eight seats fitted into the back to carry the handlers and their dogs. It was also common practice whenever a regular RAF driver was unavailable, for one of the more trustworthy German prisoners-of-war to be detailed to drive the vehicle to and from the various units.

Although, there was much celebration with the victory in Europe, the savage war against the Japanese still continued out in the Far East where British and Commonwealth troops, along with their Allies, were fighting hard gruelling battles in their attempts to force the Japanese out of Asia. In mid July, the 'Big Three'; Josef Stalin, Winston Churchill and Harry H Truman met in Potsdam, just outside Berlin, where they estimated that the invasion of Japan would result in the unacceptable loss of over a million and a half Allied troops. However, on the 6th August, in an effort to reduce the predicted Allied losses, the Americans, dropped their first newly developed atomic bomb on the Japanese city of Hiroshima killing eighty thousand people and completely destroying the city. Before the fact that an atomic bomb had been used in war for the first time could register on the world, a second atomic bomb destroyed the city of Nagasaki, three days later, killing a further forty thousand people. Although the new weapon brought about mass destruction on a scale never before witnessed, it did bring about the sudden and unconditional surrender of Japan on the 14th August, thereby ending the war in the Far East, and after six long and bloody years the war finally ended. World War II had been a global military conflict that, in terms of lives lost and material destruction had been the most devastating war in human history. It began in 1939 as a European conflict between Germany and an Anglo-French coalition but eventually widened to include most of the nations of the world either directly or indirectly. It ended leaving a new-world order dominated by the United States of America and the Soviet Union. During six years of conflict, World War II had claimed the lives of some fifty million people. More than any previous war, it involved the commitment of nations' entire human and economic resources, the blurring of the distinction between combatant and non-combatant, and the expansion of the battlefield to include all of the enemy's territory. By the end of the War, the overall establishment of the Royal Air Force had reached 1.2 million personnel and there were some five hundred and forty operational airfields scattered around the United Kingdom supported by many more non-flying units and headquarters formations. The size of the RAF Police had also reached its peak with an establishment of five hundred commissioned officers and twenty thousand non-commissioned officers, making it one of the largest British police forces.

In occupied Germany during the later part of 1945, Corporal A Thompson and Air Dog Gundo were on patrol on an airfield one night when Gundo indicated that there was something ahead of them. Corporal Thompson released his dog and followed. After a few minutes he found Gundo standing over a German who had been attempting to steal equipment from a storage shed. The man was promptly arrested and subsequent enquiries revealed that as a former member of the *Waffen SS* he was a wanted man. When his house was subsequently searched by British troops over thirty Red Cross parcels, intended for prisoners-of-war, were found amongst a hoard of other stolen property.

Although the war had ended, severe rationing was still restricting the sale and issue of petrol, vehicle parts, tyres and food amongst other things. As such, the RAF Police dog handlers deployed on RAF units played a vital role in preventing 'de-mob' happy airmen and local criminals, who, with an eye to getting rich quick, had intentions of making off with a wide variety of military equipment, stores and other essential commodities.

Just before Christmas Corporal R H Gregory, who was stationed at RAF Fazackerly, was posted out to North Africa. After crossing the English Channel between Newhaven and Dieppe he made the long tiring journey by rail and sea to Egypt where he eventually arrived at the RAF Police Dog Training School that had been established at RAF Heliopolis. After being teamed up with a new dog he was sent down to No 107MU at RAF Kasfareet where he remained until being discharged from the RAF in 1947.

As 1945 came to an end, so began a two-year period of National Service with the armed forces. In accordance with the National Service Act it became law for every British male citizen to register at their local branch of the Ministry of Labour and National Service as soon as they reached the age of eighteen. Detailed information about National Service and how to register for it was placed in all the newspapers and broadcast on the BBC. Schools and employers also played their part in putting the message across to the public at large. While many young men chose to go into the Army, those that elected to serve in the RAF were accepted only after successfully completing an intelligence test. Those that passed were first sent to one of the two induction centres set up at RAF Padgate near Warrington or RAF Cardington near Bedford.

The RAF Police underwent yet another significant change over the same period when they were authorised to wear white webbing equipment and the now familiar white tops to their service caps. Dog handlers of course, who worked during the hours of darkness, were given dispensation from wearing the white equipment when on operational dog handling duties so as not to stand out in the dark whilst on patrol.

In line with the post-war restructuring and demobilisation process, the overall establishment of the RAF Police by the beginning of January 1946 had fallen to around 13,000 personnel.

After the war Lieutenant Colonel Baldwin was keen to start breeding German Shepherd dogs for service with the RAF and after receiving the required approval, established a breeding kennels at Down Hatherley near RAF Staverton. During the early stages of the breeding program Lieutenant Colonel Baldwin put out an appeal to members of the public for the loan of suitable German Shepherd dogs and bitches from which to breed. It was in the spring of 1946 that one such member of the public, Collett Calverley, learned about the loan program after seeing an advert that appeared in the magazine *Our Dogs*. As he owned a German Shepherd bitch by the name of Beauty, who incidentally, had cost him three pounds to purchase, he responded to the appeal and was contacted soon after by Lieutenant Colonel Baldwin. During the subsequent conversation, Collett learned that the dog training school would breed a litter from each dog loaned to them and then they would train the dog up to elementary obedience standards before returning her to the owner with one of the puppies. After asking a few more questions about welfare and basic conditions at the school, Collett agreed to loan Beauty to the program and the standard agreement form was duly signed to that effect. Soon after, arrangements were made for Beauty to travel to the school at RAF Staverton and a day or two later one of the staff contacted Collett to inform him that his dog was found to be beyond the stipulated training standard when it had arrived at the school. It was while Beauty was at Staverton that Collett decided to join the Army. As a result, he donated Beauty to the RAF Police as an unconditional gift and Lieutenant Colonel Baldwin eagerly accepted her, adding that the school would still honour their contract and send Collett one puppy from each subsequent litter. Prior to beginning his military service, and at the invitation of Flight Lieutenant Hawkshead, Collett paid a visit to the breeding kennels to see Beauty. His guide during the visit was a Flight Sergeant MacIntosh, who had a badly scarred face, the result apparently of being mauled and bitten by a dog a few years earlier. After being shown around the kennel complex, Collett watched as Beauty was put through a criminal work-out and although she was very pregnant at the time, she still took a well-built airman playing the part of the 'criminal' to the ground in no time at all. Consequently, as a corporal instructor stationed at the Royal Armoured Corps Centre in Bovington, Collett would be visited every so often by a RAF Police corporal dog-handler, who would hand him a puppy, one of the latest of Beauty's offspring. Additionally, Collett also visited the dog training school on a couple of occasions to see Beauty, and to check on her progress. All in all, during her time with the breeding program Beauty gave birth to twenty-eight puppies in three litters, comprising twenty-four dogs and four bitches.

In September, after serving in the RAF for six years Acting Sergeant J Higson's war service came to an end and after handing in his kit he returned to Lancashire and civilian life. He had joined the RAF hoping to train as an engine mechanic at the age of eighteen in 1940, but had then transferred to the trade of administration orderly and had been posted to RAF Cranwell. It was while he was there that he saw a notice one day asking for volunteers to be dog handlers, so, thinking that it would be a far more interesting type of work he volunteered and was duly accepted. On a bitterly cold day in January 1942 he had been posted to the MAPGDS at Woodfold near Gloucester and had joined a course along with seven other trainee handlers. At the time, a rather large lady who was described as being very firm but fair with her staff and the trainees seemed to be in charge of the training program. Aircraftsman Higson had been assigned to a two-year old gold and sable German Shepherd bitch named 'Queenie', who had been donated to the school by a civilian donor. All the RAF trainees attending the month long course had been volunteers and during their training they had been taught how to use their dogs to protect vulnerable aircraft against the threat from enemy saboteurs, 'Fifth Column activists' and the Irish Republican Army. Each morning the trainees had been required to clean out the dog kennels and attend to their dogs grooming, while the afternoons had been spent on obedience training. In the evening between the hours of nine and midnight, in bitterly cold conditions, the trainee handlers and their dogs had been taught the skills of tracking and dealing with intruders. On successful completion of the course, it was policy for the trainees to be posted to RAF units as a team of eight, comprising one Corporal, one Leading Aircraftsman and six Aircraftsmen. Consequently, at the end of his training, Leading Aircraftsman Higson had been posted to the Coastal Command station at Aldergrove near Belfast, from which aircraft had hunted and attacked German U-boats threatening Allied shipping off the southern coast of Ireland. The dog handlers stationed at Aldergrove had been employed on permanent night duty, patrolling the perimeters of the airfield and the aircraft dispersal bays. Initially, each man had been armed with a rifle, but a later policy decision changed their weapon to a more easily managed Sten-gun. Additionally, they had carried a large self-charging, clip-on torch, and had worn a heavy leather type sleeveless over-jacket or jerkin to protect them from the damp and the cold winds. The shifts carried out by the dog handlers began at eight in the evening and had carried on through until six the following morning with each dog team working four hours on patrol followed by four hours rest. The challenge issued by each dog handler to any would-be intruder at the time had been, 'Halt and be recognised', followed by, 'Halt or I'll fire'. In May 1942, Leading Aircraftsman Higson had been sent back to Woodfold to train a new team of dog handlers, after which he had been promoted to corporal. After successful completion of their training course Corporal Higson and his new team had been posted to Weston Park, the large country estate belonging to the Earl of Bradford, which under the command of Wing Commander Smallwood, had been a satellite of the nearby RAF Maintenance Unit at Cosford. In June 1943, as a break from their normal duties, Corporal Higson had taken his team and their dogs to the Sports complex of the Dunlop Company in Birmingham, where a gathering of eight hundred civilian war workers had been organised. It was a beautiful day and everyone was out to enjoy a few hours break from the dogma of war work. They had not been disappointed as the RAF handlers and their dogs treated them to an impeccable performance of obedience and track-ing. In 1944, following the absorption of dogs into the RAF Police, Corporal Higson and the other members of his team had been sent to the RAF Police

School at Weeton near Blackpool where they had successfully completed their initial RAF Police training. Although Corporal Higson retained his rank the airmen on his team had all been elevated to the rank of acting corporal before being returned to their unit. In 1945 the dog section at Weston Park had been dis-established and after Corporal Higson had returned his dog to Staverton he had been promoted to the rank of acting sergeant and posted to take charge of the RAF Police section at Polebrook airfield, a former American bomber station, near Oundle in Northamptonshire. With a staff of just five RAF Police corporals, he had been responsible for looking after the police and security interests of five hundred RAF personnel and two hundred German prisoners-of-war. In those days, there were so many security passes of different colours, sizes and markings that it was impossible to memorise them all. In mid-1945 after being confronted by a visiting Air Vice-Marshal who had no pass, Sergeant Higson had threatened to arrest him unless he provided proof of his identity. The situation had quickly been resolved by the officer identifying himself and two weeks later Sergeant Higson had received a glowing letter from the Air Ministry informing him that his future in the RAF was assured, if he so desired. Sergeant Higson had chosen not to extend his service and had stayed at RAF Polebrook until being demobilised. When he enlisted in the RAF the pay for an Aircraftsman Class 2 was 1/6d (7.5p) per day, paid fortnightly. An Aircraftsman Class 1 received an extra 6d (2.5p). Promotion to Leading Aircraftsman saw another increase of 9d (4p) and a corporal received an extra 1/3d (6p). With consolidated pay, length of service increments and good conduct pay, Acting Sergeant Higson shortly before leaving the RAF was drawing the glorious sum of £4.4s (£4.20p) per fortnight.

In October, the RAF Police School and the RAF Police Headquarters moved from RAF Great Sampford to a more permanent base at RAF Staverton where they joined the RAF Police Dog Training School. The entire station was at that time under the command of Group Captain A A Newbury, who as station commander became the first RAF Provost Officer to hold such an appointment. Although, all the elements of the RAF Police training organisation were for the first time together, the new unit soon experienced severe difficulties in providing adequate accommodation for everyone serving there. As a result, a satellite unit was opened up shortly before Christmas at an old balloon repair station at Pucklechurch, situated in a rather desolate spot between Yate and Bristol. The new site was to be home for the National Service RAF Police trainees during their initial six-week police training course, while RAF Staverton continued with the main bulk of the training program, including the training of dogs and RAF Police dog handlers. At this point in time RAF Police dog teams were established and working within the United Kingdom and Northern Ireland, in France,

Belgium, Germany, Italy and in Egypt. The dogs serving overseas were however, locally recruited and training was carried out on a local basis by RAF Police NCOs who had prior knowledge of working and training dogs.

After the war, following on from their success in locating victims buried after the German V1 and V2 rocket attacks on London, the question was asked whether dogs could be trained to locate victims buried in a mine disaster. A test was arranged at a suitable coalmine and again the dogs proved to be successful in locating a number of buried victims. However, following a real disaster and explosion, doubt was cast on whether the dogs would be able to cope in such difficult conditions. Unfortunately, soon after, such a disaster occurred at the William Pitt coalmine in Whitehaven and a number of men were trapped underground. Flight Lieutenant Cooper and two of his dog handlers were authorised to attend the scene to see if they could help. As the rescue operation reached a crucial point there were still two men unaccounted for and the rescue workers were following an airline that had been in use at the time of the explosion. However, the RAF Police dogs indicated in another direction and the area of the search was switched to the area indicated by the dogs. It was a wise move, because soon after, the remaining two bodies were located and while the rescue party was investigating that part of the mine, one of the dogs, Air Dog Prince, pricked up his ears and started to back away. On the instructions of the handler every one else quickly moved back from the passage just as the entire roof collapsed in behind them.

Up until 1947, every commissioned provost officer serving within the RAF Police had been on loan from the Administrative and Special Duties Branch but with the expansion of the RAF Police organisation, authority was granted on the 1st January 1947, for the establishment of a specialised Provost Branch within the service, and all serving provost officers were transferred into the newly formed Branch. Additionally, the Air Ministry, in an effort to standardise the use by the RAF of miscellaneous guards and watchmen around the world, instructed all RAF Deputy Provost Marshals commanding overseas theatres to assume immediate responsibility for their employment and training. Accordingly, to make up for the shortfall in regular manning overseas, suitable native guards were absorbed by the branch under the heading of Royal Air Force Police Auxiliaries.

During the month of February, recently promoted Sergeant R F Young was demobilised from the RAF and returned home from Egypt. At the time, his dog Flick was still serving in Northern Ireland, and after finishing his sixty-nine days disembarkation leave, Sergeant Young travelled to the RAF Police Dog Training School at RAF Staverton where he spoke to someone regarding the return of his dog. He was delighted to hear that Flick had been brought back from Northern

Ireland and was actually there at the school waiting to be collected. Within the hour Sergeant Young and Flick were reunited and both returned to civilian life having completed 'their bit for King and Country'. Flick remained with his master until he was eleven, when sadly; he had to be put down because of severe arthritis, which had affected his hip joints.

Aircraftsman B A Stapleton and Aircraftsman D Taylor, having successfully completed their basic police training together at RAF Staverton, promptly moved across to the dog training school in April,, where they were met by the commanding officer, Flight Lieutenant Cooper and a WAAF sergeant by the name of Jones, who instructed the two trainees to go and select a dog each from the main kennels. While Aircraftsman Taylor had the opportunity to have a good look at the dogs before making his selection, it seemed that Aircraftsman Stapleton was denied that facility on account that Air Dog Bruce chose him to be his handler. Aircraftsman Stapleton had joined the RAF the previous year, and together with fifty other recruits had taken the 'oath of allegiance' at RAF Padgate on the 11th April, before being sent down to RAF Compton Bassett in Wiltshire to complete his recruit training. After successfully completing his recruit training he had been posted to RAF Staverton, and detached to RAF Manby. Then on the 5th January 1947, he had been posted to No 5 RAF Police District at Princess Gate Court in London where he had been employed as a 'policeman under-training', until being sent on his basic police course on the 19th February.

On the 30th May, newly promoted Acting Corporal Stapleton with Air Dog Bruce, and Acting Corporal Taylor with Air Dog David, were posted to RAF Middleton St George in the north-east of England, where they were employed on dog patrol duties, with the specific aim of preventing squatters from taking over buildings on the unit. During their time at that unit, both NCOs were billeted in accommodation situated about half a mile from the camp. During the same month, the newly created RAF Police journal 'Provost Parade' was printed and published. The first, issue contained forty pages of stories, sporting reports and a few cartoon drawings but on the front cover there was displayed the photograph of a RAF Police German Shepherd dog, which had been specially taken for the purpose by Lieutenant Colonel Jimmy Baldwin, himself a keen photographer.

In early June, the *Three Counties Agricultural Show* was held on the airfield at RAF Staverton and was attended by a huge public audience. It was just after the war and people wanted to be entertained and to enjoy themselves after the dismal years of committing everything they had towards the war effort. They were not disappointed and one of the biggest and most popular attractions of the day, turned out to be the parade of some forty smartly turned out, RAF Police dog handlers and their dogs, lead by the officer in charge of the RAF Police Dog

Training School; Flight Lieutenant Cooper. In addition, the parade was accompanied by suitable music for the occasion, supplied courtesy of the RAF Police Silver Band. As the parade passed by, the audience were drawn to the presence of a single dog handler; Corporal G Woodburn, whose dog was pulling a small cart on which was seated a 'German prisoner-of-war' played by Aircraftsman F Elliott. It turned out to be a splendid day for everyone and marked the start of things to come for RAF Police dog participation in major public events around the country. Incidentally, Corporal Collett Calverley, then a member of the Royal Armoured Corps School Motor Cycle Display Team, also took part in the show, and although he watched the display and the parade put on by the RAF Police Dog Training School with great interest, he did not see Beauty, the dog he had donated to the RAF two years before, and unfortunately he never saw or heard of her again.

During the same month the *'Marshall Plan'*, named after American Secretary of State George Catlett Marshall, was announced which stated that if Europe devised a co-operative, long-term rebuilding program, the United States of America would provide financial assistance to help rebuild the European nations devastated by the war. Europe's agricultural and coal production was almost at a standstill and its people were threatened with starvation. The Americans had offered their assistance to avoid European nations turning to the Soviet Union for help. Even at that early point the Americans were beginning to see the Russians as their main rival. Consequently, more than $13 billion in aid was made available to the Organization for European Economic Co-operation (OEEC), the body set up to control it. The largest sums of money were earmarked for Great Britain, France, Italy, and West Germany, in that order.

During the year, in the continuing effort to standardise the use of 'locally employed watchmen and civilian guards' in overseas theatres, the Provost Marshal announced that the first thirty members of the newly formed RAF Police Auxiliaries had reported for duty at RAF Changi in Singapore on the 18th June.

Aircraftsman C Agar reported to the RAF Police School at Staverton to begin his initial police training in July, after completing his recruit training at RAF Wilmslow in Cheshire. He recalls that the airfield at the time was not in use and that the former aircraft hangars, station headquarters, sick quarters, cookhouse, NAAFI and the hutted accommodation for the other ranks were located on the west side of the unit, while the RAF Police Dog Training School was located on the east side of the unit and separated by a public road that ran north and south. At the time the school, which was divided into 'A' Squadron and 'B' Squadron, was an extremely busy place running initial police courses for airmen on regular engagements and airmen on National Service as well as running post-graduate advanced courses. While 'A' Squadron was located at Staverton, 'B' Squadron comprising National Service trainees was located at RAF Churchdown, a somewhat isolated satellite unit situated between Yale and Bristol. Because there was an acute shortage of accommodation for the RAF Police trainees at Staverton, many of them, including Aircraftsman Agar were billeted 'under canvas' with four men sharing a tent that was devoid of electric lighting. Even so, the trainees were expected to be smartly turned out each morning for the inspection parade. Each man was issued a camp bed and five blankets; sheets were not issued, and although there were electric lights in the nearby huts there were no electrical sockets and therefore adapters fitted to the light fittings had to be used when ironing uniforms. Each week the Station Commander; Group Captain A A Newbury, personally inspected the trainees on parade. He would turn up in his private car to be met by the wing commander and while his pet German Shepherd dog ran around loose he would inspect each man in minute detail.

After being called up for National Service and successfully completing his initial RAF Police training on Course No 455, at RAF Staverton, Aircraftsman D R E Jenson moved across to the RAF Police Dog Training School, with another National Serviceman, Aircraftsman Davies, to begin their training to become dog handlers. Soon after their arrival at the school they were each allocated a German Shepherd dog; Jenson's was called Eos and Davies' was Erich. Both dogs had apparently been donated to the RAF by the same owner so they knew each other and got on well together. After successfully completing their training, the newly promoted and qualified dog handlers and their dogs were posted to RAF Shepherds Grove in Suffolk which at the time was a satellite unit of nearby RAF Watton. With dogs and kitbags, the difficult journey to their first posting on a dull November day was made by train from Gloucester to Paddington station in London, where they were collected by a RAF Police NCO from the London District Headquarters and taken by vehicle to Liverpool Street station where they caught another train up to Bury St Edmunds. When they eventually arrived rather tired at Bury St Edmunds Corporal Jenson telephoned the guardroom at RAF Shepherds Grove to request transport but the corporal in charge apparently knew nothing of them joining the unit. Indeed, when they eventually arrived, they were informed that there were no kennel facilities for the dogs, which caused a slight problem, but not one that was impossible to resolve. Consequently, as a temporary measure the two NCOs were accommodated together with their dogs in a Nissen hut located next to the RAF Police accommodation. Because the handlers worked during the hours of darkness they were not required to be up early in the morning like the other RAF personnel on the unit who mainly worked normal daytime hours. Therefore, after being at the unit for a week or so, the two NCOs, having worked through the night, were still in bed at around nine in the morning. Corporal Jenson, who was half awake, heard a noise outside and then someone saying, "I don't think we should inspect this hut today Sir, it's the billet occupied by the two new dog handlers who were working last night". In reply, another voice said, "I have to inspect a number of billets today and this will be one of them". At that point, the door opened and someone started to enter just as the two dogs growled and leapt towards the door, which suddenly slammed shut again. The two NCOs later heard that it had been a rather keen orderly officer on his rounds, who had received the fright of his life as the two dogs leapt towards him. During the weeks that followed the problem of accommodating the dogs was resolved when a former wartime air raid bunker was converted into two kennels and a compound was erected around the structure so that the dogs could move about during the day. Once the work was completed amble supplies of straw was obtained for bedding from a local farm and the two dogs were introduced to their new homes. Patrols carried out during the hours of darkness were generally uneventful, which probably indicated that the presence of the dog team was effective in keeping unauthorised persons away from the site. During the evening shift Corporal Jenson would often call into the NAAFI for his break, during which time Eos would remain quietly next to him while he drank his tea and chatted to other service personnel. It was also common practice for the two dog handlers to exercise their dogs during the late afternoon by walking them around the roads and lanes that surrounded the unit. In addition to exercising the dogs off-base, the dog handlers both got to know the areas that lay beyond the station perimeter fence. During his nights off duty Corporal Jenson would usually attend the dance in the NAAFI or visit the cinema with his girlfriend, who later became his wife, and afterwards they would collect Air Dog Eos from his kennel and he would accompany Corporal Jenson as he walked his girlfriend home to the nearby village of Stanton.

The RAF Police School and the RAF Police Headquarters hardly had time to settle down at RAF Staverton and dwell on the success of their first major public event at the *Three Counties Agricultural Show* because later that month they were on the move once again to RAF Pershore near Worcester, leaving behind the dog training school to carry on its fine work at RAF Staverton.

By now the training of RAF Police dogs was firmly under control, the Treasury had approved an overall establishment of some five hundred and fifty dogs and only thirty dogs on loan from the public remained in service. Additionally, the use of dogs by the RAF Police was beginning to attract attention from the media and a number of high profile stories appeared in the newspapers. One such story concerned RAF Police dogs being used to assist the civil police in

Norfolk to search a large wooded area in Thetford for an escaped prisoner. The man, of Polish nationality, was armed and dangerous and had evaded capture in the woods for three weeks. However, shortly after the start of the operation the dogs were able to flush him out and he was taken back into custody.

In December, Aircraftsman C Agar, having successfully completed his initial police training, was posted across to the Dog Training School to begin his training to become a dog handler. Unfortunately, at the time there was an outbreak of distemper in the kennels and as such the dogs affected were quarantined and the movement of personnel around the kennels was strictly controlled so as to minimize the spread of the disease. Initially, Aircraftsman Agar and a fellow trainee were allocated to the meat preparation area to assist in butchering the meat each morning for the dogs. It was in connection with that task that they went out on a couple of occasions with a three ton truck loaded with clean empty dustbins to the abattoirs in Cheltenham, Painswick and Stroud to collect the meat. After the 'restrictions' connected with the distemper infection were lifted, Aircraftsman Agar and his fellow trainees began their training under the guidance of corporal instructors; Darnell, Irvine and Bruce.

Continuing their public relations exercise, by the end of the year, a team of RAF Police dog handlers and their charges from the RAF Police Dog Training School had taken part in three public military events around the country. The first was at the Blackpool Air Pageant, followed by an appearance at the Daily Express Air Pageant at Gatwick Airport and finally, they gave a display for members of the British Legion and their families in Swindon. Needless to say, that all the dog displays were greatly appreciated by all of those who attended the events.

In late February 1948, with his training successfully completed, newly promoted Acting Corporal C Agar and his dog were posted to RAF Marston Moor near York where he joined three other dog handlers stationed at the unit. Although at the time, RAF Police dogs were entitled to a daily ration of two and a half pounds of meat and eight ounces of dry tack biscuits, there seemed to be a problem in justifying and obtaining it from the NCO in charge of the cookhouse. The senior dog handler, himself only an acting corporal, went to report the matter to the Station Adjutant, who was the officer nominated to command the RAF Police, but he seemed unconcerned and dismissed the dog handler with the unconvincing promise that he would deal with the matter. When the situation had not improved after a couple of days, Corporal Agar was sent to complain to the adjutant who turned out to be quite aggressive and unconcerned. After the confrontation, Corporal Agar managed to obtain a lift in the transport that was going to York and on the way he was dropped off at RAF Rufforth, which was also the home base of the RAF Police District Assistant Provost Marshal (APM); Squadron Leader Wilson. Having gained an audience with the APM, Corporal Agar explained the problems he and his colleagues were having in obtaining the daily rations for their dogs. As luck had it, the APM was on friendly terms with the Army major quarter-master in York and promised to sort out the problem. Corporal Agar returned to his unit and sure enough the following day and thereon after the allotted rations for the dogs were ready to be collected. The APM it seems had fulfilled his promise to help. Unfortunately, the Station Adjutant heard about the intervention and was furious. He sent for Corporal Agar and demanded to know who had given him permission to go and speak to the District APM. At that point, Corporal Agar stunned the officer by replying that he was not aware that he had to seek permission to speak to his brother-in-law. After that, it seems that there were no further problems with the adjutant.

On the 24th April, Corporal B A Stapleton and Air Dog Bruce arrived at RAF Tengah in Singapore. He had left the United Kingdom on the 23rd March on board the troopship SS Dunera, where he had joined up with four other RAF Police NCOs; Sergeant Gardner, Corporal Fossey, Corporal Clarke and Corporal Butterworth. During the month-long voyage the four Junior NCOs, being dog handlers travelling out with their dogs, had been accommodated on what was known as the 'isolation deck', situated above that where Senior NCOs, wives and members of the WAAF were accommodated. After quickly settling in at RAF Tengah, Corporal Stapleton and his dog were detailed to carry out night-time patrols at RAF Changi.

It had been the original intention of Lieutenant Colonel Baldwin to train and use only the breed of German Shepherd dog for RAF service but problems arose when the supply of suitable public donations failed to maintain the number of dogs required by the service. In an effort to overcome the problem, a breeding program had been started. From the beginning Lieutenant Colonel Baldwin had been adamant that only stock of the highest quality should be used in the breeding program. Consequently, he had contacted some of the country's top breeders and had asked for their help; indeed, most had been keen to help providing mainly breeding bitches. The first to produce a litter had been 'Crumstone Agate' a prize winning German Shepherd bitch provided by Mrs Margaret Griffin BEM, who proved to be a dedicated friend of the RAF Police Dog Training School long after her retirement as a trainer with the MAPGDS in the early 1940s. Equally, the stud dogs were required to conform to the very highest working breed standard outlined by Lieutenant Colonel Baldwin, and as such, the breeding kennels had been based on three outstanding dogs; the first had been Baldwin's own champion dog

'*Lucky Jim of Picardy*', the second had been a working trials champion, '*Seigurd of Jutenheim*' and the third had been '*Air Dog Rex*', who had been one of the original RAF Police dogs.

In the Far East, a state of emergency was declared in Malaya on the 18th June, following a number of serious terrorist attacks against Police stations and European owned rubber plantations throughout the country. Up until that point, the terrorist attacks had resulted in the murder of a number of European police officers and plantation managers and the destruction of a considerable number of plantations. Although security measures within the country had been tightened, the Chinese communist 'bandits' of the *Malay Peoples Anti British Army (MPABA)* backed up with logistical support from the *Min Yuen*, had mobilized in the jungles and had threatened to carry out further attacks in an effort to destabilise the country by disrupting the economy. As the situation developed and the country became more unstable RAF units were moved from the mainland and onto the island of Singapore in an effort to improve their security situation.

On the 25th June, that the first batch of RAF Police dogs arrived on the island of Ceylon from bases in Singapore. After a short period of acclimatisation after their journey and further continuation training the dogs were ready to work. Consequently, a new security deterrent became visible when the dogs and their handlers were assigned to duties protecting aircraft and military installations at a number of RAF locations on the island.

In occupied Germany, the relationship between the Eastern and Western Alliance was beginning to show signs of tension. The Soviet Union was making unreasonable demands and the West was in no mood to submit to them. As the situation deteriorated in June, the Soviet Union further increased her pressure on the West by throwing a cordon around West Berlin and cutting it off from the outside world and preventing anything entering or leaving the city by road, rail or river. The Western Allies did not want to storm in and relieve the city for fear of starting another war so, in an effort to break the Berlin Blockade, they mounted, '*Operation Planefare*', and the Berlin airlift started. During the operation, all the RAF units in Germany were used as staging posts for the mountain of food and medical supplies required to support the city's population under siege.

In the summer, Corporal Jenson and his dog were recalled to RAF Staverton for refresher training before being detached along with a number of other RAF Police dog handlers and their dogs to the School of Land and Air Warfare at RAF Old Sarum near Salisbury, where they were accommodated under canvas. The dog handlers remained at Old Sarum for a fortnight carrying out security patrols of the unit, which at the time was the venue for a series of conferences attended by senior politicians, including Winston Churchill, and senior officers from all three British services and a number of senior American military personnel. At the end of the detachment to Old Sarum the dog handlers returned to RAF Staverton and soon after, Corporal Jenson was selected to be one of the dog handlers to join the RAF Police Dog Display Team, which subsequently took part in the public military event staged at the *Three counties Agricultural Show*, which again for the second year was held on the airfield at RAF Staverton. Following the success of the previous year, the RAF Police dog parade comprised five ranks; four of which comprised dog handlers and their dogs with ten men in each rank, and a central rank of ten female kennel assistants, each with a police dog. At the end of another successful event, the dog handlers and kennel assistants who took part in the parade were visited by Air Chief Marshal Sir Arthur Tedder and his wife who were delighted with the performance staged by the team. After a hectic summer, Corporal Jenson returned to RAF Shepherds Grove and soon after, his colleague Corporal Davies was demobilised from the RAF and was replaced by Corporal R Stanton and his dog.

On the 13th July, having completed his tour of duty at RAF Marston Moor, Corporal C Agar was just one of a group of eighteen RAF Police dog handlers who arrived at Port Said in Egypt after a long and tiring voyage from the United Kingdom by troopship. Shortly after the vessel had moored in the harbour the operation to disembark the passengers began using Army landing craft to take them ashore. Once assembled on the quayside the RAF contingent, who were wearing full marching order and carrying one of their two kit bags, was marched down to the railway station. By the time they arrived there they were all sweating profusely in the scorching heat. However, they were not dismissed to rest but were lined up by a RAF Regiment sergeant and given a lecture about Egypt; the political situation and more importantly, the Egyptian people themselves. Amongst the many 'do's and don'ts' the sergeant listed was a warning not to display fountain pens in breast pockets because the Egyptians were very quick to steal them without the owner realising. When the sergeant looked down to his own breast pocket to demonstrate what he meant he realised with some embarrassment that some-one had already stolen his pen. After the lecture, the RAF contingent were told to stand easy to await the imminent arrival of the train that was taking them on to the transit unit at RAF El Hamra. However, some time later when the train failed to appear, the contingent was dismissed into the shade of a nearby railway shed while enquiries were made as to whereabouts of the train. When it was confirmed that the train was running late, the troops were given a light meal comprising a sandwich, a small cake and a mug of tea. After a couple of hours, the troop train finally appeared and the men were ordered to board it for the journey to El Hamra. After spending a week at RAF El Hamra living in tents, Corporal Agar and the other seventeen dog handlers were posted to the RAF Police dog training school that had been established at 112MU at Wadi Ysira, to be re-teamed with dogs. With the exception of one volunteer from the Woman's Voluntary Service (WVS), the unit was an all male establishment.

In August Corporal S Martin was discharged from the RAF. He had originally joined the RAF Regiment after completing his basic training in January 1941, but the following year transferred over to the RAF Police and after completing his police training at RAF Uxbridge was posted to the RAF Police Headquarters in Cairo, Egypt, which at the time was under the command of Wing Commander Udall. Initially he was employed on provost duties but in 1943 volunteered to become a dog handler. At the time, the military authorities had decided to use dogs to guard various units from the continuing threat of sabotage and large-scale theft. Some dogs were trained to attack while others were merely placed in compounds or on chains in specified areas to give warning by barking if unauthorised persons approached. As in the United Kingdom, volunteers from all ground trades who could be spared from normal duties were employed as dog handlers. The dogs it seemed comprised various types including German Shepherds and Bull Terrier cross breeds and were acquired locally from the Army and the Egyptian Police or merely rounded up from packs of wild dogs that roamed free. Corporal Martin was duly accepted for training and was sent to the recently opened RAF Dog Training School located at RAF Heliopolis which at the time was under the command of Flight Lieutenant Stewart-Watson. There were between eight to twelve students on each course which lasted for eight weeks. Corporal Martin was allocated an 'German Shepherd' type dog by the name of Boozer, and because of his seniority, after successfully completing his training he was retained at the school as an instructor but because he occasionally carried out dog patrols of the camp, he was authorised to retain Boozer, who was about two years old, had a strong personality and could be quite unpredictable at times. It was wartime and with the high risk of sabotage to essential war materials, and the theft of equipment by civilians being a constant worry, the dogs being used by the British Forces were simply trained to detect the presence of people and when released, to attack them; the fact that the intruder might be a saboteur intent on reeking havoc or a civilian thief mattered not. Indeed some of the dogs were quite ferocious beasts and Boozer; Corporal Martin's dog was amongst them. On one occasion, Corporal Martin authorised another handler by the name of Corporal Clarke, to take Boozer out for some exercise on the strict understanding that the dog be kept under control on the lead at all times. Corporal Clarke returned to the school within the hour in quite a state. Apparently, against all instructions to the contrary, he had let the dog off the lead for a free run in an isolated area but shortly after, a Bedouin woman had appeared from somewhere and before he could do anything Boozer immediately attacked and severely injured her before being pulled off. The woman had been seriously mauled and bitten during the attack and tragically died from her injuries before what medical help there was, could be summoned. The circumstances of the incident were quickly reported to Wing Commander Udall at Cairo Headquarters and after lengthy negotiations with the Bedouin Headman, an agreement was finally reached to resolve the matter and the RAF agreed to pay out a substantial amount in compensation to the dead woman's family. Sometime later at RAF Al Maza Corporal Martin had just completed a patrol with Boozer and at the end of his shift he was approached by the Orderly Officer, who wanted to inspect his notebook. Corporal Martin advised the Flight Lieutenant not to approach too close but the officer replied that he was not afraid of dogs and continued advancing. As Corporal Martin was attempting to take his notebook out of his pocket, Boozer sprang forward and bit the officer in the groin. The Station Commander, Wing Commander Aldiss initially wanted Corporal Martin court-martialled but when Flight Lieutenant Stuart-Watson arrived at RAF Al Maza and heard Corporal Martin's story, he suggested that all the dogs be withdrawn so as to prevent a similar incident from happening. The Station Commander of course, quickly realised the implications of that and when he heard the full account of what had taken place agreed to drop charges against Corporal Martin.

Meanwhile, back in England during the same period, staff at the RAF Police Dog Training School received an urgent request for assistance from the Gloucestershire Constabulary. It seemed that a dangerous prisoner, convicted of armed robbery, had escaped from Leyhill Prison. The urgency to recapture him increased when the police received a report that three people, living on an isolated farm in the area, had been brutally attacked and robbed by a man answering to the prisoner's description. In response to the request, five dogs and their handlers, under the control of Lieutenant Colonel Baldwin, were sent to assist in searching the area where the prisoner was believed to be hiding. Shortly after the search commenced, the dogs gave a positive indication that someone was hiding in a field of kale. As the dog teams went into the field to check it, a dishevelled man, answering to the description of the prisoner broke cover and tried to run off. He was challenged by one of the dog handlers and when he refused to stop, a dog was released and the man was apprehended and swiftly arrested. The search for, and capture of the convict had been witnessed by Mr A H Carter, the Assistant Chief Constable of the force, who it seemed, was most impressed by the professionalism of the RAF Police dog teams involved and of course, the speed in which the convict had been recaptured. In another case during the year, it emerged that stores to the value of £61,000 had been stolen from a RAF Station in the South of England. The investigation began with the apprehension by a RAF Police dog team of a civilian who was attempting to steal equipment. The subsequent joint enquiry, by the RAF and civil police, highlighted the fact that, during the previous three months, a considerable amount of crown equipment had been stolen by the same gang. As a result of the investigation, property to the value of £50,000 was recovered and three airmen and five civilians were sentenced to terms of imprisonment totalling sixteen years.

By early September, having successfully re-teamed with a new dog Corporal C Agar was posted initially onto the 'B' Mobile Dog Section. The Mobile Dog Section provided RAF Police dog teams on a random basis to patrol RAF units at night along the Suez Canal Zone. Shortly after joining the team he was patrolling one particular unit with his dog when suddenly the sound of a bullet passed close to him. It transpired that one of the RAF guards, thinking he was an intruder, had opened fire on him. Apparently, no-one had bothered to inform the armed guards that a dog team was patrolling their area. After that incident Corporal Agar was always a little wary when patrolling new areas in the still of the night.

In Singapore on the 3rd October, Corporal B A Stapleton and his dog were on night duty patrolling the area around the officer's mess at RAF Seletar where there had been a spate of reported thefts. The NCO and his dog had been posted from RAF Tengah on the 26th June, where they had been detailed to patrol the huge area of the airfield, an area that was packed with surplus ex World War II military vehicles awaiting disposal. At the time, large-scale thefts of military equipment by local people was a huge problem in Singapore and the deployment of RAF Police dog handlers were certainly one effective method of controlling the situation. As Corporal Stapleton kept watch on the officer's mess from within the shadows, his dog became anxious and the hair on the back of the dog's neck began to bristle, a sure indication that someone was in the area. At that point Corporal Stapleton saw the figure of someone climbing down from a balcony. He approached and challenged the person to stand still, but the person started to run off. Air Dog Bruce was released and quickly brought the running man down. Although the Malayan thief had covered himself in grease to avoid being captured by human guards, he had not counted on the fact that the grease would be an ineffective precaution against a fully trained RAF Police dog. The Malayan was duly handed over to the civil police and he later received a two-year prison sentence for theft. His capture was apparently the first achieved by the use of a RAF Police dog in the Far East Air Force area.

Towards the end of 1948 in occupied Germany, a team of eighteen RAF Police NCOs, from their headquarters at RAF Buckeburg, were formed into a special flight in order to provide high profile escorts and personal protection for the British High Commissioner for Germany, General Sir Brian Robertson, the former military governor. The team comprising a flight sergeant, a sergeant, eleven corporals and five dog handlers had all been specially selected, trained and equipped to carry out a wide range of duties connected with the task. In addition to guarding the general's official residence and escorting him around Germany, the team were responsible for escorting and protecting his official visitors. Up until that point, the list of VIP's provided with that service had included, the Right Honourable Ernest Bevan, the Foreign Secretary, Viscount Montgomery, Lord Henderson the Defence Secretary and Lord Tedder Marshal of the RAF, as well as the French and American Governors. In addition to wearing their normal RAF Police uniform and accoutrements, members of the elite team, were also authorised to wear the British Army on the Rhine (BAOR) shield emblem, on the right arm of their tunics, just above their badges of rank.

In December 1948, a press release from the Air Ministry reported:

> *...security patrols by RAF Police dogs have released hundreds of men from guard duties at RAF stations throughout the world, and by doing so have saved the country thousands of pounds on the defence budget. The employment of dogs by the RAF began during World War II, when a number of dogs of various breeds, obtained by gift or purchase, were trained and used in places where it was necessary to leave quantities of valuable aircraft, stores and equipment on dispersed sites, or otherwise inaccessible places. After the war the decision was made to increase the use of security dogs and to place it entirely in the hands of the RAF Police. Some of the original gift dogs were returned to their owners and those of assorted breeds were gradually phased out, keeping only the best of the German Shepherds and adding to them a few distinctive dogs of the same breed. German Shepherds were chosen because they are intelligent, have stamina and good noses and also because they can cope with the extremes of the climate met by dogs whose duty may take them to any part of the world where the RAF is operating. An additional reason for the choice of breed is that many people, particularly those with a tendency towards criminal activities, are afraid of German Shepherds, and as such, there is no need for the dogs to be savage beasts. The next decision taken by the RAF was to breed its own dogs so as to maintain a succession of*

dogs with the special qualities required for police and security work. The result is that the RAF now has about five hundred magnificent dogs including one hundred and fifty puppies of various ages. Taking into consideration that one dog with his handler can, in certain circumstances, do the work which would otherwise need anything from ten to twenty men, the value is obvious and the cost is remarkably low; there is no purchasing of expensive dogs and the training is all done by the RAF Police at their training centre at RAF Staverton.

The breeding kennels on the station, under the control of Lieutenant Colonel J Y Baldwin DSO, have been constructed using 'self-help' and salvage materials inside existing wooden huts. The puppies stay for six weeks with their mothers and then have six weeks out on the 'ranges', which are spacious kennels with large outdoor runs surrounded by chain link fencing. At the end of twelve weeks they are all sturdy, healthy youngsters and have been inoculated against the disease Distemper; they are magnificent specimens and much admired by visitors, amongst whom are experts from all over the country and many from abroad. Particularly noticeable is the even size of the puppies in each litter. Some litters have as many as nine puppies with only the slightest variation in weight. They then go out for about six months to various RAF stations around the country to be 'walked' with special instructions that they are to be petted and spoilt and are to mix with people, especially children. This makes them thoroughly friendly and receptive to future training.

Formal training begins when they are about twelve months old, when they are recalled back to the training centre at RAF Staverton. Each young dog is allotted to a RAF Police dog handler, who has already done some training himself with a trained dog, known as an 'instructor dog'. Normally, the handler and his dog stay together until one or the other is posted overseas. After a period of training at Staverton, the handler and his dog are posted for duty to a RAF Station where the handler is required to continue the training he has been taught. The training of a RAF Police dog begins with a response to simple words of command, at first with the dog on the lead and then as things progress the dog is let off the lead.

After learning the basic commands the dog learns to scent, track, leave, and guard a prisoner. Every dog has a name and a number, the latter tattooed inside the dog's ear. After completing this phase of training the dogs are classified as 'Air Dog u/t' (under training). After six months out working on a RAF station the handler and his dog are recalled to the training centre where the dog is graded by the Central Trade Test Board (CTTB). To become an 'Air

Dog 2' he must achieve at least 60% marks for obedience on the lead to certain key words of command, and an elementary standard of obedience to the same commands working off the lead. The dog must also show potential in clearing obstacles, scenting and tracking.

The first trade test that was held at RAF Staverton on the 11th and 12th of November 1948, showed that the dogs examined had, on the whole, achieved the required standard and that all of them were willing to learn and had confidence in their handlers. A few, however, were inclined to shyness because of the isolated locations in which they had been working, but they will probably be returned to the centre for refresher training. They would all scent, follow and attack a criminal, who was equipped with a padded sleeve to receive their bite. However, not all of them would let go of the padded sleeve on the word of command to leave. For classification to 'Air Dog 1' the dog must attain at least 80% marks on normal training, plus 60% marks for any two special items. [1]

At the first board a few dogs achieved 'Air Dog 1' status direct from 'Air Dog u/t', which showed a high level of care and training by their handlers. A 'Leading Air Dog' must gain 100% on normal training plus 60% on four special items, such as refusing to leave his guard except when called away by his handler; attacking a man whilst being shot at (blanks are of course used during the training sessions); attacking through flames; locating dead bodies; tracking a human through various degrees of old scent; identifying property or an individual; message carrying and mine detection. The need for a dog to be trained to let go on the word of command will be readily appreciated as instances may occur when an intruder may be scented, followed and attacked, and who may prove to be an innocent, if careless, person. Usually, the warning notice posted that RAF Police dogs are working in the locality prevents unauthorised people from entering the area, and invariably acts as a deterrent to service personnel who might otherwise be tempted to take short cuts through restricted areas. A highly intelligent and well trained dog may become a 'Junior Instructor Dog', and to do so, must satisfy the CTTB that it has all the 'Leading Air Dog' qualifications plus all the special items and then just that little bit more.

Having been a successful 'Junior Instructor Dog' for a year, it is possible for the dog to be promoted to a 'Senior Instructor Air Dog'. Food for RAF Police dogs are

---

[1] Special items include things such as guarding a prisoner for ten minutes on his own without moving; refusing food except from his own normal bowl; passing other dogs without paying undue attention to them; working through cattle, horses, sheep, cats etc without paying undue attention to them; clearing obstacles; scenting up to four hundred yards with favourable winds and locating live bodies in fields, aircraft, trees etc.

provided by the RAF station on which they work and comprise a daily ration of around 2½ lbs of meat plus any amount of dry tack biscuits that the dog may care to eat. At the training centre the meat is stored in large refrigerators formerly used on naval ships and is obtained from local abattoirs. Although classified as 'unsuitable for human consumption' the meat is perfectly safe for the dogs to consume and is only cooked for puppies and for dogs placed on special diets. The RAF Police have won world-wide renown for their efficiency and high standard of discipline, and also for the tact and patience with which they carry out their many functions. It is all the more appropriate therefore that they should be responsible for the selection, training and employment of their dogs, which give them so much help. The steadily increasing number of trained and qualified dogs has already made its mark both in the security of valuable stores and in the saving of manpower required to guard them. An opportunity for the public to see a demonstration by the RAF Police dogs will be provided at the Royal Tournament at Olympia next spring, when it is hoped that as many as one hundred dogs and their handlers will show off the high standard of proficiency which has been achieved so far.

After completing his two years National Service, Corporal Jenson had been due to be demobilised from the RAF in January 1949, but at the time relations between East and West were not at their best and following the Russian blockade of Berlin, the Berlin Airlift was in full swing to sustain the besieged city. As a result, he along with many other National Servicemen were retained in the services until the crisis eased. Later that same month, Corporal Jenson and Corporal Stanton were exercising their dogs off the lead one afternoon in an area just outside the air raid bunker that had been converted into kennels. After playing normally for a while, the two dogs, for some unexplained reason, ran off into the nearby woods and despite being called back, disappeared. The two handlers quickly searched the immediate area but found no trace of their dogs. As a result, Corporal Jenson informed his commanding officer what had happened and then was left to telephone Flight Lieutenant Cooper at RAF Staverton to inform him that their two dogs were missing. Not surprisingly, Flight Lieutenant Cooper was not at all happy with the news and ordered the two handlers to find the dogs as quickly as possible. Having one fully trained RAF Police patrol dog on the loose in the public domain was a serious enough matter, but having two out on the loose was something else. The two handlers were frantic, after all, if the dogs attacked anyone or for that matter any livestock then there would be serious trouble. After notifying the local civilian police officer, Constable W Richardson, who agreed to help, a full search of the local area was carried out but there was no sign of the two dogs anywhere. By nightfall the search was called off and the two extremely worried handlers returned to their accommodation but had little sleep that night. The search resumed again the following morning but there was still no sign of the dogs anywhere. Things looked about as bad as they could get and just as Corporal Jenson was about to make the dreaded telephone call to Flight Lieutenant Cooper again, Constable Richardson telephoned the unit to report that two German Shepherd dogs matching the description of the RAF Police dogs had been reported playing on a haystack on the estate belonging to the Duke of Grafton, some five miles from the unit. Without wasting any further time a RAF driver and a van were made available and the two dog handlers were transported to the estate. When they arrived, they saw their two dogs lying on a pile of straw. They called out to them and the two dogs, obviously pleased to see their masters, came straight to them. They were returned to the kennels after being fed and watered, a much relieved Corporal Jenson telephoned Flight Lieutenant Cooper to report that the dogs had been recovered and were unharmed. Flight Lieutenant Cooper was pleased with the news and nothing further was heard about the incident thereon after. It seemed that the two dogs had perhaps caught the scent of a bitch on heat somewhere near where they were being exercised and just did what dogs do in such circumstances; ran off to find her.

In Singapore on the 2nd February, Corporal B A Stapleton and his dog were on night duty patrolling the area around the airman's married quarters at RAF Seletar, when Air Dog Bruce indicated that there was someone ahead of them. At that point, a man broke from the undergrowth and started to run off. He was challenged but when he refused to stop the dog was sent after him. After a successful arrest the Malayan, who was in possession of stolen items, was handed over to the civil police and he later received a one-year term of imprisonment for theft. Unfortunately, just after that incident, it became obvious that Air Dog Bruce was going blind however, because the dog had such a good personality, he was released from RAF service and went to live with a local doctor for the rest of his natural life. Consequently, Corporal Stapleton was re-employed on general police duties at the unit.

The Berlin blockade and the deterioration of relations with the Soviet Union had spurred the United States of America, Great Britain, France and other countries within Western Europe to create a counter-balance to the threat from Soviet aggression. As a result of their combined political and military efforts, twelve nations signed up to the North Atlantic Treaty on the 4th April, and in so doing, formed the western Alliance which became known as the *North Atlantic Treaty Organisation* (NATO). Eight days later, the Berlin Blockade, which had been in force for three hundred and twenty-two days, was called off by the Russians.

In May, eighteen-year old Corporal P J Mason successfully completed his training on Course No 42 at RAF Staverton to become a RAF Police dog handler, and was posted with Air Dog Ranger to RAF Henlow in Bedfordshire. Corporal Mason had joined the RAF the year before in June and after completing his recruit training he had been sent to RAF Pershore where between early December 1948 and late February 1949 he underwent initial RAF Police training. He recalls that although there was much talk of the 'infamous' Colonel Baldwin during the six-week course, he never actually saw him. At the time the principal members of staff at the Dog Training School were Flight Lieutenant Cooper, Flight Sergeant Legg, Sergeant Darnell and the course instructor, Corporal Davies. Additionally, Leading Aircraftswoman Kathryn Hodgson was one of the many kennel-maids employed at the school looking after the dogs. Corporal Mason recalls that when he arrived at the school he found it strange to see many of the instructors and other students with bandaged arms. However, when he saw many of the dogs in the kennels, the mystery was solved. Air Dog Ranger, a German Shepherd dog had been donated to the RAF by a lady who lived in Cardiff. During his dog training he recalls that the students were required to visit a nearby slaughterhouse to collect meat for the dogs, and a farm to collect straw for the dogs' bedding. At that time RAF Henlow was being used for the experimental testing of newly designed parachutes. He recalls how Dakota aircraft used to fly over the unit dropping the rubber weighed parachutes onto the grass airfield. He also recalls that there were a number of old wooden huts on the airfield that had been used to house German prisoners-of-war who, during their internment, had beautifully decorated the interiors with religious paintings. Additionally, there was also an old farmhouse on the edge of the airfield that was reputedly haunted.

In June, much to the delight of the general public, an impressive turn out of eighty-eight personnel from the RAF Police Dog Training School appeared for the first time at the Royal Tournament in London, along with fifty-nine adult dogs and twelve puppies. Of the dogs that took part in the display at Olympia, forty-two were bred by the RAF and twenty-nine were dogs donated as gifts by the public. Marching smartly into the arena the RAF Police Dog Demonstration Team was lead by the commanding officer, Flight Lieutenant R D Cooper and RAF Police Mascot Leading Air Dog Storm, a pure white German Shepherd dog. The dramatic commentary throughout the performance was delivered by Deputy Provost Marshal, Group Captain C Richdale, who described the RAF Police German Shepherd dogs as '£2,500 worth of high explosive dog'. The public loved them and as such, they were an instant success, proving to be a first rate publicity campaign for the branch and indeed the service. Both the *Daily Telegraph* and the *Manchester Guardian* newspapers reported that,

'The RAF Police Dog Demonstration Team, under the command of Flight Lieutenant R D Cooper, stole the whole show with their marvellous performance'.

After their first and highly successful public appearance at the Royal Tournament, there were no further problems in obtaining suitable gift dogs from the general public, who it seemed, were only to willing to donate their German Shepherds to the RAF Police. A nominal role of the personnel and dogs that took part in the Royal Tournament is included at the end of this chapter.

On the 7th July, their Majesties the King and Queen, together with Princess Margaret and the Duchess of Kent, attended the opening day of the first post war RAF Display, which was held over two days at RAF Farnborough and attended by some 80,000 members of the public. During the highly successful show, some 5,400 members of the RAF were on duty at the unit, with 400 of them being RAF Police personnel carrying out a wide spectrum of police and security commitments in support of the event. In addition, the RAF Police Dog Demonstration Team also appeared during the display to entertain the crowds.

During the same month with the emergency in Berlin over, Corporal Jenson was demobilised from the service, but before leaving had the extremely stressful task of returning Air Dog Eos to RAF Staverton and walking away from his kennel knowing that they would never see each other again.

At the end of the summer Corporal P J Mason was placed on an overseas draft and shortly after, he left Henlow for the transit camp at RAF Hednesford. At the time, it was common practice for RAF Police NCOs awaiting their draft to be employed with the local civil police patrolling the town. During his brief stay at Hednesford, Corporal Mason, operating from the local police station, carried out a number of patrols with his civilian counter-parts.

On the outskirts of Bristol, during the early hours of the 3rd September, a newly developed passenger aircraft called the Brabazon was, for the first time, towed out from a large hangar at RAF Filton. The new aircraft, which was equal in length to six double-decker London buses, drew a considerable amount of interest from the media and the general public, who had lined the perimeter fences of the unit, in the hope of catching a glimpse of it. In fact, so great was the interest and their numbers, that most members of No 6 RAF Police District, and a number of carefully chosen RAF Police dog teams were tasked to assist the station police in preserving the security of the station. Although the aircraft was only conducting engine tests and was soon safely back inside the hangar, the media and a large number of the public remained at the perimeter fences all day, just in case the aircraft was brought out again. However, the real event took place the following day, when the aircraft took off on its short but successful maiden flight. The crowds were out in abundance, accompanied by a considerable number of the world's media. Once again, the RAF Police and especially the dog handlers were kept extremely busy in maintaining the security of the unit and preventing the more enthusiastic spectators from running amok in their keenness to get closer to the runway and of course the aircraft.

In mid October, Corporal Mason boarded the troopship *Dilwara* bound for Egypt, and was immediately placed in charge of the ship's detention area 'the Brig' and given his first prisoner, a soldier who had a reputation for 'jumping ship'. The voyage however, turned out to be uneventful and shortly after arriving in Egypt, Corporal Mason handed over his prisoner to the waiting escort and was then sent to the newly established RAF Police Dog Training School at Kasfareet to await the arrival of his dog Ranger, who was being shipped out on a freight ship. At the time, the dog school at Kasfareet, previously located at 112MU Wadi Ysira, was under the command of Warrant Officer Hobson, who was later succeeded by Flying Officer Stromquist and a Sergeant Smith, both of whom had previously served in Greece.

With a growing reputation for training dogs, the Air Ministry in London received a request from the Commissioner of Police for the Federation of Malaya, who asked for RAF Police assistance to help establish a dog training program for his force and to assist with counter-terrorist operations. In response, two RAF Police dog handlers, Corporal B A Stapleton, who was stationed at RAF Seletar and Corporal P Thackray who was stationed at RAF Changi were detached to the Malaya Federation Police Training School in Kuala Lumpur on the 18th October. Upon arriving in Kuala Lumpur, the two NCOs were allocated accommodation with No 210 Provost Company Royal Military Police, and the following day they reported to the civil police training school where a police lieutenant welcomed them both and took them along to the dog section, which comprised a large compound containing around thirty dogs of all sizes and breeds. After checking them all out the NCOs chose two dogs each, and almost immediately began the task of training them to track in the jungle. Corporal Stapleton named his two German Shepherds Lassie and Lucky, while Corporal Thackray named his two dogs as Bobbie and Jasper.

On the 19th November, Corporal's Stapleton and Thackray were attached to the 2nd Battalion of the Coldstream Guards for administrative purposes, but remained under the operational control of the civil police. With dogs that were trained the two NCOs joined a police counter-terrorist jungle squad that was under the command of Lieutenant N R McGill, a former colonial police officer from Palestine and an experienced terrorist fighter. On joining his squad, Lieutenant McGill gave the NCOs two important pieces of advice to stay alive; the first being that the terrorist always endeavours to kill, when under fire or even when wounded. In the latter situation the terrorist will usually have a primed grenade in his hand, which he will detonate when approached by the security forces. Additionally, even the dead bodies of terrorists can be booby-trapped. The second piece of advice concerned hornet nests that might accidentally be disturbed whilst on patrol. "If that happened", he said, "it was every man for himself in trying to get as far away from the angry insects as quickly as possible to avoid being strung to death".

On the 30th November, Corporal Stapleton was called out to an area where three terrorists had been killed in an earlier confrontation with the soldiers from the Coldstream Guards. A fourth terrorist, who had been wounded, had escaped into thick undergrowth and Corporal Stapleton was asked to mount a search for him. As it was difficult for Corporal Stapleton to handle his two dogs and his Sten-gun he was given an American Carbine by the civil police which was a vast improvement on the heavy Sten-gun; it held fifteen rounds in the magazine and could be held and fired quite easily in one hand. Soon after, he began the search using Lassie and Lucky and it was Lassie who picked up the scent, which they followed. Soon after, Lassie indicated that the terrorist was close by, and at that point Corporal Stapleton saw him still armed and, remembering what he had been told by Lieutenant McGill about wounded terrorists being dangerous, he opened fire and shot the terrorist dead.

In Egypt at the beginning of December, Corporal P J Mason and Air Dog Ranger were posted to RAF Spinney Wood, a radio communications unit close to RAF Ismailia. Because of the anti-British problems in Egypt at the time, it was unwise for British service personnel on guard duty at night to leave the sanctuary of the shadows and venture into the glare of any lighting, as Corporal Mason quickly found out. He had not been in Egypt long when during a night patrol he walked into the glare of the lights illuminating the unit's perimeter fence. Suddenly, two rifle shots rang out from the desert and narrowly passed over his head. He quickly took cover in the dark but by then, whoever had fired the shots had fled. It was a lucky escape and a stark reminder that there were people lurking about at night intent on murdering British service personnel. Some time later, Corporal Mason had another frightening encounter when he challenged an Egyptian civilian who was acting suspiciously. The man pulled out a large knife and threatened Corporal Mason with it. Mason however, produced his revolver and ordered the man to drop the knife. The man reluctantly complied and Mason arrested him and handed him over to the Egyptian Police.

On the 15th December, whilst Corporal Stapleton and Lieutenant McGill were out on patrol, they suddenly came under attack by someone using an automatic weapon. Both men instantly took cover and remained on the ground until the attack had stopped. A short time later they searched the area but their assailant had gone leaving behind a quantity of spent 9mm shell cases. Using Lassie, Corporal Stapleton followed the scent of their attacker for over a mile to an unmanned rubber collection station before finally giving up the search. A number of subsequent patrols were conducted in the area of the Slim River over the following weeks and although there was ample evidence of terrorist activity in the area and various hide-outs were destroyed, there were no further direct confrontations.

Although the RAF Police dog breeding program had been well thought out, it nevertheless proved to be problematic. Basically, it was not cost effective because the dogs had to be looked after for about fifteen months until they were old enough to be trained. Even at that point, many of the young dogs were rejected simply because they did not have the right qualities required of a police dog. As a result, the experimental breeding program was abandoned and in addition to the German Shepherd dog other suitable large breeds, offered by the public, were tried out by the service on an experimental basis.

In Malaya on the 2nd January 1950, Corporal Stapleton was called to a place called Serenban where a civil police convoy had been ambushed and many policemen had been killed and injured. A Ghurkha unit had been called in to help hunt down the terrorists and soon after, they reported finding an abandoned jungle hideout capable of housing up to two hundred terrorists. Corporal Stapleton and his dogs picked up on a scent and started to follow it into the jungle. He remained with the Ghurkhas until he was recalled to Kula Kuba Bahru Depot. However, the Ghurkhas continued their hunt and some time after Corporal Stapleton's departure they caught up with the terrorists and in the fire-fight that ensued, a large number of the terrorists were killed.

During the same month, Corporal C Agar, having served as a dog handler at six different units within the Suez Canal Zone was posted to RAF Habbaniya in Iraq with Corporal Alexander to form a new dog section there. During his twenty months spent in Egypt the RAF Police dog teams had played an important role in helping to protect RAF assets from theft and damage and indeed, on a number of occasions those seeking to steal or destroy RAF material, who were routinely armed, had been apprehended by the dogs on patrol. After a short while two other dog handlers and their dogs were posted into Habbanyia bringing the section strength up to four teams. For Corporal Agar, Habbanyia was the best RAF station he had served on up to that point. It was like a small town and well appointed with amenities. The food being served in the cookhouse was good and plentiful and the daily rations for the dogs were of an equal standard. Unlike Egypt, the Iraqi people seemed friendlier towards the RAF and were not as inclined to steal anything not guarded. Once settled in to their new environment the dog handlers concentrated their night-time patrols around the technical and domestic areas of the camp while NCOs from the RAF Police Mounted Section with their horses patrolled the airfield and outer reaches of the camp.

Unfortunately, around this period, the political tension both within Europe and around the world was beginning to increase again and the relationship between the Americans and the Russians was entering a state of rapid deterioration. The Russian leader; Stalin, was steadily absorbing all the countries of eastern Europe into the Soviet Union and the Russians were particularly active in recruiting new allies elsewhere around the world. In addition they were also rapidly building up their military strength again and were eager to develop a nuclear capability all of their own. Consequently, the whole situation fuelled American suspicions of Russian expansion and likewise the Russians were wary of the Americans. As such, the 1950's heralded the start of the period known as the *'The Cold War'* between NATO and the Soviet Bloc alliances.

During the same month, Corporal P J Mason and Air Dog Ranger left Egypt and were posted over to RAF Habbaniya in Iraq, which was a large airfield located west of Baghdad. He recalls that one of the high points of his tour of duty in Iraq were the occasional visits to the leave centre at RAF Seramadia, situated close to the border with Turkey. After the heat and the dust of the desert, the lush vegetation at the leave centre was a real paradise to experience.

On the 21st January, both Corporal's Stapleton and Thackray were called out to assist soldiers of the Green Howard's Regiment in locating a wounded terrorist who had escaped into an area of swamp. As soon as the NCOs had been briefed they set about searching the area with their dogs for a scent to follow. Soon after, two of the dogs, Bobby and Lassie jumped into a stretch of water and something appeared to go tragically wrong; Bobbie just disappeared below the surface, while Lassie convulsed, bit her back and immediately sank below the water. At that point Corporal Stapleton saw that there were lots of dead fish floating on the surface and then noticed a cable running into the water. A later enquiry, established that it was a live electric cable, which had been severed by a bullet and which had dropped into the water. Although both police dogs had been instantly killed by the 30,000 volt current, their loss had actually saved their handlers and other members of the patrol from being electrocuted.

During the month of March, the battalion of Coldstream Guards were replaced by the Scots Guards and during their first operational patrol together

Corporal's Stapleton and Thackray were tasked to cover the possible escape route in an area where terrorists were known to be operating. They were told that the area of jungle concerned was going to be bombed by RAF aircraft sent in from Singapore. The aircraft arrived soon after and the jungle area concerned was blasted by a series of explosions. As soon as it was safe to do so the NCOs began to search the affected area where the ground had been churned up by the force of the blasts, which would, without a doubt have killed anyone in that area. It was therefore surprising that the search failed to find any evidence of the terrorists. A few days later, both NCOs were tasked to assist the civil police during a series of patrols up in the Cameron Highlands. In between actual patrols to locate the terrorists, as part of winning over the local population, the civil police and the two NCOs visited many villages in the region where terrorists had murdered members of the community.

On the 5th May, after being deployed on jungle patrols for almost two months, Corporal's Stapleton and Thackray returned to their base depot at Kula Kuba Bahru but after only a few days rest were back out helping to search for terrorists in the Batu caves and along the Slim River. Again, although the patrol found amble evidence of terrorists operating within the area, they encountered no direct contact with them.

In Korea on the 25th June, North Korean troops crossed the 38th parallel and invaded South Korea in support of their government's claim of sovereignty over all the territory in the Korean peninsular. As a result, the matter was brought before the United Nation's Security Council who deemed the invasion to be unlawful. As a consequence, the United States of America, Great Britain and a number of other British Commonwealth countries, assembled troops and went to war once again in the defence of South Korea.

Air Commodore de Putron the Provost Marshal, and his wife lived in a bungalow located just outside the main entrance to RAF Biggin Hill, the unit made famous as a fighter station during the *Battle of Britain*. Each morning the Provost Marshal's driver; a RAF Police sergeant, drove him up to the Air Ministry in London and returned him home each evening and the routine was only interrupted whenever the Provost Marshal was away visiting units around the globe. Unlike today, his residence was not especially guarded because in those days it was not necessary because no particular security threat existed. The Provost Marshal's wife was a frequent visitor to the RAF Police guardroom on the unit and adored dogs so much that apparently, she often took the unit's RAF Police dog out for a walk with her during the afternoon.

On the 7th July, their Majesties the King and Queen, together with Princess Margaret and the Duchess of Kent, attended the opening day of the first post war

RAF Display, which was held over two days at RAF Farnborough and attended by some 80,000 members of the public. During the highly successful show, some 5,400 members of the RAF were on duty at the unit, with just under 400 of them being RAF Police personnel carrying out a wide spectrum of police and security commitments in support of the event. Prior to the war events such as this had been policed by the civil police on a repayment basis with the costs coming from the profits destined for the RAF Benevolent Fund. With the expansion during the war of the RAF Police, a decision was reached whereby the RAF Police would take on the role. Accordingly, this was the first time that the RAF Police had managed such a massive public event and despite the youth and relative inexperience of many of the NCOs on duty, all commitments were carried out professionally and with tact. In addition, the RAF Police Dog Demonstration Team also appeared during the display to entertain the crowds.

During the month of August, Corporal Stapleton and his dog teamed up with a RAF Regiment unit at Kajang, and shortly after they started out on a four-day jungle patrol. At one point the Chinese interpreter knocked over a hornets nest and was quickly overwhelmed by the disturbed and angry insects. Needless to say, that he was so badly strung that his body swelled up to twice its normal size. After administering first aid on the spot, the patrol retraced a two-hour trek through the jungle to reach the main road where the injured man could be taken away to hospital for treatment. The patrol resumed and some time later came across and searched some caves that had been used by Colonel Spencer Chapman's *Force 136*, a British-led underground resistance group that had operated in Malaya during World War II, co-ordinating acts of sabotage and espionage against the Japanese. During the night of the 15th August, the patrol was summoned to meet the civil police at Bentong, from where an English lady, who was a former member of *Force 136*, and her two bodyguards had been kidnapped by terrorists. The patrol quickly searched the immediate area where the three people had been abducted and in the process detained a Chinese man for questioning. Shortly after, another patrol out searching for the three missing people, reported hearing a woman's scream. At that point, Corporal Stapleton and his dog were transported to the site where the scream had been heard and he and a Ghurkha patrol continued to search the dense jungle but found nothing. Three days later, however, the bodies of the woman and her two bodyguards were found some two hundred metres from the place where the Chinese male had been detained; all three had been murdered. Back at Bentong, Corporal Stapleton and police dog Lucky joined a number of local patrols to track down the terrorists who were stopping and searching buses for particular passengers who they promptly murdered before making good their escape along the many narrow tracks that ran through the rubber plantations.

Having enjoyed his short, but exciting time in the RAF, Corporal D R E Jenson decided to rejoin the RAF in October 1950. Although he again chose to join the trade of RAF Police, he decided against becoming a dog handler. Although in the years that followed, he never came across Air Dog Eos, he did learn that he had joined the RAF Police Dog Demonstration Team and had appeared at the Royal Tournament in London.

On the 20th December, Corporal Stapleton and a number of civil police officers were returning to the police station in Bentong after completing a patrol when they were stopped by a Ghurkha patrol that had flushed out an ambush set up by the terrorists on the only road leading into the village. Had the Ghurkhas not discovered the terrorists when they did, perhaps the ambush may have been set-up to take the returning police patrol out. As a stark reminder of just how dangerous things were, Corporal Stapleton heard, three days later, that the terrorists had killed his friend, Lieutenant McGill at Kula Kuba Bahru.

Corporal C Agar arrived at Southampton two days before Christmas on the Troopship *Empire Ken*, after serving almost two and a half years out in Egypt and Iraq. After completing his disembarkation leave he was posted onto station police duties and was later promoted to the rank of sergeant.

On the 31st December, Corporal Stapleton and his dog were part of a patrol operating in an area where terrorists had been reported. As the patrol closed in on the target it was starting to go dark and Corporal Stapleton and Lucky were instructed to remain on the outer fringe to engage any terrorist trying to escape. After a great deal of gun fire, Corporal Stapleton and his dog went into the area to look for bodies, and at that point he saw two figures start to run off. He followed, shooting at each one in turn, but they separated. Corporal Stapleton and Lucky followed one of them through thick undergrowth until he came into view. At that point, Corporal Stapleton opened fire and shot the terrorist dead.

During the same month, the RAF Police branch as a whole where delighted when His Majesty King George VI, graciously approved a badge for the RAF Police. The idea of a badge had first been discussed in September 1943, when a request was circulated to units asking for the submission of suitable designs. Unfortunately, nothing suitable was produced and because of the war effort the idea was suspended. However, in early 1949, Group Captain A A Newbury decided that the design for any suitable badge, had to be based on fact and not fancy. He therefore investigated the symbols of Nemesis, the goddess of vengeance and bringer of swift and terrible retribution to those doing wrong. Of the four attributes of Nemesis, the griffin emerged as the most attractive and appropriate for the badge, mainly because it was the symbol of guardianship. The motto, or any reasonable suggestion for one, seemed as difficult to design as the badge. However, after much thought, the motto 'Fiat Justitia' which freely translates as 'Let justice be done', was chosen. Although Group Captain Newbury was the driving force behind the design two other provost officers; Wing Commander P Henniker-Heaton and Flight Lieutenant G F McMahon DFM, came up with a design acceptable to the college of heralds.

During the year adequate numbers of suitable German Shepherd dogs were being given to the RAF as unconditional gifts by the public and as such the RAF Police Dog breeding program was brought to an end.

In Malaya on the 3rd February 1951, a RAF and Naval air strike was called in by the civil police against an area of jungle suspected of containing a terrorist base. On the ground, Corporal Stapleton and police dog Lucky were part of the military operation to round up any terrorists attempting to escape. When the air strike ended, there was no sign of the terrorists and the search was called off. However, as Corporal Stapleton was making his way back to his vehicle he saw the face of someone who was hiding in the undergrowth. He immediately raised the alarm and started firing his weapon into the area where the person was hiding. As the area was searched a rifle, a grenade and a trail of blood was discovered. Corporal Stapleton and Lucky followed the trail until they caught sight of a man. He was challenged but started to run off. Corporal Stapleton opened fire and the man dropped to the ground dead. He was later identified as Lan-Jang-San, a dangerous terrorist who was wanted 'dead or alive' and for whom a reward had been offered. Corporal Stapleton's detachment with the civil police came to an end a week later and he returned to RAF Kuala Lumpar. As for the dog he had trained and, who had performed so well in such dangerous circumstances, he was donated by the civil police to the RAF and became Air Dog Lucky 3610.

During the same month, the RAF Police Dog Training School moved from RAF Staverton and joined the RAF Police Driving School at RAF Netheravon situated on the edge of the Salisbury Plain. At the same time, plans were also made to move the RAF Police Training School, from RAF Pershore in the Vale of Evesham, to the same unit later that year. Netheravon was one of the most historic RAF stations, having been one of the first permanent airfields built for the Royal Flying Corps during the Great War. However, during World War II, it had also taken on an active role when it was used to train glider pilots and to plan 'Operation Market Garden', the ill-fated Allied airborne landings at Arnhem in Holland.

In Iraq on the 4th April, in the early hours of the morning, Corporal H T Raybone, a twenty-year old RAF Police dog handler, attached to No 3 RAF Police District, was on patrol at RAF Habbaniya near Baghdad, when his dog suddenly indicated something suspicious ahead of them. Although the night was pitch black he started to investigate and soon discovered four bandits, two of which, were armed with rifles, standing not far from his position. He challenged them to surrender but they started to run off so he immediately released his dog to round them up. As the dog quickly closed the gap between him and the intruders, it was shot as it fearlessly attacked one of the intruders. Despite the fact that his dog lay dead, Corporal Raybone, who was armed, continued to pursue the four men and in the process, one of them turned and aimed a rifle at him. In response, Corporal Raybone shot the man dead but the other three continued and made good their escape. The bandits were all armed and were out to steal explosives and whatever else they could lay their hands on. Indeed, they would have done so, had the Corporal Raybone and his dog not been on patrol that night. In recognition of his prompt and courageous action that morning, Corporal Raybone was subsequently awarded a Commendation for Bravery from the Commander-in-Chief Middle East Air Force (MEAF). His dog, which had died simply doing its job, was buried with dignity at the RAF Police Dog Section at RAF Habbaniya.

At RAF Pershore on the 26th April, before an assembled parade, Air-Vice Marshal A C Sanderson CB, CBE, DFC, formally and proudly presented the newly authorised RAF Police badge to Air Commodore de Putron. In his speech before the presentation, the Air-Vice Marshal spoke warmly about the branch as he said:

'It is appropriate, I think, before presenting this badge, to look back and see how our Royal Air Force Police first came into being. You will remember how on the 1st April 1918, just thirty-three years ago, the Royal Flying Corps and the Royal Naval Air Service merged to form the Royal Air Force. At the same time, the Army Provost Marshal of Great Britain was made responsible for the policing of this new force. He appointed Major Pryor to act as Provost Marshal of the Royal Air Force.

In 1919, Major Pryor was demobilised and Lieutenant Colonel Brierley, who later became a Wing Commander, took over the provost duties in addition to his normal personnel staff duties at the Air Ministry, and for some years, the duties of discipline and Provost Marshal were combined.

By 1920, the RAF Police School had been opened at Halton with intakes of fifteen trainees, undergoing six-week courses. It was commanded by Flight Lieutenant Bishop who had been appointed Assistant Provost Marshal and the instructors were loaned temporarily from the Military Police School, until such time as RAF Police instructors could be trained to supersede them.

By 1931, Squadron Leader Stammers, who was struggling with the dual role, found that because of the expansion of the Royal Air Force, it was necessary for him to concentrate all his energies on the full time duty of Provost Marshal. By 1934, the global establishment of the RAF Service Police at home was, 254 and 160 overseas.

In the spring of 1939, Provost Officers were recruited for the first time and were posted for duty at Command and Group Headquarters, whilst by the summer, the RAF Police strength had increased to 1,470 men all told.

When war was declared, the RAF Police were ready and in fact, a small party under the command of Squadron Leader Richdale, now the Command Provost Marshal, Middle East, was already serving with the Advanced Air Striking Force in France. Naturally, with the rapid expansion, there were mounting demands for Service Police and although the school had by this time moved to Uxbridge and had increased it's intake considerably, we were not able to meet all our requirements and were in fact some 1,500 men deficient.

It is interesting here to mention that the WAAF Police were formed in 1940 and gradually grew in numbers as the war progressed. When Group Captain Stammers' eleven year tour as Provost Marshal came to an end in 1942 and he was replaced by Air Commodore Owen de Putron, the RAF Provost Police had already been formed and were active in Iraq and the Middle East in addition to the United Kingdom. As the war increased in size, so RAF Police were needed in almost all theatres.

The Special Investigation Branch which had been formed in 1931 with one officer and four NCOs, had expanded considerably and was now handling many thousands of cases. The RAF Police took a very active part in the invasion of Europe in 1944 and received numerous commendations for gallant work. The Provost Branch has received twenty-five British awards for officers and thirty three for airmen and a solid tradition of service has been built up. The RAF Police reached it's peak in January 1945, when it consisted of 468 officers, 20,300 airmen, 56 WAAF Police Officers and 400 airwomen.

In 1947, the Provost Branch was officially recognised and became a separate branch of the Royal Air Force. Amongst it's many commitments today, it includes participation in 'Escape and Evasion' exercises, in which many of you have, I believe, already taken part, ceremonial parades such as the presentation of the Kings colour to the Royal Air Force next month in Hyde Park, escort and convoy work including the movement of ammunition by road and sea and security cover for USAF airfields. Nor must we overlook the police dogs which are a most important and growing commitment. We now have 570 dogs and hope to go up to 900 as soon as possible. Apart from their normal duties of guarding maintenance units and patrolling airfields, they have already been used successfully on active service in Malaya.

The introduction of the new trade structure this year has done much to improve pay and prospects for the RAF Police and I feel sure that you having those two paramount qualities required of police in the services, outstanding integrity and loyalty, will continue to uphold the fine traditions which the provost branch, young as it is, has already moulded for itself.

I should just like now to make a short reference to Air Commodore de Putron, his term of office as Provost Marshal, lasting nine years is about to end. I should like on behalf of the RAF, to congratulate him for his loyal and efficient handling of the RAF Police during this long period. He has every reason to be proud and satisfied with his work, the results of which can be seen wherever the RAF is serving.

It now becomes my very pleasant duty to hand over to the Provost Marshal this badge, which His Majesty the King has been graciously pleased to approve. The Griffin in the centre is the symbol of retribution, whilst the motto, Let Justice be Done, aptly epitomises the role of the Royal Air Force Police'.

Air Commodore de Putron retired as the RAF Provost Marshal during the month of May, after nine extremely productive years. He was succeeded by an officer from the General Duties (Flying) Branch, Air Commodore B C Yarde CBE, who had been the station commander at RAF Gatow during the Berlin airlift. Although not a professional policeman, he was certainly impressed with the work carried out by the branch, and was extremely happy to take on his new appointment.

During 1951, Air Dog Rex and Air Dog Whiskey, two of the smallest German Shepherd dogs taken on by the RAF Police, completed their training and together with their handlers; Corporal K Crossland (Whiskey) and Corporal R Long (Rex), were posted to RAF Tengah in Singapore. Their lack of size however, did not prevent the two dogs from attacking anything or anybody, anywhere at any time. Rex in particular, would regularly eat his way through kennels, even those that had been reinforced with metal sheets. He was an acclaimed escapologist and would regularly be reported as being out on patrol around the airfield alone. Consequently, Corporal Long would be urgently summoned to take control of his charge. At the time, the dog section at RAF Tengah occupied a bungalow situated quite a way from the main camp. As such, the building also served as home for the single handlers serving on the section. Additionally, the section was proud to have standing in front of their building, an old Japanese field gun left at the unit following the Japanese surrender at the end of World War II. Although the gun no longer functioned, some of the handlers took great delight in simulating it being fired by dropping 'thunder-flash pyrotechnics' into the barrel. When the thunder-flash went off it produced an effect similar to the gun actually being discharged.

As Her Royal Highness Princess Elizabeth, Duchess of Edinburgh, was leaving the Royal Tournament on the 19th June, she commented on the fact that the Royal Air Force Police guard of honour were not accompanied by any RAF Police dogs. Her Royal Highness suggested that the Queen would undoubtedly like to see RAF Police dogs, when she visited the tournament later that week. Accordingly, two days later, Sergeant F Holland together with six handlers and their dogs, were presented to Her Majesty, as she left the Royal Box. At first Her Majesty was a little hesitant in approaching the fearsome looking dogs and even commented that she hoped they would not bite her. They did not of course, and the presentation was a great success for the branch.

At RAF Netheravon on the 10th July, Corporal B A Stapleton, having completed his tour in the Far East, reported for duty as an instructor at the RAF Police Dog Training School. After being interviewed by Lieutenant Colonel Baldwin, it was decided to take advantage of the experience he had gained out in the Far East. At the time, Lieutenant Colonel Baldwin was keen to improve the training of RAF Police dogs to track and to be an effective tool in rescue operations such as mine disasters. Consequently, Corporal Stapleton was instructed to select two dogs, which showed potential to be trained in both disciplines. After inspecting a number of dogs, Corporal Stapleton selected two German Shepherd dogs; Air Dog Ralph and Air Dog Prince, as being suitable for the specialist task. The additional training program however, was only to be carried out in between the normal basic dog training courses held at the school.

In the Far East, an estimated 30,000 people attended the 4th Singapore Air Display, which took place on the 1st September 1951, at Kallang Airport in Singapore. Accordingly, a large number of RAF Police personnel were on duty there carrying out a wide range of police and security duties at what was undoubtedly, the finest display of it's kind ever seen in that part of the world. While the flying displays of various aircraft, including the Vampire, the Meteor, the Dakota and the Sunderland Flying Boat, thrilled the assembled crowds, one of the highlights of the show was of course the excellent display staged by the local and specially trained RAF Police Dog Demonstration Team. The demonstration commenced with the six handlers and their dogs being marched onto the arena by Warrant Officer T B Whittaker, from No 2 RAF Police District, and included the full range of obedience, search, obstacle and criminal work. It was an excellent display which gave a great deal of pleasure not only to the assembled crowds, but also to Air Commodore J L F Fullergood CBE, the Air-Officer-Commanding Malaya.

During September, after completing his recruit training, Aircraftsman J Bastard reported to the RAF Police School at RAF Pershore where he joined No 35 Initial Police Course. Pershore being in the Vale of Evesham was extremely isolated, making visits off camp a very expensive business, and the accommodation was rather poor and comprised wooden huts that were sparsely furnished and which were very cold and damp in the winter. As there were very few lockers available, uniforms had to be hung up on nails in the walls and turned periodically to prevent them from going mouldy. The floors of each hut occupied by trainees, was kept highly polished and felt pads were used by personnel to 'glide' over the surface without spoiling the shine. The ends of each bed were blancoed white as was the inside of the pot belly coke stove when not in use. Coke bins were highly polished with brass cleaner and the wooden handles and broom heads were scrapped clean each day with a razor blade. The wash house was located in a separate building and comprised a long trough which served as the sink fed by numerous taps which provided only cold water, even in winter, and the 'Bath Book' had to be signed at least once a week by all trainees indicating that they had bathed. Additionally, Aircraftsman Bastard recalls that the standard of the food served in the cookhouse was not particularly good and meals were rushed. As there were so many students on No 35 Initial Police Course it was divided into A and B Flights, with A Flight comprising regular airmen and B Flight comprising National Servicemen. During his training Aircraftsman Bastard had volunteered to become a dog handler and so in November after successfully completing the course with a pass mark of 75%, he reported to RAF Netheravon to begin his training as a dog handler. After being assigned Air Dog Rex 3788, an eighteen month old German Shepherd dog, the training began under the direction of the course instructor; Corporal C Jones.

After five months of training his two dogs to track and to detect the presence of trapped humans, Corporal B A Stapleton was invited to the Civil Defence Centre at Easingwold on the 14th December, to give a demonstration of what Air Dog Prince had been trained to do. During the demonstration a number of 'trapped victims' were hidden in a variety of damaged buildings throughout the site, and on checking each building, Prince successfully located all of them. At the end of the demonstration, Corporal Stapleton was invited to stay on at the centre where he received from the civil defence instructor's additional information regarding personal safety and search techniques whilst operating within damaged buildings.

Personnel and Dogs from the RAF Police Training School That Took Part in the Royal Tournament at Olympia in London in 1949

Flight Lieutenant R D Cooper – Officer Commanding
with 3227 LAD Storm (Mascot).

1562533 Sergeant Darnell – with 3192 SI Rex
Opening Individual Criminal Display.

MASS OBEDIENCE DEMONSTRATION

No 1 TEAM					
2399238	Cpl Roper	-	V.6	ADI	Van
3115829	Cpl Howorth	-	IN4	ADII	Nomad
2405008	Cpl Knight	-	3292	ADII	Vicky
2396659	Cpl McNab	-	3245	ADII	Bruce
3114218	Cpl Stewart	-	N4	ADII	Nero
2400238	Cpl Willett	-	3309	ADII	Don
4030256	Cpl Burrows	-	1A3	ADII	Ajax
2396507	Cpl Baxter	-	1G1	ADII	Garry
2396507	Cpl Sutherland	-	N2	LAD	Nolan
2395304	Cpl Oakes	-	J6	ADII	Juno
4018055	Cpl Pestall	-	3246	ADI	Gift
2399020	Cpl Leigh	-	3322	ADII	Rob
No 2 TEAM					
2402825	Cpl Hastwell	-	F3	ADI	Flicka
2399211	Cpl Taylor	-	M1	LAD	Monty
2404379	Cpl Finch	-	1J6	ADII	Jolly
3114211	Cpl Woodward	-	V2	LAD	Viking
4030363	Cpl Holden	-	1A2	ADI	Ace
2362880	Cpl Gallop	-	3299	ADI	Don
2387193	Cpl Lakin	-	A3	ADII	Andy
2399302	Cpl Stevens	-	1D1	ADII	Desperate
4029064	Cpl Mowbray	-	1D41	ADI	Devil
3107375	Cpl Collins	-	C1	LAD	Caro
4030488	Cpl Burnett	-	R1	ADII	Richdale
2234314	Sgt Irvin	-	E7	LAD	Eos
No 3 TEAM					
2402765	Cpl Fyfe	-	1H4	ADII	Hugo
4030497	Cpl Hondaley	-	1D2	ADII	Demon
4006026	Cpl Donloavy	-	3260	ADII	Rex
2396367	Cpl Howes	-	1I5	ADII	Irish
4003160	Cpl Collins	-	J2	ADI	Jason

2386190	Cpl Pike	-	1B1	ADII	Buster
2399226	Cpl Welch	-	1N5	ADII	Noble
3116954	Cpl Salter	-	N1	ADI	Noel
2399026	Cpl Iley	-	G1	LAD	Guy
2405596	Cpl Clark	-	3259	ADII	Prince
2397972	Cpl Jamieson	-	1N8	ADII	Nettle
2404682	Cpl Hewitt	-	3365	ADII	Grant

JUMPING & TRICK DISPLAY

NCO in Charge – 1318315 Sgt Holland					
3500279	Cpl Sutton	-	3236	SI	Mick
2362435	Cpl Morgan	-	3271	JI	Max
2350814	Cpl Pate	-	3241	LAD	Wolf
2362441	Cpl Pickering	-	3247	LAD	Rex
4030107	Cpl McDermott	-	1H8	LAD	Homer
2388032	Cpl Thomas	-	3364	ADI	Billy
4029748	Cpl Crowther	-	3356	ADI	Silver
2386528	Cpl Ryan	-	V4	ADI	Vincent
2399431	Cpl Ronaldo	-	3361	ADI	Deane
2390374	Cpl Gillespie	-	V5	ADI	Voss

MASS TACKLING DISPLAY

NCO in Charge – 2362064 Sgt Tustin					
3115523	Cpl Shutt	-	1489	JI	Prince
2362064	Cpl Livey	-	3262	LAD	George
2558449	Cpl Hedley	-	3197	LAD	Brady
3307417	Cpl Legg	-	264	ADI	Ranger
2395011	Cpl Ring	-	1152	ADI	Tony
4028892	Cpl Wood	-	3242	ADI	Mowgli
2398876	Cpl Malsom	-	3251	ADII	Wolf
2389816	Cpl Hall	-	3324	ADII	Feter
3106818	Cpl Newman	-	3264	ADII	Rex
2391636	Cpl Forrest	-	3342	ADII	George

'CRIMINALS'

4027878	AC Whyte	3116949	AC Wilkinson
2410998	AC Langley	2399102	AC Swinburne
2399101	AC Bentley	4018509	Cpl Reid
3113964	Cpl Sharp	4006936	AC Lahiff
2410923	AC Allam	4028924	Cpl Nowstend

Trolley Team	Dogs Pulling Trolley		
1233318 FSgt Foster NCO in Charge	3064	ADII	Jan
2809232 ACW Bridges	3366	Puppy	Max
2809236 ACW Davies	1U3	Puppy	Unera
	1V2	Puppy	Valiant
	1V5	Puppy	Vulcan
	1W4	Puppy	Waverley
	1Y5	Puppy	Youth

In Charge of Puppies	Puppies in the Trolley		
2803189 ACW Miller	2T1	Puppy	Tactful
2807323 ACW Livingstone	2T2	Puppy	Trust
	2T3	Puppy	Tar
	2T4	Puppy	Teak
	2T5	Puppy	Tally
	2T6	Puppy	Timber

General Administration	Arena Assistants
?541033 FSgt Legge	2089172 Cpl Donleavy
?532877 FSgt Clark	2804252 ACW Saffon
???4713 FSgt Toseland	2804191 ACW Hazell
??03780 FSgt Thorrington	2803339 ACW Hodgson
2?64523 Cpl K Wareham IC Feeding	2804231 ACW Hill
2378119 AC Wright Driver	
4018112 AC Lewington Driver	
2595077 AC Pritchard CO's Batman	

TOTAL PERSONNEL & DOGS INVOLVED IN DISPLAY

RAF Officers	1
RAF NCOs & Airmen	78
WRAF NCOs & Airwomen	9
Adult Dogs	59*
Puppies over 6 months	6*
Puppies under 6 months	6*
RAF Bred Dogs	42
Gift Dogs	29

Mr Charles Fricker inspects students and dogs at the MAPGDS Woodfold in 1942

Lt Col Baldwin inspects RAF Dog handlers at MAPGDS Woodfold in 1943

RAF Police Dog Training Course No 376 RAF Staverton 1945

RAF Police Dog Breeding Program1946 – Lt Col Baldwin with Kennel Assistants and puppies.

For Loyal and Faithful Service
1939 — 1945

This Certificate *is awarded to R.A.F. Police Patrol Dog*
Nº 3066 MICHAEL
in grateful recognition of tireless effort and constant devotion to duty willingly rendered to Britain and all the free peoples of the World in time of War.

Provost Marshal
Chief of Royal Air Force Police

Certificate of War Service for Air dog Michael issued by the Provost Marshal in 1947

Disk issued to RAF Dog Flick by the PDSA 1942 – 1947

RAF Police Dog handlers and their dogs on parade at the Royal Tournament at Olympia in London in 1949 – Flt Lt R D Cooper and Sgt Darnell

RAF Police Dog handlers on duty at RAF Gatow (Berlin) during the Berlin Airlift – 1949

2.   1952 – 1961

In January 1952, the RAF Police School and No 1 RAF Police Wing (formerly the headquarters), finally completed the move from RAF Pershore to RAF Nethera-von, and in doing so, joined up with both the RAF Police Dog Training and the RAF Police Driving Schools, which had moved there at the end of 1951. In compliance with a directive from the Air Ministry, the new station, commanded by a RAF provost officer; Group Captain T R Champion, was duly re-titled as the Royal Air Force Police Depot.

The British people and the people of the British Empire were shocked on the 6th February to hear the sad news that His Majesty King George VI had died in his sleep at Sandringham in Norfolk, aged fifty-six. Her Royal Highness Princess Elizabeth, the Duchess of Edinburgh, together with her husband were on holiday in Kenya when she was informed of her fathers death. She returned home im-mediately and at the age of twenty-five became the new monarch, Queen Elizabeth II.

Diplomatic relations between Egypt and Britain worsened when Egypt re-nounced its twenty-year treaty of 1936 with Britain and reiterated its claim on the Sudan. The recently elected Egyptian government had at first, seemed friendly enough towards British interests in the region, but severe domestic problems and pressure from extremist groups within the country had combined to make the dispute with Britain a welcome distraction. Britain reacted to the announcement by refusing to accept the cancellation of the treaty, or indeed to recognise King Farouk as the King of the Sudan. As hostility towards the British developed within Egypt military units within the Suez Canal Zone were rein-forced to deal with increased attacks and hostility against them.

In Kenya at RAF Eastleigh, situated on the outskirts of the capital Nairobi, a number of RAF Police dog handlers and their dogs had been established to enhance the unit's overall security measures during the *Mau Mau* terrorist campaign being waged by the Kikuyu tribe. Within a short space of time, the dogs had proved themselves to be a very effective deterrent to any would-be terrorists. That was highlighted one night when a German Shepherd dog indi-cated the presence of some twenty native intruders who had been quietly approaching a radar site. The dog handler located the intruders, called for assistance and challenged them but they quickly fled from the area. The dog was subsequently used to track them but unfortunately, it lost the scent near an isolated farm. As a result, the Kenyan Police searched the farm buildings and seven members of the Mau Mau terrorist organisation were duly arrested and a number of weapons and a vast quantity of ammunition were recovered. As a result of that incident, No 7 RAF Police Flight Detachment, commanded by Flying Officer F D Edge, tightened up the security measures on the station and made good use of the dog patrols to prevent any further attempted acts of terrorism and sabotage from taking place. No chances were taken and accordingly all Africans entering and leaving the station were thoroughly searched and their identities validated.

On the 9th June, at RAF Habbaniya in Iraq, a strike by native employees developed into a riot. The RAF Police were called out to deal with the troublemakers and accordingly, personnel from the RAF Police Mounted Section on horseback together with dog handlers and their dogs from the RAF Police Dog Section managed to restore calm and order amongst the strikers quite quickly. Consequently, the strikers returned to work three days later and their grievances were taken up by the RAF authorities.

In June, after successfully completing the training to become dog handlers, newly promoted Acting Corporal J Bastard and Air Dog Rex 3788, together with National Serviceman; Acting Corporal R Merrill and Air Dog Rex 3868, left Netheravon and were posted to RAF Patrington, a radar unit located east of Kingston-upon-Hull. Although the unit had a small staff of station police under the command of Sergeant R Fryer which operated out of the guardroom, the unit was also established for three dog teams. Corporal's Bastard and Merrill were taking over from Corporal's J Bacon and T McHaffie who were posted while the third dog handler at the unit was initially Corporal G Collins, but he was later replaced by Corporal C Whitwell a veteran from Palestine and Egypt who had been very badly mauled by a dog that went mad in Egypt. Facilities at the dog section were very basic and comprised a small wooden hut where the handlers could prepare the dog's food and four kennels, each with a run-wire attached to allow freedom of movement but also to contain the dogs in the vicinity of their kennels. The task of the dog handlers was to provide security during the hours of darkness at the site housing the radar and the operations centre. Additionally, the duty dog handler would also be tasked with carrying out 'wake-up calls' for duty personnel and lighting the cooking range in the cookhouse at 0400 hours, which allowed the duty cook to have an extra hour in bed before he was woken up to prepare breakfast. Because of that arrangement, the duty dog handlers and their dogs were always well looked after by the cooks in respect of rations. Socially, for sixpence personnel from the unit could make the return journey by RAF transport each evening to Withersea on the North Sea coast, or for 2/6= a bus or train journey would take personnel into the 'bright lights' of Hull. During his time at RAF Patrington Corporal Bastard was chosen to represent No 12 Group Fighter Command at the Annual Small Bore Shooting Competition at Bisley and was promoted to the substantive rank of Corporal.

On the 3rd July, Corporal B A Stapleton arrived at the RAF Police Dog School at RAF Kasfareet, located in the Suez Canal Zone of Egypt to be re-teamed with a new police dog. Prior to leaving the United Kingdom in mid May, he had handed over his two fully trained dogs, Air Dogs Prince and Ralph to Corporal T McHaffie, who himself in 1976, would become the Chief Training Officer at the RAF Police Dog Training School. After successfully re-teaming with Air Dog Rex, Corporal Stapleton was posted to RAF Devorsoir.

On the 3rd October, Britain tested her first nuclear weapon on the Monte Bello Islands, to the west of Australia. Then between the 5th and 9th October, a RAF Police team from No's 64, 65 and 66 Flights, assisted by dog handlers from RAF Kuala Lumpur mounted 'Operation Hengist', the security operation designed to protect the Duke and Duchess of Kent during their five-day official visit to the Malay Federation. Over the period, the Royal couple used the RAF airfield as a transit point during their visits to Singapore and other destinations within the federation. Given that at the time of the visit, the jungle surrounding the airfield was infested with bandits, the operation mounted by the RAF Police ensured that the Royal couple were not subjected to any type of security incident during their stay in the region.

During the same month, Corporal Stapleton was tasked by senior officers from No 4 RAF Police Wing, to intensify dog patrols at RAF Abu Sultan, where large amounts of ammunition were being stolen from the storage sheds during the hours of darkness. A few nights later during a patrol of the storage sheds in company with Corporal Gillespie and his Air Dog Voss, the two NCOs disturbed someone who ran off towards the perimeter leaving two boxes of ammunition on the ground. Unfortunately, the NCOs were not able to send the dog after the intruder who made good his escape because they believed that the area beyond the perimeter fence was mined and they did not want to put the dog in danger. However, the following night, the NCOs again encountered a group of figures creeping into the camp over the sand. Corporal Stapleton challenged them to stand still but they ignored him and continued to advance. At that point, he opened fire with his Sten gun and they fled. The following morning, when the area was checked, they found one dead Arab and trails of blood leading through the barbed wire fence. The Egyptian Police were summoned, who confirmed that the dead Arab was inside the camp boundary, which was a designated 'Restricted Area'. They also confirmed that four other Arabs had been arrested earlier that morning when they attempted to get treatment at a local hospital for gunshot wounds. Not deterred by the fact that one man had been shot dead and four others had been wounded and arrested, there were further intrusions during the subsequent three nights, but on each occasion the intruders were arrested by the RAF Police dog handlers on duty.

In October another RAF Police landmark was reached, when for the first time, fifteen RAF Police German Shepherd dogs and their handlers, from the RAF Police Depot, were transported by air from RAF Abingdon in Oxfordshire to RAF Gutersloh in Northern Germany. The whole journey, by road and Valetta aircraft, had taken less than ten hours, compared to a much slower and more stressful journey for the dogs by road to the port of embarkation, then by sea to Germany and then by road again to their new unit.

At the end of 1952, Corporal P J Mason's tour of duty in Iraq came to an end and, leaving Air Dog Ranger behind, he was posted back to the United Kingdom. After successfully re-teaming with a new dog at RAF Netheravon, he was posted first to RAF Wilmslow in Cheshire, then to RAF Great Orton in Cumbria, and finally to RAF Stafford. It was at Great Orton one day that he thought his time in this life was about to suddenly come to a dreadful end. At the time, the unit was in fact one very large bomb dump, containing some of the most powerful conventional weapons in use at that time. He was on patrol one day in the bomb dump and was watching a team of armourers using a crane to lift one of the larger bombs onto a truck parked nearby. As the crane slowly started to lift its load, the winch suddenly came to a grinding halt with the bomb hanging about ten feet off the ground. The sudden halting of the operation caused the load to swing and the bomb started to slowly slip out of its harness. As those nearby realised what was about to happen, they started to run as fast as they could from the scene. Spurred on by what was happening, Corporal Mason and his dog did likewise just as the bomb slipped from the harness and struck the ground with a dull thud. For a moment there was an almost deafening silence before most of those who had run off realised that nothing had happened. The bomb, of course, was inert and totally harmless having not been primed. At the time however, Corporal Mason had no knowledge of that and thought that the day had come to meet his maker.

At RAF Eastleigh, situated on the outskirts of the Nairobi, a number of RAF aircraft were being used with great effect to target the Mau Mau terrorist encampments located in the dense forests around Mount Kenya and the Aberdare Mountains. Accordingly, security in and around the base was tightened up to prevent any attempts at sabotage. Airmen guards were armed and posted around the unit and RAF Police dog handlers were reinforced to further enhance the unit's overall security measures and the perimeter.

Severe gales and floods, resulting from extremely high tides in the North Sea, caused widespread havoc along Britain's East coast, on the 2nd February 1953, leaving many dead and thousands more homeless.

In March, Corporal P J Mason, having successfully completed his NCOs course at RAF Hereford, was posted to Egypt once again. After successfully re-teaming with a new police dog he was posted to No 109 MU at RAF Abyad near Fayid, where he became the NCO in charge of the RAF Police Dog Section. He recalls that at the time some of his colleagues at that unit were, Corporals Gibson, Smith and Bromham. Theft of both government and private property was a big problem at the unit; it seemed that unless it was nailed down or physically guarded then the local population would simply walk off with it. In order to control the problem, Corporal Mason, increased the use of dog patrols around the unit and in addition to apprehending many would-be thieves, the number of reported thefts fell sharply.

In Hong Kong during the month of April, eleven well groomed RAF Police dogs and their smartly turned out handlers, under the command of Flight Lieutenant G Innes (later to become Provost Marshal), appeared on a public parade for the first time in the colony in order to celebrate the official birthday of Her Majesty Queen Elizabeth II.

Air Commodore Yarde was promoted to the rank of Air-Vice Marshal on the 20th April, and shortly before taking up his new appointment as the Air-Officer-Commanding No 62 Group he relinquished his appointment as Provost Marshal. He was succeeded as Provost Marshal by Air Commodore North Carter CB DFC, who prior to taking on the top job in the Provost Branch, had been a senior staff officer with No 205 Group, Middle East Air Force (MEAF).

On the 29th May, the world's highest peak, Mount Everest, was finally conquered by Edmund Hilary and Sherpa Tensing and four days after, the splendid Coronation of Her Majesty Queen Elizabeth II, took place in Westminster Abbey. Incidentally, it was the first time that the Coronation ceremony of a British monarch was broadcast live on British television to millions of people around the country.

Aircraftsman C Gilmore had enlisted in the RAF in February 1953, having signed on for a five-year regular engagement. Having worked on a farm in Wiltshire for three years prior to joining up he had grown fond of working with a wide variety of animals especially dogs and as such it was his intention to become a RAF Police dog handler. Having successfully completed his recruit training at RAF West Kirby, he reported to the RAF Police Depot at Netheravon to begin his initial police training. He was accommodated in Hangar 94H, which had been turned into a huge barrack block for airmen undergoing initial police training. At that time Corporal Drinkwater was the NCO in charge of Hangar 94H and the daily inspections were carried out by Flight Sergeant S Grayson, the training supervisor, who it seems had a terrifying reputation amongst the trainees of missing nothing during the morning parade. After successfully completing his nine-week initial police training, newly promoted Acting Corporal Gilmore moved across to the Dog Training School to begin his training to become a dog handler. In doing so, he moved out of the draughty and noisy Hangar 94H and into slightly more comfortable accommodation reserved for trainee dog handlers. On the first morning of training the students were met by their instructor, Corporal Walchester, who carefully briefed them on the 'do's and don'ts' of the Dog Training School before allocating each student a dog. Because he had volunteered the information that he had worked with dogs before and had been a member of a dog training club, Corporal Gilmore was allocated Air Dog Prince. Shortly after, all the students were taken by Corporal Walchester to meet their dogs in the Quarantine and Isolation Section, which was housed in a number of former billets, each of which, contained between six to eight dogs in separate compounds. Air Dog Prince however, was outside running around on a run-wire set-up between two of the billets and given the sudden appearance of strangers he was barking quite aggressively. At that point, Corporal Gilmore was ordered by his instructor to approach the dog and put it on its lead and take it for a walk. Although the dog seemed quite agitated, Corporal Gilmore, remembering what he had been taught at the civilian dog training club, calmly walked forward and took command of the dog and within seconds, much to the surprise of Corporal Walchester, had Prince on the lead and was walking him quite normally. Apparently, the reason why Prince was on the run-wire and not kennelled inside with the other dogs was that no-one could exercise him without being bitten and so the run-wire allowed him to run around. After getting acquainted with their dogs the students transferred them from the Quarantine and Isolation Section out to the kennels in the training ranges. Later that day Corporal Gilmore could not help noticing a large sign hanging up in the hangar used by the Dog Training School which declared, 'Don't Punish Your Dog – Train it'. After the initial meeting Corporal Gilmore and Prince quickly bonded and both went on to enjoy the training course that followed. Eventually, the course drew to a close and on the final day the legendry Lieutenant Colonel Baldwin, who they had not seen during training, appeared to carry out the final assessment of each dog team. After a full-day of practical and oral tests all students were notified that they had passed the course and were, from that point on, qualified RAF Police dog handlers.

Aircraftsman R Allsopp arrived at the RAF Police Depot Netheravon on the 3rd June to commence his basic police and thereafter his training to become a dog handler. It was a very hot day and he and other trainee policemen had to wait outside the guardroom wearing their hats, their greatcoats and webbing belts and holding their heavy kit bags until enough trainees arrived to make up a flight. The last man to arrive was appointed 'Senior Man' and at that point they were allowed to march up the hill to Hangar 94H which was to serve as their accommodation. When they were halfway up the hill however, they met Warrant Officer J James riding towards them on his bicycle. He stopped and ordered them to halt and after informing them in no uncertain terms that their marching was not up to the required standard, ordered them to 'about-turn' and return to the guardroom and start again. Whilst at Netheravon, Allsopp remembered that Flight Sergeant Grayson used to parade the trainees of five or more training courses each morning on the peri-track with the latest and most junior course at one end of the formation and the most senior course at the other end. Flight Sergeant Grayson had the voice of a Regimental Sergeant-Major and could see from one end of the parade to the other, no matter how thick the fog was at certain times of the year. He also clearly remembers that the *daily defaulter's parade* outside the guardroom for those trainees that had been charged with some minor infraction was usually thirty strong, with sometimes considerably more.

After, successfully completing his basic police training under the supervision of Corporal C Learmonth, Aircraftsman Allsopp moved across to the Dog Training School to begin his training as a dog handler. He remembers during his time there seeing a lot of the 'legendry' Lieutenant Colonel Baldwin who was preparing for retirement and Miss Dobbins who worked in the dispensary. The dogs were housed in cages inside one of the hangars and were bedded on straw which had to be changed regularly; there was always a bonfire burning at the school fuelled by the old straw. After completing his training he was posted with his dog to No 61 MU Handforth, near Manchester. The unit consisted of seven sites but the dogs were accommodated at the rear of the guardroom on No1 Site. There were no proper compounds and the dogs were kept on run-wires but during the winter the runs got very muddy and the dog handlers eventually built them more suitable accommodation. In the days before tinned dog food and special biscuits, the dogs at the unit were fed on raw meat which was collected twice a week from a slaughter house in Altringham. The dog handlers took it in turns to cut the meat up and the dog handlers finishing the night shift were responsible for feeding all the dogs before going off duty. Each day a couple of the dog handlers were assigned by roster to clean the dog section, groom the dogs and exercise those not assigned for duty. In addition, it also gave the handlers the opportunity to carry out continuation training. Because there was no suitable living accommodation at RAF Handforth the dog handlers were accommodated at RAF Wimslow but the station commander there was completely unsympathetic to the fact that the dog handlers, except for the occasional day shift, worked permanent night shifts. As such, he was not prepared to find anyone still in bed during his weekly morning inspection of the barrack accommodation occupied by the airmen and airwomen. Eventually however, the dog handlers moved to much improved accommodation at RAF Ringwood which was situated just across the road from Manchester Airport, which at the time had one small refreshment facility. It became practice for the dog handlers to use the refreshment facility as a waiting area and pick-up point for the transport which collected the handlers and then the dogs before dropping them off at the various MU sites each evening for duty. At the time some of the dog handlers working at Handforth included; Corporal T Convey the NCO in charge of the Dog Section, Corporal T Blumberg, Corporal G Shaw who was a former Rhodesian policeman, Corporal G Barker and Corporal Frowen. A dog handler and his dog was assigned to each site and would use the site guardroom, manned by a member of the Air Force Department Constabulary (AFDC) to take their breaks. Prior to leaving the RAF transport each dog handler would be issued with his nightly rations which came from the cookhouse at RAF Wilmslow and which usually comprised, a sausage, an egg, two rashers of bacon and two slices of bread, all of which had to be fried at some stage during the shift. The Shift supervisor was an AFDC sergeant who had a key for the padlock which secured the gates to each site and he used to approach the sites with no lights showing on his vehicle to carry out his checks and treated the AFDC constables and the RAF Police dog handlers in exactly the same professional manner.

On the 15th July, Her Majesty Queen Elizabeth II, arrived at RAF Odiham in Hampshire, to review the Royal Air Force and the largest parade of aircraft ever to have been assembled in one place. The RAF Police of course, were there in force helping to control the public and the traffic attending the venue. In addition, they provided escorts and security for the visiting VIP's and a large number of dog handlers point-guarded some of the newly developed and still secret aircraft that were for the first time on public display. Two days later, after some of the longest negotiations to bring about a cease-fire, Korea became a divided country as fighting there ended, and a truce was declared with the signing of an armistice at Panmunjom.

In Egypt on the 5th August, the RAF Police Dog School at RAF Kasfareet was closed down and the instructors and the nineteen dogs that remained were used to form the basis of an operational RAF Police Dog Section. At the time, in order to reduce the number of burglaries and thefts occurring in the bungalows occupied by married service personnel, a scheme was hatched by the RAF Police to supply guard dogs to each household. The dogs were either police dogs that were too old for operational police duties, or stray dogs obtained from other sources, which were trained to deter thieves from breaking into premises by barking and alerting their owners that intruders were close-by. As the crime prevention scheme gathered pace it became highly successful with the dogs helping in a major way to control the crime wave affecting the unit.

From Netheravon, Corporal Gilmore and Air Dog Prince had been posted to RAF Lyneham in Wiltshire, which had a section comprising four dogs. Sadly after only being at Lyneham for a few months, Prince died suddenly from a twisted gut and Corporal Gilmore found himself back at Netheravon teaming up with a new partner; Air Dog Sonny, who had previously been the *criminal attack dog* with the RAF Police Dog Demonstration Team at the Royal Tournament. The re-teaming was swift and uncomplicated and Corporal Gilmore and Air Dog Sonny returned to RAF Lyneham but after only a few months more, they were recalled to Netheravon; Corporal Gilmore to assist in training other dogs for the 1954 Royal Tournament and Air Dog Sonny to resume his role of *criminal attack dog* with the demonstration team. After a few days Corporal Gilmore was notified that he was being retained at the school to take charge of the Quarantine and Isolation Section from Corporal R Jarvis who was leaving the RAF. It was a very important promotion for Corporal Gilmore who after all had only been in the RAF for just over a year. The Quarantine and Isolation Section housed up to sixty dogs awaiting handler allocation, and the dogs were looked after on a daily basis by a team of WRAF kennel assistants. The section was also kept on constant standby to deal with any dog thought to be showing signs of any contagious disease such as distemper, which was quite common in the 1950s. As previously mentioned, the Quarantine and Isolation Section was housed in former billets; basically old wooden huts that had been condemned for human occupation. Accordingly, they were not the most secure of premises and 'break-outs' by some of the dogs at night were not uncommon. Fortunately, the dogs that did manage to escape did not venture far and were quickly rounded up the following morning. Prompted by that problem, the Quarantine and Isolation Section moved into to new premises sometime later, taking over a more secure building that had formerly been the meat preparation facility. Secure purpose built kennels were constructed for the dogs; an office and restroom were included for the staff and a storeroom was provided for their equipment, all of which was a vast improvement on the old premises. Additionally, the new premises also provided living accommodation for one of the staff and therefore Corporal Gilmore moved in permanently to live on-site. The section was an extremely busy and noisy place with new dogs arriving on a daily basis, mainly as unconditional gifts from the public. Each new dog was examined and assessed for temperament on arrival and kept in isolation for a few days to ensure that it was disease free. Paperwork was raised and each new dog received a personal number that was tattooed into its left ear. As each new dog handling course assembled, dogs were selected and allocated to each trainee. During his time in charge, Corporal Gilmore managed to work with many dogs, each possessing a different temperament and personality and as such his experience in handling the German Shepherd dog developed very quickly. Before joining the RAF Corporal Gilmore had worked on a farm under a manager who prided himself for his overall efficiency and who insisted on a very high degree of animal husbandry. Corporal Gilmore had been very impressed with the manager's attitude and therefore successfully adopted a similar system in managing the Quarantine and Isolation Section; indeed, despite the fact that Sunday was the only non-working day of the week, he and his staff put in many hours of overtime to ensure that the dogs in their care were well looked after. At the time, the Dog Training School was under the command of Squadron Leader Parker, assisted by Flying Officer Edwards and Warrant Officer Legg. Some of the staff at that time included; Flight Sergeant's Farley and Foster, Sergeant's G Irvine and Donlevey, Corporal's E Johnson, P Trehane, R Coulson, B Dowl, A Simkin, Robertson, J Wardley, H Fox, J Batley and J McWhirter. Pat Dobbin, as we have seen earlier, was the civilian who ran the dispensary and the kennel assistants included; Stella French, Chris Collins, Joan Quantill, 'Chunky' Kline, Laurie Churchill and 'Sandy' Sands. During his time at Netheravon Corporal Gilmore got married but because he was still under the age of twenty-one, he was not entitled to a married quarter and therefore his new bride Sheila, lived some fifty miles from the unit. As such, whenever a thirty-six hour pass was approved, Corporal Gilmore would make the long journey to see his wife but as he was not earning a great deal at that point and because the public transport system between the unit and home was complicated and expensive he used his bicycle to make the trip back and forth. Socially, staff from the dog school would meet up in the Corporal's Club during the evening to play darts or snooker over a mug of strong tea. Alcohol was expensive but occasionally whenever there was a dance or similar function organised in the club Corporal Gilmore and his colleagues, some of whom included; Corporal's E Snaillum, T McHaffie, G Rowe, B Lillicrap, J Ford and J McGlade, would purchase bottles of cheap wine from the NAAFI shop to drink during the evening. Sometimes the cheap wine produced a rather 'heavy head' in the morning but that was always resolved by a good strong mug of tea served up by one of the kennel assistants with a knowing smile.

After an impressive career, Lieutenant Colonel Jimmy Baldwin finally took up his retirement in October. For thirteen years he had been the inspiration of the RAF Police Dog Training School, which had, over that period, gone from strength to strength, earning for itself an extremely high reputation in very wide circles. Although it was a sad day, the work of the dog training school continued and he was succeeded as the Chief Training Officer (Dogs), by Mr Charles Edward Fricker, who himself, had joined Baldwin right at the start when the school was formed at Woodfold. Unfortunately, it was during the war and after only a short period of working at Woodfold, Mr Fricker had been conscripted to work in the coalmines as a *Bevin Boy*. After the war ended however, he had eagerly returned to the world of dogs and had started his own kennels, breeding and showing off German Shepherd dogs. He had also formed his own dog display team, which had proved to be extremely popular, and had even performed before the Royal family at the Royal Inverness Show in 1948.

In mid October, Corporal B A Stapleton was on night duty patrolling the stores complex at RAF Kasfareet, when his dog Rex, became restless at something ahead. At the same time, a figure emerged from the perimeter fence and entered the camp. Corporal Stapleton challenged the figure to stop but the intruder started to run off. Rex was released and quickly brought the intruder down to the ground. The Arab man was later handed over to the Egyptian civil police for processing.

Since its creation in 1920 the RAF Police Training School (later joined by the RAF Police Dog Training School and the RAF Police Driving School) had come under the functional control of the Provost Marshal. However, on the 2nd November, it was transferred to the command of the Air Officer-in-Chief Technical Training Command, who could if he wished seek the advice of the Provost Marshal on matters regarding the training of Provost Officers and RAF Police NCOs.

After working for two years in the guardroom at RAF Sandwich in Kent, Corporal I Soulsby decided that he wanted to work outdoors. He consequently applied to become a dog handler and in November found himself back at the RAF Police Depot on a dog-handling course under the control of two instructors; Corporal's M Fox and J Laing. Initially, there was a slight problem in that there were eight students and only seven dogs available. Unfortunately, Corporal Soulsby was the 'odd-man out' and initially was without a dog of his own. However, after a few days a German Shepherd dog by the name of Prince arrived at the depot for re-allocation. Prince was a large, heavy-jowled black and tan dog and when Corporal Soulsby saw him he knew it was the dog for him. Corporal Fox on the other hand, had recently lost his dog to a fatal illness and therefore using his seniority claimed the dog for himself. The following morning, Corporal Fox brought Prince out with him to the morning parade but when he ordered the dog to sit it grabbed the instructor by the pocket of his trousers and refused to let go. As Corporal Fox moved around attempting to release himself from the jaws of the dog, so the dog followed, refusing to let go. After a few more minutes Prince released his grip and was promptly put back into his kennel to calm down. Over the days that followed Prince revealed that he was completely unpredictable and each time he was taken out of his kennel to be exercised someone got bitten. Despite the dog's obvious bad temperament, Corporal Soulsby still had desires on teaming up with the dog and spent time outside Princes' kennel calmly talking to him. Additionally, every time Corporal Soulsby entered the hangar where the dogs were kennelled he would give a special whistle just to let Prince know that he was about. After a while Corporal Soulsby volunteered to exercise the dog and quickly learnt that Prince had no respect for authority when the dog turned on him and bit his hand. The dog was returned to his kennel and Corporal Soulsby was taken to the medical centre to have his injured hand treated. In two weeks Prince had mauled nineteen people at the dog school and his reputation was such that whenever he was taken from his kennel a warning would be shouted and everyone within the hangar would flee to safety out of his path. After being treated, Corporal Soulsby was advised by Corporal Fox to take Prince out of his kennel and take him for a 'long walk'. It seemed that what Corporal Fox was implying was that the trainee handler should take the dog out and show him who was in charge; the Alpha Dog. Corporal Soulsby did as he was told and after counselling his dog sat on a bale of straw to await his next move. Prince calmly approached and sat between his handler's knees and carefully licked his heavily bandaged hand and his face before laying his chin on his shoulder. They sat like that for a while and then Corporal Soulsby took Prince out for a long walk. It was at that point that Corporal Soulsby realised that there was a special bond between them. A few days later while Corporal Soulsby was in class, a young kennel-assistant entered the classroom to inform the instructor that Corporal Soulsby was urgently required in the hangar. It seemed that for a dare, another trainee dog handler had taken Prince out of his kennel and whilst parading him up and down the hangar, the dog had turned on him and savaged him quite badly. As a result, everyone else who had been in the hangar had dashed off to various points of safety while Prince roamed around inside the hangar. Corporal Soulsby entered the hangar and saw Prince at the other end. He quickly gave his special whistle and called Prince to come to him. The dog responded calmly and Corporal Soulsby ordered him to 'heel' and was thus able to walk him back into his kennel without any further incident. An ambulance was called and the injured trainee was taken off to hospital having won his dare, but at a painful cost. At a subsequent meeting to discuss the future of the dog, Corporal Soulsby was asked if he would consider taking the dog out to the Far East on operation duties. However, when he explained that he had only been married for four weeks, the officer in charge decided that Corporal Soulsby would take Prince back to RAF Sandwich after he graduated from the course. The rest of their training however, was no easy task. Prince was a very powerful dog with a headstrong personality and it was quite a job to graduate and prove that they had what was required to form an effective team. After leaving the depot Corporal Soulsby and Prince, who was muzzled, were standing on the platform at Salisbury station waiting for the train that would take them to London on the first phase of the return journey to Kent. Suddenly, a cat appeared before them and almost provoked Prince into reacting. Prince of course reacted just like any other dog in similar circumstances and started to give chase. Unfortunately, Corporal Soulsby who was in uniform and wearing hob-nailed boots that did little to help him stand his ground. As a result, he was literally pulled along the platform as if he was roller skating, scattering other waiting passengers as they went. Luckily, after travelling some thirty yards or so the cat disappeared from view and Corporal Soulsby managed to gain control of Prince and calm him down. Mercifully, the cat had not decided to leave the platform and cross the lines. Somewhat embarrassed by the ordeal, Corporal Soulsby returned to his kitbags apologising to the other travellers on his way. After only being at RAF Sandwich for two weeks Prince actually chewed his way out of his kennel and quickly brought the entire radar unit to a standstill. Such was his reputation that everyone had immediately dashed indoors and refused to go out again until the dog had been rounded up. Corporal Soulsby was summoned; the dog was located and returned to his kennel and repairs were quickly made to reinforce the kennel to prevent any further escapes. After nine months, Prince, although very loyal to Corporal Soulsby, was getting worse and becoming more of a serious risk. After being examined by one of the RAF Police dog inspectors, Prince was taken off operational duties and Corporal Soulsby was ordered to return him to the depot. Shortly after doing so, he was teamed up with a new dog; a pure white German Shepherd dog named Ambrose who was trustworthy and who had a much more pleasant personality. However, even before Corporal Soulsby had left the depot, Prince broke out of his kennel again and attacked another trainee dog handler.

Sadly, Prince proved to be so unpredictable and dangerous to anyone in his vicinity that the decision was made to put him down.

During the year, Her Majesty Queen Elizabeth II, carried out her first Royal visit as head of the British Empire to the colony of Aden. During the occasion members of the RAF Police stationed there, together with their military colleagues, provided enhanced security cover. Not surprisingly, RAF Police dog teams played an important part in the security operation.

In Egypt at RAF Abyad in January 1954, Corporal P J Mason, was awarded a commendation from the Air-Officer-Commanding, in recognition of the hard work he had done in order to reduce the reported cases of theft at the unit by the use of effective RAF Police dog patrols and the introduction of 'alarm dogs' that barked a warning whenever intruders were nearby.

In March the rules changed with regard to the rank of RAF Policemen and women passing out from training. Whereas before they left the RAF Police School after passing their initial training as Leading Aircraftsman Acting Corporal with two chevrons on the arm of their uniform, the new system scrapped the use of the acting corporal rank and the chevrons and so they passed out as Leading Aircraftsman.

In Northern Malaya, just after sunrise on the 23rd May, Corporal J T Elvin and Air Dog Charlie, who were stationed at RAF Butterworth, responded to a request for assistance from the commanding officer of the 12th Royal Lancers, who had been on jungle patrol in the state of Kedah, some fifteen miles from the airfield at Butterworth. It seemed that during the previous night, the patrol had engaged a number of terrorists and a fire fight had taken place. In spite of the swift response, the gang had quickly made good their escape into the surrounding jungle and the Army patrol had lost all trace of them. However, during a search of the skirmish site at first daylight, a patch of blood soaked earth had been discovered, which indicated that one of the terrorists had probably been wounded. After a quick examination of the scene, Corporal Elvin and Air Dog Charlie, supported by the Army patrol, began tracking the wounded terrorist into the dense jungle. After some time the dog stopped and started barking towards a patch of thick undergrowth. Corporal Elvin carefully went forward and discovered the wounded terrorist hidden at the base of a large tree. Although he was still alive, he was barely conscious having been shot in the thigh, and consequently, he had lost a considerable amount of blood. A rifle lying near him had also been damaged in the skirmish the previous night and was not capable of being fired. Nevertheless, no chances were taken with the terrorist who was was promptly arrested and taken away for medical treatment and questioning. As a result of their efforts, both Corporal Elvin and Air Dog Charlie were given celebrity status when the story was featured in *The Singapore Straits Times* on the 26th May. In addition, Corporal Elvin also later received a commendation from the Provost Marshal, Air Commodore North Carter, for his dedication and professionalism.

On the 16th June, the first four members of the United States Air Police arrived at the RAF Police Depot at RAF Netheravon to begin their RAF Police dog handling course. Although American personnel from the United States Army Air Force had been trained as dog handlers, by the RAF at the MAPGDS during World War II, they were the first policemen to become qualified dog handlers with the United States Air Force. The four eager students were named as Airman 1st Class C Crutchfield from Virginia, Airman 2nd Class C Misner from Missouri, Airman 2nd Class E Johnson from Wisconsin and finally, Airman 2nd Class L Lynn from Texas.

In June, Corporal J Bastard's tour of duty at RAF Patrington ended and he was posted to 2TAF West Germany. Initially, he reported to the RAF Police Headquarters situated at Buckeburg to be re-teamed with a new dog and to learn details of his new unit within 2TAF. After successfully re-teaming with Air Dog Lola, he was posted to Holland and RAF Eindhoven on the outskirts of the town made famous by the large Phillips Radio & Television Company. As was normal practice by then, the station was supported by a contingent of RAF Police. Additionally, a dog section had been established at the station to patrol, during the hours of darkness, No 401 Air Stores Park, which was a mile away from the main camp. The stores park, located within a pine forest, covered a huge area and also included an ammunition and bomb dump. When normal work ceased each evening, all personnel left the park and returned to their accommodation at the main camp, leaving the dog handlers to secure the gates and patrol the site. Rations were sent up to the park for the duty dog handlers and they were able to cook them using the huge wood burning cooking range located within the guardroom. At the time, other members of the dog section included; Corporal's T Betteridge, R Irons, Roy, and Ferguson. Initially, the senior NCO in charge of the RAF Police at RAF Eindhoven was Sergeant Palmer but later replacements were Sergeant Kertan and Sergeant S Muller a former military policeman. Some time after Corporal Bastard's arrival at the unit a Dutch Sabre aircraft crashed near the bomb dump and Corporal Betteridge who was on duty at the time managed, at some personal risk, to rescue the pilot. Corporal Betteridge was also on duty one night when a young orderly officer thought it would be a good idea to 'play commando' by climbing undetected into the stores park to check on the dog handlers. Unfortunately for him, his every move towards the site had been observed by Corporal Betteridge, who waited silently until the officer was at his most vulnerable on top of the high gate before he and his snarling dog rushed out from their concealed observation point to frighten the wits out of him. After being kept on the gate for some time until his identity was confirmed, the terrified officer was allowed to climb down and return to the main camp having learned the harsh lesson that trying to creep up on a RAF Police dog team undetected rarely works. The kennels for the dogs had been made by the handlers using wooden crates that had previously contained RAF equipment. There were no separate compounds for the dogs and so they were contained on run-wires. Food for the dogs, comprising 'horse meat on the bone', came from Belgium and was butchered and prepared for the dogs by the dog handlers using a work bench located at the back of the guardroom.

Corporal R Allsopp was posted from No 61 MU Handforth to RAF Butterworth in Malaya but before leaving he had to return his dog to the Holding Unit at the RAF Police Depot, which at the time was no easy task because there was a national rail strike in progress. Eventually both man and dog were transported to RAF Netheravon in a three ton truck and after leaving his dog at the Depot Corporal Allsopp then hitched a lift home to Birmingham to take his embarkation leave. The journey out to Singapore by aircraft took three days to complete with refuelling stops at Brindisi, Cyprus, Beirut, and Bangkok and overnight stops in Karachi and Calcutta. When the aircraft arrived in Singapore the passengers were met by RAF administrators armed with the details and internal travel arrangements for those posted to units within the Command. Additionally, those being posted to RAF Butterworth were lectured on the dangers of sexually transmitted diseases and the precautions to be taken and were informed that Butterworth was experiencing 'a particular problem' at that time. The train journey from Singapore to Butterworth took twenty-four hours and despite the fact that he held acting rank, Corporal Allsopp was appointed NCO in charge of the guard because of his two chevrons. Two very drunk Australians were also placed in his charge during the journey but once sober they turned out to be thoroughly reliable and were a tremendous help to the young inexperienced NCO. Fortunately, the train was not attacked during the long tiring journey north, much to Corporal Allsopp's relief since he had no experience of commanding men, especially in a crisis. After arriving at RAF Butterworth and being re-teamed with a dog he was employed on night patrol duties guarding the aircraft but occasionally the dog handlers were assigned to assist the civil police or units of the Australian Army in setting up ambushes around a particular place which was known to be used by terrorists as a food collection point. It was the task of the dog handler and his dog to pursue and capture if possible any terrorists who broke through the ambush cordon. Two of the other dog handlers serving at Butterworth at the time included, Corporal Williams and Corporal T Convey who had also been posted from No 61 MU, and Corporal B Kelly and Corporal Hawthorn were two of the station police employed within the guard-room at RAF Butterworth.

During the night of the 21st July, Flying Officer Edge, at RAF Eastleigh, was given reliable information which suggested that a Mau Mau oath taking cere-mony was going to take place, on a deserted part of the airfield. At very short notice, he decided to investigate and consequently, a short time later, as he and a handful of armed RAF Police NCOs including a number of dog handlers and their dogs approached the area concerned, but they were seen by a look out who raised the alarm. Although some escaped, twenty-two members of the Mau Mau were arrested and a number of weapons and literature associated with their cause were discovered. In recognition of his efforts, Flying Officer Edge was later awarded the MBE.

In August, Greek Cypriots, who made up fourth fifths of the island's popula-tion, wanted full unity with Greece but the Turkish Cypriots, who made up one fifth of the island's population and the British government objected strongly to the proposal. With no hope of a compromise, the Greek Cypriot terrorist move-ment; EOKA, under the leadership of General Georgios Grivas, started a violent terrorist campaign against the British, living on the island and any Cypriot who worked for them or collaborated with the British. As a result, security at all British military units on the island was reviewed and enhanced.

It was during 1954 that the RAF Police Dog Demonstration Team appeared for the very first time at the Edinburgh Military Tattoo in Scotland and became a huge success with the audience.

During October, Air Commodore North Carter retired as the Provost Marshal and was succeeded in post by Air Commodore H J G E Proud CBE. Prior to taking up his appointment as Provost Marshal, Air Commodore Proud had been the Air-Officer-Commanding No 67 (Northern Ireland) Group Headquarters.

On the 2nd December, the Air Ministry in London circulated Order No A.300 on the subject of RAF Police dogs to the Air-Officer-Commanding RAF Records Office, the Commandant RAF Police Depot, RAF Police District Commanders and Station Commanders within the United Kingdom and to Command Provost Marshals and Station Commanders overseas. The broad contents of the general order included;

The Provost Marshal from the Air Ministry is responsible for the control of all RAF Police dogs. In the United Kingdom control is exercised by the Command-ing Officer RAF Police Depot, and in commands overseas through the Command Provost Marshal. The Air-Officer-Commanding RAF Records Office is however, responsible through their Detachment Office at the RAF Police Depot for the posting or attachment of RAF Police dog handlers and their dogs and for the maintenance of all such records. The service number of each dog is tattooed inside its left ear and is to be used together with the name of the dog in all official records and correspondence, for example; 6503 Air Dog Rex.

A ceiling establishment of police dogs has been approved and proportional allocation between the United Kingdom and commands overseas has been made by the Provost Marshal. All proposals for the raising of a dog section or for variations to existing establishments must be supported by the recommendation of a provost officer before the proposal is forwarded to the appropriate command headquarters for transmission to the Air Ministry for consideration.

RAF Police dog handlers with their dogs are normally employed on security patrols at remote and widely dispersed airfields and other units outside normal working hours and throughout the night. The dogs are normally to be kept on a leash while on patrol and are trained to indicate the presence of an intruder within a reasonable distance. The daily tour of duty for a RAF Police dog handler and his dog is not to exceed six hours with one or more break periods not exceeding a total of thirty minutes. Because of the personal attention a handler must give to his dog, he is not to be employed on guardroom or other RAF Police station duties, or to make good any deficiencies in the manning of RAF Police employed on station duties except when he is posted to a unit unaccompanied by a dog or when his dog is unfit for duty. At units employing RAF Police dogs, conspicuous signs in red lettering on a white background are to be displayed around the perimeter of the unit, worded as follows; 'Warning – RAF Police Dogs are on Patrol'.

The responsibility for the supervision of RAF Police dog sections on stations rests with the Officer in Charge of the RAF Police. Dog handlers are responsible for the general welfare, grooming, feeding, exercising and kennelling of their dogs, which are to be brushed and combed each day to keep their skin clean and free from dust. Providing that daily grooming is done properly, bathing should not become necessary, except that a bath may be beneficial when a dog is changing coat. They are not to be petted or controlled by anyone other than their handlers. It is important that nothing should be done to destroy the dog's confidence or the result of its training. They are not to be taken into any station building, private quarters, NAAFI, dinning rooms or institutions. They are given adequate training at the RAF Police Depot to make them reliable guard dogs, but their continued efficiency depends primarily on the continuation of their training after leaving the RAF Police Depot, and secondly upon their health and general well-being. It is therefore the responsibility of the Station Commander to ensure that the regular practice of lessons and exercises are carried out daily for a minimum of one hour. Without this regular repetition, the efficiency of the dog, however good at first, will rapidly wane. When conveyed to and from places of duty the dog handler is always to travel in the same compartment of the vehicle as his dog and the latter must not be secured to any vehicle by any means nor left unattended. When being conveyed by public transport dogs are to be kept muzzled, although this precaution may be dispensed with in vehicles if no persons, other than the handler are in the same compartment. On long journeys the muzzle is to be removed periodically subject to the handler having full control of the dog. A RAF Police dog handler on the staff of each RAF Police District Headquarters in the United Kingdom is available to advise Station Commanders on the organisation, administration, training and employment of police dogs when required. His services can be obtained through the RAF Police District Commander or his Provost & Security Liaison Officer.

Under no circumstances are RAF Police dogs to be used for stud purposes, or bitches to be mated. When a bitch comes into season the senior dog handler is immediately to ensure that all necessary precautions are taken to prevent mating from taking place.

In the United Kingdom RAF Police dogs posted or attached to stations are not to be used for demonstration purposes. Application for a demonstration team for the purpose of giving displays at organised shows, tournaments etc, is to be made through command channels to the Air Ministry. Demonstrations may be given by dogs on the strength of commands overseas subject to the approval of the Commander-in-Chief. All out of pocket expenses incurred by the RAF involved in such demonstrations should be recovered from the organisers of the event.

The Commanding Officer of the station or unit to which RAF Police dog handlers and their dogs are posted or attached is responsible for providing kennels and compounds to the satisfaction of the appropriate Provost & Security Liaison Officer at home, or other qualified provost officer overseas. Kennels provided by units at home are to be manufactured to the approved design. Those supplied overseas are to be of a similar design but may be modified as approved by the Command Provost Marshal to suit local conditions. In tropical climates addition shade is to be provided in addition to the kennel and at home and overseas in cold seasons a bed of dry wheat straw is to be provided. Each kennel is to be enclosed within a compound measuring 20 feet by 10 feet with a smooth 4-inch concrete base and completely enclosed by a 7 foot chain link fence with the top foot bent inwards to an angle of 45°. The base of the fence is to be embedded into the concrete base and drainage is to be provided. On no account is barbed wire to be used. The kennel is to be placed at one end of the compound with a gate placed at the opposite end. 'Run wires' are not to be used unless their use has been approved by the appropriate officer at the RAF Police Depot. Whenever possible, each compound is to be detached to help contain the spread of disease, but when that is impracticable solid sheeting material to a height of 4 feet is to be used to shield the dogs from each other. A building is also to be provided for the preparation of the dog's rations and for the storage of wheat straw.

Dog Occurrence Reports are to be compiled by the RAF Police Depot, the Command Provost Marshal and units to which RAF Police dogs are posted or attached. They are to be serial numbered and are to contain the dogs number, name and details of such occurrences as for example; by whom it was presented to the RAF, losses, sales, serious illness, movements and death. RAF stations at home are to forward copies of the report to the Air-Officer-Commanding RAF Records Office and the RAF Records Office Detachment at the RAF Police Depot. Overseas, stations are to send one copy to the Command Provost Marshal who is to forward two copies of a consolidated dog occurrence report to the Air-Officer-Commanding RAF Records Office and the RAF Records Office Detachment at the RAF Police Depot. Dog Record Cards are to be completed when a dog is taken on charge and will be the authentic record of the dog during its service in the RAF. It is to be raised by the Air-Officer-Commanding RAF Records Office and is to be maintained from the information contained in dog occurrence reports. In commands overseas, the Command Provost Marshal may if he wishes maintain cards of the dogs within his command.

To ensure the proper care of RAF Police dogs, the establishment of RAF Police dog handlers at any RAF station will not be less than two. If for any reason, the strength should fall below this figure, or if one handler is absent for more than ten days the RAF Police Depot must be informed immediately. RAF Police dog handlers with their dogs will be posted to stations at home and to commands overseas for duty by the Air-Officer-Commanding RAF Records Office. They are not to be transferred subsequently from one station to another without the prior approval of the Air-Officer-Commanding RAF Records Office at home, or the Command Provost Marshal overseas. On completion of training each dog handler posted to a station at home will be provided, at the RAF Police Depot, with a British Transport Commission Permit BR 2462, without which the movement of RAF Police dogs by rail will not be permitted. Units are to apply to the RAF Police Depot for renewal of permits by the 1st December each year and expired permits are to be returned to the RAF Police Depot. All authorised movements are to be reported in Dog Occurrence Reports.

Whenever a dog becomes sick the services of a Royal Army Veterinary Corps officer are to be obtained where possible, but when these services are not available a local veterinary surgeon may be employed. All RAF Police dog handlers have been given elementary training in the detection and treatment of the initial symptoms of sickness, but all RAF Police dogs are to be inspected by a qualified veterinary officer at least once a month. A veterinary officer's recommendation of unfitness for duty is to be reported immediately to the Commandant RAF Police Depot or to the Command Provost Marshal overseas using a dog occurrence report. First aid treatment will normally be covered by the following list of basic medical supplies which are to be obtained from the Station Sick Quarters and kept readily available in the RAF Police dog section:

- Clinical thermometer
- Antiseptic fluid
- Mixture Kaolin and morph
- Liquid paraffin
- Unquentum Boric acid
- Absorbent Cotton Lint 1-ounce pack
- Absorbent Cotton Wool 1-ounce pack
- Loose woven 2-inch Bandage
- Loose woven 4-inch Bandage
- Absorbent Gauze 2-yard pack

A Veterinary Treatment Register is to be maintained to show the date, number, and name of the dog, the ailment diagnosed and the treatment given. Both simple treatment given by a dog handler and that prescribed by a veterinary surgeon are to be recorded.

A personal issue of all the RAF Police dog equipment detailed in Air Publication 830, Volume 3, Scale E45 (except the kennel), is to be made to each dog handler on completion of his initial training. Replacements are to be demanded under normal equipment procedures. Personal issued items are to be retained by the dog handler on change of station, on posting, or detachment. All other articles in use at the dog section are unit equipment and are to be accounted for in accordance with normal procedures.

The authority for placing a police dog on the ration strength of a unit is the RAF Records Office posting or attachment notice. The daily ration scales for dogs employed on police duties or under training are 2½ pounds of raw meat and ½ pound of dog biscuits. For sick dogs the ration may be varied as recommended by an approved veterinary officer. Dogs should be fed once a day, after patrol duties or not less than three hours before beginning duty. Unconsumed food is to be removed from the compound after dogs have finished feeding. Catering officers are to obtain and take on charge all supplies; they are to record receipts, issues and stock balances, on a suitable form or tally card.

As a general rule, dogs having attained 8 years of age are no longer fit for the strenuous duties required by the RAF. Therefore, when a dog reaches 7½, and every 6 months thereafter, it is to be submitted to a special examination by a veterinary officer. The value of a fully qualified dog is £125 sterling, while that of a dog which has not completed its training is assessed at £5 sterling for write-off purposes. It is the responsibility of the Commanding Officer of the unit to which a dog is posted or attached, to convene a board of officers, of which a provost officer is to be a member, to investigate the loss, theft or death (other than by natural causes) of any RAF Police dog. RAF Form 2, is to be completed and two copies forwarded to the Air Ministry for approval. In overseas commands two copies are to be forwarded to the Command Provost Marshal who is to transmit one copy to the Air Ministry.

If a Commanding Officer in the United Kingdom considers that a dog is unfit for further service by reason of ill-health, old age, or general unsuitability for police duties, he is to render a report to the RAF Police Depot who will withdraw the dog by arrangement with the Air-Officer-Commanding RAF Records Office and obtain a veterinary officer's report. If the veterinary officer advises disposal, a board of officers is to be convened to recommend the method of disposal, for example; returning the dog to its original owner, by sale, or when necessary by humane destruction. In commands overseas suitable arrangements are to be made by the Command Provost Marshal. In an emergency such as when a dog has been seriously injured or becomes ill and is in great pain, a Commanding Officer may authorise the immediate destruction without prior approval of the RAF Police Depot or Command Provost Marshal overseas, when he has obtained a certificate from a veterinary officer stating that course of action is necessary on humanitarian grounds.

The sale of a RAF Police dog following the recommendation of a board of officers must be authorised in the United Kingdom by the Provost Marshal or Command Provost Marshal overseas. When a sale is authorised, dogs are to be sold at their current market value, but not for less than £5 sterling. Three copies of the sales voucher are to be prepared with the purchaser signing the voucher and retaining a copy. A copy is to accompany a dog occurrence report and must be forwarded to the RAF Records Office and the third copy accompanies payment and is forwarded to the accounts officer at the unit concerned.

It can be seen from the above instructions that for the first time since the RAF Police began working with dogs a standardised set of orders concerning everything to do with dogs had been formalised and circulated to everyone throughout the *RAF world* to ensure that this important asset was managed in the best possible way. Although the provision of purpose built kennels took some time to procure, the specifications were indeed an important step in the right direction, and the detailed rules not only provided authority but guidance to all those concerned with working or managing RAF Police dogs around the globe.

Having completed his tour of duty in Egypt, newly promoted Sergeant B A Stapleton was posted into No 5 RAF Police District on the 9th January 1955, where he became the RAF Police dog specialist responsible for supervising and inspecting the dog sections of thirty units within the No 5 RAF Police District area.

In early 1955, the RAF Police dog section at RAF Sandwich in Kent was closed down and the four dog handlers employed there were posted to new assignments. Corporal I Soulsby and Corporal K Matthews, together with their dogs were posted to a small radar unit at Scarinish on the isle of Tiree, way up in the Inner Hebrides. The two NCOs were issued with travel warrants and given instructions to travel to their new unit by train and a ferry. A few days later, on a dull Thursday evening, they were driven to the station by the other two dog handlers; Corporal W Sanderson and Corporal A Killam, to catch the train up to London. After seeking out the guard on the train the two NCOs and their muzzled charges were surprised to be escorted to a first class compartment that had been especially reserved for the first part of their journey. After a short but uneventful trip in relative comfort, the train pulled into Waterloo Station, and the two NCOs were met by a RAF driver who transported them across the capital to catch the night train up to Glasgow. Because the train was packed to capacity and the guard's van was also full of mail and luggage, the guard suggested that the NCOs and their dogs should travel in an empty parcel van at the front of the train. Under the circumstances the NCOs had no choice and therefore agreed. Consequently, the sight of two RAF Police NCOs in uniform together with two fierce looking and muzzled German Shepherd dogs attracted a lot of attention from their fellow passengers as they made their way past several carriages up to the front of the train. Additionally, Ambrose, the dog handled by Corporal Soulsby was pure white and that in itself was a rare sight to see in that particular breed. After exercising the dogs briefly on the end of the platform the guard instructed the NCOs to board the train. The interior of the van in which they were travelling was sparse and not particularly clean; and a big difference from 'first class' compartment used during the first phase of their journey. There was a long bench style seat running up each side of the carriage under the windows but there were no toilet facilities. The guard provided a large bucket of water for the dogs and as he left them he closed and locked the door behind him. Shortly after, the train pulled out of the station and as it began its journey north the two NCOs made themselves as comfortable as they could and settled down to sleep. After a long night the train pulled into Glasgow station just before seven on Friday morning and after being released from the van the two NCOs were met by the sergeant dog specialist from No 1 RAF Police District who was taking them to RAF Bishop Briggs on the outskirts of the city for the weekend. After arriving at the unit their kit was taken to the police accommodation while the two NCOs and their dogs were taken over to the dog section. The sight that met them was not particularly impressive; it seemed that the station commander had been using the spare compounds to house his chickens and as such, they were in no state to accommodate the dogs. Although highly unusual, the dogs were taken over to the police accommodation and during the weekend were chained to the side of their respective handler's beds when not being exercised. On Sunday evening, fully refreshed, the two NCOs and their dogs were transported back to Glasgow station to catch the midnight train over to Oban. On that occasion they were delighted when directed to a compartment in the first carriage that had been reserved for them. Shortly after, the train pulled out of the station and later stopped for an hour in Stirling where the two NCOs, again attracting considerable public attention, were able to exercise their dogs out on the platform. After the break they resumed their journey and arrived in Oban just after five on Monday morning. The journey from the train to the ferry, the SS Claymore, was within walking distance, which gave both the handlers and their dogs a chance to stretch their legs. Soon after boarding, the ferry cast-off and the two NCOs together with their dogs made their way out on deck to take in the sea air and the splendid view. However, they were soon approached by a rather cautious looking steward who informed them that a private saloon had been provided for them and that breakfast was also being served, both for them and their dogs. As they settled down to eat, the ferry pulled into its first port of call, Tobermory on the isle of Mull. After finishing a hearty breakfast and freshening up, the two NCOs returned to the deck as the ferry started to berth at Arinagour on the Isle of Coll. From Coll they began the final leg of the journey that would take them to Tiree and that is when the two NCOs were treated to the sight of a couple of large basking sharks swimming close to the ferry. It was just after eleven in the morning when the ferry finally berthed at Scarinish. It seemed that news of their arrival had preceded them because the quayside was packed with local people all eager to catch a glimpse of the two RAF Police dogs and of course their handlers. As the gangplank was lowered two airmen from the radar unit boarded the ferry and collected the kit belonging to the two NCOs and loaded it into a waiting truck. At that point, the Station Commander, Flight Lieutenant Bull carefully approached and welcomed them all to Tiree before he began introducing them to some of the more prominent islanders. After a long and tiring journey the 'celebrity status' was quite an experience for the two young NCOs. The islanders gathered around to take a closer look at the two muzzled dogs but decided to keep their distance after the dogs started growling at them. Indeed, the islanders had never before seen a pure white German Shepherd dog and later it became known that many referred to it rather unkindly as the 'Devil Dog'. Having said that, after quickly settling into their new posting, both the NCOs and their dogs became very popular with both the RAF and the civilian community.

At the beginning of the year, Corporal P J Mason and three other dog handlers together with their dogs were posted from RAF Abyad in Egypt to RAF Nicosia in Cyprus where the terrorist problems with EOKA were beginning to cause concern. In June, Corporal Mason's RAF service came to an end and after a most rewarding few years of working with RAF Police dogs he returned to his life as a civilian in the United Kingdom.

On the 5th May and almost ten years after the war ended, West Germany was once again given sovereignty over its own territory and consequently became the Federal Republic of Germany and a member of NATO. On the 14th May, the Warsaw Pact was signed by eight Eastern European countries under the influence of the Soviet Union. The pact had been largely brought about as a result of West Germany regaining its sovereignty and being allowed to form its own defence force in order to join NATO.

Despite the widespread ongoing EOKA terrorist activity on the island of Cyprus the new RAF airfield at Akrotiri, located on the South-western point of the island, was completed on schedule on the 1st January 1956, and was made ready for operational use soon after. As part of the RAF Police section established on the new unit, a brand new dog section was built there.

When Corporal C Gilmore's tour at Netheravon came to an end he was posted overseas to 2TAF in West Germany. Accompanying him was Sergeant G Irvine, a very experienced dog handler who had joined the RAF Police in 1940. Both NCOs were to become instructors at the Dog Training School based at RAF Wahn with Sergeant Irvine taking on the role of senior NCO in charge. Corporal E Heart was the third RAF instructor there at the time. RAF Wahn was also home to the 2TAF RAF Police School and the RAF Police Driving School, both of which were under the command of Squadron Leader Bracken assisted by Warrant Officer S Grayson, the former flight sergeant training supervisor so feared by the RAF Police trainees at Netheravon. At the time, many of the dog sections established on RAF units within 2TAF were manned by Germans from the General Service Orderly Watchman Service (GSOWS) with a RAF Police corporal dog handler in charge. The dog school at RAF Wahn was capable of holding sixty dogs, most of which were sent out from the RAF Police Depot at Netheravon, while the remainder were recruited locally as unconditional gifts from the public. The school also had three GSOWS personnel on strength; one acting as an instructor for GSOWS dog handlers attending the school on courses, while the other two were employed as kennel assistants. Corporal Gilmore quickly settled into his new posting and after being there for only a few months his colleague Corporal Heart was promoted and posted back to the United Kingdom and his place was filled by Corporal P Trehane who was posted in from the RAF Police Dog Demonstration Team. The main bulk of the instructors' work at Wahn was re-teaming experienced dog handlers posted into 2TAF, including units in Holland, with new dogs; a process that could take up to two weeks to complete. Although the instructors were kept rather busy, they still managed to build a small social club at the dog school which they duly inaugurated as 'The Tail Waggers' Inn'.

On the island of Cyprus EOKA terrorist activity continued at an alarming rate with the violence being directed towards not only the British but also towards the Turkish Cypriot population. On the 11th February, the terrorists launched a surprise attack against the RAF airfield at Nicosia and as a result, three airmen were killed and one was seriously injured. The RAF Police were quickly mobilised and the three terrorists concerned in the attack, were arrested in the area soon after. However, it did little to deter such terrorist activity and on the 4th March, EOKA terrorists destroyed a British Hermes civilian transport aircraft that had been parked on a dispersal area at Larnaca civil airport. The aircraft was being used to bring troops in and out of the island and an investigation revealed that a bomb had been loaded on board the aircraft packed inside a suitcase. Although no one had been hurt, it was still an embarrassment to the authorities and in order to prevent further attacks, the RAF Police, including a number of dog handlers, were called in and shortly after, commenced security duties at the airport. Consequently, every piece of luggage or cargo taken onto any RAF or civilian chartered aircraft after that event was thoroughly searched before being loaded on the aircraft.

After an agreement on the 17th May, between the British government and President Nasser, all British forces were withdrawn from their bases along Egypt's Suez Canal Zone. The years leading up to the withdrawal had been extremely troubled and many British servicemen and women had been killed, attacked and injured. There had been widespread open hostility towards the British presence in the country; the withdrawal of local labour; riots and sabotage, bordering at times on the outbreak of all-out war. As for the RAF Police dogs that had served in the Canal Zone, those that were fit were transferred to other units within the command such as Cyprus and the Persian Gulf and those that were too old or medically unfit for further service were humanely destroyed.

Corporal R Allsopp left RAF Butterworth and was posted back to the United Kingdom to RAF Honington but because there was a shortage of dogs at the time, he was posted to his new unit without one and in fact was never employed as a dog handler again after that. Although he was primarily employed within the RAF Police Flight Counter-Intelligence office, he did carry out the occasional patrol of the unit and patrols, in company with Sergeant M Brown, of the local dance halls which were used by RAF personnel and soldiers from nearby Bury St Edmunds.

In September, Air Commodore Proud retired as the Provost Marshal and from the service. He was succeeded in post by Air Commodore W I G Kerby CBE. The appointment was extremely welcome by everyone in the branch because since its formation, the office of Provost Marshal had been filled by officers from the General Duties Branch, who, in all fairness, had done a considerable amount of work moulding and developing the RAF Provost and Police organisation. However, Air Commodore Kerby was the first RAF Policeman to have attained the appointment who had held every rank along the way, from aircraftsman, right up to Air Commodore. He had initially joined the Royal Flying Corps in 1917, but was later commissioned during World War II. Prior to taking up his appointment as the Provost Marshal, he had been the Command Provost Marshal with the 2TAF in Germany.

On the 11th October, a Valiant bomber of No 49 Squadron dropped the first British nuclear bomb, *the Blue Danube*, during *Operation Grapple* over the Maralinga Test Area in South Australia. From that moment on the RAF Police and especially the dog teams would be fully committed to the protection of nuclear weapons held by the Royal Air Force.

On the 31st October, following the illegal take-over of the Suez Canal by Egyptian President Nasser, British and French forces launched *Operation Musketeer*, in an effort to recover and restore international normality to the canal. The military operation started with a successful series of bombing raids against the Egyptian Air Force which was followed up on the 5th November, by the landing of a joint Anglo and French force of paratroopers, who invaded the area of Port Said at dawn. In addition to recovering the Canal Zone, the operation was also described by the politicians, as a *policing role* to restore order in the region following the invasion of the Sinai Peninsular by Israeli forces.

For a number of years, the important day-to-day routine of feeding, grooming and exercising RAF Police dogs at the RAF Police Dog Training School had been carried out by members of the WRAF (Women's Royal Air Force), who had been 'borrowed' from the trade of Administration Orderly to act as kennel assistants. Unfortunately, there had been no formal training course involved in their employment at the kennels, and that particular type of employment limited the career prospects of the girls who continued to serve in that capacity. Indeed, many of them never attained the rank of Leading Aircraftswoman but enjoyed the job so much that they were prepared, in most cases, to tolerate the many drawbacks involved. However, in early 1957, as part of an overall restructuring of ground trade groups, the trade of Kennel Maid was, for the first time, officially recognised, and the sixteen kennel maids serving at the RAF Police Depot at Netheravon, became for the first time, part of the RAF Police trade group structure. A formal training course was developed shortly after, during which the girls were taught not only how to care for the dogs on a daily basis, but also basic treatment techniques and how to prevent the spread of diseases and finally, general dog section administration.

In addition, promotion prospects were opened up for the first time, and successful candidates could if they wished, attain the rank of corporal. Although the girls who enlisted as kennel maids thoroughly enjoyed their work, it was nevertheless a difficult, and at times, a very strenuous job, especially during the long British winter months. Of the sixteen girls serving at that time only one had worked as a kennel assistant in civilian life. The others had held various occupations such as shop assistants, baker's assistants, farm-workers and press operators, but all shared one thing in common, they had always wanted to work with dogs. Two of them, Julia de Candia and Patricia Crawley, had already reached the rank of corporal. Indeed, Corporal de Candia had been one of the very first airwomen to be employed as a kennel assistant when those duties were carried out by Administrative Orderlies. She had served for five years up until 1949, caring for RAF Police dogs. She left the service and joined the Woman's Land Army, but after three months she realised that she missed working with dogs and so she rejoined the WRAF and took up from where she left off. Corporal Crawley had joined the WRAF in 1955 as an Administrative Orderly and soon after found herself looking after the RAF Police dogs, a job she really enjoyed. At the time, Sergeant Bell WRAF, was the Senior NCO in charge of the kennel maids, and while it was the job of the kennel maids to control the dogs, it was her job to control the kennel maids and she quite often wondered who exactly had the more difficult task. During the year, the kennel maids had received a great deal of publicity from photographers and newspaper reporters keen to highlight to the public at large what a splendid job they were doing at the Depot. Indeed, their daily routine had even been the subject of a short documentary recorded by *Pathe News*. Despite having their photographs published by WRAF recruiting publications, magazines and the national press, they continued to look after their dogs in the most professional manner.

Corporal J Bastard, having completed his tour of duty at RAF Eindhoven, was posted to RAF St Mawgan in Cornwall with his new dog; Air Dog Lady. Although the dog section there was established for four handlers and four dogs, for a variety of reasons, during Corporal Bastard's tour of duty there were rarely more than two dog teams available for duty for long periods of time, which resulted in the two handlers working rather a lot of hours each week on patrol and on kennel duties.

The Blackburn Beverley was a heavy-lift transport aircraft which descended from the tank carrying heavy-lift GAL50 Hamilcar glider that saw service in World War II. It was not an attractive or elegant aircraft by any means. It had an enormous box-like body with a large tail boom that had been modified into a passenger area. Four powerful Bristol Centaurus engines were mounted on the high wings and a large fin and rudder were fitted on each side of the tail plane. The propellers had a then novel reverse pitch feature which made for a very short landing and enabled the Beverley to reverse under its own power. Access to the freight bay was by rear opening clamshell doors and the undercarriage was a fixed tricycle type. The first Beverley aircraft entered RAF service in March 1955 with No 47 Sqn and with a crew of five could carry ninety-four passengers in the freight bay and thirty-two in the tail boom. It was capable of carrying a considerable payload of bulky frieght in its cavernous hold including helicopters, missiles, small aircraft, and various types of vehicles. Tragedy struck just after 11.05am on Tuesday the 5th March, when Blackburn Beverley XH117/Z, belonging to No 53 Squadron, and flown by Flight Lieutenant N E H Gilbert, crashed in poor weather conditions, shortly after taking off from RAF Abingdon on route to RAF Luqa in Malta and RAF Nicosia in Cyprus.

Shortly after take-off, and at a height of 1,000 feet, a serious fuel leak developed in the vicinity of No 1 engine and to prevent a fire from developing the engine was shut down. At that point the captain, with three remaining engines, turned the aircraft around and headed back for the airfield at RAF Abingdon but as he did so, the No 2 engine suddenly failed and the aircraft quickly lost height. In doing so, it struck a set of power cables and then several elm trees in the village of Sutton Wick, Drayton, some two miles south of the airfield, before cartwheeling into a row of farm buildings and a house and landing on a caravan where it burst into flames. On board the aircraft were eleven RAF Police dogs and eighteen people:

53 Squadron (The crew):
Flight Lieutenant Norman Henry Gilbert - Pilot and Captain – killed.
Flying Officer M J Ludlam – Co-pilot – Injured.
Flight Lieutenant Reginald Gordon Wilcox - Navigator – Killed.
Sergeant Gordon McLennan Woodhouse – Air Signaller – Killed.
Corporal John Leonard Arthur Spoel - Air Quartermaster - Killed.

47 Squadron Slip-Crew:
Flight Lieutenant V J R Hurring DFC – Pilot – Injured.
Flight Lieutenant Leonard A Andrew - Navigator – Injured.
Flight Sergeant Jindrich Zarecky – Pilot – Killed.
Sergeant Walter James Owen – Air Signaller – Killed.
Sergeant Douglas Robinson – Air Quartermaster – Killed.
RAF Police Dog Handlers (All Killed):

Leading Aircraftsman Thomas Arnison Jones from Gossip.
Leading Aircraftsman Tony Fredrick Blakey from Boston.
Leading Aircraftsman William H Gorst from High Heysham.
Leading Aircraftsman Raymond Thorley from Leeds.
Leading Aircraftsman George Raymond Croucher from Roslin.
Leading Aircraftsman Colin James Elsegood from Middlesborough.
Leading Aircraftsman Robert Rose-Harvey from Poole.
Leading Aircraftsman Michael John Corden from Auckland New Zealand.

With the exception of three members of the aircrew, all the other people and the police dogs onboard the aircraft perished. In addition, two civilians on the ground; a nineteen year old electricity meter reader, Mr James Matravers and a fifty-one year old lady, Mrs Muriel Binnington were killed and another lady, Mrs Margaret Stanton, was trapped inside her demolished house and seriously injured. A witness to the crash, Mr Philip Richards, heard the aircraft and when he looked up, saw it flying low and then in the next instant it crashed in flames against nearby farm buildings and a cottage. After the initial noise of the crash subsided he could hear dogs howling from within the wreckage and together with other witnesses, Mr Eric Webb and Mr William Dawson, ran over to the wreckage to help survivors. At great personal risk, the rescuers began their search of the wreckage despite the fire and intense heat and managed to take an injured passenger away from the aircraft but he died soon after. They went back to the mangled wreck and managed to take another injured passenger away to safety and then they came across another injured airman who had apparently been thrown clear of the wreckage. His clothes and hair were smouldering and he was in a very confused state. They quickly lead him to a horse trough and poured water over his head and shoulders to cool him down. At that point, the emergency services started to appear at the scene and took over. Some of the dogs survived the crash and although badly injured two managed to escape from the wreckage. Two other seriously injured police dogs that were still trapped inside the wreckage were destroyed by a local vet who was called to the scene. Senior Aircraftsman G Smart, a dog handler from the depot, was a member of the party dispatched to help track down the two missing dogs and recapture them. One dog in particular had escaped having been badly burnt and had lost one of his hind legs. The dog was tracked across farmland until it was cornered in a farm yard, where it was found to be in a dreadful state and too dangerous to approach. The farmer was very distressed about the state of the animal, and was asked to shoot it, which he did, mercifully putting it out of its misery.

The young RAF Police dog handlers had recently completed their training under the guidance of Corporal's E T Snailum and J Ford to become dog handlers, and together with their dogs had been posted out to Cyprus. As the investigation began into the cause of the crash, it transpired that the doomed aircraft had been damaged the previous month when it collided with a similar aircraft during taxiing. It also transpired that the ill-fated flight 3052 had apparently been postponed a number of times during the previous few days as a result of various problems and bad weather forecasts. The final outcome of the accident investigation blamed the crash on a non-return valve in the No 1 port fuel tank that had been fitted incorrectly by a senior technician and which had caused the fuel leak and the fuel starvation to No 2 engine. The tragic event stunned the two squadrons who lost personnel but the RAF Police Branch and particularly the instructors and staff at the RAF Police Dog Training School, who had recently trained and graduated the eight NCOs and their dogs, were devastated by the news. Aircraftsman Michael John Corden, one of the RAF Police dog handlers killed in the crash was born in Mitcham Surrey and after being bombed out in 1940 the Corden family moved to Rainham in Kent. In 1951, the family decided to make a new start and emigrated to Australia but then moved over to New Zealand where they settled. Michael was described by his brother Barrie as the 'wandering type'. He did not stay long in New Zealand but returned to the United Kingdom and joined the Merchant Navy for a while before heading back to Australia where he enlisted in the Army. After completing his engagement he headed back to the United Kingdom and joined the RAF Police in 1956. Being fond of animals, he volunteered to train as a dog handler but during the course his stay at the RAF Police Dog Training School was extended because his dog required further training to reach the required pass-out standard. As a consequence, he left the school later than scheduled and instead of being posted to Northern Ireland, was re-drafted to a posting in Cyprus and thus boarded the ill-fated flight number 3052.

In 1957 the RAF Police dog section established at RAF Nicosia on the island of Cyprus, comprising sixteen handlers and their dogs, was under the firm control of Sergeant Frankland who was assisted in his task by Corporal Coulson. With the exception of the dog kennels, the entire RAF Police dog section was at that time undergoing renovation, with existing buildings being redecorated and the construction of a new demonstration and obstacle training compound and a grooming area.

Between the 19th and 21st May, the first Annual United Kingdom RAF Police Dog Championship Trials were held at the RAF Police Depot, Netheravon, before a large audience of service personnel and members of the public. The object of the trials was to encourage RAF Police dog handlers serving on stations to take a keen interest in the continuation training of their dogs and to improve their overall efficiency. At the same time it also allowed individual dog teams to demonstrate their initiative and commitment to the task of dog handling. The strict standards that were set for the championship trials equalled those imposed on the various civilian German Shepherd dog training societies within the United Kingdom. The championship was open to all members of the RAF Police who were employed on dog handling duties within the United Kingdom. However, handlers serving, or indeed under training at the Depot were excluded from taking part in the competition.

From the outset the contest was designed to be between individual RAF Police teams and was not intended to be a competition between RAF command formations or indeed RAF units. Provost officers and the dog specialists from each of the United Kingdom RAF Police Districts were tasked with carrying out an inspection of all dog teams working within their respective areas. Each officer was invited to select three prospective candidates, which, with the permission of their respective station commanders, were then invited to attend the championship trials at the RAF Police Depot. It was emphasised that the details of all those taking part in the trials were to be notified to the depot by the 19th April. Three awards were prepared for the winners; the Championship Trophy known as the 'Sabre Trophy', which would be retained by the winners' unit for twelve months, was to be awarded to the dog handler whose dog gained the highest number of points during the competition. In addition, the dog handler would be presented with a personal award that he could keep on a permanent basis. A 'First Class Diploma' was awarded to the runner-up in the competition and finally, the dog handler who came third in the competition was awarded with a 'Second Class Diploma'. After a combination of assessments throughout the year to determine which units had the most efficient teams, twenty dogs and their handlers were rigorously tested at the depot over a two-day period before a panel of judges. In all, some twelve separate aspects of discipline were stringently tested, emphasising that the trial was not a circus act or drill display but a real test of the dog team's skills. The standards required by the judges were very high and not surprisingly, so were the performances.

Each team was put through a set routine, which included basic obedience, a criminal attack under gunfire, obstacles, searching, wind scenting and finally the condition of each dog and the handlers' dog equipment was thoroughly checked to ensure it was being maintained to the highest standards. At the end of a very tough competition, the winner of the first trial and the 'Sabre Trophy' was announced as Acting Corporal D Hodgson and Air Dog Cindy from RAF Waddington near Lincoln. Second place was taken by Corporal Cruickshank and Air Dog Raksha, and third place went to Acting Corporal Davies and Air Dog Lassie. The 'Sabre Trophy' donated by Lieutenant Colonel and Mrs Douglas Bain, was presented to the winner by Air Commodore C M Stewart CBE, Air-Officer-Commanding No 27 Group. The four judges involved in the first competition were naturally, Lieutenant Colonel Baldwin DSO, who had done so much to establish RAF Police dogs in the first place, Mrs G Hester of Croydon, Mr R M Montgomery of Guilford and Mr C H Belcher of Bingley.

At RAF Luqa on the island of Malta a serious security incident occurred when some one attempted to blow up one of several Valiant bomber aircraft that were parked in an isolated spot on the airfield. As was normal practice, the aircraft dispersal area concerned was being patrolled by a RAF Police dog team, and it was the dog handler who noticed a parcel lying under one of the aircraft as he did his rounds. Thinking that there was a piece of string attached to it, the NCO pulled on it and, what in fact turned out to be a length of fuse came away in his hand. He immediately reported the matter and shortly after, a full security investigation began, which quickly confirmed that the parcel was indeed a home-made improvised bomb. When the dog handler was later interviewed he told investigators that some time before finding the parcel, he had ordered a couple of what he thought were local Maltese shepherds out of the area. It seemed that they may have actually been in the process of laying the bomb, but because of the dog handlers' intervention were unable to light the fuse. At the time, RAF Luqa was continually at odds with local shepherds who wandered onto the airfield with their flocks regardless of aircraft movements. Although the investigation continued for some time afterwards, no suspects were identified.

By the end of 1957, the RAF Police instructors at the 2TAF RAF Police Dog Training School heard that the school would be closing the following year with dog training being transferred from RAF Wahn to Sennelager where it would join forces with the Army's War Dog Training School. Fortunately, the transfer of training was not going to affect Corporal C Gilmore because his five-year RAF engagement was almost at an end.

In early 1958 Corporal C Gilmore left Germany when his service in the RAF came to an end. After completing his discharge procedure in the United Kingdom he returned to his former occupation; working on his step-father's farm in Wiltshire. His passion for working with dogs however, remained strong and he really wanted to find some form of employment in that capacity. His time in the RAF had helped him to establish many useful contacts in the 'dog world' and he therefore hoped that one of them would 'open the door' to allow him back into that line of work.

In Aden, on the 2nd May, the British Governor declared a state of emergency as Egyptian sponsored civil unrest, violence and anti-British protests continued to escalate within the colony. Although Aden was a somewhat hot, dusty and barren place, RAF personnel serving there were given the chance to escape from it all by taking leave in the Services Leave Centre situated at the coastal resort of Mombassa in Kenya. A similar scheme had also been introduced for the RAF Police dogs serving within Aden. Although the German Shepherd dogs stood up to the incredible heat in the colony pretty well, they were prone at times, to suffer from various skin complaints, which proved difficult to treat in the uncomfortable climate of Aden. To resolve the problem, the dogs were flown out of the colony to the more temperate climate of Kenya to recover. Unfortunately, they did not get to see the Indian Ocean at Mombassa but instead went to the RAF Police dog section kennels at RAF Eastleigh, where they received the best veterinary treatment and were put on 'light duties' until completely recuperated.

Ever since their formation, the RAF Police had always taken on unusual tasks whenever their assistance had been called for, and in 1958, at the height of the *Cold War* they were confronted with another unique challenge when they took on the major responsibility for safe guarding the nuclear weapons assigned to the RAF as part of the British defence policy to thwart any attack from the Soviet Union. As such, armed RAF Police NCOs found themselves responsible for providing the constant security measures required to protect Britain's nuclear deterrent. At night security at those important sites was enhanced by the deployment of RAF Police dog handling teams who patrolled the outer perimeter of the sites to detect the presence of intruders before they even reached the fences. The assignment, although extremely important, was nevertheless, very monotonous for the non-dog handlers and involved carrying out static guard duties and mobile patrols of the sites, known as Special Storage Areas (SSA), that contained the weapons and the Quick Reaction Aircraft (QRA) that were on constant standby armed with nuclear weapons. Additionally, the RAF Police provided escorts for nuclear weapon convoys.

During the second Annual RAF Police Dog Championship Trials which were held in May at the RAF Police Depot, Acting Corporal B Fear and Air Dog Tess took first place after a gruelling competition, while Acting Corporal C Hayburn and Air Dog Rangi took second place, and Corporal J McWhirter and Air Dog Bruce finished in third place. As the idea of the Annual United Kingdom RAF Police Dog Championship Trials became popular, similar competitions were organised in Cyprus for dog units serving within Headquarters Middle East Air Force (HQ MEAF) and in Singapore for dogs units serving within the Headquarters Far East Air Force (HQ FEAF). The first competition held in HQ MEAF was won by Acting Corporal Turner and Air Dog Rex, with Acting Corporal Burnett and Air Dog Duke taking second place and Acting Corporal T Wright and Air Dog Bruce coming third. During the HQ FEAF dog trials, Acting Corporal James and Air Dog Rex came first, while Acting Corporal Richardson and Air Dog Duke came second, and Corporal Esplin and Air Dog Bint came third.

During the month of July, the Bloodhound surface-to-air missile entered service with Fighter Command at RAF North Coates in Lincolnshire. In due course the security of all Bloodhound surface-to-air missile sites deployed along the United Kingdom's East coast would be trusted to the RAF Police and patrolled during the hours of darkness by RAF Police dog teams.

The RAF Police Dog Demonstration Team were still extremely popular with the public nine years after their first appearance at the Royal Tournament at Olympia in London. During the 1958 show held at Earls Court the thirty-four man team, under the command of Squadron Leader C W Hobgen, assisted by Flying Officer I G Mackie and Sergeant K C Hart, continued to thrill the crowds with their skill and professionalism. In the 1958 publicity pamphlet the following was written about the RAF Police dogs:

In war or peace, at home or abroad, the RAF Police dog is now recognised as an indispensable weapon in our security armoury. Whether in the torrid heat of Aden and Malaya or in the chill of a Scottish moor, whether seeking out terrorists in Cyprus or guarding vital installations in the very heart of England, the

RAF Police dog is in its element. Tenacious, loyal, intelligent, strong, these are the sterling qualities of our dogs; no wonder their handlers have such immeasurable faith in them, little wonder they are known as the finest police dogs of their kind in the world today. Most of the dogs now serving in the RAF have been presented by civilian owners whose one desire was to find a suitable home for their dog where it would be usefully employed and well cared for. Gifts of suitable dogs would be gladly accepted and owners of German Shepherd dogs who feel disposed to present them to the RAF Police are invited to write to the Commandant at the RAF Police Depot at Netheravon in Wiltshire. The commandant will always be pleased to supply donors with details of their dog's health and progress.

The mascot dog leading the RAF Police Dog Demonstration Team into the arena this year is Number 4686 Air Dog Comet with his handler Corporal J Tait. Comet, a white German Shepherd dog, is a fully trained RAF Police dog and the only animal honorary life member of the RAF Association. Training is carried out at the RAF Police Depot, where the RAF Police handler, a volunteer for this work, is trained with the dog. Training is done by firmness and kindness; cruelty, however slight, is never tolerated; a German Shepherd dog works to please its master, not because it is forced to do so. The order given more often than any other to the trainee handlers is 'Praise your dog'. The handlers and instructors must display great patience during training, but they are rewarded by the knowledge that the handler will leave the depot with a dog completely under his control and unswerving in its loyalty and affection. The working and living conditions of the dogs are governed by detailed regulations and inspections by veterinary surgeons and service inspections are frequent and rigorous. With its acute sense of smell the dog will detect and apprehend an intruder who might otherwise escape a sentry whose vigilance has been defeated by darkness. A dog will seize an intruder and hold on to him until recalled; should the intruder be unwise enough to assault the handler his dog will attack without command. Indeed, a number of RAF Police dogs have died in defence of their handlers, so undivided is their loyalty. A fully trained RAF Police dog is valued at £125; the dogs before you today are therefore valued at £4,000. However, the value of their work and loyalty to the men they serve cannot be reduced to figures; in this respect they are priceless.

With nuclear war then a global possibility, 1958, saw the formation of the *Campaign for Nuclear Disarmament* (CND), within the United Kingdom. The organisation, headed by the philosopher Bertrand Russell quickly gained a great deal of public sympathy and recruited numerous members from all areas of the country. As a consequence, the group had organised their very first protest march at Easter, when thousands of peaceful demonstrators from around the country had joined forces and marched the fifty miles from London to the *Atomic Weapon's Research Establishment* (AWRE), at Aldermaston, where they demanded that the British government should give up her nuclear deterrent and the research into nuclear missile systems. Although the demonstration ended peacefully, future protests were soon mounted against RAF units thought to hold such weapons and accordingly, RAF Police dog teams played an important role in keeping unauthorised personnel away from secure sites and more especially during organised anti-nuclear demonstrations.

During the year, Corporal D Wardell, who had joined the RAF in 1955, was serving at the technical site at No 210 SU (Signals Unit), RAF Borgentreich, which was situated up a mountain just north of Warburg in Nordrhein-Westfalia. Although it was a very small 'stand alone' site it was nevertheless a totally independent RAF station in its own right. The RAF Police Flight at the time was under the control of Flight Sergeant Blucher. Corporal Wardell, who had the distinction of being bitten by his own dog on the day he passed out of training, had served at RAF Sopley, RAF Trerew and RAF Wahn prior to being posted to RAF Borgentreich. He had volunteered to become a dog handler because at that time, dog handlers wore blue webbing equipment unlike their colleagues on basic duties, who wore white webbing equipment on duty. White webbing of course, required an incredible amount of effort each day to keep it up to the required standard and that seemed to be incentive enough to cause many recruits who wanted to join the RAF Police to volunteer to become dog handlers. Having said that of course, it must be pointed out that the dog handlers committed an incredible amount of their off-duty time to the welfare and the continuation training of their dogs and as such, the job was certainly not a 'soft option'.

During the third Annual RAF Police Dog Championship Trials held in May 1959, at the RAF Police Depot, Acting Corporal B Fear and Air Dog Tess proudly took first place for the second year in succession, while Corporal R Grey and Air Dog Susie took second place, and Corporal D French and Air Dog Butch came third. At the HQ MEAF dog trials held at RAF Episkopi in Cyprus, the top three places were attained by Corporal McBay and Air Dog Luke, Corporal D Hogan and Air Dog Monty, and Corporal H Cheswick and Air Dog Winston. During the HQ FEAF dog trials the top three places were awarded to Corporal Jessiman and Air Dog Beri, Sergeant Clark and Air Dog Franz, and Acting Corporal Cunningham and Air Dog Rex.

Corporal J Bastard, having completed his tour of duty at RAF St Mawgan, was posted overseas again to Aden. After a long but uneventful journey by troopship, he arrived in Aden and joined the dog section at RAF Steamer Point, which at that time was under the control of Sergeant Martin an experienced dog handler who had spent many years as an instructor at the RAF Police Dog Training School. The section was quite large having some twenty dog handlers on strength; two of whom included Corporal J Finch and Corporal Wallace.

On the 8th June, RAF Habbaniya and RAF Basrah were closed down and after forty years of service in the region, the RAF finally withdrew from Iraq. It was a sad end brought about by the revolutionary government who had seized power in the country the previous year following the assassination of their king. As the overall political situation worsened pressure had been placed on the British government to withdraw their forces from the country. As part of the pressure, the RAF were denied the use of their units for flying operations and as such, there was no point in trying to keep them open. The horses however, which had been used so successfully by the RAF Police Mounted Section up until then, and the RAF Police dogs that were fit were all transferred to RAF Akrotiri in Cyprus, where they continued to give the same valuable operational service.

In June, Corporal B T Drew completed his four-year engagement as a RAF Police dog handler and returned to life as a civilian. Prior to joining the RAF in July 1955 he had been a police cadet with the Metropolitan Police. After success-fully completing his recruit and initial police training he had elected to become a dog handler. To ensure that the dogs were fed and exercised each day of the week the students were detailed to work either on a Saturday or a Sunday and it was on one of those occasions that Corporal Drew took pity on the dog that was kennelled next to his own dog; Air Dog Skipper. Having struck up a friendship with the dog; Air Dog Prince, over a couple of weeks he decided to take it out for a walk with the others. Prince was delighted and after trekking for a few miles they came across Corporal J Wardley, an experienced dog handler and a member of the RAF Police Dog Demonstration Team, who asked if the dog Corporal Drew had with him was Air Dog Prince. When Corporal Drew confirmed that it was, Corporal Wardley instructed him to take the dog straight back to the kennel. Corporal Drew complied and Corporal Wardley followed and as soon as Prince was back in the compound his temperament suddenly changed and he went berserk. It was at that point that Corporal Wardley revealed that Prince, not to be confused with Prince of the same nature mentioned earlier in the book, was extremely unpredictable and dangerous and was waiting to be destroyed because he had bitten so many of the staff. The following morning Corporal Drew was summoned to see Flight Lieutenant Parker, the unit's commanding officer. At first Corporal Drew thought he was in trouble but as it turned out the Flight Lieutenant seemed impressed with the way he had confidently handled Prince.

The situation with Prince was explained and at that point the Flight Lieutenant asked him if he could take Prince to the dispensary to be humanely destroyed. He agreed, and despite the dog's reputation, had no trouble whatsoever with Prince even when he put the muzzle on him and held him while the lethal injection was administered by the vet. Upon completion of the course, Corporal Drew was retained with his dog at the dog training school and soon after, he was detailed to go to Wales to collect a dog that was being donated to the RAF. After a long and tiring journey by train he arrived at his destination late in the evening and therefore decided to make the house call the following morning. He needed somewhere to spend the night and luckily, the station master who was extremely obliging, allowed him to sleep in the station's waiting room, heated by a blazing log fire. He was awoken just before eight the following morning by the station master who handed him a mug of strong hot tea and indicated where he could wash and shave.

After leaving the station Corporal Drew walked into the town and located the address he had been given. After knocking the door, he had been given a really warm welcome and after being shown into the kitchen was served a hearty breakfast by the lady of the house. After a couple of hours of polite conversation whilst getting to know the dog, Corporal Drew and his new charge left the house and returned to the station to make their way back to Netheravon. Although the night staff had gone off duty, the station's day staff were equally obliging and when the train arrived they ensured that Corporal Drew and his dog were shown to a compartment reserved just for them. The journey back to Salisbury had been very comfortable and uneventful. Back at the school he helped out the instructors by acting as the 'criminal' for the students and their dogs, but the padded suit always seemed to cause him problems with remaining in the upright position and that was before he was even attacked by a dog. Helping to conduct 'training patrols' at the top end of the unit during the summer months was very pleasant but in winter the place was freezing. Additionally, the standard issue leather sleeveless jerkin provided very little protection against the bitter winter winds that constantly cut across the Salisbury plain.

One of the other 'training patrols' carried out at night was known as the '*White Lady Patrol*' on account of it being conducted along a lane bordering the camp that was supposedly haunted by the ghost of a white lady. The purpose of the patrol was to meet members of the WRAF and families off the bus and escort them safely along the dark and haunted lane to the camp. While he was there he quickly learned just how invaluable the kennel assistants were and what a terrific job they did in looking after the dogs in their care. Some of the kennel assistants employed at the school at the time included; Jonnie Banks, Maureen Sadler,

Margaret McKay, Sue Hunt, Veronica Grace, Maureen Crocker and Avril Taylor. At some point during his time at the school, officers from the Royal Society for the Prevention of Cruelty to Animals (RSPCA) arrived to investigate a complaint of cruelty made by a concerned member of the public who thought the idea of making RAF Police dogs leap through rings of fire during public demonstrations was going a little too far. The RSPCA officers were given free access to the school to view for themselves the training methods used and to see first-hand the confidence the dogs and their handlers had in dealing with such obstacles as the fire ring. After a full briefing they left convinced that the staff at the RAF Police Dog Training School and the methods they were employing were indeed the best and we able to brief the complainant that none of the animals were being cruelly treated. In early 1956 it was decided to establish a RAF Police dog section in Malta and so in April, Corporal Drew was posted overseas to RAF Luqa.

While he and seven other dog handlers were flown out to the island to set things up, two other handlers and the nine dogs made the long journey by sea. Sergeant Davies from the depot, acting as a dog specialist, was there to meet them and to oversee the project. Their arrival on the island made the headlines in the *Daily Mirror* soon after with the statement declaring that 'RAF Police dogs battle with goat herders'. Maltese shepherds, as previously mentioned, had been using the airfield as pasture for as long as anyone could remember, but their presence on the patrol areas conflicted with the interests of the dog teams and it was a daily battle to keep them away.

In September and October 1956, RAF units in Malta were placed on alert when *Operation Muskateer* was launched to recover the Suez Canal from the Egyptians. At Luqa a constant flow of RAF transport aircraft came and went, loaded with troops and equipment required for the impending strike against Egypt. It was during that period that Corporal Drew and Air Dog Skipper, whilst on patrol one night, encountered four Royal Marine Commandos who had just jumped over the perimeter wall to test security on the base. The dog handlers had been issued with a flare pistol a few days before, to use if they encountered intruders. When the commandos saw the snarling dog and the dog handler drawing the flare pistol, they ran for their lives and leapt back over the wall, no doubt thinking that he was about to fire at them. In January 1957, Corporal Drew's father was taken seriously ill in the United Kingdom and the family contacted the Orderly Officer at RAF Luqa asking that Corporal Drew be informed of the circumstances. It was just after 7pm and Corporal Drew was on duty with Air Dog Skipper patrolling the airfield when the Orderly Officer arrived in a car to collect him. After breaking the news, the Orderly Officer transported Corporal Drew and his dog back to the dog section before taking

Corporal Drew back to his accommodation to change and pack a bag. From the barrack block Corporal Drew was taken to the Air Malta Desk at the airport and shortly after he was flying home to London. It was just over four and a half hours later when he arrived at Heathrow Airport and was met by immigration officials who whisked him through the airport to meet his uncle who was waiting with the car. Shortly after, Corporal Drew was at his father's hospital bed and was able to spend a few hours with him before he passed away. At the end of 1958 Corporal Drew's tour in Malta came to an end and after leaving Air Dog Skipper behind to re-team with a new handler, he returned to the United Kingdom and after completing his disembarkation leave was posted into RAF Feltwell, the home of the Thor Missiles in Norfolk. It was late evening when he arrived at Brandon railway station and as he was about to telephone the guardroom at Feltwell for transport a uniformed American Air Force officer and his wife offered him a lift to the unit.

After spending the night in temporary accommodation in one of the guardroom cells, he was taken on a tour the following morning of his new unit and the 'site' where three ninety-foot Thor missiles were maintained on constant readiness for launching. The huge brilliant white rockets adorned with RAF roundels certainly looked impressive on the launch pads and to Corporal Drew resembled something from a futuristic sci-fi movie. After completing the usual arrival procedures, he was detailed to take charge of the dog section but having hardly had time to settle in, he and the rest of the dog section were called out on Christmas Day to assist the two local constables at a nearby construction site where the foundations for a new missile silo were being laid. During the day over a hundred members of CND had invaded the site to stop the work being carried out. Unfortunately, the Irish construction workers, who were being well paid for working on Christmas Day, had not taken kindly to their work being interrupted and had come to blows with some of the protestors.

When Corporal Drew and his fellow dog handlers arrived at the site the construction workers were physically dragging protestors away from the silo through the mud and cement but as they did so more protestors moved in to take the places of their colleagues. A RAF fire engine was called for and shortly after it arrived the firemen were ordered to turn their hoses onto the protestors. It was a bitterly cold day and after a good soaking the protestors seemed to lose all interest in the site and moved away without further trouble. After settling in to his new unit Corporal Drew found the Americans working on the base to be a particularly social group of people when off-duty and very much enjoyed their company. On duty however, the US Air Police who were detailed to guard the site containing the Thor missiles, tended to be just a little keen to use their firearms and one or two of the dog handlers patrolling the exterior of the site at night were lucky not to have been shot by them.

On the 9th September, Sergeant B A Stapleton arrived at RAF Wildenrath, in West Germany where he became the senior NCO in charge of the RAF Police dog section.

The beginning of the 1960's marked the final stages of the close down of what was once a vast British Empire around the world. It also highlighted the continued expansion of yet further specialist roles being undertaken by the RAF Police. The first was of course the detailed development of the security protection required for the nuclear weapons held by the RAF, as part of the national defence deterrent, and the second was the establishment and formation of what became known as Travel Control Security (TCS) measures. Up until that time, the majority of troop movements to and from the distant reaches of the British Empire had been undertaken by using huge troop ships. However, as British influence around the world grew smaller and many of the British military bases closed down, it became much cheaper and faster to carry out troop movements either by RAF transport aircraft or indeed civilian aircraft chartered for the purpose. However, the procedure was seriously prone to attack by terrorists, either hijacking the aircraft in flight or sabotaging it while it was on the ground. Indeed, there had been several such terrorist attacks mounted against civilian aircraft during the preceding years and the RAF desperately wanted to avoid similar problems and so introduced the system of Travel Control Security.

Over on the island of Cyprus on the 2nd February, the first ever dog handling course to be held especially for the locally employed native RAF Police Auxiliaries, was successfully completed at RAF Nicosia. In all, seven Cypriot auxiliary policemen, trained by Corporal P Regan, successfully completed their training and during the subsequent passing out parade, the inspecting officer, Squadron Leader A Smart BEM, from No 24 RAF Police District, congratulated the handlers and their instructor on their smart appearance, the condition of their dogs and the high standard of training which they had achieved. Shortly after, all seven took up their role as qualified dog handlers patrolling and guarding various RAF installations around Cyprus. In addition, because the scheme proved to be so successful, the idea was copied soon after in the Far East, where twelve volunteers from the RAF Police Auxiliaries, under the instruction of Sergeant J A Pearson, successfully completed a locally organised training course to become qualified dog handlers at RAF bases in Singapore. During the same period, Air Dog Tiger, the last Boxer dog in service as a RAF Police dog was retired from 'active service' during a short ceremony held at RAF Nicosia. Tiger had previously served in the Egyptian Canal Zone and upon being retired was immediately adopted by HQ MEAF as their official mascot.

Having only been in Aden for a year, Corporal J Bastard broke his ankle playing sport and complications set in which resulted in him being sent back to the United Kingdom for treatment. Initially, he was detached to No 6 RAF Police District based at RAF Filton on light duties but when that unit disbanded he was transferred to No 4 RAF Police District based at RAF Innsworth, where he ended up accompanying Sergeant Gilltrap, the Police District dog specialist, during his visits to RAF Police dog sections within their area of responsibility.

An estimated total of over a quarter of a million people attended the thirty performances of the 1960 Royal Tournament Show, at the Earls Court Exhibition Centre in London, between the 22nd June and the 9th July. Amongst all the things provided to thrill the crowds, it seemed that the star of the show turned out to be a three-year old RAF Police dog by the name of Judge, and the crowds just loved him. The scenario for his popular performance happened to take place at a simulated RAF guided missile base, being patrolled by a RAF Police dog handler and his dog. As the lights in the arena dimmed, the team commenced their patrol, and the dog indicated the presence of intruders. Suddenly the base came under a surprise attack from a group of armed saboteurs. The handler, Corporal J Black, quickly challenged them and released his dog, but unfortunately, as Judge made his way towards the intruders, they shot him dead, and he immediately dropped to the floor of the arena and lay there motionless.

As you can imagine, nearly every person in the audience gave out a loud sigh in shock as they witnessed poor old Judge being cruelly gunned down. Indeed, night after night, many in the audience attempted to revive Judge by whistling at him and calling out his name, but Judge, the perfect actor, remained quite still and played his part wonderfully. After the demonstration ended and the team took up their positions in front of the Royal box, Judge remained quite inert on the floor where he had fallen. At that point the public were really getting concerned that Judge may really have been hurt. However, they need not have worried because just as the Royal salute was about to be given, he suddenly sprang to life and quickly joined his handler in the line up to pay their respects. The audience loved him and of course their loud cheers filled the entire house night after night. By then of course, the professional reputation of the RAF Police dog teams was indeed an excellent public relations exercise in itself and accordingly there was no shortage of German Shepherd dogs being offered by the public as unconditional gifts.

After a mere forty-three colourful years of loyal service to *King and Country*, the Provost Marshal, Air Commodore W I G Kerby, retired from the RAF on the

11th July. However, he maintained his connections with the branch in the years that followed and continued to offer his services as the President of the RAF Provost & Security Association. He was duly succeeded in post as Provost Marshal by Air Commodore W S Gardner CB, OBE, DFC, AFC, who was not a professional policeman, but a pilot. Prior to taking up his appointment as Provost Marshal, Air Commodore Gardner had been the Head of Plans, Training and Operations Division of the Central Treaty Military Planning Organisation.

On the 31st July, the twelve-year state of emergency within Malaya finally came to an end. The United Kingdom government had granted Malaya her full independence on the 31st August 1957, which had effectively ended one hundred and seventy years of British rule within the colony.

Although it was RAF policy that man and dog remained teamed up for as long as both were together, an exception occurred at RAF Colerne due to an unusual set of circumstances. Three of the unit's dog handlers had been selected to represent RAF Colerne at the 1960 United Kingdom RAF Police Working Dog Championships; Corporal B Fear, a previous RAF Dog Champion, teamed with Air Dog Tess; Corporal M J O'Neill with Air Dog Bess, and a young National Serviceman, Corporal C O'Hanlon with Air Dog Elke 5271. Unfortunately, soon after, the plans started to fall apart. Corporal Fear broke his leg whilst playing rugby for Headquarters Transport Command, and therefore could no longer compete. Soon after, Air Dog Bess went down with a debilitating virus, which prevented her from competing, and if that was not disaster enough, Corporal O'Hanlon, in the face of such adversity, lost confidence in his ability to represent the station alone. So, in the end the unit had one champion dog, Tess, fit and raring to go, but with no handler and one fit handler, Corporal O'Neill, who had no dog.

Dog handlers always have had a fierce loyalty to each other and towards the animals they handle, however, the handlers at RAF Colerne knew that drastic action was needed if their unit was to be represented at the championship. After discussing the matter, it was agreed that Air Dog Tess was good enough to win again for a third year and that was an opportunity that could not be given up easily. Although never before contemplated, it was possible that Corporal O'Neill could team up with Air Dog Tess and save the day. Additionally, it would also give Corporal O'Hanlon the confidence to compete in the competition. The suggestion was put to Squadron Leader H M Shepherd at No 4 RAF Police District, and after seeing their predicament gave Corporal O'Neill a fortnight to re-team with Air Dog Tess and then arranged a full-scale demonstration of the trial at RAF Colerne to access their performance. It was the break that the station needed, and two weeks later Corporal O'Neill and Air Dog Tess were put through the routine. As always, Tess was brilliant and they were given permission to enter the championship at the RAF Police Depot Netheravon to defend the title won on two previous occasions by Corporal Fear and Air Dog Tess. Unfortunately on the day, amidst stiff competition and a great deal of hard effort, Corporal O'Neill and Tess did not win, but came seventh.

The top three winning positions at the dog trials held in the United Kingdom at RAF Netheravon were Corporal M Black and Air Dog Wolfe, Corporal A Faichney and Air Dog Bonnie, and Corporal Grey and Air Dog Susie. At the HQ MEAF dog trials held in Cyprus the top three winning positions went to Corporal Seago and Air Dog Rusty, Corporal J McBay and Air Dog Luke, and Corporal P Regan and Air Dog Duke. At the HQ FEAF dog trials held at RAF Seletar the top three positions were taken by Acting Corporal C Scott and Air Dog Dominic, Acting Corporal Elder and Air Dog Beri, and Corporal Barnes and Air Dog Sabre. Given the popularity of holding annual dog trails, two new formations joined the process; HQ 2TAF (Germany) and Hong Kong. In Germany at the trials held at Monchengladbach the winner and runner up were Corporal P Lettice and Air Dog Thunder, and Corporal D Johnson and Air Dog Kim. In Hong Kong at a competition held at RAF Kai Tak between dog handlers from the RAF Police, the Army and the civil police, the top three places were taken by the RAF Police; Corporal D Guy and Air Dog Rajah, Sergeant R Clarke and Air Dog Franz, and Corporal G Lambert and Air Dog Simon.

During August and September, the RAF Police School moved home once again to RAF Debden, which was situated three miles South East of Saffron Walden in the county of Essex. No 2 (Driver Training) and No 4 (Advanced Training) Squadrons were the first units to move, followed shortly after, by No 1 (Basic Training) Squadron. However, No 3 (Police Dog Training) Squadron had to be left behind at RAF Netheravon, until suitable accommodation and training facilities could be built at RAF Debden to house it.

On the 21st September, Cyprus was finally granted her independence and Archbishop Makarios, who had been exiled by the British on suspicion of his connection with EOKA, was allowed to return to the island, where soon after, he was duly elected as the first President of the new republic. Although Cyprus became a fully independent nation in its own right, Britain, as part of the overall independence agreement, still maintained her two Sovereign Base Areas (SBAs) on the island. The first, protecting its bases in Dhekelia on the South East part of the island and the second, protecting the area around Akrotiri and Episkopi on the South West part of the island.

The buff coloured envelope arrived in the morning post. It was addressed to Mr P J S Waller and had the 'HMS' logo on the front. The message inside was precise and to the point, 'You will report to RAF Cardington by 1700 hours on the 10th October 1960 to commence your National Service in Her Majesty's Royal Air Force'. Thinking that he had managed to evade *call-up* it came as quite a shock to Mr Waller. Consequently, on the appointed day he arrived at Bedford railway station along with many more young men who had received identical instructions and seemed equally bewildered as they gathered on the platform. They were not waiting for long because a number of very tall and severe looking RAF corporals wearing peaked caps appeared from nowhere and started barking various instructions and threats at the startled new recruits. Waller recalled that while everyone was running around in a general state of panic, he noticed a couple of railway porters sitting on a nearby bench who were smiling and had no doubt witnessed the same *reception* many times before. After loading everyone up in a number of three-ton trucks the convoy set off for RAF Cardington and everyone sat in silent reflection of what lay ahead for them.

At Cardington, the corporals began barking more instructions and everyone swiftly disembarked from the transport and lined up outside their accommodation; a thirty-two man barrack hut. After quickly leaving suitcases inside the hut the men were told to line up again outside and were then taken over to the Stores hut where each man was issued with the first of many essential items; a knife, fork, spoon and a pint mug. From the Stores hut they were taken over to the cookhouse to try out their new equipment and to sample the delights of RAF cooking. Over the days that followed, the new batch of National Servicemen were documented, injected, medically examined, dentally examined and paraded here there and everywhere. During the procedure, one or two of the intake were found to be medically unfit for military service and were delighted to be sent home. Uniforms of rough blue/grey serge material were issued to each man and the tailor promised to alter them so that at least they fitted reasonably well. At one point, the corporals lined the men up and began reading out a list of names and the official service number that had been allocated to each man. At the end, the men were told that they had to remember their number and that in five minutes each man would be tested to ensure that they had duly remembered it. In the five minutes that they had been given Aircraftsman Waller indelibly printed in his mind his service number; *5081320*.

In between all the above mentioned activities the airmen were instructed by their corporals how to march as a squad between the barracks and the cookhouse, something easier said than done in a number of cases. Each man was required to hold his knife, fork, spoon and mug in his right hand behind his back at waist height, whilst swinging the left hand up to shoulder height as they marched along. Of course, there were always one or two who could not coordinate the movement of their arm and their legs and invariably ended up *tick-tocking* much to the frustration of the corporals.

After spending a week at RAF Cardington, the National Servicemen were put onto a train, which arrived in the middle of the night at Bridgenorth in Shropshire. Again they were met by three stern looking RAF corporals who did nothing but rant and roar at them, in fact, Corporal's Hoth, Hoast and Stewart, who were to be the airmen's drill instructors, made the corporals at RAF Cardington look rather like saints in comparison. Arriving at nearby RAF Bridgenorth soon after, the men were directed to their accommodation; another thirty-two man barrack hut, and told to get some sleep. It was 0530 hours when they were abruptly woken from their slumbers by the three drill instructors who seemed to be roaring louder than ever. The men washed and shaved in cold water and once dressed were assembled and marched across to the cookhouse for breakfast. After breakfast they were marched back to the barracks and one of the corporals issued each man with a sheet of thick brown paper and some string and informed them that from that point on they would wear only uniform and that all their civilian clothes were to be packed up and sent home. After completing that task, the men were marched over to the camp barber and given a very short military style haircut, regardless of how short their hair was to start with. After an exhausting first day, the men were assembled in their barracks and one of the corporals briefed them about the standards he expected from them during their stay.

"You will stand to attention every time an NCO enters the barracks. You will make up a bed pack every morning as shown in the poster on the wall. You will lay out your kit and equipment on the bed and your small locker as per the poster on the wall. You will use only *Cherry Blossom* shoe polish, *SR* toothpaste, and *Gillette* wet shaving equipment (electric shavers will not be used). You will never walk on the floor of the barracks without putting bumper pads under your feet. Whenever an NCO walks into the barracks, the first person to see him will shout 'Attention NCO present' and everyone will stop whatever they are doing and come to attention. You will blanco your webbing equipment blue. You will remove every pimple from your boots with a heated spoon until they are smooth".

In effect, to get everything prepared for the morning inspection meant getting up at around 0300 hours. So to avoid that, everything was prepared the evening before; the bed packs, the layout of their kit and equipment, and consequently, each airman slept on the floor. At that time the weekly wage, issued to RAF National Servicemen at a formal pay parade was fourteen shilling, from which the airman had to purchase polish, dusters, toiletries and other essential items from the NAAFI. Needless to say, that many of the men wrote home requesting food parcels to keep them going. As the airmen settled into the routine at Bridgenorth it was drill, drill, and more drill, and for a change, physical training during the day, and cleaning and polishing kit and the barracks during the evenings. Part way through their initial training, the men were sent out on a field exercise to RAF High Ercal near Shrewsbury. However, the weather turned really nasty and the exercise had to be terminated and the men returned to Bridgenorth. A week or so after that, each man was interviewed to ascertain what trade they wanted to volunteer for in the RAF. Unfortunately, many of the trades on offer could only be applied for by *signing on* for a minimum of five years service as opposed to two years National Service. As Aircraftsman Waller had intentions of joining the civil police after completing his National Service, he volunteered for the RAF Police. After eight weeks of intensive training, the big day finally arrived when the group passed out and were posted. Aircraftsman Waller was given seven days leave and then told to report to RAF Debden to begin his initial police training.

After a short but well earned rest at home on leave, Aircraftsman Waller reported to the RAF Police Depot at Debden where to his surprise he found that RAF corporals were actually capable of talking to people rather than shouting and screaming at them. After settling down to his initial seven week RAF Police training course he found the new unit to be a far more pleasant place when compared to Cardington or Bridgenorth. Unfortunately, the blue/grey webbing equipment he had worked so hard to bring up to the accepted standard was taken from him and in its place he received another set that had to be scrubbed and blancoed white. During his subsequent training the students were taught amongst other things, service law, unarmed combat, traffic control and of course the Judges Rules that explained the procedure for dealing with persons suspected of committing offences. Although it was hard work it was nevertheless a most interesting course, which Aircraftsman Waller enjoyed.

Halfway through the syllabus the students were introduced to members of the RAF Police Dog Demonstration Team who came up from RAF Netheravon to show off their dogs and to recruit new dog handlers. Shortly after the visit, the instructor let it slip that anyone who volunteered for dog handling duties stood a very good chance of completing their National Service in the United Kingdom, rather than going overseas. As Aircraftsman Waller was not particularly keen to go abroad he immediately volunteered and was accepted provided he completed his initial police training. At the end of a very intensive seven week training course the students were promoted, and Leading Aircraftsman Waller and his fellow students passed out and out of a course of thirty four, six were posted to the RAF Police Dog Training School, while the remainder were posted either to Aden in the Persian Gulf, or to RAF Bruggen in West Germany.

As the *Cold War* dragged on and the Soviet Union continued to develop and expand its intermediate range weapon systems, the threat of nuclear attack against the United Kingdom increased in size and reality. When intelligence sources indicated that the Russians had the capability of destroying the British *Blue Streak* missile sites well before the weapons could be prepared for launch, the program was scrapped, leaving the *Thor* missile and airborne V Force to provide the nuclear sting. However, that did little to please the CND, who by then were holding large demonstrations around the country almost every weekend. The RAF had taken on the role of providing Britain's nuclear deterrent by using the *Thor* missile to strike into the heart of Russia and the V Bomber Force to deliver free fall nuclear weapons. As such, the CND mounted various protest meetings at a large number of RAF stations around the country, with the aim of disrupting the operational role of the base and highlighting their demands to have nuclear weapons scrapped. As you can imagine, their activities took up a considerable amount of RAF and civil police time in trying to prevent them from succeeding in their aims. Consequently, RAF Police personnel backed up by dog teams from non-nuclear units were quickly drafted into the stations at risk, in order to reinforce and supplement the existing establishment in maintaining an adequate level of security cover. Indeed, many of the demonstrations turned out to be quite violent affairs and most were covered by the media, who it seemed by their very presence, tended on a number of occasions, to incite trouble.

In early 1961, Leading Aircraftsman Waller and his colleagues travelled across to RAF Netheravon on the edge of Salisbury Plain to begin their training to become dog handlers. Again, the initial impression they formed of the new unit was favourable; it was a friendly, smallish camp with comfortable accommodation in the form of six man rooms. Additionally, the food in the cookhouse was good and there was plenty of it. Once the course got underway, the RAF men were joined by two American airmen from RAF Alconbury near Huntingdon, who immediately became the focus of attention especially as they seemed to have access to an inexhaustible supply of duty free alcohol and cigarettes, items that were expensive to buy in the NAAFI or British shops. Just before the students were introduced to their dogs, the instructor told them that the first impression they made on the dog was very important and that as such, they should not show any sign of under-confidence as the dog would know and immediately take advantage. When Leading Aircraftsman Waller first saw Tarzan (5183), his German Shepherd dog, it sat looking at him as if to say, "If you come in here, I will have you". However, after feeding the dog a couple of bars of fruit and nut chocolate, they became immediate friends. The course lasted seven weeks and covered all aspects of dog training, welfare, obedience, criminal work and wind-scenting. Although the majority of the training was carried out out-doors, there was also a great deal of classroom work involved.

By May, Leading Aircraftsman Waller successfully completed the training and was promoted to the rank of Senior Aircraftsman, and posted with Tarzan to RAF Coningsby located between Lincoln and Skegness. Arriving on his new unit, Senior Aircraftsman Waller was pleasantly surprised to find himself accommo-dated with the United States Air Police, who were also stationed on the unit. Of course, living and working with the Americans again brought with it numerous perks and made for a very pleasant life indeed. At the time, it was the height of the *Cold War* and No 9 Squadron operated from the unit with their Canberra bomber aircraft and the main task of the dog handlers was to patrol the armed aircraft that were on constant standby for rapid deployment, and of course the weapon storage areas.

Corporal J Bastard, having been declared medically fit again, was posted to RAF Geilenkirchen in West Germany. After being re-teamed with Air Dog Rex at the RAVC War Dog School at Sennelager, which at the time had two RAF Police dog handlers on strength; Sergeant J Babbs and Corporal P Truslove, Corporal Bastard and a colleague Corporal J Lamb, returned to the dog section at Geilen-kirchen, which was under the control of Sergeant K C Hart. The section located behind the guardroom was pretty basic and comprised a meat preparation room and a large compound in which twenty or so kennels were arranged with the dogs secured on run-wires that allowed them to move about without making physical contact with each other. Plans however, were in hand to construct a brand new section. The dog handlers at the unit were required to patrol the outer perimeter of the Special Storage Area, or 'the site' as it was referred to, which allegedly contained nuclear weapons. Shortly after his arrival at the unit, Corpo-ral Bastard and a colleague, Corporal J Watts, were at the dog section preparing the meat to feed the dogs when suddenly two RAF jets collided over the nearby estate that contained the married quarters and the primary school. While the bulk of the aircraft came down to earth in open ground, some of the debris did land on the estate and in the school grounds. Both pilots were killed but luckily, no-one on the ground was seriously injured. Later, work began to build the new dog section and when it was finished comprised an office, dispensary, meat room, storage facilities and individual kennel compounds for the dogs. At that point, Sergeant Hart returned to the United Kingdom and until his replacement arrived Corporal Bastard was nominated to take charge of the section. Some other members of the section at that time included; Corporal's R Pike, J Henry, D

Johnson, D Wigmore, Lamb, R Franks, Wilson, P Figgins, M Moore, Street, Boswell and E Eagles.

On the 16th July, Air Commodore Gardner relinquished his appointment as the Provost Marshal on being appointed Director General of Personal Services at the Air Ministry and promoted to the rank of Air-Vice Marshal. He was succeeded in post by Air Commodore J C Millar DSO, another pilot, who prior to taking up his new appointment had been the Commandant of the Central Signals Establishment at RAF Watton in Norfolk.

Having only been at Coningsby for a few months, the unit was closed down operationally while work was carried out to extend the runways for the imminent arrival of the much larger Vulcan bomber. Accordingly, the Canberra aircraft were re-deployed to other airfields and the dog handlers, including Senior Aircraftsman Waller, were posted to RAF Finningley near Doncaster, which at the time was home to the larger Vulcan and Victor bombers. Soon after and exactly one year after joining the RAF, Senior Aircraftsman Waller was promoted to the rank of Senior Aircraftsman Acting Corporal, and after being presented with his 'stripes' by Warrant Officer Pringle, was introduced into the Corporal's Club to celebrate. Security at the unit was strict for various operational reasons and in order to test just how effective it really was, members of the local RAF P&SS region would regularly carry out security exercises to test just how effective security was on the unit. The term P&SS, standing for Provost & Security Services, was the new title of the RAF Police operating outside RAF units under the direct control of the Provost Marshal; formerly the RAF Police Districts. The Station Commander, by virtue of his appointment, would be told when the tests were to be carried out, but he was sworn not to disclose that information to anyone else. However, whenever he paid a visit to the weapons storage area to chat with the dog handlers, it was a certain sign that the *Test Team*, as they were called, were about. Accordingly, all off-duty RAF Police NCOs in civilian clothes were mustered to check the local area outside the unit, and the cafes on the Great North Road A1, for their presence.

As the vehicles used by P&SS were invariably unmarked black Austin 1800s, the task was not that too difficult and once the team were located, their every move would be monitored and the details passed back to the unit. Given the level of surveillance brought into play, it was not often that the *Test Team* managed to breach the security defences of that particular unit, and that of course kept the station commander very happy. On one occasion, HRH Princess Margaret paid an official visit to the unit to present colours to one of the squadrons and as part of the program she was to be shown one of the Vulcan bombers. Consequently, Corporal Waller and another dog handler, together with their dogs were posted on guard at the aircraft concerned. It was sometime later when the Royal visitor arrived and upon seeing the dog handlers she started to approach Corporal Waller and Air Dog Tarzan. The dog however, had a job to do and showed no favouritism as he snarled at her. Although he was firmly under control, the Royal visitor wisely backed off and went instead to view the aircraft. Friday evenings were always busy for the dog handlers on duty because a great number of airmen from the unit would attempt to take a short cut across the airfield back to their accommodation after spending the evening in Finningley village. The airfield was strictly out of bounds to unauthorised personnel, and the dogs were very efficient in locating them as they attempted to cross the airfield in the dark. Needless to say, after receiving that stark challenge, *"Halt, or I will release my dog"*, they spent up to thirty minutes face down spread eagled on the damp grass awaiting the arrival of the RAF Police patrol to take them to the guardroom.

On the 20th August, work began to construct the *'Berlin Wall'*. The stark barrier was completed very quickly and was patrolled by armed East German border guards, with orders to shoot anyone trying to cross over into the west. A number of hopeful escapees tried and while some were successful, unfortunately, many more lost their lives in the attempt. The building of the wall effectively cut the city into two zones and divided its population, relatives, friends and colleagues. In addition, it isolated West Berlin from the rest of West Germany and travel in and out of that half of the city was tightly controlled and directed along special *'corridors'* into and out from the city. As for the western Allies stationed in the city, the wall meant nothing and as such, they continued to exercise their right to move about within the entire area of Berlin unrestricted.

During the Annual United Kingdom RAF Police Dog Championship Trials held at the RAF Police Depot, The top three NCOs and dogs judged to be the best dog teams serving in the United Kingdom were named as; Corporal E George and Air Dog Sabre, Corporal J Savill and Air Dog Sheba, and Corporal J Perry and Air Dog Kurt.

The retirement party held for Lt Col Jimmy Baldwin in 1953.

RAF Police Dog handlers and their dogs on Parade in Hong Kong – 1953

The 1958 RAF Police dog trails Singapore with Mr Charles Fricker Senior Training Advisor (RAFP Dogs) in centre of picture

The three Amigos Circa late 1950's

RAF Police Dog handlers and their dogs on parade – Circa 1960

Air dog Tiger, the last Boxer dog to serve as a RAF Police dog – Nicosia Cyprus 1960

Cpl Waller (R) and colleague on patrol during his National Service – 1960

RAF Police dog handlers and dogs on patrol in the Tower of London 1962

3.   1962 – 1971

Madge Chapman joined the WRAF on the 6th February 1962, wanting desperately to become a kennel maid; a trade in the RAF, that many, including her instructors at recruit training, had no idea existed. After completing her basic training at RAF Spitalgate, 2837778 Aircraftswoman Chapman was posted to the RAF Police Dog Training School at Netheravon and shortly after her arrival there faced her first crucial test. The WRAF sergeant in charge of Administration and the kennel maids at the school interviewed her and then took her on a tour of the kennels as an introduction to her new job. It was then that the sergeant pointed to a drain around which a pool of foul looking sludge had accumulated, and told Aircraftswoman Chapman that it was blocked and needed to be unblocked. There seemed only one way to deal with the problem and so Chapman calmly rolled up her sleeve, plunged her arm into the smelly sludge and the drain beneath and pulled out a handful of muck and straw which quickly resolved the problem. In response, the sergeant merely said, "You'll do" and as soon as Chapman had washed her hands at a nearby tap they quickly continued with the guided tour. It was at that point that Chapman wondered what the sergeants response would have been if she had flinched from the task. Over the days that followed, she began to settle in and was introduced to her new colleagues and of course the dogs she would be caring for. At first, she was very wary about some of the dogs, which seemed so big and full of snarling teeth. Although she had worked in kennels before joining the RAF, she had been dealing with Poodles, Dachshunds and Chihuahuas; a world away from the German Shepherds that seemed about as docile as 'Attila the Hun'.

She had only been at Netheravon for a couple of days, and was walking from the WRAF accommodation to the kennels, when she saw an airman in uniform walking towards her and immediately she went into a state of panic when she realised he was wearing a peaked cap. Her mind was working fast and she was not sure if it was an officer or not, and if he was, would she have to salute him? But then on the other hand he might be a warrant officer and they were not saluted. It was all too much for the shy young eighteen-year old and so she decided to do nothing and hope for the best. Unfortunately, her decision was wrong; it was a young officer and he was not too pleased at not being saluted. She tried to explain that she was not sure whether he was an officer or a warrant officer, but that just seemed to make the situation worse and he immediately started to berate her for not knowing the difference between an officer and a warrant officer. After what seemed like an age, he finished his lecture and she was dismissed, she quickly saluted and went on her way. Luckily, nothing further was heard about the matter but she was a little more careful after that.

Without having time to dwell on the matter further, she started her trade training with a group of new inexperienced dog handlers that had just completed their initial police training. Chapman was assigned 5371 Air Dog Tim, a fully trained German Shepherd who had a calm temperament and was usually used for training new dog handlers, who apparently in most cases did not know one end of a dog from the other. Her training took three weeks to complete during which she was taught various aspects about dogs; their health, their welfare and how to train them to a basic standard of obedience. Training had been divided between theory taught in the classroom and 'hands on' experience outdoors. Once her course was over she was assigned six dogs to look after. They were dogs that had already been trained and were waiting to be allocated to a dog handler. One of the dogs in her charge was Air Dog Chum and a fellow kennel maid quickly warned her about him and told her to be careful because the dog could be somewhat unpredictable. She had looked after him once before when he had been returned to the school and had been caught out when he suddenly turned on her one day. Although Chapman accepted the advice given, she nevertheless though that perhaps her colleague might be over-reacting slightly; personally, she could not see anything wrong with the dog having looked after him for several days without any problem. A day or so later she was out exercising Chum when she stopped to chat to a passing dog handler, Corporal Wass who was exercising his dog, 5530 Major. Chum was sitting quietly by her side when suddenly without warning he changed into what could only be termed as a snarling angry 'devil dog'. Before Chapman could react, Chum lunged at her with such force that he knocked her to the ground and at that moment all she could think about was keeping the dog away from her face. In the next moment Air Dog Major came in and the two dogs started to fight. Everything was happening so fast but then Corporal Wass and one of the instructors came to the rescue. Before the dogs could be separated the instructor was bitten and so was Chapman, so much so, that wounds on her hands and arms needed a number of stitches. Both dogs however, were unscathed and were swiftly returned to the kennels to calm down while Chapman and the instructor were taken off to the Medical Centre to be treated. On her return to the school she was just a little nervous about getting into trouble over the incident, and of course her colleague saying "Told you so" but in the end all that was said was, "You're a proper kennel maid now you have been bitten, welcome to the club". Because of her injuries she was unable to work at the dog school until her wounds had healed and the bandages were taken off, so she was sent to work in the station telephone exchange. She was just a little disappointed with her change of employment because the week before, one of the male trainee dog handlers had been bitten and he had been sent home on two weeks sick leave. Perhaps, she thought, "The girls are made of sterner stuff".

The NAAFI bar at Netheravon was frequented by kennel maids and dog handlers alike, and it was not long before Chapman was introduced to *Newcastle Brown Ale*, a brew popular with the kennel maids at the time, many of whom could out drink some of the young dog handlers going through the school. Evenings were usually spent exchanging amusing stories about dog handlers, kennel maids or indeed the dogs. She remembers one night being told about a dog handler who had been stationed out at RAF Changi in Singapore. Apparently, there was one corner of the airfield where the dogs refused to go when out on patrol, so the dog handlers kept well away from the area; that is until one night when one of the bolder dog handlers decided that enough was enough and took his dog into that particular area. The dog apparently was found back at the dog section the following morning a quivering wreck, and the dog handler was found later in the area after a search, with a look of total terror on his face. He was so upset by the experience that apparently he was unable to tell anyone what he had seen. Whether the story was true or not Chapman never found out but it certainly made the hairs on the back of her neck rise as she thought about it later that night as she walked back to the WRAF accommodation in the dark.

In November 1961 former Corporal C Gilmore had returned to RAF Netheravon as a Civilian Instructional Officer (Grade 5) at the Dog Training School. Although the post had been advertised the year before the process to join the Civil Service had been a long and drawn out affair. After successfully completing the 'Trade Instructional Techniques Course' at the RAF School of Education at RAF Uxbridge, he began doing the job he dearly loved; working with and training dogs. At that time, the school was a very busy place with a new eight-week basic dog handling course, averaging between twelve and sixteen students, starting every week. When Mr Gilmore joined the school there was only one instructor allocated to each course which subsequently meant that the instructor was actively involved with the students all day and every day of training. Moving between theory lessons in the classroom to practical lessons outdoors also involved the instructor changing from his normal suit, collar and tie into overalls and a padded suit and then later having to change back again to continue teaching in the classroom environment. Mr Gilmore quickly settled into his new position and found that what made his job so interesting was that no two days at the school were ever the same.

In Aden during the early days of 1962, the Service Police element had been subjected to a number of changes and comprised four units. The first being the Headquarters Provost & Security Services; a joint unit, under the command of a provost wing commander, and made up from personnel from the Royal Navy Regulating Branch, the Royal Military Police (RMP) and the RAF Police. Secondly, 24 Infantry Brigade Provost Unit, commanded by a captain RMP, who was responsible to the Brigade Commander. Thirdly, the Port Unit RMP, commanded by a captain RMP, who was responsible for security to the Royal Navy Captain at HMS Sheba. Finally, the Travel Control Security (TCS) Unit at Aden civil airport, commanded by a provost squadron leader who was responsible for air transport security to the Command Provost Marshal and the High Commissioner. The joint Headquarters Provost & Security Services, which also had detachments in Bahrein and Kenya, comprised five sections. The first being the Provost Section, commanded by a captain RMP, which was established for four RN Regulators, twenty-seven RMP and twenty-three RAF Police NCOs. The Special Investigation Section, commanded by a provost flight lieutenant, was staffed by five RMP and seven RAF Police NCOs. The Counter-Intelligence Section, commanded by a provost flight lieutenant, comprised seven RAF Police NCOs. The TCS Unit, commanded by a provost squadron leader, was established for nine RAF Police NCOs. Finally, the Dog Section, also commanded by the TCS squadron leader, was established for thirty-three dog teams. Although the headquarters was described as a 'joint service unit' there were limitations, because of the variations in training, in employing the RN Regulators and the RMP NCOs on some duties because for instance neither was trained to carry out security work or dog handling like their RAF counter-parts and therefore could not be employed on counter-intelligence, TCS or dog handling duties.

The coming of 1962, saw the world, for the first time seriously on the brink of nuclear war as the two superpowers, The Soviet Union and the United States of America, defiantly faced each other over what became known as the *Cuban Missile Crisis*. In 1960 Soviet Leader Nikita Khrushchev launched plans to supply Cuba with intermediate-range ballistic missiles that would put the eastern United States of America within range of nuclear missile attack. Unfortunately, Khrushchev mistakenly assumed that the Americans would take no action and when questioned denied that any missiles were being supplied to Cuba. President John F Kennedy consulted secretly with advisers, discussing options; invasion, air strikes, a blockade, or diplomacy, and decided on a naval blockade to prevent the arrival of more missiles. He demanded that the missiles on Cuban soil be dismantled and returned to the Soviet Union. Consequently, the United States military were put on full alert and the Navy was ordered to impose a complete blockade around the island. Shortly after, both the American and Soviet governments were locked into dialogue in an effort to defuse the situation and prevent it from developing into all out war.

The Tower of London has a very interesting history; on the 14th October 1066, William of Normandy met Harold at Hastings and conquered him at the Battle of Hastings. William, then known as *William the Conqueror* was crowned King of England later that year and immediately began building forts up and down the country to symbolize his power. One stood in the southeast corner of London, near an old Roman wall on the north bank of the River Thames. William ordered it to be demolished in 1078 and replaced it with a huge stone fortress which he named the Tower of London. Rising nearly one hundred feet high, with its walls fifteen feet thick in certain places, it contained a chapel, apartments, guard-rooms, a prison and crypts. The Tower was protected by a wide ditch, a new stone wall, the old Roman wall, and the River Thames. King Henry III made the tower his home in 1240. He whitewashed it and extended the grounds to include a church, a great hall, and other buildings. He named the entire area the Tower of London, and renamed the original tower as the White Tower. Although the tower remained a prison, Henry turned the White Tower into a beautiful palace and entertained many important visitors, many of which came with animals as gifts. Near the drawbridge of the tower, he built the Lion Tower; a zoo where visitors would be greeted by roaring beasts. Several monarchs met violent deaths in the Tower of London. One was thirteen-year-old King Edward V. When his father, King Edward IV died, his uncle Richard, the Duke of Gloucester, plotted to take the throne for himself. Richard had the thirteen-year-old king and his younger brother the Duke of York, taken to the tower where they were later murdered. King Henry VII formed a personal bodyguard at the Tower in 1485 after killing Richard III on the battlefield. His protectors were called the Yeoman Warders, a force which still guards the tower today. After the death of Henry VII, the Tower of London was never again used as a Royal residence but the dungeon was still used to hold England's enemies, many of whom were tortured and executed. On the 19th May 1536, Anne Boleyn, the wife of King Henry VIII, was executed at the Tower Green and for a while their daughter Elizabeth, who would later become Queen of England was held prisoner in the Tower for two months by her half sister, Queen Mary. In 1603, part of the Tower of London became a museum. King James I, ordered that the Royal jewels be kept in the Tower Jewel House and be put on display for important visitors to view when visiting the tower. From the beginning of July until the end of August 1962, the RAF Police became a part of the towers' history when for the very first time they were invited to assist in guarding the Tower of London; which still housed the high security depository for the famous and priceless Royal Crown Jewels. A theatre company had been invited to perform an opera entitled, 'Yeomen of the Guard' within the site and in order to ensure that security was in no way compromised over the period, the assistance of RAF Police dog teams was requested to patrol the moat area. Consequently, twelve extremely smart RAF Police dog handlers and their charges were divided into three four-man teams to patrol the grounds of the fortress where they provided a very real deterrent to any would-be intruder with desires of getting his hands on the Royal gems. With the exception of Corporal M Lawford with Air Dog Remus, all those who took part in the operation had recently completed their training to become dog handlers and so it was a really exciting start to their RAF service. The dog handlers and the dogs were accommodated at RAF Northolt and each evening they were transported to the Tower where foot patrols were carried out between 6pm and 6am. One other member of the detachment was Leading Aircraftsman I Paterson with Air Dog Kim.

Corporal Waller's time in the RAF Police as a National Serviceman was coming to an end very quickly, and before he knew it he found himself on the train from Doncaster taking his dog back to RAF Netheravon. As he said goodbye to Air Dog Tarzan for the last time he felt quite emotional as he recalled the events that they had both been a part of over the previous two years. However, he quickly composed himself and shortly after arriving back at RAF Finningley, he was demobbed to continue his life as a civilian. In retrospect, when he looked back on his time as a National Serviceman, he thought it was the best two years of his life up to that point. He had met lots of interesting people and had learned the value of teamwork and comradeship.

During two days of gruelling tests involving twenty-four dogs and their handlers, the top three winning positions at the Annual RAF Police Dog Championship Trials held in the United Kingdom at RAF Debden were Corporal G Herd and Air Dog Bonnie, Corporal A Brown and Air Dog Krista, and Corporal J Perry and Air Dog Kurt. RAF Champions Corporal Herd and Air Dog Bonnie, a four year-old dark sable German Shepherd bitch serving at RAF Hemswell in Lincolnshire gained 471 points out of 500 and were awarded the *Sabre Trophy* and the RAF Police Champion Dog Coat. It was a third try triumph for Bonnie, acquired by the RAF in 1958. During the 1959 trials she was judged best dog of the opposite sex to the winner, receiving the *Crumstone Storm Trophy* and in 1961 she was awarded a Second Class Diploma. Corporal Herd joined the RAF in 1951, after advice from his father who had also been a RAF Policeman. He had served at Hemswell since 1959. Second prize went to Air Dog Krista, a gold and brown four-year old German Shepherd bitch handled by Corporal Brown from RAF Waddington near Lincoln, who picked up 469 points in the competition. Only six marks behind in third place came five-year old Air Dog Kurt, a sable and black German Shepherd dog handled by Corporal Perry from RAF Cottesmore in Rutland, who were awarded the *Crumstone Storm Trophy*. The three judges at the 1962 event were television personality Mr Stanley Dangerfield and two dog breeding and training experts; Mr A G Morrow from Cumberland and Mr E Sandon-Moss from Birmingham. At the RAF Germany dog trials the top two places were taken by Corporal D Martin Air Dog Rex and Corporal G Ringer and Air Dog Simba. During the dog trials held in Cyprus the top three places were taken by Corporal Burnett and Air Dog Limey, Corporal Tait and Air Dog Simba, and Corporal Down and Air Dog Kim.

On the 26th October the Russians agreed to Kennedy's demands to remove all the missiles from Cuba and offered the Americans a full on-site inspection in return for a guarantee not to invade Cuba. Kennedy accepted and halted the blockade. The missile crisis had been brought to a successful conclusion by the intervention of the United Nations Security Council who had prevented the situation from developing into a further global conflict. Although nuclear war had been narrowly avoided, the episode added further fuel to the CND movement within the United Kingdom, and other like groups abroad, who used the 'near war crisis' to promote their cause even further.

Flight Sergeant F Authers arrived in the port of Aden and after spending his first night in the Red Sea Hotel; a transit facility run by the RAF, he reported for duty at the joint Headquarters Provost & Security Services. During his subsequent arrival interview with the Deputy Command Provost Marshal, he was informed that a number of security incidents had occurred up in Bahrein and as a consequence the RAF were in the process of enhancing the overall security measures at their base there. At that point, he was informed that he was being sent there to establish the security section at the airport and that three RAF Police sergeants, twenty corporals and ten RAF Police dogs would be joining him from the United Kingdom the following Sunday. The following day Flight Sergeant Authers flew up to Bahrein in the Persian Gulf to begin the task. As promised, the NCOs arrived on time from the United Kingdom, and were divided into three shifts, each under the control of a sergeant, and rostered to provide twenty-four hour cover. The section took over the old watchtower on the airfield and all RAF aircraft at the airport were enclosed within a barbed wire compound, which was patrolled at all times by armed RAF Police NCOs. Additionally, RAF Police dogs were deployed during the hours of darkness to further enhance the security measures in place. Although it was still winter in the region, the average daily temperature was around 40°C in the shade with the average rainfall being around fourteen millimetres per year. Although water from natural springs was plentiful in the tiny state it was highly mineralised and so de-mineralised water had to be bought for consumption at about one shilling and sixpence a gallon, which just happened to be the same price as petrol there.

As previously mentioned, RAF Netheravon was situated on Salisbury Plain and in the summer it was delightful but in winter it was a different matter. Leading Aircraftswoman Chapman remembers quite often during the winter of 1962/1963 waking to see an inch of ice on the inside of the windows. In fact, the accommodation was so cold that the kennel maids used to practically get dressed for work and then get into bed. Those that did not actually go to bed dressed became experts in dressing under the bedclothes in the morning. At the time all WRAF personnel were issued with knee length silky bloomers known as 'passion killers'. While they may not have been fashionable they nevertheless came into their own during those cold winter days. The weather at the beginning of 1963 was particularly bad and on one occasion after being hit by strong blizzards all night, the kennel maids literally dug their way through to the kennels the next morning to find most of the dogs sitting on top of huge snowdrifts that had accumulated in their runs.

At around the same time, Aircraftsman G R Phillips arrived at the RAF Police Dog Training School to begin his training as a dog handler and immediately developed a fondness for Netheravon and being a young man brought up with rationing still in force, he especially remembered the food as being wholesome and plentiful. Initially, because of the severe blizzards affecting the unit, he and his colleagues were employed on clearing snow drifts from around the dog training school, which was hard work but great fun and a good way of developing teamwork. Eventually, once the blizzards abated he and his fellow trainees started their course under the watchful eye of their instructor Corporal R Schlanker. He was allocated Air Dog Lassie 4979, a German Shepherd bitch who had been donated to the RAF by another 'Mr Phillips' who apparently came from the Amesbury area. Lassie was a splendid dog who had a very good temperament and a thick heavy coat which certainly protected her from that terrible Wiltshire winter weather. He remembers that the course was hard work and very physical but certainly something which he enjoyed immensely. After successfully completing their training, both passed out at around the same time that volunteers were required for training in preparation for the next Royal Tournament. Although Leading Aircraftsman Phillips did not volunteer, he and Lassie were nevertheless selected and joined the team soon after. He remembers other members of that team as being, the Andrews brothers, Warren, M Manning, J

Field and D Remnant who were all 'mothered' by Sergeant's Darnell and K Hart and Flight Sergeant Logue.

CND were active in May 1963 when they organised two major anti-nuclear demonstrations at RAF Marham near Kings Lynn. During the first on the 11th May some three hundred and fifty demonstrators suddenly appeared at the unit and stopped all movement in or out of the station. The civil Police arrived to assist the RAF Police in containing the situation and seventy-nine protestors were arrested and later charged for a variety of offences. During the second demonstration a week later, fifty-eight of the two hundred and fifty protestors were arrested by the civil police for similar offences.

On Saturday the 29th June, RAF Waddington in Lincolnshire received at very short notice, the President of the United States, John F Kennedy, who paid a brief official visit to the station. As you can imagine, given such short notice, the security arrangements were hastily, but successfully arranged with the help of RAF Police reinforcements, including a number of dog handlers and their dogs, from neighbouring stations at RAF Scampton, RAF Hemswell, RAF Conningsby and RAF Finningley. After a rather hectic but successful day, the president flew out from the station on board his Boeing aircraft, *Air Force 1*, and everything on the station reverted back to normal.

Although Netheravon could be quite a bleak and exposed place at certain times of the year, many of the kennel maids and the dog handlers who worked there or passed through during training held very fond memories of the place. It was therefore quite a wrench when the RAF Police Dog Training School closed in June and July 1963, and everything was moved to RAF Debden. At that point, the part-time services of a veterinary surgeon were required by the RAF to look after and advise on the health of the large number of dogs in service with the branch. Accordingly, Mr John Allan Fleming, a veterinary surgeon running his own private practice in nearby Saffron Waldron accepted the offer and was subsequently titled as the Veterinary Advisor to the RAF. After settling into their new accommodation, Mr Charles Fricker introduced the 'Annual Working Dog Efficiency Competition'. In order to obtain the required results, he had to travel to every RAF station, which had RAF Police dogs established on it and subject both the handlers and their dogs to a number of rigorous efficiency tests. As soon as the results were known, the best teams were invited to the RAF Police Depot, where, to compete for the title, 'RAF Police Dog Champion of the Year', they demonstrated their skills before an assembled and excited audience. To present the prizes to the winners, Mr Fricker enlisted the assistance of the Provost Marshal, Air Commodore J C Millar, and other notable officers of air rank and before long the trials proved to be a very popular annual event, so much so, that similar procedures were subsequently organised in every overseas command.

After successfully taking part in the Royal Tournament at Earls Court and proving his worth, Leading Aircraftsman G R Phillips was posted onto the RAF Police Dog Demonstration Team and allocated a new dog, Air Dog Sabre, formerly handled by Corporal J Ansell. While Lassie returned to the Depot for re-allocation, Leading Aircraftsman Phillips and Sabre quickly settled down to become a part of the busy and high-profile team. He particularly remembers one performance carried out during the interval of a rugby match at a town in the north-west. The weather was appalling and the heavy rain had turned the pitch into a quagmire, which was enough to deter other exhibitors from performing. However, the *more robust* dog demonstration team decided to carry on and marched smartly out onto the soaked pitch to great applause from the spectators. Although the demonstration was carried out to plan, both the dogs and the handlers were drenched and caked in mud at the end of the performance.

The kennels at RAF Debden had been newly built, and the modern facilities for both the dogs and the staff were excellent and a great improvement on the facilities left behind at Netheravon; Debden was indeed, comfortable. The rest room used by the kennel maids actually had toilet facilities incorporated into it which was a great improvement. However, the luxury of the new facilities did tend to 'retain' the girls for longer than the old facilities; that is until Sergeant H Patterson cut through the cigarette smoke to call them back to work. Additionally, the standard of the WRAF accommodation was a great improvement on that left behind at Netheravon, which had been built during the Great War. Because the new accommodation was centrally heated, the kennel maids were no longer forced to go to bed dressed because of the cold during the winter months.

For Mr C Gilmore the move to Debden had been an exciting time and he had been delighted with the purpose-built dog training environment that had been established there. After a few initial teething problems, training quickly settled into a routine and while the majority of the students attending the basic dog handling course were RAF Police NCOs, they were joined by a growing number of American Air Police who were stationed at various bases within the United Kingdom that had been leased to the United States Air Force (USAF). Because of the strict quarantine regulations in force in the United Kingdom the USAF did not want its dogs brought over from America to suffer six months in isolation before becoming operational. Therefore, RAF Police dogs were leased out to the USAF on the understanding that all their handlers attended and passed the initial RAF Police dog handling course at the RAF Police Depot. In addition, the Air Force Department Constabulary also sent its dog handlers to Debden to be trained by the RAF Police. Although there had been a large Quarantine and Isolation Section established at Netheravon, when the school moved to Debden the section that looked after all unallocated RAF Police dogs underwent a name change and became known as the Police Dog Holding Unit (PDHU).

It was at RAF Debden that Senior Aircraftswoman Chapman first came into contact with personnel from the United States Air Force who were serving at bases within the United Kingdom and who had been sent to Debden to be trained as dog handlers. She had never actually met an American before and at first it had been quite strange to be addressed as 'Maam', whilst engaged in conversation with them. At one point, the American trainee dog handlers from one particular course decided to throw a party and of course invited all the kennel maids to attend. The girls however, were a little surprised initially to find that the venue for the party was not the NAAFI as was usual, but a disused war time air-raid shelter situated right in the middle of the airfield. It had been rigged out with red lighting which gave the old place something of a face lift and beer crates had been brought for people to sit on. As the evening got into full swing, and the American beer started to flow, a good number of guests from all around the station converged on the party and everyone was having a really enjoyable time; so much so that a few of the kennel maids were late reporting back to the WRAF accommodation for bed check. At the time, in a very protective RAF, airwomen under the age of twenty-one were required to be back in the accommodation one minute before midnight to be accounted for by the duty WRAF senior NCO or WRAF officer. It was a system introduced many years before to ensure that the girls came to no harm with the RAF authorities taking on the role of guardian. Anyway, as the girls made their way off the airfield that evening and dashed into their accommodation, they were confronted by the WRAF officer who was waiting for them. Although she was not at all happy, it seemed that there was little she could do about it that night as the girls were just a little under the influence of all the American hospitality.

In the early hours of the 3rd August, the night mail train from Glasgow to London was stopped and robbed at an isolated spot called Sears Crossing in Buckinghamshire by the gang now known as the 'Great Train Robbers'. During the violent attack, the gang disguised as soldiers, managed to escape with just over two and a half million pounds in used bank notes.

At the Annual United Kingdom Dog Championship Trials held at RAF Debden Corporal A Clare and Air Dog Jackson were awarded first place receiving the *Sabre Trophy*, while Corporal D Dimbylow and Air Dog Ranee took the second prize, and Corporal A Brown and Air Dog Lynn came third. At the RAF Germany dog trials the two winning teams were declared as Corporal Poad and Air Dog

Bruce and Corporal Pike and Air Dog Jack. In Cyprus the three winners emerging from their dog trials were Corporal Bolton and Air Dog Limey, Corporal Winsor Air Dog Cobber, and Corporal Robertson and Air Dog Wolf.

On the 22nd November, American President John F Kennedy, who was forty-six, was assassinated by Lee Harvey Oswald during a visit to Dallas in Texas. At RAF Debden later that day a number of the kennel maids went into the NAAFI as usual and found out the news from the Americans who were dreadfully upset, with a number of them in apparent shock and openly crying. At first, the girls were very confused by the atmosphere around them but quickly realised just how the shooting of President Kennedy had affected the young American servicemen. It was one of those very sad occasions when the kennel maids were at a loss of how to deal with the situation or what to say under the circumstances.

By the start of 1964, the *Thor* intermediate ballistic missile system had been withdrawn from service in favour of the newly developed *Polaris* deterrent and all the *Thor* nuclear warheads were duly returned to the United States of America. The RAF however, retained the V Force and their free fall nuclear weapon systems, for which the RAF Police continued to provide *'around the clock'* security protection.

The Beehive Café situated just down the road from the main gate at RAF Debden was definitely not the Ritz, but was nevertheless, an extremely popular meeting point for many of the personnel from the camp including of course, the kennel maids. Indeed, 'Les' the proprietor was described as not being the most attentive or enthusiastic of people and the customers were quite often forced to make their own bacon or chip sandwiches or pour their own tea or coffee but having said that, the place did have a good atmosphere and that supposedly made up for any deficiencies. The small back room held the pinball machines, and the main cafe area the jukebox which had a great range of music on it from The Beach Boys, Elvis Presley, Fleetwood Mac, Tony Bennett and Andy Williams.

At the time, all dogs serving with the RAF continued to be donated by members of the public and from the several hundred that were offered each year about two thirds were rejected because of their age or their temperament. The RAF accepted as unconditional gifts, any German Shepherd, dog or bitch, between eighteen and thirty months old with a pedigree. Once a dog had been offered and its pedigree checked an experienced RAF Police dog handler would visit the owner to view the dog on its home territory. If it seemed to be fit and of the correct age and temperament and provided that it passed a number of simple tests, the dog would be accepted for training and the owner would be required to sign a *'Deed of Gift'* form, before handing the dog over to the RAF. Some dogs of course failed to complete the training course and under such circumstances the owners were given the option of taking their dogs back. As soon as the dog arrived at the RAF Police Depot at Debden it would be examined by Mr Fricker, the Chief Training Officer (Dogs), to ensure that it was of the correct size and temperament before being subjected to a few more tests. After that, the dog would be placed in local quarantine for fourteen days during which it would have its service number tattooed inside its left ear and it would be examined by Mr Fleming the RAF Veterinary surgeon, to confirm that it was healthy and fit for training. At the end of the quarantine period, the dog would be transferred to the Holding Section to await selection by a trainee dog handler. Once teamed up with a handler, the seven to eight weeks which followed were spent training, during which time the handler and the dog were taught to work together as a team. The training for the dog would be carried out in short but frequent periods to ensure that it continued to give full attention. However, in between training periods, the dog would receive ample opportunity to play and to rest, while the handler continued with the theory part of his studies in the classroom.

Training of the dog would begin by building up a bond of affection, confidence and trust between the dog and the handler. The lessons would start with basic obedience; learning simple commands such as 'sit', 'down', 'stay' and 'heel'. The next stage concentrated on the dog's aggressive instincts, building on its desire to defend himself and his handler in the face of danger. The dog was taught to chase, apprehend and guard a person as well as being taught to break off from a chase at any point. The dog was taught to guard and escort, off the leash, an apprehended prisoner and to attack without command should the prisoner try to escape. As training progressed the team were taught how to patrol down wind in order to detect the scent of a human in a variety of terrains over various distances. While the pass-out standard at the time was two hundred yards, most German Shepherds are capable of detecting the scent of a human over three times that distance. Finally, at the end of the course the fully trained handler and his dog would be posted onto the strength of a RAF station somewhere within the United Kingdom. Normally whenever a dog handler was posted within the United Kingdom both man and dog usually moved as a team. However, if a handler was posted overseas then he rarely took his dog with him but was re-teamed with a new dog already serving in-theatre. The original dog was returned to the Depot to be re-teamed with another handler destined to serve in the United Kingdom.

One day in May, quite unexpectedly, Senior Aircraftswoman Chapman was summoned to see the warrant officer. As she entered his office her first though was 'what trouble am I in now', however, she was delighted to hear that she had been chosen to escort five dogs out to Singapore the following month, which were replacements for a number of dogs killed by an epidemic in Changi. Having never been overseas before she was really excited at the prospect but at the same time somewhat apprehensive, because it would also be the first time that she had flown.

On the day of the task in early June the dogs were loaded into transit kennels and placed onto a truck for the journey to RAF Lyneham for an overnight stop ready to embark early the next day. The following morning it was bright and early as Senior Aircraftswoman Chapman began the task of loading the dogs, which had not been sedated, onto the transport aircraft; it seemed odd but during the operation everyone else seemed to have disappeared and no one returned to the aircraft until all the dogs had been safely installed inside the transit kennels, which in turn were packed within crates. Shortly after, the aircraft took off and began what for Chapman, was a huge adventure. The route took them via RAF El Adem in Libya and Gan in the Indian Ocean where the aircraft would refuel and, or, stop-over for the night. Chapman recalls that when she stepped off the aircraft at El Adem it was like walking into a red hot oven because it was so hot. However, she still had work to do and quickly set about exercising, feeding and watering the dogs one by one while the aircraft was refuelled. After watering and exercising the dogs she ensured that they were properly secured in their kennels before the aircraft took off again a few hours later for Gan. If she thought flying over Africa and the Indian Ocean was spectacular, she was so excited when she was invited onto the flight deck as the aircraft began its approach towards the tiny coral island of Gan, which to her looked just like paradise. However, from their position in the air the runway ahead and below them looked awfully short and Chapman asked what would happen if the aircraft overshot the runway, "Pray" came the reply back from one of the crew.

As the aircraft came around and started its descent Chapman returned to her seat and strapped in. Shortly after, the aircraft made a perfect landing; perhaps due to all the praying she did on approach. Shortly after landing Chapman again began the task of exercising and watering the dogs only on that occasion she had help from a number of the resident dog handlers. After finishing her work, given that she was perhaps only the second female on the island base, she was invited by the aircrew to join them in the Officers Mess for lunch. Holding the non-commissioned rank of Senior Aircraftswoman even entering the Officers Mess was not the done thing, but to be invited to take lunch was all too much and she quickly started to panic. However, her hosts quickly put her at her ease and during the meal which followed she realised that transport aircrew officers were a different breed from all the others; they were human and interesting. Later that evening after being entertained by members of the resident RAF Police Flight, Chapman, exhausted by the long journey and the excitement of it all collapsed into bed in the room that had been especially reserved for her, unaware that an RAF Police dog handler had been posted to patrol the area to make sure her slumber was not interrupted. After leaving the paradise island of Gan the following morning the aircraft began the final leg of the journey to Singapore flying over the vast expanse of the Indian Ocean. The descent into Changi was just as exciting for Senior Aircraftswoman Chapman. Shortly after landing the aircraft was met by the senior NCO in charge of the dog section who made arrangements for the dogs to be unloaded and taken to their new home. The humid heat of Singapore was as much a shock to the dogs as it was to Chapman and after arriving at her accommodation she spent some time under a cold shower trying to cool down before being whisked off to see the local sights and to taste the famous *Tiger Beer*, which she remembers was definitely not up to the standard of *Newcastle Brown Ale*. After a hot and restless night, she was taken over to the dog section the following morning where she was surprised to find the dogs being dunked in what looked like a sheep-dip. After the previous problem which had killed off so many of the dogs it was a procedure introduced to protect them from the ticks, fleas and other parasites that could invoke disease and sickness. The dogs, however, failed to appreciate the benefits of the system as they were introduced struggling into the solution by the handlers. After spending five days at Changi she said goodbye to her hosts and embarked onto the aircraft and started the long journey back to RAF Lyneham.

During the month of August on the Maldive Islands minor disturbances at Hittadu caused the formation of two rival groups, each headed by prominent island leaders. As a consequence of the disruption, a strike took place and the local population of Addu Atoll, most of whom worked on the base walked out of the RAF unit at Gan on the 5th August in order to sort out their differences. A local leader Afif Didi, who had been educated at Cairo University realised that he could take advantage of the situation. For sometime the RAF personnel stationed on the island were aware that trouble was brewing and their suspicions were borne out when the RAF Police stationed on the Atoll increased security patrols and a detachment of RAF Regiment personnel arrived from Singapore. A few days after a speech by Afif Didi inciting trouble, six members of the Maldivian government were flown into Gan and at the same time the Duke of Devonshire arrived from the United Kingdom. There were rumours that the islanders of the next atoll to Gan had sympathy with Afif but that acts of civil disobedience there had been put down very quickly by the Maldivian government. At the first sign of trouble on the island the fire section were instructed to set up a line of hoses on the shore adjacent to the hut known as the '*Parliament building*' close to the jetty. Soon after, dozens of native boats loaded with angry men waving heavy sticks and iron bars and all shouting loudly, arrived to confront the government officials who were meeting in the parliament building. The whole building was surrounded by fully armed members of the RAF Regiment and the RAF Police were deployed nearby. The firemen received instructions to use the hoses should the protestors try and come ashore. At that point, a RAF Police flight sergeant walked to the waters edge and attempted to get the boats to turn back by shouting at their occupants; unfortunately, his instructions were ignored and he withdrew. At that point a number of angry women from the neighbouring island were wading across to Gan near the old causeway. However, they were eventually stopped by the sight of RAF Police dogs deployed to turn them back. During the disturbances approximately eighty-seven islanders were arrested including the RAF Police interpreter before calm was eventually restored.

After her flight out to Singapore Senior Aircraftswoman Chapman had only been back at Debden for a couple of months when she and another kennel maid; Senior Aircraftswoman V Hart, were summoned to the see the warrant officer. Again, just before stepping into his office the pair quickly scanned their consciences for anything untoward. The warrant officer explained that the internal security situation in Aden had deteriorated and that as a result more RAF Police dogs were being sent out there from the Depot. He then told the two kennel maids that they would be travelling out to Aden with the dogs and to go and get prepared. A week or so later in early September both kennel maids travelled down to RAF Lyneham with ten dogs and the following day boarded the flight out to Aden, stopping on the way in Malta and Bahrain to refuel. After a long flight the aircraft touched down at RAF Khormasker on the 13th September and was met by the senior NCO in charge of the dog section who arranged for the dogs to be off loaded and conveyed to the dog section at RAF Khomarsker. The girls received a very warm welcome and were then taken to their accommodation. Aden was hot and dusty and because of the security situation they were confined to camp. However, during their brief stay they were very well looked after and enjoyed seeing a small part of the colony. In fact, the only problem the girls encountered during their visit was with the wildlife; the small gecko lizards were common in Aden and were often heard and seen running about on the rafters in the ceilings or on the walls inside the barrack rooms. They were totally harmless but nevertheless their presence terrified the two girls. They left Aden a few days later and returned home all the wiser for their experience.

Having completed a number of engagements around the country, Senior Aircraftsman G R Phillips was posted at his own request onto operational dog handling duties and as such, was posted to RAF Benson where he joined the two other handlers on strength; Senior Aircraftsmen P Madden and R Roddis. Air Dog Sabre, being a dog trained mainly for the dog demonstration team, had been retained at the depot and prior to being posted, Senior Aircraftsman Phillips had re-teamed with his third dog, Air Dog Rex. Unfortunately, after only a few months Rex who was under-weight from the start failed to put on weight despite being put on various special diets. After being examined by the local veterinary surgeon; Mr J Holmes, Rex was diagnosed as being unfit for duty and had to be returned to the depot. At that point, Senior Aircraftsman Phillips was re-teamed with his original dog, Lassie. It was during his tour of duty at Benson that Senior Aircraftsman Phillips' dog demonstration skills came into their own when he very successfully organised a small demonstration during the units' annual Families Day to show off what the RAF Police dogs could do.

In October Corporal J Bastard, having completed his tour of duty at RAF Geilenkirchen was posted home to RAF Honington near Bury St Edmunds. Again, the dog handlers at the unit were required to patrol the outer perimeter of the Special Storage Area that was a facility for the storage of nuclear weapons, or guard static aircraft parked out on isolated dispersal areas. Not surprisingly, after enjoying the responsibility of running a dog section in Germany, he immediately took a dislike to the unit and the mundane duties he was called upon to perform. Consequently, he and a colleague, Corporal J Williams successfully applied to join the RAF Police Dog Demonstration Team for the 1965 season.

At the Annual United Kingdom Dog Championship Trials held at RAF Debden Corporal Watson and Air Dog Paul were declared as the champions, while Corporal A Turnbull and Air Dog Sabre came second, and Corporal Kinglake and Air Dog Bruce came third. The two winning teams at the RAF Germany dog trials were declared as Corporal McClennan and Air Dog Bruce and Corporal Cockerill and Air Dog Rikky.

After a most rewarding tour of duty at the RAF Police Dog Training School, Senior Aircraftswoman Chapman left the Depot in early 1965 and was posted to RAF St Mawgan outside Newquay in Cornwall. Her new unit was totally different from either Netheravon or Debden. The dog section there was also a lot smaller and Chapman more or less quickly became her own boss, and was left to get on with her work. The dog handlers at St Mawgan, like those on every other dog section, regularly met up during the afternoon at the kennels for a period of continuation training and it was during one of those periods that Chapman volunteered to act as the 'criminal'. Her offer was accepted by the dog handlers and she was helped into the padded suit. At the time, RAF Police dogs were not specially trained to go for the arm of a criminal and as such, would bite onto any particular area of the body. So, in order to afford the *'criminal'* maximum protection during the training session, the suit was thick, heavy and extremely warm to wear. Additionally, because it was so bulky, the person wearing it could just about walk let alone run off from the dog. When she and the handler and his dog were ready the exercise began and she was required to walk into the view of the patrol. At that point, the handler standing some way off would give the standard warning. *"Halt or I'll release my dog"*. She ignored the warning and looking something like the Michelin Man attempted to waddle off. At that point, the dog was released. Because of the high collar on the suit she could not turn to see what was happening but in the next instance a dog weighing around eighty pounds travelling at speed hit her with all the force of an express train, knocking her instantly to the ground. The dog had hold of the suit until he was called off by the handler. After a while she was helped to her feet and soon after, climbed out of the suit having probably lost a few pounds in weight. Again, it had been an experience for her but not one to be repeated to often.

In the Far East, during March, the first units of American troops were sent into Vietnam in an effort to stop the Communist take over and to stabilise the region. Consequently, anti-war and peace movements in the United Kingdom and Germany organised demonstrations at United States military establishments to register their disapproval of the American action.

Having completed his tour of duty at RAF Benson and returned Air Dog Lassie to the depot, Acting Corporal G R Phillips was posted overseas for the first time to the dog section at RAF Khormasker in Aden, where he was a little surprised to be allocated a Doberman by the name of Carlos I, which had formerly been used by the Army in Kenya. Although he looked the part of a good police dog, he nevertheless possessed an unpredictable temperament and on a couple of occasions turned on his handler. The one good thing about him was that because his coat was so short it made the daily task of grooming and de-ticking the dog a straightforward affair compared to the problems the other handlers had with their German Shepherds. At the time, the dog section was under the firm control of Sergeant Darnell, late of the dog demonstration team, and the handlers were accommodated in a stone built building adjacent to the kennels, which had once apparently been used as a stable. After a few months in Aden, Corporal Phillips contracted a serious bout of dysentery and was taken into the military hospital until he recovered.

During her time at St Mawgan Senior Aircraftswoman Chapman used to exercise the dogs around the perimeter of the airfield but some of the helicopter crews thought it was great fun to hover low enough overhead to blow her beret off, and then would take great delight in watching her trying to catch it, whilst controlling the dog. Although they were not supposed to, now and again during weekends she and one of the dog handlers used to take a couple of the dogs to a secluded beach to let them swim in the sea, which they really enjoyed. Eventually, Chapman was joined at St Mawgan by another kennel maid from Debden, Senior Aircraftswoman Gane, and together they looked after the dogs and kept the dog handlers firmly under control.

The PDSA (People's Dispensary for Sick Animals) founder Maria Dicken introduced the *Dicken Medal* in 1943 in order to honour animals that had served with the Armed Forces and the Civil Defence units during World War II. Since its inception, the award has been made to carrier pigeons, horses, a cat and dogs. The *Dicken Medal* is considered to be the animal's *Victoria Cross* and is awarded to an animal that displays conspicuous gallantry and devotion to duty associated with or under the control of any branch of the Armed Forces or Civil Defence units. It is only awarded on recommendation and is exclusive to the animal kingdom. The medal is made of bronze and the top it bears the letters PDSA, and in the middle *'FOR GALLANTRY'* is written whilst underneath *'WE ALSO SERVE'* is written. In 1964 an incident occurred at RAF El Adem, near Tobruk in Libya, which demonstrated the bravery and loyalty of a RAF Police dog. Air Dog Prince 6073 was on patrol one night with his handler; Corporal R McCall, when they encountered three armed men on the base area. Corporal McCall, who was later awarded the British Empire Medal for meritorious service by the Queen at Buckingham Palace, was knocked unconscious by a blow to the head and his dog was struck by a rifle butt and hit in the side by one of seven shots that were fired by the intruders as he stood guard over his handler. Air Dog Prince later died of his injuries and was posthumously awarded the *Dicken Medal* which was presented to Corporal McCall during the 1965 Royal Tournament. The citation states;

'In spite of severe injuries, from which he later died, Prince persisted in his attacks on the intruders and in loyally defending his handler, who had been rendered unconscious, displayed outstanding devotion and courage as a result of which his handler's life was saved'.

It was during 1965 that Corporal J Henry, a RAF Police dog handler, stationed at the RAF Police Depot Debden, became one of the NCOs responsible for visiting homes around the country as a RAF Police Gift Dog Collector. He had joined the RAF Police in 1961, and had since completing his training been employed on dog handling duties. As previously stated, many of the dogs in service with the RAF Police at the time had been donated by members of the public. Indeed, before those dogs had been accepted into service, their owners had been visited by a RAF Police Gift Dog Collector who had made an 'on-site' assessment of the dog to confirm its suitability for training and service as a RAF Police dog. To many within the branch, including many dog handlers, the role of the RAF Police Gift Dog Collector was very underrated. The job called for an experienced dog handler and trainer who could quickly assess a dog's personality to tell whether it could be trained and if so whether it would make the grade as a police dog. Certainly a dog accepted by the dog collector, which lacked the basic standards made it far more difficult for the instructional staff and the student at the depot when it came to training. On that matter, Corporal Henry adopted a simple philosophy when he inspected a dog being offered by a member of the public. He asked himself whether he would be happy to have that dog on patrol with him. If the answer was no, then he would simply reject the dog. Some collectors, he knew, found it difficult at times to reject a dog as being unsuitable, but he had no problem with rejection and knew that at times he had to be focused and honest, even if rejection upset the owner, which sometimes it did.

In those days the majority of the journeys around the country by the dog collectors were by rail. The method of course, had its drawbacks from time to time and it could be daunting for a dog collector having to escort an unknown dog on a long train journey and uncomfortable, as officially the collector and the dog were required to ride in the guards' van. Corporal Henry's first collection was in Cornwall, and luckily there were no problems with the dog being suitable because it had previously been assessed by the NCO in charge of the dog section at RAF St Mawgan. That was normal procedure when the donor lived a significant distance away from RAF Debden. However, the system was not always infallible; occasionally a dog that had been provisionally accepted by a dog handler from a nearby RAF station would be rejected by the collector on-site for a variety of reasons. Gradually, with the closure of many lines and stations in a national review of the railways, the use of vehicles became the normal method for collecting dogs, and as the offers increased, so the driving hours and the mileage increased. It was routine for a dog collector to drive down to Cornwall at the beginning of the week and to drive back down from Scotland at the end of the same week. Often Corporal Henry would leave RAF Debden early in the morning and arrive back from a task in the early hours of the following morning.

Driving such long distances around the country in a vehicle containing dogs that were probably unused to travelling could again be problematic. Although Corporal Henry was never involved in a traffic accident whilst out on the road, he recalls one journey back to RAF Debden from somewhere in the south-west region, on a Friday afternoon when the windscreen shattered on the Morris van that he was driving. It was mid winter but luckily he was close to RAF Andover and as such decided to drive there for assistance. Unfortunately the motor transport servicing section did not have a replacement windscreen in stock and although they were willing to order a new one it would not arrive until Monday. As Corporal Henry had to get back to his base with the two dogs he was carrying he decided to continue his journey. The NCO in charge of the motor transport servicing section, however, was most helpful in providing Corporal Henry with a pair of goggles and a scarf as protection against the icy wind blowing into the cab of the van. It was a very cold and wet journey home and the two dogs experienced a tough test of their initial entry into RAF.

Initially, the vehicles used by the dog collectors were not customised for carrying dogs and more often than not the rear seats were taken out and a transit kennel was merely placed in the back of the vehicle. The transit kennels used at that time were rather heavy metal items, which required at least two people to lift them in and out of the vehicle which in itself could be a problem at times considering that the dog collector was usually out on the road on his own. Still, as Corporal Henry recalls, it was better to have a transit kennel than none at all, as was the case with a mini van that was used at RAF Debden for collections. Opening the back door of a vehicle without a transit kennel and trying to place a lead on a strange dog was a skilful art. Indeed, several dog collectors using that particular vehicle had lost their dogs when they arrived back to the depot trying to do just that. Corporal Henry remembers one dog collector spending a long night on the airfield at RAF Debden trying to locate a dog that had escaped from the van before he had chance to put the lead on it. On one particular occasion a dog who had escaped spent a number of weeks wandering around the Saffron Walden area, avoiding all attempts to recapture him. He was eventually caught and went on to complete his training course without difficulty.

After serving for a year on the barren rocks of Aden, Corporal G R Phillips returned home and after re-teaming with a different Air Dog Rex to one he had at Benson, was posted to the dog section at RAF Wyton where he joined the team comprising; Corporal's M Rundle, J Allen, F Grimson, J Gilmore, P O'Shaughnessy and Cantrell. The unit at the time was home to a squadron of Victor tankers and Canberra aircraft and the task of the dog handlers was to patrol around the aircraft parked on the dispersal areas close to the perimeter fence during the hours of darkness.

On the 15th September, Senior Aircraftswoman Chapman, otherwise known as 'Chappy' left the RAF after a most rewarding and enjoyable three and a half years working as a kennel maid. During her service some of her colleagues included; Corporal De Candia, Jan Green, Jean Grover, Vivian Hart, Cindy Rathbone, Patrica Sheckley, Jonah Laidlaw, Angela Hatton, Min Toulmin, Taff Legge, Patrica

Sheckley, Diane Sewell, Susan Milburn, Maureen Smith, 'Blodwyn', 'Queenie', Paula, Dodie and Kate.

The winner of the Annual United Kingdom Dog Champion Trials held at RAF Debden was judged to be Corporal J Tait and Air Dog Bruce. While Corporal Oliver and Air Dog Bonnie took second place, 1965 was the first year that two teams, Corporal Cooper and Air Dog Paul and Corporal R Nuttal and Air Dog Beauty, tied for third place. In the RAF Germany dog trials Corporal Mallon and Air Dog Rusty took the top position while Corporal Cockerill and Air Dog Rikky took second place, and Corporal McGlenn and Air Dog Champ came third.

In November, Air Commodore Millar DSO, retired from the RAF and was subsequently succeeded in post as Provost Marshal by another former pilot, Air Commodore W I C Inness CBE OBE ADC.

At RAF Changi in Singapore a serious illness amongst the RAF Police dogs resulted in the loss during the year of fourteen dogs. At one point the situation was so severe that only one of the twenty-three dogs on strength was fit for duty. Biological tests carried out locally and in the United Kingdom were inconclusive and at first it was suspected that the dogs had been poisoned through the use of a pesticide dip which when analysed turned out to be toxic. The dip was immediately withdrawn from use and substituted with a non-toxic agent but the dogs failed to make a recovery and the RAF Police Depot was asked to assist by sending out replacement dogs.

At the start of 1966 Corporal J Bastard, having completed a successful season with the RAF Police Dog Demonstration Team, had been retained at the RAF Police Depot at Debden as an instructor with the dog training school. It did not take him long to settle into his new environment and the first task he and his colleagues had been given was to train up a batch of twenty-one dogs for an overseas posting to the Far East. It was hard work but at the end of the training all the dogs had been trained and were posted to Singapore along with Corporal Bastard. On the 19th February a team comprising Corporal's Bastard, D Holmes, J Hemmings and Allsop and Leading Aircraftsmen Scutt and Richardson, took the twenty-one dogs to RAF Lyneham on the first leg of their long journey out to RAF Changi in Singapore. The following morning with the dogs and the handlers onboard, the Britannia transport aircraft took off but after only a few hours it developed a fault which forced it to return to RAF Lyneham. Although it was a different aircraft type, the handlers could not help recalling the delays that had occurred before the tragic crash in 1957 of the Blackburn Beverley at Abingdon that had claimed the lives of nineteen people including eight dog handlers and eleven dogs. The aircraft took off again the following morning and after a very long and tiring flight and several stops along the way, landed at RAF Changi where a reception committee comprising the Command Provost Marshal Group Captain H M Shephard, Squadron Leader Harrow, the RAVC veterinary surgeon Captain Forgrave, the Dog Inspector Flight Sergeant Ogle and the local press were waiting to meet them.

It seemed that the arrival of such a large number of RAF Police dogs was a major news item in Singapore and the press wanted to know all about the dogs and the men who had brought them out from the United Kingdom. Of the twenty-one dogs that had been brought out, four were sent to RAF Butterworth in Malaya, one was sent to RAF Labuan in Borneo and the rest remained in Singapore. At the time the dog section at Changi was under the control of Sergeant J Wilcox, who was not a qualified dog handler but had been detailed for the job after the sergeant dog handler had been returned to the United Kingdom because of ill health. Unfortunately, the section was experiencing serious problems because a great percentage of the dogs there were sick suffering from the mysterious illness which caused severe internal bleeding and was thought to have been caused by ticks or mosquitoes. While the dogs brought in from the United Kingdom were healthy replacements, they too were at risk and the urgent search continued to find out the cause of the illness and a cure for it.

The medical staff working at the British Military Hospital were tremendously supportive and provided all the medication required by the section. Additionally, under the guidance of Captain Forgrave the RAVC veterinary surgeon, blood samples were taken from each dog at night once a week to be analysed. At the time, the dogs were secured on run wires under canvas that had been erected overhead and although it provided shade from the blazing sun, it did not provide any protection to the dogs from the heat and the insect life of Singapore. As a result, it was decided to construct a new purpose-built kennel complex for the dogs and the Royal Engineers were asked to take on the project. Although the dogs were regularly bathed in a disinfectant solution, tick infestation was a major problem to be tackled on a daily basis. Minor cuts or grazes quickly attracted flies that laid eggs in the wound which regularly became infested with maggots in the humid heat, and of course infected wounds proved extremely difficult to heal.

After a while, Sergeant Wilcox returned to normal duties and Sergeant W Franklin was posted in briefly to take over the dog section with Corporal Bastard acting as his deputy. Sergeant Franklin was replaced by Sergeant C Jones, who arrived just in time to see the opening of the new dog section. The new kennels were a great improvement as was the grooming range and the bathing area for the dogs. With improved facilities, the health of the dogs slowly improved together with the morale of the men. Training increased and a number of successful dog displays were organised for service families and the local community.

In Cyprus, with the closure of RAF Nicosia, a new RAF Police Dog Training School was opened in March at RAF Episkopi under the control of a RAF Police sergeant dog handler.

During the month of May, the dog handlers throughout the branch were somewhat alarmed when the Provost Marshal announced that a study was being conducted into the feasibility of amalgamating RAF Police and Army dog training.

Each day in the life of a RAF Police gift dog collector was different; in addition to visiting all areas of the country, the dog collectors met a wide variety of people living in diverse environments. Often it was heartbreaking to see some of the conditions that the dogs lived in. Corporal Henry, in the course of his job as a dog collector, visited scrap yards where dogs were chained to a post or were confined within small yards which prevented them from getting any proper exercise. On one occasion, he was called to assess an adult German Shepherd dog that was kept on a high-rise balcony outside a London block of flats and was appalled to learn that the dog had never been outside the flat for exercise. The reason many owners had for donating their dogs to the RAF were many, but the main reason was that they were simply unable to look after them. Although Corporal Henry was always sympathetic with owners who were in difficult situations, he never allowed those situations to affect his assessment of a dog. If the dog was not suitable then he had no problem in rejecting it. On a number of occasions after rejecting a dog as being unsuitable he was offered cash or other incentives by desperate owners to take the dog away. However, he always remained resolute and quickly rejected any offer of a bribe. On one occasion he was called to a rather large house near Newbury to see a dog. A delightful and well developed young lady greeted him wearing only a pair of skimpy shorts and a tight top. Throughout the course of the conversation the she kept telling Corporal Henry that her husband was away working in all week. He dismissed the remarks and asked to see the dog, which turned out to be a powerful looking German Shepherd dog with a long coat and in excellent condition. Unfortunately, when assessed the dog was found to have a soft temperament and in Corporal Henry's opinion would never have made a police dog. As such, it was rejected, however, the lady persisted in telling Corporal Henry of her problems looking after the dog, problems that were complicated by the fact that her husband was away a lot and was not due back for some days. It was clear that the lady was lonely and needed companionship but Corporal Henry remained professional, made his apologies and quickly left.

On another occasion he was called to a house on an Army camp located just outside Oxford. When he arrived at the house just after lunch he discovered the front door ajar, he knocked and a female voice shouted for him to come upstairs. On entering a bedroom he discovered a large lady sitting up in bed wearing a nightgown and with her hair in curlers. She was smoking and drinking whisky and when she spoke seemed a little under the influence of the drink. Corporal Henry ascertained that the dog was in the back garden and after carrying out his assessment found that the dog was indeed suitable. However, he still had the problem of the drunken owner waiting for him. He returned to the bedroom and whilst sitting on her bed managed to complete all the relevant paperwork, which the owner then signed. After declining her kind offer to have a glass of whisky, Corporal Henry placed the dog into the van and continued on his way. On yet another house call, Corporal Henry while inspecting a German Shepherd bitch noticed that she was pregnant and explained the fact to the lady owner who appeared shocked and suddenly started to cry. As Corporal Henry attempted to console her she pleaded with him to take the dog away because she could not look after it. When Corporal Henry explained to her that it was against RAF regulations to accept a bitch that was pregnant she persisted with her pleas, even offering him money to take it. When he repeated that the school would not accept the dog in that condition she begged him to take the money and abandon the dog somewhere out on the road. It seemed unbelievable but it was true, it appeared that some people were really desperate to have their dog taken off their hands. Corporal Henry during the course of assessing dogs even came across cases where people had offered their dogs to the RAF without their partner's knowledge, intending that once the dog had been accepted and taken away, they would explain to their partners that the dog had simply run off.

During the Annual United Kingdom Dog Championship Trials held at RAF Debden Corporal Kendall and Air Dog Leo took first place and received the *Sabre Trophy* while Corporal White & Air Dog Duke came second, and Corporal Carlton and Air Dog Bruce came third. The winning three teams in the Cyprus dog trials held at RAF Episkopi were, Corporal Ray and Air Dog Limey, Corporal Scrase and Air Dog Duke, and Corporal McMillan and Air Dog Prince. During the dog trials held at RAF Germany, the top three teams were, Corporal McMillen and Air Dog Prince, Corporal J Corner and Air Dog Sultan, and Corporal B Uzzell and Air Dog Kim.

In early 1967, Corporal G R Phillips, having completed his tour of duty at RAF Wyton, was posted overseas once again to the dog section at RAF Changi in Singapore. Being rather impressed with his new posting it did not take him long to re-team with Air Dog Kim, previously handled by Corporal P Lawry, before he joined one of the shifts. Other members of the dog section at that time included; Sergeant C Jones and Corporal's C Harris, A Frankham, R Jordan, Williams, J Bastard and kennel-maid Angie DeVoll. He recalls that Sergeant Jones was exceptionally keen and expected very high standards of professionalism and cleanliness around the dog section. If the kennel compounds had been scrubbed spotless and disinfected then they still were not up to his standard and if a handler had exercised his dog for an hour then it still needed more. The result of course, was that the section was gleaming and the kennels were totally tick-free and efficiently run. After the previous health and hygiene problems experienced prior to Sergeant Jones' arrival and the loss of so many dogs it was little wonder that the man in charge took the job seriously and almost everyone appreciated his commitment.

Corporal Henry was always careful when meeting and assessing potential police dogs in the course of his visits around the country. Although he had never been bitten there had been a number of occasions when he had narrowly escaped injury. Normally, if the dog was out of sight during his visit he asked the owners to bring their dog to him on a lead, although more frequently the owners simply let their dog run into a room where he was sitting. The majority of dogs were quite happy to issue a warning that they were guarding their territory by barking and displaying boldness in their own domain and that was something that Corporal Henry was quite prepared for. Having said that, he knew all too well that he had to be very careful in those circumstances, and never once did he fully trust the owners to maintain control of their dog. On one occasion in early 1967 he was in Yorkshire inspecting dogs and he had to visit a doctor's surgery where the owner, a doctor, had brought the dog in for him to assess. At the time he was accompanied by another RAF Police NCO, Corporal W Booth, who had travelled up with him to visit his relatives who lived nearby.

The dog turned out to be a handsome looking German Shepherd dog with a definite bold temperament. Although the owner had the dog on a lead it sat staring at Corporal Booth who was standing directly in front of him. Suddenly, without any warning whatsoever the dog lunged forward and went straight for Corporal Booth's groin. Luckily for Corporal Booth the dog was on a short lead and Corporal Booth also had the sense to quickly push backwards to avoid being bitten. Once the dog was back under control Corporal Henry and the doctor reassured a rather shocked and pale faced Corporal Booth that had he been bitten he was in the best place to receive immediate medical treatment.

Another colleague who was not quite so lucky to escape being attacked was Corporal J Bolton. The pair had left RAF Debden to inspect a number of dogs in the south-east area of the country. At one point they arrived at a grand house located in the Surrey *stockbroker belt*. The lady of the house greeted them and invited them into her home. Sitting chatting to her in the lounge Corporal Henry asked her the usual questions about the dog before asking where it was. The lady stood up and opened a serving hatch to the kitchen and suddenly a huge long coated German Shepherd dog appeared and filled the entire frame of the hatch and growled at the two NCOs. At that point the lady advised them that only her husband could handle the dog and that he would soon be returning from his job in the city.

After further conversation on a variety of topics the husband entered the house. He looked the typical city gent type, dressed in a pin stripe suit, wearing a bowler hat and carrying a brolly and a briefcase. After introductions, Corporal Henry asked him to place the dog on his lead so that they could view it outside on the lawn in the large garden. Corporal Henry, for some reason felt just a little apprehensive about the whole episode but quickly dismissed it and they all duly trooped out onto the lawn. The dog was even more impressive when seen outside the house; he weighed about 100lbs and was indeed a wonderful specimen of the breed. However he knew that the two NCOs were strangers on his territory and he continually kept his eyes on them both. At the same time the husband was occupied singing the praises of his dog and Corporal Henry asked him if he had done any training with the animal. The husband replied that he had done a lot of obedience training, including off the lead work with the dog. At that point, the husband bent down and unclipped the lead, which given the circumstances was not the most sensible thing to do.

Two things happened at once, the dog realised that the lead was off and Corporal Henry realised that he and Corporal Bolton were in big trouble. The husband and his dog were about thirty yards away when the dog suddenly launched his attack at full speed. Corporal Henry realised what was happening a split second before his partner and reacted just that bit quicker. Given the circumstances, it was every man for himself and so Corporal Henry got behind his partner and hung on to him for dear life using his colleagues body as a shield, which was no mean feat as Corporal Bolton was a strong chap who played for the station rugby team.

Suddenly, the dog was upon them and bit Corporal Bolton high up on his chest. Then it was chaos as Corporal Bolton fought with the dog while its owner tried desperately to get it back on the lead and under control. At the same time Corporal Henry was trying to keep out of harms way and the wife was screaming and that was getting the dog more agitated. At that point Corporal Henry seized the opportunity and managed to grab the dog's collar to get him off his partner. Thankfully, it was all over fairly quickly and the dog was returned to the kitchen, while the wife and the two NCOs returned to the lounge to recover. Corporal Bolton had sustained puncture wounds to his chest and had to be cleaned up by the lady. The husband was most apologetic saying that the dog had never done anything like that before, that is until he was reminded by his wife that the dog had attacked the postman a few months before. As the husband poured everyone a whisky, he asked what he should do with his dog. Unfortunately, the suggestion returned by Corporal Bolton is subject to censorship. The dog however, was accepted and later became a RAF Police dog. Corporal Bolton recovered from his ordeal with no lasting effects.

In September former Air Dog Elke 5271 passed away peacefully in the arms of her owner Mr David Lascelles after collapsing on a beach the day before. Elke had been retired from the service the year before after having completed eight years of loyal service and was first mentioned within this book in 1960 at RAF Colerne. At the time, she was being handled by a young National Serviceman, Corporal C O'Hanlon, and was one of the unit's two dogs entered in the 1960 United Kingdom RAF Police Dog Championship Trials. Although she did not win any prizes that year she certainly gave a good performance during the competition helping to boost the confidence of her handler. In March 1966, Air Dog Elke and her last RAF Police handler, Corporal H Neill were posted onto the strength of the dog section at RAF West Raynham in Norfolk where their primary duty was to patrol the Bloodhound surface-to-air missile site operated by No 41 Squadron. At around the same time, Senior Aircraftsman Lascelles, a clerk secretarial, was posted into the unit from RAF Gatow and after a short time got to know Corporal Neill and Elke quite well. In September of that year Corporal Neill's engagement with the RAF was nearing its end and in conversation one evening he told Senior Aircraftsman Lascelles that although Elke was being sent back to the RAF Police Depot, it was unlikely that she would be re-teamed with another handler because she had already completed eight years service and was getting too old. As such, it was a possibility that she would be put down. Unfortunately, Corporal Neill was unable to take Elke into retirement because he was getting married and would be moving into a flat in London.

After quizzing him about Elke's temperament, Senior Aircraftsman Lascelles was satisfied enough to try to save her from the inevitable. After consulting with his mother, he wrote to the Commandant at the RAF Police Depot at Debden asking if he could purchase Elke into retirement. After several days he received a telephone call from a Flight Sergeant King at the depot who asked him various questions, before confirming an appointment to visit the depot that weekend. On Saturday the 10th September Senior Aircraftsman Lascelles and a friend arrived at the Debden and met the Flight Sergeant and together they completed the necessary paperwork to retire Elke before the princely sum of £5 was handed over by Senior Aircraftsman Lascelles. After the formalities had been completed the Flight Sergeant sent a corporal dog handler to collect Elke from the row of kennels nearby. He returned a few moments later with Elke on a rope lead. At that point Senior Aircraftsman Lascelles was not sure whether the dog would accept him or attack him, however, he need not have worried because as soon as he called her she came and ran straight around him and sat down at his left side. From Debden Elke was taken to her new home in Mablethorpe on the Lincolnshire coast where she quickly settled in to her new environment. She was gentle enough to pick up a rabbit that had been dazzled by headlights before being put down unharmed and yet she was very loyal and protective towards her owner. She soon became very well known in the locality but she had developed a heart murmur and was under treatment for several months. The day before she passed away she had collapsed on the beach near Sutton-on-Sea; Senior Aircraftsman Lascelles knew that she was in a bad way and had carried her for over half a mile through dunes to a friend's van. They got her home and called out the veterinary surgeon who gave her some treatment but in the small hours of the morning he was called for again and gave Elke an injection in an attempt to stop some internal bleeding. Senior Aircraftsman Lascelles sat up with her all night and just before dawn she raised her head to him, then laid it down again and died. He had only had Elke for a year, but it was a year of good and memorable times which she might otherwise not have had.

The top three winning teams of the Annual United Kingdom Dog Championship Trials held at RAF Debden were Corporal Adrain and Air Dog Sheila, Corporal Jones and Air Dog Rikki, and Corporal Kendall and Air Dog Leo. In the Cyprus dog trials held at RAF Episkopi Corporal Barber and Air Dog Storm took first place, Corporal Clarke and Air Dog Bruce came second, and Corporal Moore and Air Dog Duke came third. In the colony of Aden the RAF Police organised a local dog trials competition for the first time and the winning three teams were judged to be, Corporal Dean and Air Dog Prince, Acting Corporal Johnstone and Air Dog Trushka, and finally, Corporal Egglestone and Air Dog Vickie.

In January 1968 the rules were again changed by the Air Ministry with the reintroduction of the Leading Aircraftsman Acting (unpaid) Corporal rank for all RAF Police NCOs graduating from initial police training.

All around the world on the 1st April 1968, the RAF and of course the RAF Police celebrated their Golden Anniversary in a number of different ways that had been organised to mark the occasion. Despite being the junior service with uncertain beginnings, the RAF had achieved an incredible amount and had earned for itself a first class reputation during its brief and rather colourful fifty-year history. Likewise, in parallel, the RAF Police organisation had also grown from very humble beginnings to become a well-disciplined and professional branch. At that point, it was working at all levels within the service and in every theatre around the world. Despite the occasion, the RAF Police were kept fully employed over the celebration period and were seen carrying out police and security commitments at all the functions that had been laid on the mark the special occasion. Indeed, the RAF Police were also honoured when Flight Lieutenant D Stevens LRAM ARCM, from the RAF Central Band, composed a piece of music entitled *'March of the Royal Air Force Police'* early that year which was first played in public to accompany the appearance of the RAF Police Dog Demonstration Team at the Royal Tournament at Earls Court.

During the same period, Sergeant S G Corry, a technician serving at the RAF Police Depot, was summoned to see the Commandant. He was informed that the RAF Association at nearby Clacton-on-Sea wanted a float to represent RAF Debden during their forthcoming carnival. Accordingly, Sergeant Corry set about building a suitable float using a RAF three ton Bedford truck as the base. After much hard work the finished item finally emerged from the workshops and all was revealed. Given the theme *'Fifty Years of the RAF'*, the rear of the float displayed a large model of a 1918 DH9A biplane, suitably guarded by an airman dressed in the appropriate uniform of that period. At the front end of the float, a large model of a surface-to-air missile had been built and again it was suitably guarded by a RAF Police dog handler. Miniature RAF ensigns were flown from each corner of the float and it was escorted by two kennel-maids and two RAF Police dogs. The RAF crest was displayed at the front and rear of the vehicle and along each side was a large sign announcing *'Fifty Glorious Years of the RAF 1918 – 1968'*.

One of the largest events by far to mark the anniversary took place at RAF Abingdon, in Oxfordshire, on the 14th June. Her Majesty Queen Elizabeth II, Prince Phillip, the Queen Mother, the Duchess of Gloucester, Princess Marina and some 25,000 former and serving members of the service attended the largest RAF exhibition ever assembled. An incredible amount of work had been put into organising the event and not surprisingly it turned out to be a huge success and a superb way of celebrating the Golden Anniversary. Amongst the many items on a packed program of events, the RAF Police Dog Demonstration Team put on a splendid display, which was enjoyed by everyone who watched it. To promote the occasion even further and to add another sparkle to the celebrations, the feature film *The Battle of Britain* produced by Mr Harry Saltzman, and starring, Kenneth Moore, was also being filmed over the same period at the RAF Police Depot and at RAF Duxford. During the filming, as on previous occasions at other units, a number of RAF Police NCOs, many from the dog training school, eager no doubt to make the correct impression, were recruited into the production as film extras.

In August after an extremely challenging tour of duty at RAF Changi in Singapore, Corporal J Bastard returned home and after being re-teamed with a new dog was posted to RAF Lyneham in Wiltshire. At the time, the dog section was under the control of Corporal D Byrne and the task of the dog handlers was to patrol the airfield and the technical site and the outer perimeter of the 'transit accommodation' provided for passengers embarking on flights overseas. For Corporal Bastard, the first surprise of working again on a dog section within the United Kingdom was discovering that canned dog meat had been introduced, which certainly made the daily task of feeding the dogs a much easier affair.

On the 8th September, Earl Louis Mountbatten of Burma, wrote from his home, *Broadlands* in Hampshire, to Group Captain H M Shepherd at the RAF Police Depot to thank him for the recent gift of a retired RAF Police Dog. The dog had been named *'Bond'* and given the service number '007', after the fictional special agent, James Bond 007 created by Ian Flemming. Earl Mountbatten stated that the dog had settled in well to his new surroundings and seemed to like the huge estate.

In the United Kingdom Annual Dog Championship Trials the top three teams were, Corporal Allan and Air Dog Kruger, Corporal Spence and Air Dog Duke, and Corporal Cater and Air Dog Bob.

Corporal Henry, working with the gift dog collection unit, was asked to visit a house, which happened to be in a very run down estate in Gateshead. The street when he found it resembled something like a war-zone which worried him slightly. After locating the address he knocked the door and it was opened by a dishevelled looking youth who seemed to be under the influence of some substance or other. He invited Corporal Henry into the house and upon entering he was immediately hit by the foul smell of stale urine and excrement. In fact, he almost stood in a pile of it as he walked through the hallway to the front room where he met the young man's mother who also seemed to be under the influence of something. She was dressed like a beggar woman, was filthy and the odour wafting from her was foul. The house was in fact a stinking mess and Corporal Henry just wanted to get out of there as quickly as possible. Fortunately, the dog was in the room and without asking the usual questions Corporal Henry just put a lead on it and took it outside to examine it. The dog however, had a suspected problem with its hip joints and had to be rejected. It was returned into the house where Corporal Henry quickly explained to the woman his reasons for rejecting the dog. As he left carefully avoiding the foul mess in the hallway he felt sorry having to leave the poor dog in such misery. Sadly some of the dogs examined could not be accepted because they were extremely aggressive and uncontrollable. During a visit to a house in the Doncaster area Corporal Henry went outside to the back garden to look at the dog being offered. It was tied up to a clothes line pole and when he saw Corporal Henry he just went berserk. Unable to get at the stranger on his territory the dog took out his frustration on the clothes hanging on the line. He kept jumping up tearing the clothes to shreds. His owner could not do anything to stop the dog and so he continued to rip up all the clothes. Had the dog not been tied to the pole Corporal Henry believes that he would not have escaped from the garden without being seriously mauled and badly bitten. It was almost impossible to control that type of aggression and therefore the dog had to be rejected on the spot.

Corporal Henry and Corporal R Scorer were tasked to visit an address in Suffolk. After some difficulty they came upon a very run down cottage that was miles from anywhere. Walking to the front door Corporal Henry felt apprehensive and knew that it was not going to be a simple inspection. After knocking, the door was opened by an old woman who had dirty matted hair, was extremely filthy, and looked and smelt as if she had not washed herself or indeed her clothes for many months. The two NCOs were invited into the house and on entering the front room were shocked at the state of the place. All the furniture had been gnawed and chewed. The settee only had an upholstered back piece; the rest was just the internal wooden structure. The table and chairs had been bitten or chewed away and what was once the carpet was in shreds. There were scratch marks on all the doors and the walls. Corporal Henry's initial reaction was to leave but after quickly refusing the offer of tea, he enquired as to where the animal was that had inflicted such damage on the house. The woman loudly shouted for her son Rupert, who came into the room from the kitchen. Rupert was a young man who could only be described as mentally and physically handicapped. He stared at the two NCOs with his one good eye and grunted. Eventually, through simple English and sign language Corporal Henry got through to him that he was to bring the dog in on a lead. Rupert went out and the two NCOs heard the animal before it came into the room. When Rupert brought the dog into the room it went absolutely crazy. It attacked the nearest chair leg in frustration then put all of its effort into getting at the two strangers. The dog's eyes were bulging and it was frothing at the mouth. Indeed, Corporal Henry had never seen such a ferocious animal before and knew that there was no way that they were going to accept it. Rupert was having difficulty holding onto the dog and both NCOs quickly explained that they could not take the dog. However, the old woman shouted at them to take the dog off their hands because they could not look after it. Again, the NCOs explained that it was impossible and attempted to leave. At that point and to both NCOs disbelief she shouted at Rupert to set the dog on them. She was screaming and Rupert started laughing as the dog became more and more aggressive. Both NCOs quickly left the house followed by the old woman, Rupert and the snarling dog. The NCOs started to walk rather quickly up the path as the woman continued to shout at them to take the dog. However, she also continued to order Rupert to release the dog on them; thankfully he had not quite understood the order. By then Rupert was laughing hysterically and his mother continued shouting for him to let go of the dog then to the horror of the two NCOs he let the lead fall from his grasp and the dog lurched forward. Without even thinking, the two men ran to the front gate and both leaped over it just as the dog reached them snarling and growling. As the two men quickly got into their van they could still hear the old woman screaming at them and saw Rupert who was jumping up and down in fits of laughter at the sight before him.

Air Commodore W I C Inness retired as the Provost Marshal on the 1st October and was succeeded in post by Air Commodore A D Panton OBE DFC. Prior to taking up the appointment of Provost Marshal, Air Commodore Panton had been the Project Director organising the RAF Golden Jubilee celebrations.

In early 1969, Corporal G R Phillips, having completed his tour of duty at RAF Changi, was posted home after quite an emotional departure, to RAF Fairford near Gloucester. He had really enjoyed his tour in Singapore and would readily have stayed there had it been possible. At the time, Fairford, with its exceptionally long runway, had been temporarily taken back from the USAF, so that final tests on the newly developed supersonic aircraft *Concorde* could be conducted by British Aerospace. Shortly after his arrival at the unit Corporal Phillips successfully re-teamed with Air Dog Max, a dog that had previously been handled by the USAF dog handlers. As such, Max, a huge long haired German Shepherd who possessed a strong personality and in true American tradition saw no reason whatsoever to walk anyway if transport was close-by. One night, Corporal Phillips was on foot patrol with Max on the lead when a vehicle passed by and Max, expressing his desire to go 'mobile', suddenly lunged forward towards the vehicle. Corporal Phillips immediately checked the dog but it swiftly turned and bit him on the wrist. After receiving medical attention for his wounds and exchanging his torn jacket, Corporal Phillips realised that he had let Max off lightly and vowed to correct the situation should it happen again. He did not have to wait long when the same thing occurred, only on that occasion as the dog bit his arm, he was able to apply pressure to its check chain until the dog let go. At that point the dog was taken straight back to the kennel where Corporal Phillips reiterated who was the boss before going off to the medical centre to have his arm treated again. After that occasion, it seemed that Max clearly understood the 'pecking order' and gave his handler no further trouble.

The majority of dogs accepted by the RAF as gift dogs from the public possessed a good temperament and there was usually few problems in transporting them from their homes back to the depot. Sometimes however, difficulty was encountered by the dog collector when it came to putting the dog into the transit kennel, which was for some dogs an unknown experience. Such a problem happened to Corporal Henry one day during a visit to Southampton. Having completed his assessment, he had accepted the dog as being suitable and after completing the relevant documentation he lead the dog out to his waiting van and then tried to place him into the transit kennel. Unfortunately, the German Shepherd dog had other ideas and going into that cage was not one of them. Corporal Henry, using all his experience as a fully trained police dog handler applied a little pressure to the dog, which growled at him as a warning to back off. At that point, Corporal Henry took the transit kennel out of the van and placed some meat inside it to tempt the dog inside but he stubbornly refused to enter. Even throwing his favourite cuddly toy inside had no effect, and coaxing by his owner also failed to get the dog into the kennel. As a last resort, Corporal Henry tied a long lead to the dog's collar and threaded the other end through the kennel until it came out of the back. He then attempted to gently pull the dog into the kennel. Of course, that had to be done using minimum force as by then all the neighbours were out keenly watching a professional at work. However, the dog dug in his heels and flatly refused to go into the kennel and Corporal Henry admitted defeat. At that point the dog was sitting on the pavement and as Corporal Henry opened the passenger door to place his briefcase inside the dog suddenly jumped up onto the passenger seat and sat himself down. Not wanting to lose face in front of his audience, Corporal Henry quickly closed the door with a sigh of relief. It was only then that his owner remarked that the dog loves to travel in a car like that. Shortly after, Corporal Henry drove off with his new recruit sitting next to him and he remained there quite contented all the way back to the depot. Shortly after that particular job, Corporal Henry was posted to Cyprus as an operational dog handler.

One day 'out of the blue' Corporal G R Phillips, serving at RAF Fairford, was instructed to report to the depot for an interview with a view to him becoming an instructor at the dog training school. Although he had liked Netheravon very much, he disliked Debden and certainly did not want to be posted there. In addition, his time in the RAF was nearing an end and he was quite content to sit out the remainder of his RAF service at Fairford. Having attended the interview he was informed that he had been successful but clearly upset somebody when he turned the post down and was returned to Fairford soon after.

The RAF Police Dog Demonstration Team, under the command of Flight Lieutenant P Brough, had become so popular by this period that towards the end of the summer of 1969, the Parachute Regiment, who were organising a public relations tour around Canada and the United States of America, extended an invitation for the team to join them. The Provost Marshal, Air Commodore A D Panton, duly approved the request and later in the year the trip went ahead. Sixteen dog handlers were chosen to represent the RAF Police and each dog was sedated for their flight aboard the Boeing 707 to New York. Upon arrival, all the dogs were checked by veterinary surgeons from the United States Army and were found to be fit and well and showed no adverse effects from their transatlantic flight. The tour in America opened to a packed audience at Maddison Square Gardens in New York and was an instant success. Accordingly, as the team worked their way through the hectic but enjoyable schedule they covered some 8,000 miles. In all, sixty-five performances were given in twenty-three cities over a period of seventy-four days. While it was hard work, it was worth it because the public on that side of the Atlantic showed their great warmth and admiration for the British Military display and in particular, the RAF Police Dog Demonstration Team who trilled the crowds at every venue. Needless to say, the tour proved itself to be a very successful venture indeed.

During the same period, on the other side of the Atlantic, a secondary RAF Police Dog Demonstration Team, formed from operational dogs and their handlers serving in Germany were, for the first time, invited to demonstrate their skills at the Berlin Military Tattoo. Although the team was only required to perform at two public performances, they were, nonetheless, an instant success with the audience which numbered many thousands.

During the 1969 United Kingdom Annual Dog Championship Trials held at RAF Debden the three winning places were awarded to, Corporal Higgins and Air Dog Monty, Corporal Warwick and Air Dog Kasan, and Corporal Bennett and Air Dog Tanya. In the RAF Germany dog trials held at RAF Rheindalen Corporal Wilson and Air Dog Sure took first place, Corporal D Devonshire and Air Dog Rondo took second place, and Corporal M Browne and Air Dog Sally came third. During the dog trials held at RAF Bahrein in the Persian Gulf Corporal Eltis and Air Dog Melody came first, Corporal Singleton and Air Dog Kim came second, and Corporal Fox and Air Dog Wolf came third in the competition.

In the early summer of 1967, Leading Aircraftsman S Lamacraft, having recently completed his training at the RAF Police Depot to become a dog handler, had been posted to RAF Akrotiri in Cyprus and shortly after settling in there was allocated a Cypriot bred German Shepherd dog, Air Dog Simba CY33, who had been donated to the RAF Police by the resident company of the Royal Engineers based at nearby Episkopi. Apparently Simba had been what was described as the 'Block Dog' employed by the soldiers to ensure that no unauthorised persons gained entry into their barrack accommodation, and particularly no Cypriot's with designs on stealing anything within the block. Unfortunately, Simba had been too good at his job and had refused to let the garrison sergeant-major enter, which quite understandably made him a very unhappy man. Consequently, he had issued his men with an ultimatum, either they made arrangements to have the dog put down or they donated him to the RAF Police. Fortunately for Simba the soldiers chose the latter. So Leading Aircraftsman Lamacraft had taken Simba over as an untrained dog and shortly after, work had begun to turn him into a fully trained police dog. Simba, as it turned out, had been very responsive and on successfully completing the course, Leading Aircraftsman Lamacraft and his new charge had commenced duties at RAF Akrotiri. In 1968 the pair had been entered into the HQ NEAF dog trials and had taken second place. However, during the HQ NEAF dog trials held at RAF El Adem in Libya in 1969, Corporal Lamacraft and Air dog Simba won the trials with a score of 493 out of a possible 500. Additionally, Simba became the first Cypriot trained dog to win the trials, while Corporal Oliver and Air Dog Rebel took second place, and Corporal Henry, recently posted to Cyprus, and Air Dog Storm came third.

In November after having only been at RAF Lyneham for just over a year, Corporal J Bastard was posted overseas again to the Gulf State of Oman and RAF Sharjah located on the Trucial coast not far from Dubai. The unit had first been established as a RAF base in 1933. The dog section at Sharjah was well appointed and comprised an office, restroom, dispensary, isolation kennel, meat preparation room and a store room. The individual kennel compounds were shaded from the sun, connected to a central drainage system and even had electric fans to keep the dogs cool. After settling in at his new unit, Corporal Bastard began organising a 'local' RAF Police Dog Demonstration Team that in between normal duties was soon giving displays to service families, Army units, personnel employed on the oil rigs and the local community. Besides looking after the welfare of the RAF dogs, personnel from the dog section were called upon once a month to check on the condition of the dogs owned by the two fourteen-year old nephews of the ruling sheik. One of the dogs was a German Shepherd type and the other a mongrel and each month their ticks were removed and they were given a general medical check-up. Likewise, the wives of the men who worked on the off-shore oil rigs would seek assistance from the RAF Police dog handlers whenever their pet dogs came to grief.

In January 1970, the Provost Marshal, Air Commodore Panton, advised the Ministry of Defence about the increased involvement of service personnel in the abuse of illegal and dangerous drugs. Throughout the *'Hippie decade'* of the sixties the RAF Police had been monitoring the use of illegal and controlled drugs by society in general and had become alarmed with the increased ease at which the drugs could be obtained and used. At the time, drug abuse happened to be a major problem within the United States' own armed forces and the problem continued to grow. To prevent that situation from developing within the RAF, the Dog Training Flight at the Depot was tasked with training two RAF Police dogs in the detection of the drug Cannabis in all its associated forms. During the previous year two members of the RAF Police Dog Training School; Mr C Gilmore and Corporal M Chidgey had attended a Drug Dog Observers Course held at the Metropolitan Police Dog Training School in Kent, where they had watched the training techniques developed by the Metropolitan Police who had been successfully using their dogs to detect Cannabis for a number of years.

During the course the Metropolitan Police had provided invaluable advice and assistance to the RAF Police Depot in setting up their own training course which it was envisaged would take between ten and twelve weeks to complete. Mr Gilmore was nominated as the course co-ordinator and the selected handler was quite naturally Corporal Chidgey. One Labrador; Air Dog Sam and one German Shepherd dog; Air Dog Rex, were programmed into the course. The experiment proved successful and both dogs achieved a good standard and were passed out and became fully operational almost immediately. Air Dog Sam a two-year old yellow Labrador, and an unconditional gift from a member of the public, was the first of its breed to serve with the RAF Police and his success opened the door to many other suitable breeds of gun dog thereafter.

Breaking into new ground was always an exciting prospect for Mr Gilmore and the drug search course was no exception. What also added spice was the new breed being tried out and tested. While the German Shepherd had a very successful and trusted track record, the Labrador was at first an unknown quantity but Air Dog Sam settled into his new service environment smoothly and quickly adapted to being trained in his new specialisation. Air Dog Rex was six years old and had formerly been a patrol dog. Unfortunately, he had been involved in an accident and had sustained an injury to one of his hind legs causing him to limp, which according to the veterinary surgeon left him unfit to continue as a patrol dog. As for their handler; Corporal Chidgey, he was described by Mr Gilmore as being experienced, motivated and tremendously enthusiastic which made him the ideal choice. Initially, Mr Gilmore and Corporal Chidgey encountered one slight problem; they had no Cannabis with which to start training. Of course they could quite easily have purchased some but possession of the drug was an offence unless special authorisation had been obtained from the Home Office. After a few telephone calls were made to certain key figures in the Ministry of Defence, the drug samples and the necessary authority to possess them for training purposes was obtained and training commenced. Unsurprisingly, tremendous interest was taken in the project by senior RAF officers and accordingly, a number of high-level visits were made to the depot to see the training in progress. At the end of the course, both dogs and their handler were assessed by Mr C Fricker the Chief Training Officer (Dogs), who being delighted with the results, passed them out to go operational. Initially Corporal Chidgey and his dogs were assigned to the Provost & Security Services Support Squadron based at RAF Debden, and were on call to assist RAF investigators around the country with their search for Cannabis. At the same time another pilot course was being run in tandem with the drug detection training and that was the training of dogs to detect the presence of firearms and explosives: something that would help in the fight against the bomb planters and terrorists of the IRA. The initial course was of the same duration as the drug detection training and the course co-ordinator was Mr T McHaffie and the selected handler was Corporal W Sanderson. Again, the pilot scheme proved highly successful with two German Shepherds; a dog and a bitch, going operational in the later part of 1970. Later, the drug detection training moved on to include the detection of other dangerous drugs and as a consequence, senior officials from Her Majesty's Customs and Excise Service began to show a particular interest in the break through which they thought could help them in the continuing battle to detect illegal drugs being smuggled into the country.

Corporal J McNulty had joined the RAF in 1967 on a three-year engagement, and after completing his basic police and dog handling training at RAF Debden had initially been posted onto the strength of the dog section at RAF Waddington. His first overseas posting followed later when he had been sent to RAF El Adem in Libya, just prior to the 1969 revolution that saw Colonel Ghadaffi taking over the country. However, shortly after his arrival at El Adem he received a lucky break when Corporal W Bernard, who had been the NCO seconded onto the RAF Police Mounted Section, moved on to other duties. As Corporal McNulty had previous horse riding experience he had volunteered to take over Corporal Bernard's position and had been given the job. At that stage, the section had two white Arab stallions; Briggy and Shepp that had been acquired to form the mounted section in December 1963. Corporal McNulty quickly settled into his new job and enjoyed it immensely. He remembers that the horses were very popular with the service families and more especially the children as they did their daily rounds of the station perimeter.

During the 1970 United Kingdom Annual Dog Championship Trials held at RAF Debden the top three winning teams were declared as, Corporal Bishop and Air Dog Sindy, Corporal Hearl and Air Dog Kim, and Corporal A Fellows and Air Dog Ricky. In the trials held at RAF Germany Corporal D Devonshire and Air Dog Rondo took first place, Corporal Lambert and Air Dog Zardi took second place, and Corporal Riche and Air Dog Shane came third.

Following on from their successful North American tour the previous year, the hugely popular RAF Police Dog Demonstration Team had successfully carried out another hectic round of displays for the public around the country during the year, which included appearances at the Football Association Cup Final Replay, the Scottish Football Association Cup Final, The Birmingham International Spring Show, the Plymouth 'Mayflower 70' Celebrations, the Edinburgh Tattoo and of course the Royal Tournament at Earls Court London, but to name just a few of their engagements.

On the 18th February 1971, the RAF Police Auxiliaries stationed in Singapore and the FEAF celebrated the Silver Anniversary of their formation at RAF Changi in 1946. The establishment of the force had grown considerably with some four hundred multi-racial officers and other ranks being employed on a wide range of duties at various stations throughout Malaysia and Singapore. One of the very first tasks the force was called upon to carry out in 1946 was guarding Japanese prisoners-of-war. During their brief but very successful history, the force had worked extremely hard from humble beginnings to earn the highest respect from their regular RAF Police counterparts and the remainder of the RAF. Indeed, they had continually distinguished themselves in all manner of ways and some 800 members of the force held the General Service Medal for their valuable campaign service in Malaya and in Borneo.

In addition to their combined contribution to the emergency situation in the region, reports of individual distinguished service had also been rewarded. Two British Empire Medals had been awarded; one to Sub Inspector Mohamed Kassim Bin Mahat in 1956, and the other to Inspector Abu Hassin Bin Haji Ibrahim in 1965. Additionally, Commendations from the Air-Officer-Commanding (AOC), the Air Commander and the Provost Marshal had also been awarded to ten other members of the force. The occasion was marked by a splendid parade made up of four flights, including nine dogs and their handlers from the dog section at RAF Changi, which were reviewed by the Air Commander FEAF, Air-Vice Marshal N M Maynard CB, CBE, DFC, AFC, who was accompanied throughout the day by the Command Provost & Security Officer

Group Captain A A Witherington. During the parade, ten year-old Air Dog Rex 6211, handled by RAF Police Auxiliary Constable H Stewart, took pride of place close to the saluting dais, while the other eight dogs and their auxiliary handlers marched smartly besides the four flights. One of the dogs included a dark German Shepherd bitch called Neta who had blues eyes and was handled by RAF Police Auxiliary Constable Teo Ban Lai. The parade was followed by the *Beating of the Retreat* performed by the band of the Australian Army, who had kindly offered their services for the occasion. The Parade Commander was Assistant Superintendent Tajri Bin Haji Ali, assisted by Sub Inspector Abd Samad Bin Said the Parade Adjutant, and Sergeant Tahir Bin Awang the Parade Warrant Officer. At the conclusion of the parade the Reviewing Officer was presented with an inscribed outsized truncheon, of the type first issued to the Auxiliaries in 1946, by Sergeant Tahir bin Awak and in turn, the Reviewing Officer presented each member of the force with a copy of their famous cap badge mounted onto a wooden shield. The formal ceremony was followed later by the *'Ronggeng'* the Malay festival of feasting and dancing to which everyone taking part in the parade together with the spectators and their families were invited. Although the celebration turned out to be a huge success, it did unfortunately herald the start of the intended withdrawal of the RAF from that region of the Far East.

With the RAF Police commitment at RAF Fairford over, members of the section were posted to other units. With just over nine months to serve before his ten year engagement in the RAF came to an end, Corporal G R Phillips was just a little surprised to find himself posted overseas again on a nine-month tour to RAF Gan in the middle of the Indian Ocean. Having confirmed that the posting was not in fact a mistake, he made the long journey out to the Maldives and shortly after arriving teamed up with Air Dog Dante and joined the three other dog handlers who had the daunting task of patrolling *paradise*. During his tour, two unusual events occurred. The first was when RAF Gan was honoured with a visit from the Provost Marshal, Air Commodore Panton, and the second was a trip to Cyprus. At that time, the British withdrawal from the Far East was gathering pace and the Army's veterinary surgeons that looked after the dogs on Gan, were transferred to Dhekalia in Cyprus. As that was now the nearest British veterinary support for Gan, Corporal Phillips was sent there to learn more from the RAVC about being able to recognise symptoms of ill health in the dogs and how to treat minor problems. While he was there the RAVC celebrated their *'Corps Day'* with a barbecue on the beach and Corporal Phillips was invited along. Unfortunately, later that evening he and his host, who was the duty veterinary officer, were called back to Dhekalia to carry out a post-mortem on a horse from the RAF Police Mounted Branch at RAF Akrotiri.

In early April, the branch was saddened to learn of the death of Lieutenant Colonel J W Baldwin, DSO, the *father* of the RAF Police dog organisation. Although he had been in retirement since 1953, he had continued to maintain his strong links with the branch and was immensely proud of his connection with the service and of course, the highest standard of achievement, which he had worked so hard to attain during the time spent working with the RAF Police. Five years after he had retired and as a mark of gratitude and respect for all that he had done, a room in the RAF Police Museum, dedicated to the dogs, which he loved so much, was named as '*The Baldwin Room*'.

One of those who recalled dealing with him during his time at the depot was Corporal M Tucker, who prior to joining the RAF as a National Serviceman in January 1953, had written to Baldwin asking what his chances were of being accepted into the RAF as a dog handler. Baldwin, no doubt impressed with the fact that Tucker was an active member of the Epsom & Ewell Branch of the Associated Sheep, Police and Army Dog Society (ASPADS), had replied saying that if he was successful in getting accepted into the RAF then he would ensure that he was sent to the RAF Police Dog Training School. Tucker remembered very clearly the day when he first met Baldwin in person in his office at the dog school. The first question Baldwin asked him was, "What do you know about dogs?" to which Tucker had replied, "Not nearly as much as I would like to know. I just want to keep learning more and more." Baldwin stared at him for a while and then said, "And so you shall."

During the brief interview Tucker could not help noticing that on a shelf behind Baldwin's desk was a ceremonial German helmet from the Great War, which he later learned had been picked up from the battlefield by Baldwin during the Battle of the Somme in 1915. The subsequent six-week dog training course, under the guidance of instructor Corporal H Fox, passed by very quickly and Corporal Tucker remembers that at the end of their training, Baldwin entered the classroom and talked to them about how he got involved with the German Shepherd dog and how he and Lord Brabazon of Tara had introduced the breed into England at the end of the Great War. He also talked at length about how the MAPGDS had been established and how the RAF had become involved in using dogs to guard its assets. Corporal Tucker had been subsequently posted to RAF St Mawgan in Cornwall with Air Dog Prince 3259. In January 1954, Tucker had been posted to the dog training school as an instructor. However, Baldwin had retired some five months previously leaving the German helmet behind in his former office. Shortly before completing his two years National Service, Tucker wrote to Baldwin and asked him if he still wanted the helmet. In response, Baldwin wrote a letter to the commanding officer at the dog training school asking that the helmet be conveyed to Corporal Tucker with his pleasure. Tucker was delighted with the kind gesture.

At the Annual United Kingdom Dog Championship Trials held at RAF Debden Corporal M Brown and Air Dog Cindy, Corporal McIlwaith and Air Dog Panther, and Corporal R Gray and Air Dog Monty took the top three prizes. At the RAF Germany dog trials held at RAF Wildenrath, the two winning teams were declared as Corporal Sayers and Air Dog Marcus and Corporal King and Air Dog Simba.

Air Commodore Panton retired as Provost Marshal on the 16th October and was succeeded in post by Air Commodore H M Shephard OBE MBIM, who became the second provost officer, to have reached the top appointment within the branch. Prior to being promoted and taking up his appointment, Air Commodore Shephard had been serving in Germany as the Command Provost & Security Officer.

Since the end of the last war, with the introduction into service of much heavier and more sophisticated aircraft, the flying stations became static bases, comprising of the airfield and runway, the technical, operational and domestic areas. As such, the overall routine security commitment at that type of unit was relatively easy for the RAF Police to maintain on a day-to-day basis. However, with the introduction into service of the Harrier V/STOL jet fighter aircraft, that principle quickly changed along with the required security measures needed to protect the new aircraft. The Harrier being capable of vertical or short take off and landings, did not require conventional runways and airfields from which to operate from and could be deployed into and out from any location away from its parent station. In Germany for instance, the aircraft were based at RAF Wildenrath as part of NATO's first line of defence against the threat of invasion from the Eastern Bloc Alliance. However, as part of the constant preparation for war, the aircraft and their supporting elements were regularly deployed around Germany, taking part in the numerous military exercises throughout the year. Consequently, nominated RAF Police NCOs from both Wildenrath and other units within Germany, found themselves living under canvas in field conditions, whilst providing the necessary police and security support to the field air commander at their assigned site.

During those exercises, the aircraft regularly operated out of military training areas, woodland, farms and even from closed off sections of the autobahns to demonstrate their full potential. In addition to providing static security guards for the aircraft, RAF Police NCOs at each of the deployment sites, under the control of a senior NCO, carried out foot and mobile security patrols of the areas, using RAF Police dogs, as well as maintaining a control of entry system into the site for visitors. In addition, whenever public roads were being used as temporary short take off runways, the RAF Police were empowered, by the German authorities, to close them off to normal traffic while the aircraft took off or landed. Obviously, the deployment site, together with its aircraft and all the associated activity, attracted considerable interest from the local population, who in many cases, were keen to get a closer look. Consequently, the RAF Police were kept extremely busy in maintaining the security of both the aircraft and its supporting elements in many unusual locations.

With his nine-month tour of duty over, Corporal G R Phillips left RAF Gan and returned home to RAF Uxbridge in the United Kingdom. Unfortunately, an administrative blunder had occurred which resulted in his return date being so close to his discharge date that it was impossible for him to take the disembarkation leave, his outstanding annual leave, and the resettlement course that he was entitled to. As such, he was asked to extend his service by a further six months which he agreed to do. It was the first time during his ten-year engagement that he had been posted anywhere without a dog and it certainly felt strange to begin with. After being discharged from the RAF, he would go on to join the Thames Valley Police; train dog handlers for the Sultan of Oman's Air Force, and manage the Surrey Police Dog Training Unit.

RAF Police Dog Demonstration Team in Battersea Park – Circa 1963

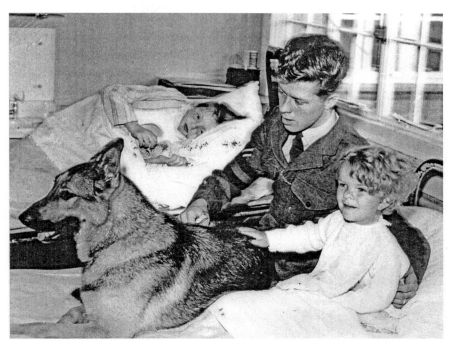

Cpl J S McArdle and Air dog Sabre visiting the Children's Ward of a Hospital in Edinburgh during a break from the Military Tattoo – 1965

RAF Police GSD being trained to walk the tight rope during a training session.

Five Kennel Maids with RAFP Dogs at RAF Dog School Debden - Circa 1968

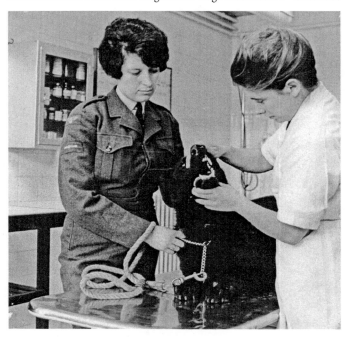

Kennel Maids examining a dog at RAFP Dog School Debden Circa 1968

RAF Police Dog handlers guarding an Armed Vulcan bomber on standby – 1970

Air dogs Sam (Labrador) & Rex (GSD) 1970
First RAFP Dogs to be trained to detect dangerous drugs.

RAF Police dog trials Debden – 1971 – Row of fire jumps known as 'Joeys Leap'

4.   1972 – 1981

In January 1972, in recognition of the work they had carried out in training and establishing drug and explosives search dogs, Mr C Gilmore and Mr T McHaffie, the training course co-ordinators, were awarded commendations from the Air-Officer-Commanding Training Command. After the success of training the first RAF Police dogs to search for drugs, Mr Gilmore remained with the Search Cell but also found time to instruct students attending initial police dog handling courses, experienced dog handlers returning to be re-teamed with a new dog and senior NCOs attending dog inspector's courses. It was in the words of Mr Gilmore, 'An extremely busy and successful time for the RAF Police Dog Training School and an exciting and rewarding time for him personally'.

On one occasion in early 1972, Corporal W Scorer, one of the dog collectors, had to travel up to Scotland to visit the owners of fifteen separate dogs who wanted to donate them as unconditional gifts to the RAF. Because of the number of dogs involved he was forced to use the specially converted coach normally used by the RAF Police Dog Demonstration Team, which was driven by a RAF driver. New to the job of collecting gift dogs, Corporal Scorer, being a rather keen NCO was looking forward to bringing back a large number of dogs from the trip, but unfortunately, it was quite a disappointing start for him because none of the dogs when seen and assessed were found to be suitable and the coach returned to Debden empty.

As already mentioned, members of the public offered up their dogs to the RAF for a number of reasons and there was always a steady supply of new canine recruits, however in the early 1970s there was suddenly a shortage of gift dogs from the public and the management at the depot decided that a publicity campaign was the answer to the problem. The RAF had always relied on low key publicity at various locations of the country and that had been adequate to maintain their demand. At one point, someone made the decision to appeal for gift dogs on national television and the RAF Police Dog Demonstration Team duly appeared on Hughie Green's talent show 'Opportunity Knocks'. At the time, the program was one of the top variety shows watched by millions of viewers. Sergeant D Mew sat next to Hughie Green, himself a former RAF pilot, and appealed for additional gift dogs for service with the RAF Police. The result was staggering and the depot was swamped with offers from the public to donate their dogs. The majority were quickly rejected because they were the wrong breed, were too old or too young or were not pedigree etc. However, at the end of the initial sorting process there were still a considerable number of dogs to be inspected. In hindsight, a hasty decision was made by the management that all suitable dogs were to be brought to the depot to be evaluated by the staff. As such, all available transport was utilised and any dog handlers not on a training course were tasked to bring in dogs from all over the country. At the time, Debden had around one hundred and twenty compounds in which to accommodate dogs and as the new gift dogs were brought in for evaluation the dog school quickly ran out of space. At that point it was decided to place two dogs in each kennel compound, which under normal circumstances was contrary to all the regulations. Actually, the idea of placing two dogs together worked out reasonably well as most were together as a dog and a bitch in each compound. At its high point there were over two hundred dogs accommodated at the depot and as fast as they were being brought in, those found to be unsuitable were being taken back to their owners. Of those found to be unsuitable, the situation was frustrated by a number of owners who just refused to take the dogs back into their homes, so there was the added problem of disposing of those dogs. Luckily there was no outbreak of disease from any infected dog coming in for assessment which given the circumstances would have been disastrous. Eventually, the situation calmed down and things gradually returned to normal. However, valuable lessons had been learned from advertising too widely and to being ill-prepared for the vast influx of gift dogs, many of which were totally unsuited to the role of becoming RAF Police dogs.

One of the fallacies of the layman is that every dog will bite, and that the German Shepherd dog is more likely to bite than the others. Regrettably, for the RAF Police, that was not always the case. In order to get the police dog to bite, and bite properly and to 'hang on', it was necessary to train it to do so. There have been previous references to 'teasing and biting', but not too many references on the business of how they achieved the good bite. The dog handlers who were involved in this particular aspect of training were called by a variety of titles over the years, but during Sergeant P Somerville's time at the school they were called Practical Training Assistants (PTAs) or, for a very brief period of time, Practical Training Instructors (PTIs). The main difference was that the PTAs were usually acting corporal dog handlers, whilst the PTIs were substantive corporal dog handlers. However, the usual title for the PTA or PTI was the same; they were known simply as 'The Criminal'.

Every dog handler on every dog section had to put a padded arm or full padded suit on at some time or other to test the dogs' bite. The individual dog sections had to rely on their own personnel for these duties or some volunteer whom they managed to cajole or hoodwink to suit up for them. The dog training school, however, had their own dedicated criminals to work the dogs out, and these were the aforementioned PTAs or PTIs. Having been a PTI for two and a half years during his career, Sergeant Somerville can assure the readers that it was one of the most challenging and exciting jobs that a dog handler could do. During his time at the depot in the early 1970s, the basic dog training courses were seven weeks long, and the dog training school was a very busy place.

There was a reasonable amount of effort to ensure that the right dog was picked for the individual handler, which was an improvement on Sergeant Somerville's time at Netheravon when his dog was allocated to him. The first part of the course was to familiarise the team with each other and that exercise varied in time and approach, depending usually on the temperament of the dog; and the dogs were of a very wide range of temperaments as well. Some dogs were very biddable from the outset, and caused no problems at all to their new handlers. Some dogs, however, could be nervous and unsure about coming out of the kennel, which involved new handlers sitting in their dog's kennel for as long as it took trying to communicate and strike up a situation of trust and the beginnings of affection and loyalty between dog and handler. The familiarisation period was followed very quickly by the obedience phase, where the handler, continuing to gain the dog's trust, started to impose his will over the dog. Basic training taught the handler that he was reverting to nature and assuming the mantle of the pack leader or *Alpha Dog*. However, it was vital that efficient control was built up very rapidly before the real work of turning the animal into a police dog began. The beginning of the course was the most dangerous period for the criminal; the handlers were new to the game and lacked a certain amount of real confidence and knowledge and that was the time when a mistake could lead to the handler or the criminal being injured by a wrong move or a lack of control over the dog. Introducing an untrained dog and handler to the biting phase took place in clearly defined stages with the first introduction to the criminal taking place in a group.

The teams were taken out as a course after a thorough briefing, and marched to the site of an old revetment which afforded cover for the criminal. Up until that point, the dog had been wearing a check-chain, but for the first time a leather collar would be put on the dog and from that moment on, the dog would associate the collar with *being on duty*. The trainee dog handlers usually placed themselves in a crescent formation and were then encouraged to start giving their dogs quiet but steady encouragement that something was about to happen. Indeed future voice encouragement such as "Whats up boy? Where is he? There's a good dog", reminds the dog that there is a situation developing and he must be alert and on his guard. Without much delay the criminal would burst out from behind the revetment with a lot of noise and shouting and get the dogs worked up. After that brief exercise the criminal would disappear behind the revetment once more and the dog would receive copious praise from his handler for seeing the 'criminal off'. It was vitally important that the dog felt that it had won the argument and that the criminal had run away. The next part of the teasing process was the bite, and that was usually achieved using a piece of Hessian sacking to begin with, which was passed into the dog's mouth by the criminal during the second teasing phase. That may sound easy but it was not, and a wrong approach from the criminal could easily spook a young dog, which then might have to go back a stage to regain its confidence.

Many people seem to feel that making a noise alone will bring out the aggressiveness of the dog. In the majority of cases that is simply not true, as just making a noise generally causes excitement, which is entirely different from the defensive and aggressive reaction required from the dog. However strong the dog was, the criminal still had to instil into the dog the feeling that he was a threat that had to be countered with some urgency. Therefore, the good criminal had to display genuine menace and aggression towards the dog to bring out its best qualities. Of course, the degree of aggression from the criminal, and indeed, the quality of the teasing was different for every dog. Some dogs had a high degree of confidence from the very beginning and required very little teasing. Others however, needed a more subtle approach to bring out the best in them. On the other side of the coin, other dogs that were overly confident, considered the threat was over and done with once the criminal was out of striking distance. So the temperament of every dog could vary quite widely and had to be worked on by the course instructor and his criminal.

After the dog had made its initial bite, training moved on to the next stage which involved the use of a padded arm, which was naturally a much more bulky item for the dog to chew on but with which the criminal could firm up the dogs bite by careful manipulation. After successfully biting the padded arm the dog would be introduced to the criminal wearing a full padded suit. In the 1970s, and for many years after, the criminals used to make their own suits. Normally a suit jacket was made up from an old uniform jacket that was built up with layers of felt and Hessian sacking. The important factors when making a padded suit were to ensure that it was well padded, as natural as possible in the circumstances, soft enough for even the softest mouthed dogs and that it allowed as much free and natural movement as possible for the criminal. In other words it was quite easy for anyone to make a suit that afforded plenty of protection for the wearer but which was totally useless for the dog. Therefore, a fine balance had to be drawn between the safety of the criminal and the needs of the dog, with the balance of course in favour of the dog's requirements. The introduction of the padded suit saw the dog begin to develop the chase. The suit phase commenced by showing the dog the criminal wearing a full suit and allowing it to bite. The next stage was for the criminal to turn his back on the dog and shuffle forward which formed the beginning of the chase. Of course, the chase then rapidly developed in length until the team were confident and competent enough to go into the training compound for the first time, where the chase and the arrest of the criminal were developed rapidly until the dog could chase a criminal the full length of the compound to make the arrest. The RAF Police dog was encouraged from the very beginning of its training to bite where it wanted to on the body of the criminal. Readers might possibly know that the civil police, other branches of the Armed Services and most other security agencies trained their dogs at the time to be 'security arm true'. In other words, the dog was trained to go for the arm, usually the right arm where the intruder or criminal might or might not be carrying a weapon. Although that system had wide approval from a variety of dog trainers to be the right method for a police dog to adopt, the RAF adopted the view that the individual dog should be allowed to bite where it wanted to. Although the RAF method makes training that much easier, an intruder entering a RAF site can never be sure where the dog will attack him. RAF Police dogs may go for the ankles, the back of the legs, the shoulders, the arms or even the feet. From the criminals' prospective, they were always wary of the dogs known as 'high flyers'; those that launched themselves for the top of the shoulders which were more likely to knock the criminal to the ground by the sheer force of the impact. It was a dangerous situation because once the criminal was prone he could not work the dog properly which was a disadvantage to its training and he could quickly lose control of the exercise and become injured. Each initial training course for dog handlers had an assigned instructor with a dedicated criminal to assist him.

Although good 'criminals', following a thorough briefing from the course in-structor on the teams' strengths and weaknesses, could work well with more than one course, it was better for each course to have a dedicated 'criminal', one who knew each individual dog and handler and was then able to get the best from them as a team. Of course, when the dog team left the dog training school that was not the end of their training, which was a continuous process that went on year after year. The main difference, as mentioned before, was that criminal work on the stations was carried out by handlers drawn from the resident dog section staff. This was quite in order, since by the time the team passed-out from the depot, the dog would be building its confidence rapidly and would be able to adapt more easily to differing scenarios. The vital requirements of continuation training carried out on stations was of course not the responsibility of the school's instructors and his 'criminal' assistant but the responsibility of the NCO in charge of the dog section and his staff, supervised by regular inspections from the Provost Marshal's Dog Inspector (PMDI). However, the 'criminals' at the depot would still become involved with trained dogs at a later stage. Whenever a trained dog was returned from a station to the depot it was assessed by a senior member of the training staff and tested by a 'criminal' before being re-allocated to a trained handler, perhaps returning from an overseas tour or requiring another dog for a variety of reasons. The team would be placed on a two-week re-team course to get used to each other, before having to undergo the same tests with the allocated course instructor, assessing officer and of course, the 'criminal'. Although the 'criminal' was mainly concerned with getting the dog to bite and chase, there were other areas during the course where his work was of vital importance. RAF Police dogs are mainly employed on night work, when the RAF station or unit is most vulnerable. The dog must be confident at night as well as during the hours of daylight. Initial night-work followed a similar pattern to the beginning of criminal-work with a group of dogs, under the control of their handlers, being teased by the 'criminal' in the darkness. Again, training progressed to chasing and arresting the criminal in the compound during the hours of darkness.

The ultimate test of the dogs' courage and the competence of the team came when the dog chased the criminal down the full length of compound in complete darkness whilst under gunfire to make the arrest. The final aspect of the work carried out by the 'criminal' is the wind scent which is without doubt the most important phase of training, considering the areas that the dog teams are required to patrol. Uniquely, in comparison with other agencies, the RAF relied upon the incredible scenting abilities of the dog to detect the presence of intruders in large open areas such as airfields, radar sites or weapons storage areas. While other agencies do use the scenting abilities of the dog to detect intruders, they never seem to use the full potential of the dog in the same way that the RAF Police have. To illustrate the point, RAF Khormaksar in Aden was a typical airfield in size and layout, and yet during the anti-British troubles, intrusions and violent terrorist incidents that took place on a daily basis during the 1960s, the RAF airfield and its aircraft and support material was successfully secured by six dog teams at any one time. Training to wind scent begins later in the course, once the dog's confidence and its bite has had time to develop. By that stage of training the dog quickly realised that as soon as its collar was fitted and it was taken from its kennel by its handler it was time for working and quite naturally it became agitated and alert, looking for the 'criminal'. To begin with the distances involved were kept short but a good dog, which is unable to pinpoint where a 'criminal' might be hiding by visual means, generally reverts to instinct and starts to use its nose to pick up a scent. Initially, the 'criminal' and the course instructor both have their work cut out in order to get the trainee and his dog to recognise a wind scent pick-up as every dog's reaction is different. Some dogs will stand, rear up and bark or growl whilst other dogs might only give the slightest of indications, leaving it to the skill of the handler to interpret his dog's reaction and act accordingly. One of the sure signs of a genuine pick-up, but not always, was the sight of the dog's ears folding down as it switched down its hearing to concentrate on picking up the scent. In all cases however, once the handler becomes aware that his dog has indicated a pick-up, the chase-in on the criminal is generally assured and of course, the reward for the dog is a bite at the end. The training quickly develops with the distances being gradually increased until the team using the wind to their advantage are able to patrol large areas efficiently.

During the late 1980s, Sergeant G Hudson, designed a tie for the 'criminals' which displayed the head of a German Shepherd dog framed by prisoners' arrows, under which the motto 'The Bitten Few' was printed. Any RAF Police dog handler who had carried out a tour of duty as a full-time 'criminal' at any of the established RAF Police Dog Training Schools was entitled to wear the tie with civilian dress and was worn with pride by the 'Bitten Few'.

During the summer of 1972, Corporal H Evans, an instructor at the RAF Police Depot, who joined the RAF in 1962, won a Certificate of Merit and a cash prize for re-designing the air-transit kennels used to transport RAF Police dogs on long journeys by air. Incorporating a sliding floor and a steel tray, the kennel could easily be cleaned without contaminating the aircraft or infringing strict quarantine regulations. With the dogs being confined within the kennel for long periods during flights, the new design definitely made life for the dogs much more comfortable, and of course cleaning them much more practical for the escorting handlers or kennel-maids.

At the Annual United Kingdom RAF Police Dog Championship Trials held at RAF Debden the top three teams were judged to be Corporal D Simpson and Air Dog Robie, Corporal G Evans and Air Dog Sindy, and Corporal A Ritchie and Air Dog Cindy. At the RAF Germany dog trials, Corporal N Durrant and Air Dog Sabre, Corporal R Allcock and Air Dog Simba, and Corporal J Bartram and Air Dog Rex walked away with the top three awards.

RAF Akrotiri on the island of Cyprus was a massive station, with its own 're-stricted' stretch of coastline. Like all RAF stations it had a technical site and a domestic site. The domestic site included hundreds of married quarters, the officer's, sergeant's and airmen's messes, offices, schools, clubs, a hospital, a cinema and numerous barrack blocks. The technical site was secured from everything else and had only two access points, both of which were manned by RAF Police and their auxiliary counter-parts twenty-four hours each day. In 1972 there were about one hundred RAF Police personnel employed on the station plus around forty dog handlers and their charges. On the outskirts of the station perimeter there was another, large, fully enclosed site, known as 'West Site', which was the main bomb storage area and was pretty well self-contained and was always manned by RAF Police NCOs during the day and dog handlers during the hours of darkness. At the entrance to RAF Akrotiri was the RAF Police piquet post that comprised a small office situated in the middle of a dual carriageway road. One carriageway was the 'in' road and the other was the 'out' road. Both roads had a barrier across them controlled by the RAF Police. Huge, dense coils of barbed wire surrounded the station marking out the perimeter fence. In addition to the security posts dotted around the station, the RAF Police also carried out mobile patrols of both the technical and the domestic sites. During evening and night shifts, dog handlers would also patrol the technical site. Everyone on duty was armed with a Browning 9mm automatic pistol and two magazines of ammunition. Each magazine contained ten rounds and one of the magazines was fitted to the weapon ready for use if required.

Although the main task of the RAF Police Dog Training School, which in 1972 was under the command of Flight Lieutenant B Ardley, was to train German Shepherds and their handlers to patrol airfields, other training courses were run at the school to train American airmen, kennel-maids, dog inspectors from the RAF and HM Prison Service, and specialist courses to detect the presence of drugs. At the time, other members of staff serving at the school included Mr C Fricker, Mr C Gilmore, Flight Sergeant K C Hart, Sergeant G Herd, Corporal L Lamb, Corporal I Horsborough, Corporal R Findley, Corporal H Evans and kennel-maids Corporal(W) C Eason and Senior Aircraftswoman G Jordan. Interestingly, because dogs donated to the RAF retained their original names, it was quite common for dogs with the same names to be serving on any particular unit; only their service number, tattooed inside their left ear identified them as individuals. The most common names in use at the time amongst serving German Shepherds included; Prince (38), Rex (24), Kim (23), Simba (18), Sheba (12) and finally Tina (7).

In early 1973, Corporal S Benson and Corporal C Booth, having successfully completed their basic RAF Police training at the RAF Police Depot Debden, made their way over to the dog training school to begin the training course to become a dog handlers. In fact, they were the only two students on that particular course. They were both given two German Shepherd dogs each to train with; Corporal Benson started off with a dog and a bitch but it was quickly realised that the dog was not up to the grade required and was rejected. As for the bitch, she also presented a problem because she had been given the wrong tattoo number in her ear, which went a long way in explaining why she seemed deaf when Corporal Benson called her by the name Sadie, when in fact her real name was Kim. As a result, Corporal Benson was given Air Dog 8045 Kyla, who happened to be a fully trained police dog. The course progressed well and one evening the two students were told to report for night training on the airfield. After collecting their dogs both students were directed to 'patrol' a specific area. As Corporal Benson set off down a dark path on the airfield, his dog indicated the presence of someone ahead. At that moment, one of the PTA *criminals*, who was wearing a padded arm, jumped out from behind a bush with a stick and started teasing the dog for a reaction. Unfortunately, the dog became confused and bit Corporal Benson on the left kneecap, and then added insult to injury, by spraying his anal glands all over his handler. The rest of the course however went well and both handlers duly graduated with their dogs in August and Corporal Benson and Air Dog Kyla were posted to RAF St Mawgan in Cornwall. The first part of their journey from Debden to London was straightforward but then things became difficult. A military driver from the Army Movements Section was supposed to meet Corporal Benson and his dog and take them through London to Paddington but for some reason they did not appear at planned. As a result, Corporal Benson was left standing on Liverpool Street station with his kit bag and one sedated police dog inside a very heavy transit kennel. Being a resourceful individual though, Corporal Benson finally found a friendly black cab driver who soon dismantled the kennel with his toolkit and then took them both on to Paddington, where the kennel was reassembled by the extremely helpful black cab driver, and both man and dog resumed the journey to their new unit.

On the 5th June, Her Royal Highness the Princess Margaret, Countess of Snowdon, arrived at the RAF Police Depot by helicopter to carry out the first ever Royal Review of the RAF Provost and RAF Police Branch. After being welcomed to RAF Debden by Air Marshal Sir Harold Martin KCB DSO DFC AFC, the Air Member for Personnel. She was then presented to the Provost Marshal Air Commodore Shephard, Colonel Sir John Ruggles-Brise Bt CB OBE TD JP the Lord Lieutenant of Essex, Group Captain R D England the Depot Commandant, and Group Captain A A Witherington the Officer in charge of the Parade. At that point, the Queens Colour Squadron of the RAF Regiment came smartly to attention and presented the Royal Salute as the RAF Southern Band played the National Anthem.

After the anthem Her Royal Highness was invited to inspect the smartly turned out provost officers, RAF Police NCOs and RAF Police Auxiliaries on parade who represented the branch serving all around the world. With the sunlight glinting from the polished brasses, medals and row upon row of white hats, Her Royal Highness seemed extremely impressed as she carried out a full inspection, stopping to chat to NCOs from every group of the parade. After the ceremony, she was taken on a tour of the RAF Police Depot where she viewed an impressive exhibition of photographs, models and static displays depicting the RAF Police at work. She then moved on to the Griffin Club where members of the RAF Police and their families were presented to her during an informal gathering. After lunch in the Officers' Mess, a group photograph was taken to mark the occasion and she was presented with a unique solid gold brooch of a Griffin, the symbol of the RAF Police, which had been subscribed to by every serving officer in the branch. Finally, she was shown around the dog training school and was clearly delighted with the demonstration arranged for her visit by Mr Fricker. At the conclusion of a most successful day, Princess Margaret returned to her helicopter and finally left the station, having had an extremely enjoyable and interesting day.

In July, Flight Sergeant M J Greenaway BEM was posted to the Headquarters Strike Command located at RAF High Wycombe, where he became one of two RAF Police dog inspectors appointed by the Provost Marshal to look after the interests of his dogs within the United Kingdom. He had originally joined the RAF Police in 1954 and had spent a good deal of his service as a corporal employed as a dog handler and as a senior NCO in charge of RAF Police dog sections within the United Kingdom and Germany. Between the years 1973-76 the two inspectors, known officially as the Provost Marshal's Dog Inspectors (PMDI), responsible for RAF Police dogs within the United Kingdom were Flight Sergeant Greenaway and Flight Sergeant Davies. During the same period, Flight Sergeant G Clapperton looked after the inspectorate within RAF Germany.

The PMDI's were responsible for visiting and inspecting all RAF Police dog sections within their area of responsibility and their role was twofold; firstly, they advised commanders at all levels on the utilisation, the training, the administration and the welfare of RAF Police dog teams required to enhance the security at RAF bases; and secondly, they carried out formal inspection visits of all units where RAF Police dogs were employed, which included all United Kingdom bases leased to the United States Air Force where RAF Police dogs were being handled by members of the USAF Security Police. In order to satisfy himself that the teams were working efficiently the PMDI would thoroughly check the compounds, kennels and section buildings for condition, cleanliness and standard of hygiene. The service records, known as the RAF form 4629, of all RAF

Police dogs were checked to ensure that they were being maintained correctly and that entries regarding continuation training and routine inspections by the local veterinary surgeon were being completed. Additionally, each dog on strength was inspected to ensure that it was fit and well cared for and both dogs and their handlers were rigorously tested during continuation training, and whilst out on their patrol areas at night. During the visit the inspector would advise the handler of any faults noted and offer recommendations to correct them. Any handler who failed to attain a particular standard could be taken off dog handling duties and any dog found lacking would if necessary be sent back to the RAF Police dog training school for retraining or re-teaming with a different handler. During the visit, which could last for a number of days and nights, the RAF Police commander on the unit would be thoroughly de-briefed and any problems noted during the visit would be discussed and recommendations offered. At the end of the inspection, observations and recommendations would be entered by the PMDI in each of the dogs' RAF F4629.

A formal post inspection report would be written and copies submitted to the Provost Marshal, the Command Security Officer at the relevant command headquarters, the Station Commander of the unit inspected and to the RAF Police Dog Training School at the RAF Police Depot. Flight Sergeant Greenaway's new appointment carried with it great responsibility and authority and he was assigned the following RAF units to supervise; Aldergrove, Bishops Court and HQ P&SS (Northern Ireland) in Northern Ireland; Machrihanish, Leuchars, Lossiemouth and Kinloss in Scotland; and, Marham, West Raynham, Northolt, Benson, Brize Norton, Lyneham, Thorney Island and St Mawgan in England. Although he was allocated a service estate car in which to travel around his large area of responsibility, he was also able to travel by air up to Scotland and over to Northern Ireland, using either routine RAF or scheduled civilian flights.

During the same period, his colleague Flight Sergeant Davies was responsible for supervising the following units; Wittering, Waddington, Scampton, Honington, Brawdy Faldingworth, Wyton and the USAF bases at Alconbury, Lakenheath and Woodbridge, which were using RAF Police dogs on loan to them. At the time, the first specialist dogs trained to detect arms and explosives, handled by Corporal's W Sanderson and J Yates, were operationally deployed with HQ P&SS (Northern Ireland). During one of Flight Sergeant Greenaway's inspection visits to HQ P&SS (Northern Ireland) an arranged exercise to detect explosives quickly turned into reality. During the exercise the Officer Commanding P&SS received a telephone call from the Army requesting urgent assistance in searching a farm where it was suspected that a quantity of explosives had been hidden. Since the troubles began in the Province in 1969 there had been just over five thousand explosions resulting from terrorist bombs and although the Army had defused a great number of the improvised bombs and had recovered an incredible amount of weapons, ammunition and explosive material, they were committed to using every means at their disposal to do it as safely as possible for the men involved. The introduction of specially trained RAF Police search dog teams and the remote controlled *wheelbarrow* used by the Army's Ammunition Technical Officers (ATO) and Bomb Disposal Teams, had undoubtedly been two of the biggest and most successful breakthroughs in the war against the terrorist bombs in Northern Ireland. As a result of the call for assistance, the exercise was quickly cancelled and Corporal Sanderson reported to the helicopter pad at RAF Aldergrove to be taken out to the farm concerned. At that point, Flight Sergeant Greenaway was invited along in order to observe the dog team in action for real. After all, the real thing was far better than a staged exercise any day. Shortly after, the helicopter containing the RAF men, the search dog and a squad of soldiers took off from RAF Aldergrove and made its way to the isolated farm.

After circling the area a few times to make sure everything was safe on the ground the helicopter went down to drop off the soldiers who were tasked with securing the area and making sure that there were no terrorist gunmen in the area laying in ambush. After the soldiers left the helicopter it quickly ascended and hovered until receiving the 'all clear signal' to land the search dog team on the ground. After quickly surveying the premises the dog team, under the watchful eye of its Army protectors and Flight Sergeant Greenaway began the slow methodical search of the farm buildings. It did not take the dog long however, to indicate the presence of something suspicious and the team were duly withdrawn so that the ATO could make a more detailed search of the site. Although no 'real explosives' were discovered that day a great quantity of spent ammunition was found which confirmed reports that para-military gunmen had indeed been using the isolated farm as a training area and range for their weapon practice. Forensically, of course, spent ammunition cases, having been expelled from a weapon during firing, left unique marks that could later be matched to the weapon they had been fired from. Additionally, the forensic scientist could obtain finger-prints from the shell cases and also tell intelligence specialists exactly what type and how many weapons had been used at the site and if any of those weapons could be matched to previous incidents. As such, the spent shell cases were gathered up and handled as important evidence. During that period, the dog teams had regularly discovered explosives and weapons concealed in a variety of locations, earning for themselves the respect of the ATO's and the various Army units they worked with.

In a tragic incident a little later, another RAF Police specialist dog handler; Corporal D I'anson, working in Northern Ireland, narrowly escaped serious injury and death when a terrorist bomb went off close to where he was working. The blast occurred at number 72 Straban Old Road in Londonderry, which at the time was part of the 4th Battalion IRA (Waterside) Division. At 3.20pm on Sunday the 9th December, an anonymous caller telephoned the Area Army Operations Room using the *Confidential Phone* stating that a bomb had been planted in either number 70 or 72 Straban Old Road. An Army patrol had been despatched and they had requested the presence of a specialist dog team trained to detect the presence of explosives and firearms. For some reason that afternoon, the duty dog handler from the Royal Welsh Fusiliers Regiment was absent from the office and could not be contacted. However, Corporal I'anson having just completed an earlier assignment heard the request for assistance and took the call and drove over to a pre-determined point on Straban Old Road, where he met up with the patrol from the 1st Battalion Royal Regiment of Fusiliers. At that point, the young 2nd lieutenant in charge of the patrol briefed Corporal I'anson on the nature of the anonymous telephone call and confirmed that the area had been secured. After sorting out his equipment and his Labrador dog, Air Dog Bruce, Corporal I'anson carried out an external inspection of both houses and noted that number 70 was totally bricked up and that the only way inside was via number 72. Although local enquiries revealed that children had been playing in and around number 72 earlier that day, Corporal I'anson's thoughts were of number 70, the inside of which was in total darkness, and that any bomb inside could be triggered by light sensitive devices or by pressure pads or trip wires.

It was always a nightmare scenario to consider that the objective of the terrorist was simply to kill members of the security forces at every opportunity. It was also known that the IRA used the *Confidential Telephone* hotline to report incidents in an effort to get the security forces into a position where they could be ambushed or blown up by a hidden bomb. Conscious of all those factors, Corporal I'anson and Air Dog Bruce carefully entered number 72 through a ground floor window and not through the door. Just like those fearless *'warriors'* of the bomb disposal units, the work of the specialist search dog teams, was extremely dangerous and for the team involved in a search of that nature it was a particularly lonely time knowing that the terrorist had spent a great deal of his time designing and placing his bomb so as to kill those sent in to try and find and disarm it. Having carefully checked the ground floor and confirming that it was all clear, Corporal I'anson and Air Dog Bruce carefully checked under the stairs for evidence of any new floorboards, pressure pads or anything else unusual. Noting that there were none, they made preparations to go upstairs. At that point, Corporal I'anson was standing at the bottom of the stairs and gave the command for Bruce to start his ascent. Air Dog Bruce went up the first three stairs to a point where they turned up and to the left. Corporal I'anson clearly remembers that the last sight he had of his dog was that of his wagging tail disappearing from view around the bend in the stairs. At that moment things changed and everything seemed to be happening in slow motion and Corporal I'anson describes seeing a large hot orange ball rolling down the stairs and a strong force hitting him in the chest and lifting him from the ground. As he looked up he saw the roof falling in on him. Knowing there was what he assumed to be a window to his right he quickly picked himself up and dived through it. However, what he had not realised at that point was that the blast had lifted him back and upwards through the ceiling into the bedroom above where he had been originally standing. It was not the ceiling coming down to him but him being forced up in the air to ceiling. As a consequence, the window he jumped out of was in fact the first floor bedroom window and not the ground floor window. The reason he remembered that fact was that it took what seemed like ages for him to land on the back yard paving stones. At that point, everything seemed to speed up again and realising what had just happened he quickly managed to scale the eight-foot back yard wall to get out into the street where soldiers immediately came to his aid.

Shortly after, he was taken to Altnalgelvin Hospital in Londonderry where a six-inch nail, from the bomb, was removed from his left elbow and he was treated for various cuts, bruises and perforated eardrums. He was indeed a very lucky man that day and although injured, he had been able to walk away from the incident, which had been arranged by the IRA to kill him. Unfortunately, Air dog Bruce his Labrador, was not so lucky and died instantly doing the job that he so much enjoyed. His remains were recovered from the house and he was later buried with dignity in front of the Headquarters of the 1st Battalion Royal Regiment of Fusiliers in Londonderry. At the time, all the RAF Police specialist search dog handlers who worked in Londonderry had a special affinity with the Royal Regiment of Fusiliers who were serving in the Province on a two-year tour of duty. The dog handlers were also granted honorary 'Geordie' status and were issued with a regimental cap badge, which included the regiment's red and white hackle.

The terrorist responsible for planting the bomb that injured Corporal I'anson and killed Air Dog Bruce; a sixteen-year old boy, was later arrested by Major Moore the officer commanding 'Y' Company, 1st Battalion Royal Regiment of Fusiliers and his men. Later at his trial, held in Belfast Crown Court, the boy, who despite his age, held the rank of quartermaster sergeant with the 4th Battalion

IRA (Waterside) Division, was found guilty as charged and sentenced to thirty-five years imprisonment.

Shortly after recovering from the incident, Corporal I'anson returned to normal duties at the RAF Police Depot Debden. He had joined the RAF in 1967 and after completing his police and dog training at RAF Debden he had first been posted to RAF Machrihanish, on the west coast of Scotland. In 1968 he had been detached to RAF Ballykelly in Northern Ireland just as the troubles were starting to get serious. After returning briefly to Machrihanish he had been posted overseas to RAF Seletar in Singapore but when that unit closed he had been transferred over to RAF Tengah. Shortly before RAF Seletar was formally handed over to the Singapore Armed Forces (SAF) Corporal I'anson had occasion one night to release his dog against two intruders inside the weapons storage area that he was guarding. While his dog had tackled one of the intruders Corporal I'anson had tackled the other. The two men, however, turned out to be members of the SAF who had not been told that a RAF Police dog team were on duty at the site. Unfortunately, the man tackled by the dog had his leg very badly bitten. After completing his tour of duty in the Far East, Corporal I'anson had been posted back to the RAF Police Depot where he became one of the men responsible for touring the country inspecting and receiving gift dogs from the public. Later, after qualifying as a specialist search dog handler he and Air Dog Bruce had been posted to Londonderry in Northern Ireland.

During the 1973 Annual United Kingdom RAF Police Dog Championship Trials the top three prizes were awarded to, Corporal D Simpson and Air Dog Roby, Corporal A Ritchie and Air D0og Sindy, and Corporal B Lambert and Air Dog Zaine. During the first dog trials held by the RAF Police on the island of Malta the top two awards went to, Corporal R Laird and Air Dog Kim and Corporal Cook and Air Dog Max.

Although 1973, saw the withdrawal of American forces from Vietnam and the ending of the war there soon after, the troubles continued in Northern Ireland and tension was further escalated when the IRA terrorists moved their bloody bombing campaign onto the British mainland, with a view of bringing their struggle closer to the minds of the British people and of course in the hope of blackmailing the government into withdrawing its troops from the Province.

In January 1974, Air Commodore Shephard retired as the Provost Marshal and was succeeded in post by Air Commodore B C Player CBE, another professional Provost Officer, who prior to joining the RAF in 1942, had been a former member of the Hampshire Constabulary. Initially, he had qualified as a pilot, but became a provost officer in early 1947. During the period leading up to independence in August 1947, he had served in troubled India. Prior to being promoted and taking up his appointment, he had been the RAF Germany Command Provost & Security Officer.

The IRA campaign of violence on the British mainland continued to kill and maim mainly innocent civilians. An IRA bomb detonated inside the Tower of London killed a female tourist from New Zealand and seriously injured forty-one school children, while a bomb placed on a military coach travelling along the M62 motorway killed ten soldiers, a woman and her young child. Public houses were bombed in Birmingham, Woolwich and Guildford, killing and horribly injuring many more innocent and vulnerable victims, whilst continuing to sicken and anger the British population.

In the spring, Corporal A Oliver, who had joined the RAF Police as a dog handler the year before, was posted into RAF Wildenrath in West Germany with his German Shepherd dog; Air dog Ben. At the time the RAF Germany Harrier *'jump jet'* Force was based on the unit and three times each year the Harrier squadrons would leave the comfort of RAF Wildenrath to take part in NATO military training exercises and as such, would deploy somewhere out in the German countryside at various improvised sites. Because the sites chosen were usually on non-military owned property such as farm land, they attracted a lot of interest from the public at large and anyone else for that matter that might have an interest in what the RAF were up to. Therefore, security at the sites was provided by the RAF Police NCOs from various units within Germany, backed up with NCOs from the HQ P&SS(UK) Support Squadron based in Wiltshire. During the hours of darkness security was enhanced around the sites by RAF Police dog teams who prevented unauthorised persons from getting anywhere near the aircraft or its supporting equipment. All members of the RAF Police engaged on that commitment were 'live armed', that is to say, they carried weapons with live ammunition, as opposed to the 'blank ammunition' carried by other RAF personnel who were involved in the exercise. As such, they were not classified as being involved in the *'exercise play'* and remained on operational duty and whenever an exercise incident occurred at the site, the RAF Police quietly withdrew to the background until the incident was terminated by one of the *umpires*. Having said, that, the RAF Police NCOs worked extremely hard during the deployment to integrate and were always on hand to assist the site commander, the aircrew, ground crew and the Army engineers in resolving all sorts of problems that invariably cropped up. During one such deployment, Corporal Oliver and his colleague Corporal L J Martin designed and erected a sign at the entrance to the field that was being used by the Harriers to take-off and land. The sign read in both English and German, 'Attention: If you can run across this field in twenty-five seconds you are in big trouble, because RAF Police dogs Ben and Bruno can do it in ten seconds'. It seemed to have the desired effect.

On the island of Cyprus on the 15th July, a military coup took place by senior officers of the Greek National Guard against the government of Cyprus and a state of emergency was declared. The officers were seeking union with Greece. All British military personnel were confined to camp while the families of British service personnel living in off base rented accommodation were trapped in their homes. As the day progressed personnel at RAF Akrotiri could hear the sound of heavy gunfire emanating from the direction of Limassol. Over the days that followed the overall situation in Cyprus began to deteriorate, it was decided to evacuate all the families of British service personnel from the outlying towns and bring them onto the military bases. Refugees of all nationalities began arriving at RAF Akrotiri, including thousands of tourists of different nationalities who had been caught completely off-guard by the military coup. A refugee reception centre was set up to cope with their needs. All refugees, except for families of service personnel, were being flown out of Cyprus as soon as possible. With hundreds of refugees leaving RAF Akrotiri each day their cars were being left on the camp and it was starting to pose a further problem. A RAF Police sergeant was given the task of sorting the problem out and from that point on, any refugee leaving the camp was instructed to write out a label showing their name, address, passport number, registration number and the make of their car. They were then instructed to attach the label to their car keys and leave them in the guardroom for the sergeant to collect. A large temporary car park was marked out on land at the rear of the dog section and half a dozen dog handlers were employed on rounding up the cars, parking them and taking the keys to back to the sergeant for safe keeping. As the situation continued to deteriorate Turkish Armed forces invaded Cyprus on the 20th July, in order to protect the Turkish Cypriots living there. As the situation became clearer it seemed that the Turks were only intent on occupying the Northern half of the island. Consequently, Greek Cypriots in the north fled south and Turkish Cypriots in the south fled north, and in the confusion many were killed, wounded or simply went missing.

During the summer, Corporal J Bastard, having completed twenty-three years service, left the RAF. After completing his overseas tour of duty at RAF Sharjah in December 1970 he was posted briefly to the dog section at RAF Waddington before moving a few months later to his final posting at RAF Abingdon where he was employed on general police duties within the guardroom.

Corporal S Benson and Air dog Kyla, having only been at RAF St Mawgan for a year, were posted to RAF Bishops Court in Northern Ireland during the month of August. During his time at St Mawgan he remembers being on duty with another dog handler during the unit's Annual Open Day and Air Show, when a distressed member of the public came up to them carrying a little black dog all wrapped up in a jacket. Upon investigation however, it actually turned out to be a little white dog that had fallen into an oil waste pit behind one of the aircraft hangars. The dog was in quite a mess and the owner had no idea what to do. However, the two RAF Police dog handlers, being knowledgeable about such matters, knew that grease applied to the dog's coat would be of great benefit in lifting out the oil from its fur. So, the owner and his dog were sent directly to the Airman's Mess, where quantities of butter applied to the dog's coat had the desired effect of bringing out the oil. A warm, soapy shower afterwards had the dog back to normal, much to the delight and gratitude of its owner.

The journey over to RAF Bishops Court started early one Friday morning when a RAF driver took Corporal Benson and his dog to Bodmin railway station where they caught a train up to Crewe. As was normal practice at the time, RAF Police dog handlers and their dogs travelled in the guard's van during journeys by train and although the dog was not in a transit kennel on this occasion, she was, for safety reasons, wearing a muzzle. Unfortunately, the journey was not quite as straightforward as it should have been. After only a couple of hours into the journey the rocking movement of the train upset the dog's stomach, causing a diarrhoea attack. After dealing with that problem the train duly arrived in Crewe, which was where they had to change to catch the train to Heysham Ferry. Unfortunately, they had just missed the connection and were told that the next train to Heysham Ferry was not until the following day. At that point, Corporal Benson contacted the local police who were very helpful indeed and while Corporal Benson was taken to RAF Stafford for the night, his dog was accommodated in the local police dog kennels.

The following day they were reunited and returned to Crewe station where they caught the train to the ferry terminal. However, when they arrived, they discovered that they had several hours to wait before the ferry sailed. As a consequence, Corporal Benson and his dog passed the waiting hours by joining forces with a British Transport Police officer and his dog, and together they went off to conduct a foot patrol around the docks, an event that certainly raised a few eyebrows from a great many of those employed at the docks.

It was early evening when they finally boarded the ferryboat to Belfast, and as Corporal Benson secured his dog in the kennels, which were on the car deck way below, he wondered whether the rest of his journey would be trouble free. After leaving his dog to settle for the night he went off to find his own cabin, which turned out to contain four bunks with no room for anything else. At least it was a bed, he thought, as he went off to find something to eat. Shortly after, the boat set sail and pretty quickly encountered very rough seas. As the vessel seemed not to possess stabilisers the boat was tossed about and the many of the passengers, including Corporal Benson and a great number of Irish Manchester United football supporters who were returning home, started to feel seasick. Consequently, Corporal Benson did not get much sleep that night and was up early to check on his dog, who it seemed had coped pretty well. Shortly after docking, Corporal Benson and his dog disembarked only to find that the pre-arranged transport to take them to RAF Bishops Court was not there. After a few hasty telephone calls, Corporal Benson and his dog were whisked off to a nearby Army barracks to await transport from RAF Bishops Court. Later that afternoon after quite an epic journey Air Dog Kyla was finally lead into her new home and given a well-earned meal, while Corporal Benson was introduced into the RAF Police Club and served a pint of Guinness. Once settled in to their new surrounding, Corporal Benson and his dog found themselves patrolling the unit during the hours of darkness to ensure that any threat from the IRA was kept well away. At the time, there was a *'Hearts and Minds'* holiday scheme in operation, whereby teenagers from conflict-torn Belfast, were taken up to Bishops Court for short breaks and were accommodated in a number of surplus military married quarters outside the camp but close to the beach. The scheme, however, was not without its problems, and it was a common occurrence for the teenagers to go on the rampage at night after consuming one or more Guinness's too many. Indeed, when fired up, a number of them, tried to break into the military base, but were unsuccessful, due mainly to the alertness of the RAF Police dog handlers on duty.

During year the RAF Police School had moved from RAF Debden to RAF Newton, near Nottingham but the dog training school had remained behind for a while longer, until work on a new kennel complex had been completed. Unfortunately, with the move to RAF Newton, the title 'RAF Police Depot' was lost once again and the school reverted to being just another lodger unit, occupying space on the station.

On the 21st September, the winners of the Annual RAF Germany dog trials held at RAF Wildenrath were judged to be, Corporal P Thompson and Air Dog Yoss, Corporal K Ryan and Air Dog Zardi, and Corporal G Pace with Air Dog Tarnia.

During the month of June 1975, the British people confirmed by referendum that they wanted to become members of the EEC and the author; Corporal S R Davies, having successfully completed his initial police training left the RAF Police School at RAF Newton for his first posting at RAF Wyton in Cambridgeshire. It had been his intention on joining the RAF in January, to become a dog handler, but after a fact-finding visit to the dog training school at RAF Debden, he had decided against specialising in that area after discovering that handler and dog were not teamed up for life as he first thought. The realisation of having a dog for a few years and then giving it up for another on posting was too distressing for the author to deal with.

On the 16th September, the winners of the Annual RAF Germany dog trials held at RAF Wildenrath were judged to be, Corporal Pace and Air Dog Tarnia, Corporal Balchin and Air Dog Sheba, and Corporal Grint with Air Dog Tex. In the Annual United Kingdom Dog Championship Trials the winner was declared as Corporal J Chapman from RAF Aldergrove with Air Dog Kelly.

During the previous year both PMDI's had been relocated from the Head-quarters Strike Command at RAF High Wycombe to RAF P&SS (Northern Region) at RAF Spitalgate just outside Grantham. Still under the control of Strike Command, the move enabled the dog inspectors to be nearer to the larger dog sections in Lincolnshire and East Anglia. Their time at RAF Spitalgate, however, was short because in latter part of 1975 the unit closed and the two dog inspectors were duly posted to the newly formed RAF Police Dog Training Squadron at RAF Newton, which had recently transferred from RAF Debden. The move of course, enabled the dog inspectors to have direct daily contact with the training staff, who could also be kept up to date with operational conditions out on the units. For the first time the training of specialist dogs and up-to-date training methods could regularly be observed by the dog inspectors and that in turn enabled a greater degree of liaison to be established between them and the staff at the training school.

At the time, increasing use was being made of drug detection dogs within the services and on one occasion Royal Navy commanders requested a drug detection demonstration from one of the RAF Police dog teams. Flight Sergeant Greenaway accompanied the team that was sent down to Portsmouth to demonstrate their expertise. Shortly after their arrival a naval commander explained that the Royal Navy was experiencing problems with drug related offences and as part of the policy they were introducing they were thinking of having their ships searched for the presence of illicit drugs as soon as they returned from foreign places. The subsequent demonstration was carried out on board a ship where a sample of drugs had been hidden inside lagging around pipes below deck. The dog team had no idea where the drugs were hidden but in any case it did not matter because as soon as the dogs entered that part of the ship they quickly indicated to their handlers where the drugs were and they were duly recovered. The naval commanders were very impressed with the demonstration and later adopted the policy of searching their ships with drug detection dogs belonging to the Ministry of Defence Police based in naval ports.

In 1976 following the move to RAF Newton Mr C Gilmore, a civilian instructor employed at the RAF Police Dog Training Squadron, moved into the Course Design Cell where the detailed planning of training courses and the constant revision and updating of existing courses and training aids was carried out. During training each student was required to pass what were known as the *Essential Skills Tests* (EST) and the *Essential Knowledge Tests* (EKT) and to ensure that each student was correctly assessed to the same standard by all the instructors, a comprehensive guide was produced by the staff of the Course Design Cell clearly outlining the specifications. So successful was the new assessment procedure that soon after its introduction it attracted a great deal of interest from other dog training establishments around the country such as the Civil Police, HM Prison Service and the Guide Dogs for the Blind.

In February, Air Commodore Player retired from the service and was succeeded in post as the Provost Marshal by Air Commodore G Innes CBE MBIM, another professional Provost Officer, and one of the RAF investigators who in 1968, had arrested Senior Technician Douglas Ronald Britten who had been spying for the Russians for many years.

Unfortunately, in the spring of 1976, in line with the United Kingdom's ongoing defence review the RAF base on the island of Gan in the Indian Ocean was closed. As the RAF made their final withdrawal from the region, they left behind the local population to re-organise their lives, which had for so long revolved around the RAF presence there. In addition, the locally recruited unit of RAF Police Auxiliaries was disbanded and the RAF Police dogs were transferred to Cyprus and other units in the Persian Gulf.

After only eighteen months of being at RAF Bishops Court, for some unexplained reason known only to the RAF, Corporal S Benson was reassigned onto general police duties for the last six months of his tour of duty. Accordingly, he had to take Air Dog Kyla back to the RAF Police Dog Training Squadron to be re-teamed with another dog handler. When they arrived, a young kennel-maid asked Corporal Benson why he was crying, but he just found it all too difficult to explain to her the bond that had been formed with his dog; living, working and playing together for two and a half years. It was a very sad NCO indeed who returned to RAF Bishops Court a few days later. At the end of his tour in Northern Ireland, Corporal Benson was offered a new posting back on dog handling duties but he declined it, not wanting to repeat the emotional upset of getting too attached to another dog. Consequently, he remained on general police duties for the rest of his career.

At RAF Debden on the 25th September, the three winning teams taking part in the Annual United Kingdom RAF Police Dog Championship Trials were, Corporal D Simpson and Air Dog Roby, Corporal S McArdle and Air Dog Justin, and Corporal N Lake with Air Dog Pax.

Later that month, after one of the hottest and driest British summers on record since the 18th Century, Mr Charles Fricker retired and handed over his appointment and responsibilities as the Chief Training Officer (Dogs), to Mr Terry McHaffie, who had been his deputy for many years. During his time in charge of training police dogs, Mr Fricker had ensured that the dogs were exposed to as much publicity as possible, which had included many appearances on television at home and abroad. Over the years his methods in doing so, had been extremely effective. The public at large had a very healthy respect for the branch and its dogs, which they had continued to donate to the RAF over the years. Indeed, whenever the RAF Police Dog Demonstration Team appeared in public, as they frequently did around the country, the shows were always very well attended and that of course proved to be one of the organisations' best public relations exercises. Mr McHaffie, himself an expert dog trainer, and a former RAF Police dog handler, possessed, like his two predecessors, a great understanding and affection for the German Shepherd dog and worked tirelessly to promote their use as police dogs. Indeed, for many years he held a special relationship with a snow-white German Shepherd dog known as Air Dog Bull, who became one of the first dogs to be successfully employed by the RAF Police on search duties. Air Dog Bull continued to serve with the branch until he was almost twelve years old.

Even the best trained RAF Police dogs can quickly revert to their natural instincts given certain circumstances. For example when two dogs get close to each other they invariably want to fight. As such, it is normal practice to keep dogs apart when they are working, especially if they have a tendency to attack and fight each other; having said that, the safeguards can sometimes fail. Such a problem occurred late one evening in October 1976 at RAF Wyton in Cambridgeshire during a shift changeover of two dogs and their handlers. Unfortunately, that evening the normal transport used by the dog handlers was in the servicing section undergoing repairs and the replacement vehicle happened to be a three-ton truck. As Corporal M P Sutton and Air Dog Simba were climbing out of the truck to begin their shift, Corporal Sutton slipped and lost control of his dog which immediately went for Air Dog Prince who was standing nearby with his handler Corporal M Greenley.

Although the fight that ensued was brief and the two dogs were quickly brought back under control, it was still long enough and serious enough for

Prince to have bitten the end off one of Simba's ears. As Prince was taken away, Corporal Sutton quickly applied a first aid dressing to the injured dog and managed to locate the bitten off piece of his ear. The police patrol was summoned and the injured dog, the piece of ear and Corporal Sutton were whisked off to the veterinary surgeon in nearby Huntingdon where Simba was examined by the duty vet. During the treatment, the piece of ear that had been bitten off was stitched back on and Simba was given a few days off in the isolation kennel to recover from his ordeal. As was normal practice under such circumstances, Corporal's Sutton and Greenley spent the rest of the night writing reports explaining what had happened. After a week or so, the bandages were taken off Simba and although he had one slightly floppy ear from that point on, the operation to reattach the ear had been successful and the dog suffered no adverse effects from the ordeal.

The Dog Training Squadron having moved to RAF Newton held the 1977 Annual United Kingdom RAF Police Dog Championship Trials at RAF Syerston, a satellite unit not far from Newton that was used for dog training. After a tough competition, the three winning teams were declared to be, Corporal G Pace and Air Dog Merlin, Corporal S McArdle and Air Dog Justin, and Corporal Davies with Air Dog Sheba. At the Annual RAF Germany dog trials Corporal Dowers and Air Dog Shane took first place, Corporal Draper and Air Dog Rebel came second, and Corporal Hodge and Air Dog Prince came in third position.

As part of the nationwide Silver Jubilee celebrations to commemorate the reign of Her Majesty Queen Elizabeth II, the largest ever Royal Review of the RAF took place on 29th July at RAF Finningley near Doncaster. Her Majesty and Prince Phillip arrived at the review accompanied by five other members of the Royal family. A huge number of her government ministers, foreign ambassadors and high commissioners, members of the Air Force Board and a host of other VIP's had also been invited to attend the review. Additionally, some ten thousand servicemen and their families and five hundred members of the media were also present.

The review comprised a ceremonial parade followed by the Royal party and the VIP's being given an escorted tour around the impressive indoor exhibition, after which they were entertained during a formal luncheon. After lunch, the Royal party conducted an informal walkabout and had the opportunity to meet and speak to some of the invited quests. Finally, the Royal party and the assembled guests were entertained by an impressive full flying display that included a demonstration given by a pilot flying his Harrier '*jump jet*'. The RAF Police were present throughout ensuring that there were no security problems but a number were present at three static display units in the exhibition hall, depicting the RAF

Police involvement in aircraft security, dog handling and special investigations. Indeed, as the Royal party were shown around the displays, both the Queen and the Queen Mother were delighted with what they saw and spoke at length to the NCOs manning the stands. At the end of the review and after an extremely busy day, the RAF Police remained in place and braced themselves for the arrival the following day, of some two hundred thousand cars, coaches and motorcycles, carrying the public for the RAF Finningley Open Day.

In 1978 following a very successful two-year trial period during which two RAF Police drug detection dogs handled by former RAF Police NCOs; Mr V Jones and Mr J Morley, had proved their effectiveness in combating the illegal importation of illicit drugs, Her Majesty's Commissioner of Customs & Excise decided to form a national force of drug detection dogs to detect the smuggling of heroin and cannabis. During the previous year the two dogs and their handlers had recovered nearly £2 million worth of drugs from ships, freight sheds, passenger luggage, letters and parcels. In May 1978, the RAF Police School was selected as the most suitable and qualified establishment in the country to undertake the program of training the forty additional HM Customs & Excise handlers and their dogs required for the task. A new training cell was established within the Dog Training Squadron and soon after, the twelve-week training program commenced under the watchful eye of Flight Sergeant J Coulson.

Mr Jones had served in the RAF Police for twenty-three years prior to being offered an initial two-year contract with HM Customs & Excise. In May 1953, having been a police cadet with the Devon Constabulary, he enlisted into the RAF and after completing his recruit and initial police training had been selected to train as a dog handler. Unfortunately, because of an outbreak of disease within the kennels, all dog training courses were cancelled and the dogs were quarantined. In November he was posted to RAF Hereford where he carried out station police and provost duties, however, after being promoted to substantive corporal he was posted to RAF Padgate and St Merryn. In early 1956 he was posted overseas and was sent to join the Provost Detachment based at RAF Akrotiri in Cyprus. At the height of the EOKA terrorist campaign, Corporal Jones carried out mobile patrols and anti-assassination duties within the town of Limassol and it was during that tour that he was mentioned in dispatches.

During February 1959, his tour in Cyprus came to an end and he was posted home to RAF Northolt for a brief period. After successfully completing his Counter-Intelligence training he was promoted to sergeant and posted to Headquarters Transport Command. In July 1964 he was posted overseas again to RAF Tengah in Singapore and was initially employed on general police duties, however, half way through his tour of duty, he was detailed by the officer commanding the RAF Police, to take charge of the very large RAF Police dog section. Although he had no experience as a dog handler, his appointment came about because Flight Lieutenant A E G Hales, himself a future Provost Marshal, wanted an experienced senior NCO in charge of the section. At the time, the dog section at Tengah was a mix of RAF Police and locally appointed RAF Police Auxiliary dog handlers. Although it was a steep learning curve for Sergeant Jones, he was fortunate enough to have Corporal D Remnant, a very experienced dog handler, on hand as his deputy, to help ease him into his strange new job. During November 1966, after a most successful tour of duty at RAF Tengah, Sergeant Jones was posted back to the United Kingdom to RAF Wittering where he was employed again on general police duties, but before long found himself in charge of the dog section, which at the time, had two very capable dog handlers; Corporal's J Yates and Kennedy, on strength to assist him. During his tour, given that he had been placed in charge of two dog sections up until that point, Sergeant Jones was sent to the RAF Police Depot at Debden where he successfully completed a dog handling course.

In June 1969, having acquired a 'hands-on approach' to dog handling, Sergeant Jones was posted overseas again to the HQ FEAF in Singapore where he assumed the appointment of Dog Inspector for the RAF Police dog sections operating in Singapore, Malaya, Hong Kong and Gan. During the period leading up to the RAF withdrawal from Singapore in 1971 Sergeant Jones was involved in the planning process; liaising with the Singapore Armed Forces (SAF) in respect of training their staff as dog handlers and for handing over RAF dogs. RAF Seletar in Singapore was chosen as the base from which to conduct the training of SAF personnel and Sergeant R Chester, himself a very experienced dog handler, was detailed to take charge of the project. One of the more unpleasant tasks that Sergeant Jones undertook during that period was to liaise with the staff from the Royal Army Veterinary Corps (RAVC) to ensure that no pet dogs were abandoned in Singapore by British Forces after their withdrawal. With the help of a number of dog handlers led by Sergeant G Herd, all unwanted and stray dogs were rounded up and humanely destroyed by RAVC personnel.

After an extremely busy and successful tour of duty with HQ FEAF, Sergeant Jones returned to the United Kingdom and was posted to RAF Waddington as the senior NCO in charge of the dog section. During 1974, Sergeant Jones was promoted and after successfully completing a PMDI training course was posted to the RAF Police Depot at Debden as the Flight Sergeant in charge of dog training. Shortly after taking up his appointment, he was informed that RAF Police training was being transferred to RAF Newton and as such he would be part of the team involved in planning the move. At the end of 1975, he moved to new dog training facilities at RAF Newton and after settling in to their new environment, the Dog Training Squadron received a visit from senior officers from HM Customs & Excise who were keen to see the RAF Police drug detection dogs in action. Flight Sergeant Jones was detailed to show the customs officers around and it was soon after that he was offered the two-year contact to join HM Customs & Excise to establish their drug detection dog teams. Together with Sergeant Morley, he joined HM Customs & Excise on the 3rd May 1976 and while he teamed up with a black Labrador called Brumby, Mr Morley teamed up with another Labrador called Brandy. After being briefed on their duties at Fetter Lane; the Investigation Division HQ of HM Customs & Excise, the two former RAF Police NCOs and their dogs began work throughout England, Scotland and Wales. In addition to searching for drugs the dog teams were also tasked with educating staff in areas where drug detection was not considered a priority.

It might be hard to believe, but initially, the Customs & Excise Union were worried that the use of drug detection dogs would lead to a reduction in staff. Fortunately, in the early days the teams were working at the Port of Dover checking incoming cars, when Air Dog Brumby indicated on the back seat of a Citroen car. The rummage crew took the car away for examination and after two hours stated that the car was 'clean'. The investigation officer Mr P Cooper, who was with the dog handlers, insisted that the rummage crew should continue looking for concealed drugs. After a further examination ten kilos of Cannabis was discovered hidden in the petrol tank that had been modified with a fibre-glass partition allowing petrol to be put in one side while the Cannabis was placed in the dry inner portion of the petrol tank. As a result, a man and woman were arrested; the rummage crew were delighted with the overtime and the good detection result, and officials within the union seemed happy.

A senior Air Officer, who will remain nameless, was visiting the RAF Police Dog Training Squadron on a tour of inspection. During his visit he observed various aspects of dog training and was treated to various demonstrations to prove just how effective the training program was. He was very impressed by what he was shown but the best was, as they say, left until last. As he was about to complement the staff on their efforts he was informed about the 'latest break through' in dog training. He listened with interest when a member of staff briefed him that the squadron had just successfully completed training a dog to find 'lost' secret documents.

The Air Officer looked stunned that such a remarkable breakthrough had been achieved. He knew only to well that whenever, classified files were reported missing an investigation team would strip search the offices or the registry where the file was normally stored to ensure that it had not merely fallen down behind a filing cabinet or had even been mis-filed. The practice although being highly disruptive, invariably produced results and thereby saved an incredible amount of subsequent investigation work. Once briefed, the Air Officer witnessed a final demonstration where a police dog was brought into a registry where a secret file had gone missing.

Shortly after entering the room the dog became excited at one particular filing cabinet and tried to get behind it. The handler approached and with some help pulled the heavy cabinet away from the wall. The dog leapt into the space and quickly came out wagging its tail and with the 'missing' secret file in its jaws. The Air Officer was very impressed and asked the trainer how on earth he had managed to train the dog in such a way. At that point, various sniggers around the room informed the Air Officer that he had been had. The dog had not in fact been trained to find lost files but had been trained to detect the drug cannabis. What the trainer had done prior to the demonstration was to rub some cannabis resin onto the file. The dog, during the demonstration, had merely been doing what he had been trained to do - detect cannabis. Of course, the Air Officer concerned was known to possess a rather keen sense of humour, was very pro-police, and therefore, the commanding officer at the RAF Police School, when briefed beforehand, had agreed to allow the prank to proceed. Luckily, for him and the pranksters, the Air Officer, when informed of how it had been done that afternoon was delighted not only with the professionalism of the squadron but also by the fact that the instructors possessed a good sense of humour; a sure and genuine sign of high morale.

Back in the days when 'half-time' entertainment at football matches was in its infancy, the RAF Police Dog Demonstration Team were giving their usual polished performance at the Dell football ground in Southampton. The finale of their display was an attack by a police dog to apprehend and arrest the 'criminal'. On that particular occasion however, the dog team had not banked on the actions of a civil police constable who had probably been distracted when the attack display had started. As the criminal ran towards the centre of the pitch the RAF Police dog handler issued his warning for him to stop and stand still, a warning that the criminal ignored. At that point the handler released his dog and that is when the constable launched himself into action from the edge of the pitch, and ran towards the fleeing criminal to arrest him. Of course, the crowd thought it was all part of the display, until the commentator on his microphone screamed at the constable to stand still as it was only a display taking place. Suddenly the constable stopped dead in his tracks and in front of 20,000 hooting spectators, realised that he had made a huge error. At that point, he slowly turned around and hastily made his way back to the edge of the pitch from where he continued his foot patrol, 'tipping' his helmet to the crowd as they continued to cheer him on his way.

During 1978 Air Commodore Innes retired as the Provost Marshal and was succeeded in post by Air Commodore I Young MBE FBIM, another professional Provost Officer, who up until his promotion had been the RAF Germany Command Provost & Security Officer.

Although the RAF Police had, for a number of years, been successfully training various breeds to detect firearms and explosives, all of those trained had been male dogs. However, on the 25th August, Air Dog Bella-Donna, a young black Labrador, handled by Corporal J S McArdle, became the first bitch to be successfully trained in that line of specialist work. The team began their training at the Dog Training Squadron on the 17th May.

At the Annual United Kingdom RAF Police Dog Championship Trials held at RAF Syerston, the three winning teams were judged to be, Corporal Burgess and Air Dog Zimba, Corporal Hendrickson and Air Dog Vaughan, and Corporal Stephenson and Air Dog Shane. At the RAF Germany dog trials the winners were declared as, Corporal R Thomas, Corporal S Skouse and Air Dog Rinty, and Corporal A Rowe and Air Dog Sultan. Additionally, at the competition held within Northern Ireland for all dog teams serving within the Province, the winners were, Corporal Burgess and Air Dog Zimba the reigning United Kingdom Champions, Corporal Young and Air Dog Sheba, and Corporal Maund with Air Dog Kylie.

In the United Kingdom as 1978, drew to a close, industrial relations between the unions and the government deteriorated and the Fire Brigade nationwide were amongst those who went out on strike, causing considerable problems for the senior fire officers and the police who were left to cope with the situation. 'Green Goddess' fire engines, which had originally been used in the late 1940's by the Auxiliary Fire Service, were brought out from storage facilities around the country and the military were called in to man them. Accordingly, a large number of RAF Police NCOs from RAF stations nationwide were detached onto fire fighting operations during the strike.

The RAF finally withdrew from RAF Luqa and indeed, island of Malta on the 31st March 1979. The withdrawal brought to an end another era in the history for both the island and the British military connection with it stretching back over many years. Prior to leaving, the RAF Police dogs were redeployed to RAF Akrotiri in Cyprus.

On the 1st May, Margaret Thatcher became the United Kingdom's first female Prime Minister. With the change of government, many in the Armed Services thought that the Conservative government would improve the overall conditions and free the financial restraints that had been forced upon them by the Labour Party. However, apart from an increase in personal salaries, which had fallen way below those of their civilian counter-parts, the financial squeeze remained in place. When Michael Heseltine became the Defence Secretary he vowed that there would be no increase in manpower for the Armed Services and ordered cutbacks whenever cut backs could be made.

A report sent to the Customs Co-operation Council in Brussels dated the 21st June, highlighted some notable detections by RAF Police drug detection dogs deployed by HM Customs & Excise and stated that during the previous year the two Labrador dogs had recovered nearly £2 million worth of drugs. Cannabis resin, oil and herbal type had been recovered from ships, freight sheds, passenger luggage, letters and parcels. Examples being:

A large seizure was made in August 1978 when one of the dogs was called to examine a diesel generator engine which had been shipped out to Jamaica and later returned to the United Kingdom. The dog picked up the scent several metres away and when the engine was dismantled a total of 129 kilos of herbal Cannabis was found inside the sump, bore holes and flywheel sections of the engine. Enquiries in Birmingham resulted in two arrests.

In a London Post Office Sorting Depot in November 1978 during a routine examination of parcels from Pakistan, one of the dogs indicated on a particular bag of mail. Four wooden candlesticks in a parcel were found to contain glass phials of Cannabis oil and resin. Three people were arrested in connection.

During a routine inspection of a London freight shed in February 1979, a dog indicated on a large crate that had been shipped from Jamaica. The crate contained five items of heavy wooden furniture. Upon closer examination the wood was merely plywood covering the furniture made entirely from compressed herbal Cannabis. When dismantled 155 kilos of Cannabis was recovered. Enquiries revealed that two similar consignments had passed through the shed.

At a Heathrow freight shed in April 1979, a dog chewed the corner off a large cardboard package and uncovered one of thirteen packages, each containing Cannabis Resin. In total 1,089 kilos were seized. False details on the airway bill indicated that the consignment had come from Kuwait but investigation revealed that the drugs came from Jamaica.

At the Annual United Kingdom RAF Police Dog Championship Trials held at RAF Syerston the three winning teams were Corporal Young and Air Dog Lady, Corporal Douglas and Air Dog Bart, and Corporal Henderson and Air Dog Vaughan. At the Annual RAF Cyprus dog trials, held at RAF Akrotiri, the three winning teams were, Corporal D Smellie and Air Dog Kim, Corporal T Crowley and Air Dog Zimba, and RAF Police Auxiliary Constable Photiou with Air Dog

Tina. In RAF Gibraltar the annual competition there was won by Corporal A Milne and Air Dog Bruce, Corporal S Morris and Air Dog Shane, and Corporal M Larkman with Air Dog Jason.

In Northern Ireland, the terrorist campaign was still active and the IRA continued to mount damaging attacks around the Province. Their activity was highlighted to the world on the 27th August, when they carried out two sickening and murderous attacks which shocked the nation. In the first, Earl Louis Mountbatten, his grandson and a local boy were killed and others were injured, when a bomb, planted on his boat, was detonated, while they were fishing off the Irish coast. In the second attack, the IRA killed eighteen soldiers and injured a number of others, during an ambush at Warren Point, close to the border with Eire.

In November, the Officer Commanding P&SS (Northern Ireland), received a signal from the Ministry of Defence, urgently requiring a search dog handler to be flown across to the Shetland Islands to assist members of the Royal Marines Special Boat Service (SBS) and officers from the Northern Constabulary with a rather unusual task. At the time, Corporal D Morgan was serving as a firearms and explosives search dog handler with the unit and was subsequently selected for the job, which involved searching a number of off-shore oil support modules owned by the Shell Oil Company. It was suspected that security of the facilities had been 'compromised' in the Republic of Ireland when they were being built. At the time Group Captain Smart, a former RAF Provost Officer held the appointment as Director of Shell Security and no doubt knew just who to call on to assist with solving his problem. The search operation lasted for four days during which nothing suspicious was found. However, the tasking turned out to be a most valuable experience for Corporal Morgan and his dogs and once again, the co-operation between the RAF Police, the SBS, the civil police and the security staff employed by Shell turned out to be excellent.

At the age of eighty-six years old, Air Commodore O W De Putron, the Provost Marshal who had achieved so much for the branch during its formative years, which included the campaign for taking over control of the MAPGDS in 1944, died at his Devonshire home on the 17th February 1980. Throughout his retirement, the Air Commodore had maintained a lively and tireless interest in the activities and the progress of the branch.

At the RAF Germany Annual dog trials held on the 30th August, at RAF Rheindahlen, the three winning teams from Germany were judged to be, Corporal D Flett and Air Dog King, Corporal R Barton and Air Dog Gandalf, and Corporal I Henderson with Air Dog Brent.

In the United Kingdom, following a breakdown of negotiations between the Prison Officers' Association and the Home Office in October, the prison officer's commenced industrial action and refused to accept further prisoners into the system. That action quickly resulted in chaos with many prisoners being confined in cells at police stations all over the country. As the situation seriously deteriorated and the system was on the point of collapse, military assistance was requested by the government and 'Operation Ruddock', was quickly put into action. In order to relieve the acute problem of prisoners being held within police cells, a temporary prison was hastily established and secured at Rolleston Camp, an Army deployment encampment, located on the bleak Salisbury Plain in Wiltshire. Although the RAF Police NCOs involved in the task, were not employed on custodial duties inside the prison, they nevertheless provided the necessary outer security cordon. As such, the custodial tasks remained the responsibility of the senior prison staff and both Army and RAF personnel detached in from the military detention centres. As the operation got underway, a large number of RAF Police dog handlers were detached into the camp to carry out external security patrols to prevent escapes from succeeding.

Although the RAF Police dogs are extremely well trained, in comparison to the dogs used by the Prison Service, they quickly gained a reputation, amongst the inmates, of being rather savage beasts. Accordingly, no escape attempts were made throughout the entire five-month operation. One of the first dog teams to be deployed to Rolleston was Corporal I Warren and Air Dog Bruno. He recalled that soon after their arrival the RAF dog handlers started to patrol the site wearing their normal green combat fatigues and blue-grey berets. As a result it seemed that the local press became confused because an article in the local paper later that week announced, 'Army dog-handlers arrive at Rolleston Prison'. In response, senior Provost Officers took the unusual step of ordering the dog handlers to wear their RAF Police white hats with their combat fatigues so that everyone would see that they were not soldiers but members of the RAF Police. Unfortunately, the press again became confused and the next published headline read, 'Navy dog-handlers on patrol at prison'. Rolleston, however, quickly filled up to capacity with the new prisoners who arrived there on a daily basis and in an effort to resolve the problem, the Home Office decided to use, ahead of schedule, the newly commissioned and partly completed prison at Frankland in Durham. Obviously, members of the Prison Officers' Association wanted no part in establishing and staffing the partially built complex and so the military were drafted in to run it. However, before plans were agreed to send RAF Police dog handlers there, the industrial action was called off.

At RAF Uxbridge in West London, during the evening on the 8th January 1981, a young RAF musician noticed the smell of petrol coming from somewhere inside his barrack accommodation. When he went to investigate the source of the smell, he was shocked to find three large plastic *'home brew'* beer containers filled with petrol, hidden under the stairs of the ground floor. As he made a closer inspection, he noticed a light blue canvas satchel lying between the containers and although he had no real idea what he was looking at, he suspected the worst. He raised the alarm and had the three-storey brick building evacuated. *Sulva Block* was built just after the Great War and during the early 1940s it had been used as RAF Police School accommodation. It also happened to be the closest building to the perimeter fence and was less than a hundred yards from a bus stop, a busy dual carriageway and a large number of private residential properties, which were all placed at risk. As a result, the musician, together with the Station Warrant Officer and Ministry of Defence Police Constable Barnes, went into the building and removed the three petrol containers. Barnes checked the satchel and saw that it contained a box that held a watch, batteries and wires. He assumed it to be a bomb and therefore left it where it was. As it happened, they only just made it in time, because twenty minutes after it was first discovered, a large explosion ripped through the entire building. Although the accommodation was extensively damaged, no one was hurt. It had been the first time that the IRA had actually attacked a RAF station on the mainland and accordingly it sent a clear message to senior ranking officers that security at the unit was poor. Apparently, the terrorists had been able to take the bomb in with no trouble whatsoever; the main gate had been wide open and there was no real form of controlled entry being exercised. The unit at the time was being policed by the Ministry of Defence Police and there was no dog section established to provide security. As a result of the attack, a number of policy changes were quickly introduced and strict control of entry measures were brought into being at all RAF stations throughout the United Kingdom, in an effort to increase the level of security and of course to prevent a re-occurrence.

On the 22nd February, three RAF Police NCOs; Corporal's P Rendell, McCarthy and Griffiths arrived in Belize, Central America, with their three RAF Police dogs and became the first RAF Police dog section to operate in the region. Although the conditions in Belize were extremely harsh, the dogs quickly acclimatised to the conditions and increased the security protection for the RAF aircraft deployed at Airport Camp. In addition, the three NCOs also had their work cut out in building a makeshift dog section until arrangements could be made to construct a purpose built compound.

At the Annual United Kingdom RAF Police Dog Championship Trials the three winning teams were judged to be Corporal Cloverdale and Air Dog Fang, Corporal Thatcher and Air Dog Sabre, and Corporal Cowling and Air Dog Major. During the first RAF Police dog working trials held up in Scotland at RAF

Lossiemouth, Corporal J McMichael and Air Dog Lady took first place, Corporal D Stamp and Air Dog Rass came second, and Corporal B Warlow and Air Dog King came third. During the Annual RAF Germany dog trials held at RAF Rheindahlen, the three winning teams were judged as, Corporal J England and Air Dog Sabre, Corporal K Riley and Air Dog Tara, and Corporal R Wakefield with Air Dog Prince. During the dog trials held in Cyprus at RAF Akrotiri, the winner of the competition was RAF Police Auxiliary Corporal G Ioannou and Air Dog Todd.

Air Commodore Young retired as the Provost Marshal on the 14th December and was succeeded in post by Air Commodore M J David OBE FBIM, a professional Provost Officer, who prior to taking up his appointment had been the Deputy Director of Security at the Ministry of Defence.

RAF Police Dog Team on patrol of an aircraft dispersal area – Circa early 1980's

The winners of the 1976 UK RAF Police Dog Trials

Members of the RAF Police Auxilliaries with Auxilliary dog handler at RAF Changi in Singapore.

Cpl I Warren and Air dog Bruno guarding the temporary prison at Rolleston Camp
in 1981 during an industrial dispute by HM Prison Officers

The RAF Germany RAF Police Dog Demonstration Team on tour in Berlin

Raising Money for Charity - RAF Police Dog handlers provide an escort for Santa Claus

Obstacle training - The Crawl

Confidence training - Hoops of Fire

5. 1982 – 1991

On the 2nd April 1982, Argentinean forces invaded and occupied the Falkland Islands, an isolated British dependency in the South Atlantic Ocean. While the British government made strong representations to the United Nations Security Council, the Prime Minister, Margaret Thatcher, assembled an impressive military task force to recover the islands by force if required. As part of the process, the RAF Police were placed on standby.

In May, while the task force was heading south and making preparations to recover the Falkland Islands from the occupying Argentinean forces, His Holiness Pope John Paul II, paid his first visit to Britain just a year after he was shot and seriously wounded in Rome during an assassination attempt.

On the 14th June, after a number of fierce battles, the Argentinean forces occupying the Falkland Islands, finally surrendered to the British Task Force Commander and the islands were once again placed firmly under British control.

In London on the 20th July, the IRA detonated bombs in Hyde Park and Regents Park, which resulted in the death of eleven British soldiers, and a number of military horses that were taking part in a ceremonial event.

During the year, Air Dog Brandy one of the first RAF Police drug detection dogs to serve with HM Customs & Excise, and handled by former RAF Police NCO, Mr J Morley, retired after a most successful career to become a family pet in the Morley household. After his dog's retirement Mr Morley became a Preventive Officer at Stanstead Airport. The RAF Police had by 1982, been working with dogs for some forty years, and had earned for itself a reputation second to none. Not only were patrol dogs being trained but the specialist training of the dogs used to detect the presence of drugs and explosives had been a very successful venture. It was therefore, rather pleasing to see that during the year, a well wishing member of the public kindly donated the 10,000th dog into service with the RAF Police.

During September, in the county of Berkshire, the CND movement, which had grown from strength to strength since the late fifties, established its first 'Peace Camp for Women' one night outside RAF Greenham Common, near Newbury. Consequently, the morning press had splashed all over their tabloids just how easy it had been for the women to infiltrate the top-secret base. The unit had been leased to the United States Air Force and had been chosen for the protest because it was suspected of housing Tomahawk cruise missiles capable of carrying nuclear warheads. Within a few hours of the embarrassing incident happening at Greenham Common the telephones at the Ministry of Defence were buzzing with the news, and demands were being made to strengthen security at the base. Indeed, the Prime Minister, Margaret Thatcher, was calling for a tough shake-up of the security procedures adopted at the base. Although the Provost Marshal was given no further resources, a team of RAF Police NCOs under the control of a Squadron Leader Provost Officer was quickly assembled and sent to the base to assist the Americans and Ministry of Defence Police. During the week that followed a number of demonstrators again broke into the less sensitive areas of the unit in an effort to prove just how poor the security arrangements were at the base. Their activities of course, did no actual harm but nevertheless it attracted further attention from the media, who gave the story very wide distribution. As a result of the embarrassing coverage, a decision was taken for a RAF Police flight to be permanently established at the base. Soon after, RAF Police NCOs from stations all around the country suddenly found themselves being detached to RAF Greenham Common for short periods to help control the protestors and more importantly to keep them away from the Americans who had strict orders to shoot first and ask questions later. Once again, RAF Police dog teams played a very important role in patrolling the huge expanse of airfield during the hours of darkness, and the dogs using their keen sense of smell easily indicated the presence of intruders, even on the darkest of nights.

As the professionalism and expertise of the RAF Police Dog Training Squadron continued to grow its reputation attracted considerable interest from other military and police organisations around the world and before long various foreign and Commonwealth students started arriving at the school to be trained as dog handlers at basic and specialist levels.

Up until early 1983, RAF Marham near Kings Lynn had been quite a sleepy hollow, being the home of two Victor tanker squadrons. However, all that had changed when the unit underwent a major rebuild to accept two newly reformed Tornado Squadrons; No 617 (The Dambusters) Squadron and No 27 Squadron. Additionally, a Special Storage Area, which was capable of holding nuclear weapons, was also established at the unit. Along with the build-up of RAF personnel to support the unit's new role, the small RAF Police Flight had also been upgraded to become a Squadron so as to provide the necessary police, security and defence cover required, and lots of additional NCOs had been posted into the unit. At the time the RAF Police & Security Squadron was under the command of Squadron Leader M McGinty who as a flight lieutenant had once been the Officer Commanding the RAF Police Dog Demonstration Team. Squadron Leader McGinty was assisted by Flight Lieutenant's Robinson-Brown and T Peacock and Warrant Officer R Grapes. The squadron once organised comprised six flights; the Headquarters Flight, four flights of RAF Police who provided the daily general duties and who worked in shifts, and finally, the RAF Police dog section, which was under the firm control of Sergeant J S McArdle who had joined the RAF Police in June 1962, and who after completing his training joined the RAF Police Dog Demonstration Team until 1966 when he had been posted to RAF Luqa in Malta. After leaving Malta he completed tours of duty at RAF Waddington, RAF Bishops Court, RAF Laarbruch, RAF Machrihanish, RAF Coningsby, RAF St Mawgan, RAF Honington, Gibraltar, and RAF Aldergrove before being posted to RAF Marham. Additionally, Sergeant McArdle had also qualified as a specialist firearms and explosives and drug detection dog handler. The large newly built dog section comprised all the modern facilities including an office, dispensary, rest room, food preparation room, isolation kennel and ample storage space. The section even had its own hardworking kennel maid Carol to look after the day-to-day welfare of the dogs. The duties of the dog handlers at RAF Marham was simply to patrol the external perimeter of the Special Storage Area and the dispersal areas on which the Victor tankers aircraft were parked at night. As the Tornado aircraft belonging to No 27 Squadron and No 617 Squadron were secured in special hardened aircraft shelters that were protected by reinforced concrete, thick steel doors and intruder alarms, they did not require constant protection by dog teams. With so many young newly qualified acting corporals at the dog section, Sergeant McArdle had his work cut out to ensure that they all attended the regular periods of continuation training, during which they were teamed up with more experienced dog handlers, who quickly helped them to hone their skills and integrate into the team.

On the 23rd April, the Station Commander of RAF Waddington near Lincoln, Group Captain J Laycock, exercised his right to march personnel from his station through the City of Lincoln. Three flights were paraded; two with fixed bayonets representing Operations Wing and No 50 Squadron and a third representing the RAF Police Squadron, commanded at that time by Squadron Leader D Gibbard. The RAF Police element comprised twelve dog handlers and their dogs and a RAF Police Range Rover borrowed for the parade from the Headquarters Provost & Security Services (UK) based at RAF Rudloe Manor. The parade marched for some two miles along the High Street in Lincoln and was watched by hundreds of Saturday morning shoppers who seemed delighted by the appearance of the RAF Police dogs in public. The NCOs who took part in the parade were: Sergeant P Hall, Corporal J Henderson with Air Dog Shannon, Corporal M Pearce and Air Dog Jason, Corporal J Davage and Air Dog Elsa, Corporal D Robinson and Air Dog Zuse, Corporal A Clarke and Air Dog Bandit, Corporal B Curtis and Air Dog Sabre, Corporal S O'Reilly and Air Dog Major, Cpl G Cassidy and Air Dog Brigg,

Corporal J Kendall and Air Dog Buster, Corporal A Sargeant and Air Dog Nelson, Corporal G Whitehead and Air Dog Sultan, Corporal M Cheetham and Air Dog Czek. Finally, the crew of the Range Rover were Corporal D Brown and Corporal R Docksey.

During this time, there were three police orientated museums at the RAF Police School at RAF Newton. The first was the main and original RAF Police Museum containing details and exhibits from some of the more important investigations and incidents dealt with by the RAF Police around the world since its formation in 1918. The second was the *Baldwin Room* named after Lieutenant Colonel J Y Baldwin DSO, and dedicated to RAF Police dogs in general, while the third and newest was described as a *Search Museum* and was dedicated to the activities of the search dog teams trained to uncover explosives, firearms and drugs, which contained information and exhibits relating to 'finds' of both drugs and weapons, by the RAF Police, HM Customs & Excise and the USAF Security Police.

During the later part of the year demonstrations in Poland continued to call on the government for the restoration of the illegal trade union known as *Solidarity*. As the pressure mounted and gathered momentum, the worried Polish authorities lifted martial law, which had been established in an effort to crush the union and its support. However, further east, the Soviet Union once again demonstrated its aggressive tendencies to the world, when in September, without warning, they shot down an airliner belonging to Korean Airways, which had apparently strayed, unwittingly into Soviet airspace, close to what was described as a sensitive military installation. In all, two hundred and sixty-nine people, who were travelling on the aircraft on that fateful day, were killed.

In Central London during the afternoon of the 17th December, four police officers and three members of the public were killed and seventy-five others were injured when the IRA detonated a car bomb in a side street near the Harrods Department Store in Knightsbridge. Although a coded warning had been received, the bomb exploded and a huge blast ripped through the busy streets, which were crowded with Christmas shoppers, before the police had chance to evacuate the area.

In 1984 Warrant Officer T Figgins and Sergeant A Rowe from the RAF Police Dog Training Squadron, were detached to Thailand. Their successful three-month visit had been brought about following a request from the Thai government, for the RAF Police to assist them in training a number of their Air Force dogs to detect firearms and explosives. Throughout the detachment the two RAF men had been hosted by the Royal Thai Air Force at Korat, situated some two hundred kilometres north of the capital, Bangkok. After quickly settling in to their new environment, the two men had prepared an intensive training program, which to complicate matters slightly, had involved learning enough of the Thai language so that the basic commands could be given to the dogs which were being trained.

Having enjoyed a very interesting and exciting career in the Provost Branch, Air Commodore David retired from the RAF in June, and was succeeded by Air Commodore A E G Hales, a professional Provost Officer who had previously been the Command Provost & Security Officer in RAF Germany.

On the 12th October, the IRA struck once again on the British mainland, when a bomb they had planted in the Grand Hotel in Brighton, exploded during the early hours of the morning. At the time, the British Prime Minister and other members of her cabinet, who had been attending the Conservative Party Conference were staying in the hotel. Margaret Thatcher survived without being harmed but unfortunately, others staying in the hotel that night were killed and injured as the entire front of the building collapsed with the impact of the terrific blast.

In February 1985, many in the branch were shocked by the tragic news that a coach carrying members of the RAF Germany Band had been involved in an accident on the autobahn in Germany while on tour. As details became clearer it was confirmed that the coach had crashed into the rear of a stationary petrol tanker. As a result the tanker was severely damaged and the escaping fuel was instantly ignited. Everything happened so quickly and in a few tragic moments many of those travelling on the coach were killed and many were seriously injured as they desperately fought to escape. As details of the casualties were published it became apparent that Corporal G Crawford a RAF Police NCO serving with the Headquarters P&SS (Germany) had been killed. In addition, the young musician, who in 1981 had discovered the IRA bomb at RAF Uxbridge, was also killed in the horrific accident. Because of the continuing terrorist threat from the IRA, Corporal Crawford, a native of Liverpool, had been detailed to accompany the band as the Security NCO during their tour. He was a large and very popular figure who during the earlier part of his career had been a dog handler. A married man with two sons, he had regularly played rugby for both the RAF and the branch and prior to his tragic death he had been involved in raising funds for a number of charities and other worthwhile causes both in Germany and in the United Kingdom.

The author had been serving in Belize as the senior NCO in charge of the RAF Police since October 1984. Belize City was a very poor dirty place with a very high crime rate with prostitution, violence, robbery, drugs and burglary being commonplace offences. With the exception of a few former British colonial brick buildings, which stood in the centre of the city, all remaining buildings were no more than battered shanties. The city was divided up by a system of canals built at the end of the last century to drain the swampy terrain but they were quite filthy and smelt foul. One of the main waterways had the idyllic name of the 'Sweet Water Canal' which was anything but sweet. Almost all the houses within the poorer areas of the city had no proper sanitation facilities and accordingly small wooden huts were positioned along the banks of the canals which served as public toilets. As a result, the raw untreated sewage fell directly into the stagnant canals below. The city was chaotic during the day but at night with very few working streetlights about it was quite sinister and dangerous. Consequently, servicemen were warned not to stray off the main streets for fear of being attacked and robbed. The poorest area was the Port Loyal District in the south while the more influential area was located around the municipal airport on the western side of the city. The RAF Police along with the majority of the British forces stationed in Belize where based at Airport Camp on the opposite side of the runway from the International Airport and the Belize River and about four miles from Belize City. The airfield, airport and military camp was surrounded by thick swampy jungle. Pilfering of private and service property and stores from the camp, by local gangs was a major and constant problem and although the RAF and the Army posted armed guards throughout Airport Camp, the three RAF Police dog handlers; Corporal P Lacey, Corporal N Adam and Corporal B Chaffe, and their dogs were hard pressed each night in preventing the pilfering as they carried out roving patrols of the two aircraft dispersal areas and the technical compound known as the *Williamson Site* during the hours of darkness. Even the RAF Police dog section store, despite being fortified, was frequently attacked and supplies of tinned dog meat were stolen. The three RAF Police dogs at Belize were looked after by a very helpful Belizian veterinary surgeon who had been trained in Canada and who practised from a well equipped clinic in Belize City. In fact, his clinic was far cleaner and better equipped than the Belize City Hospital, but he did however, have problems from time to time in obtaining certain veterinary medicines and drugs. Some of the drugs concerned were required by the RAF Police dogs to prevent or treat tropical diseases, and as it was difficult getting them from the United Kingdom, the author contacted the USAF Security Police Canine Section at a base in Florida and explained the problem. They readily agreed to help out and subsequently each month after when the RAF Supply Officer from Belize flew into the base to collect supplies for the RAF he took with him a list of requirements for the RAF Police dog section, the Army dog section and the veterinary surgeon. As a result, the RAF and military dogs based at Airport Camp were probably the best cared for dogs in the entire country.

On the 11th March, following the death of Konstantin U Chernenko, Mikhail Sergeyevich Gorbachev, a little known Russian politician, became the leader of the Soviet Union. As the western world watched on, it was clear, from the very start that he did not have the same 'hard line' attitude possessed by the previous Soviet leaders. That was further demonstrated later in the year, when Gorbachev and the American President; Ronald Reagan, attended a summit, organised in Geneva. Towards the end of the talks, the western world was amazed to hear Gorbachev announce that the Soviet Union and America would be co-operating more closely from that point on in an effort to reduce the ever growing stockpile of nuclear and conventional weapons held by the two countries.

During the Annual United Kingdom RAF Police Dog Championship Trials held at RAF Newton in 1985, the top three teams were Corporal Veazey and Air Dog Zuse, Corporal Youens and Air Dog Prince, and Corporal Taylor with Air Dog Max. At the RAF Germany dog trials Corporal S Parsons and Air Dog Dutchie took first prize, while Corporal M Watson and Air Dog Sabre came second, and Corporal K Ansell and Air Dog Shep came in at third place.

On the 28th January 1986, the American Space Shuttle *Challenger* exploded shortly after lift-off from Cape Canaveral, killing the entire crew of seven.

Flight Lieutenant P Somerville was posted to the RAF Police School's dog training squadron at RAF Newton in early 1986. At the same time Squadron Leader D Martin took over the squadron from Squadron Leader K Hack. At that time dog training was a very important issue in the RAF and the squadron supported two officer posts. Under Squadron Leader Hack's command the dog training squadron had undergone a complete establishment review; every aspect of working practice had been minutely examined to ensure that it was properly manned. Every training course had its proper measure of instructors, criminals, assistant instructors and other personnel. The syllabus for every training course clearly indicated the requirements in manpower and resources needed to run the course; from the number of vehicles to the number of teaching aids, everything was included. It was an impressive training organisation, and the product it was turning out; the dog teams, was excellent. However, the dog training squadron at that time also carried the seeds of its own destruction in its very make up. Excellence was a great thing, but unfortunately cost was to be the deciding factor in the numerous defence studies that were going to be conducted over the following few years. Flight Lieutenant Somerville was no stranger to the world of dogs or indeed dog training. He had initially joined the RAF as a dog handler in

1961 serving at various units at home and abroad. In 1976 he had been promoted to sergeant and in 1978 he had been posted to the RAF Police School to train provost officers and RAF Police NCOs on security and investigation procedures. In 1979 he had been commissioned into the Provost Branch.

During the same period, the Army Dog Training School was based at Melton Mowbray, less than twenty miles away from RAF Newton. Rivalry between the two service dog schools had existed for quite some time, and it was understandable and inevitable that someone would seriously suggest a merger of the two organisations before too long. The simple question would be why two separate dog training schools, turning out a similar product to supply the Armed Forces, should not pool their efforts and thus cut costs. Of course, neither the Army nor the RAF wanted to merge, both organisations being more or less happy with the status quo. However, the Army and the RAF alike wanted to be the dominant partner should any form of merger be imposed upon them. Shortly after Flight Lieutenant Somerville's arrival at RAF Newton, a survey concerning dog training was conducted by a senior civil servant, who subsequently wrote a report that was distinctly favourable to the Army's method of training dogs, highlighting in particular the cost differences between the two rival organisations. Soon after, Squadron Leader Martin and Flight Lieutenant Somerville were removed from all squadron duties and were tasked with writing a rebuttal of the report. It was not too difficult a task, as the civil servant's report was full of anomalies and inconsistencies, and it was obvious that its author, despite his undoubted qualities as a civil servant, knew very little of dog training. The biggest difference between the two schools was the requirement for RAF Police dogs to be able to wind scent over vast areas of airfield terrain. The Army could not see the problem in the same light as the RAF. However, the RAF requirements were unique; over the course of the years the RAF Police had perfected the art of detecting intruders over vast distances very successfully, and it was considered imperative that the dog training squadron was able to have the facilities for training to perfect that skill. However, the report itself had certainly given everyone a fright, and it had definitely focussed the minds of 'certain key personnel' on the future. Although the civil servant's report was discredited, and the RAF was able to put up a forceful argument to remain as an independent training school at RAF Newton for the time being, a number of factors were against it going completely unscathed. As nearly always it all came down to cost, and the figures were self evident and conclusively proved that RAF dog training was substantially more expensive than that conducted by the Army. The reasons for this were quite simple, the Army Dog Training School was not equipped to the same standard as the RAF Police dog training squadron, and its personnel were on lower salary pay scales and lower ranking structure than their RAF counterparts. These cost differences would eventually force the two services together, whether they liked it or not. Over the years the RAF had built up an excellent training school for dogs and its reputation both at home and overseas had grown accordingly. The RAF Police had the contract for training dogs for a number of overseas organisations and also had the contract for a number of key organisations within the United Kingdom, including the *'Jewel in the Crown'*, Her Majesty's Customs & Excise. The RAF had had a *'training understanding'* with Her Majesty's Customs & Excise since the early 1970s, and it had been enormously successful. All operational customs dogs serving in the United Kingdom were RAF Police dogs on secondment, a situation which gave the RAF Police great prestige in the international market place. As successful as they were, the problem was of course, that quality is not always the key factor in determining the security of any organisation, especially in the Armed Services and to those controlling the budget.

Although it appeared that relations between America and the Soviet Union were beginning to warm up considerably, things elsewhere were not quite so comfortable. On the 15th April, America launched a dramatic air raid against Libya, from airfields within the United Kingdom. The attack was in retaliation for various terrorist activities that had allegedly been sponsored by Libya. Simultaneously, the RAF stations in both Cyprus and in Gibraltar went on full alert, in case the Libyans launched a counter-attack there. Within twenty-four hours, RAF Police reinforcements from around the United Kingdom were sent out to both RAF Akrotiri and RAF Gibraltar, to assist the resident RAF Police and RAF Regiment, in securing both stations against any form of terrorist attack.

In Russia on the 26th April, the world's worst nuclear accident occurred as the Nuclear Reactor in the Chernobyl Power Station went into meltdown sending out extreme levels of radioactive pollution. During the aftermath many people were killed trying to contain the situation and many thousands of people were evacuated from a wide area around the site.

On the 1st May, the newly commissioned RAF station at Mount Pleasant on the Falkland Islands became fully operational and took over from the makeshift facilities established at RAF Stanley, which had been operational since the end of the conflict. As such, the new unit, situated thirty two miles from Stanley, became home to the Falkland Islands Garrison Police Unit (FIGPU), commanded by Major B Atkinson Royal Military Police, and became responsible for provost operations throughout the region, while the RAF Police Flight, commanded by

Flight Lieutenant D Wilson, assumed responsibility for the internal policing and security matters on the unit.

On the island of Cyprus on Sunday, the 3rd August, without warning, terrorists from the pro Libyan *'Unified Nasserite Organisation'* launched an attack against RAF Akrotiri, and the nearby *Ladies Mile* beach, which was being used at the time by RAF families, local people and a number of tourists. Although several mortar bombs and rockets were initially fired at the station, no-one was killed but two RAF wives were nevertheless injured by shrapnel. After the mortars had been discharged, the terrorists drove their car along the *Ladies Mile* beach, firing automatic weapons over the heads of the terrified families and the tourists who were defenceless and had no means of escape. Luckily, once again, no-one was hurt in the cowardly attack and the alarm was quickly sounded. Although a RAF Wessex helicopter was promptly scrambled to locate the terrorists, they had unfortunately, made a swift get away.

Following the highlighting of certain key factors in the rebuttal report written by Squadron Leader Martin and Flight Lieutenant Somerville regarding the amalgamation of dog training with the Army, the RAF went upmarket and obtained, at considerable expense, the services of one of the leading consultancy firms in the country. The arrival of their representatives at the dog training squadron was quite impressive; they gave a very professional briefing to the squadron personnel telling them all about their background and how wonderful they were as an organisation. Over a period of several weeks they conducted a thorough survey of the Army and RAF dog training establishments and other animal issues involving the training of horses conducted by the Army. The *'other animal issues'* were in fact quite critical to the survival of the Army and the RAF schools because besides training dogs, the Army were of course responsible for training and supplying horses to the Army. The set-up at Melton Mowbray for training horses was quite excellent and well established and it was quite apparent, that as long as the Army perceived a need to train horses, the two organisations were going to have an enormous problem dealing with where to establish any future joint training school. The RAF put forward the view that the horses could be trained at Newton and its nearby satellite unit at RAF Syerston, and therefore the Army could close down Melton Mowbray. The proposal turned out to be a non-starter for a number of reasons. First of all, neither Newton nor Syerston were really suitable for housing and exercising horses, especially as RAF Syerston was an operational flying station. As the survey continued it was very apparent that the consultants had no knowledge of dog training, but in the greater scheme of things that was not considered to be a drawback. After several months their report was issued and proved once again favourable to the Army system. At first the management at the dog training squadron were not allowed to comment on the report, the Service seemed to think the situation was cut and dried and would not countenance a rebuttal similar to the one given to the previous report. However, rumour had it that the Chief-of-Air Staff himself was not very happy with the report and wanted it dismissed. The *'dog world'* had always had friends in the higher echelons of the RAF, as many former Station Commanders who had achieved air rank remembered their dog handlers with a degree of respect and affection. Eventually, the report was basically *'set aside'* and the dog training squadron lived to fight another day. However, the consultants had completed a report that again highlighted the cost differences of the Army and RAF systems, and Flight Lieutenant Somerville like many others felt at the time that the RAF case was being badly weakened.

During the Annual United Kingdom RAF Police Dog Championship Trials held at RAF Newton the top three dog teams were judged to be, Corporal M Hallett and Air Dog Ben, Corporal Ellis and Air Dog Rajah, and Corporal Boyce with Air Dog Prince. At the RAF Police (Scotland) dog trials held at RAF Kinloss Corporal N Cousins and Air Dog King took first place, while Corporal J Dalton and Air Dog Monty took second place, and Corporal A Jones with Air Dog Wolf came third. At the RAF Germany dog trials the three winning teams were, Corporal S Parsons and Air Dog Dutchie, Corporal A Sargeant and Air Dog Mac, and Corporal J Taylor with Air Dog Max.

During October Air Commodore Hales retired as the Provost Marshal and was succeeded in post by Air Commodore G E Winch FBIM who was commissioned into the RAF in 1956 as a fighter controller before transferring into the Provost Branch in 1961. As a provost officer, he had completed tours of duty in the United Kingdom, in Germany, in Cyprus, and at the Supreme Headquarters Allied Powers in Europe (SHAPE). Prior to taking up his appointment as Provost Marshal, he had been the Deputy Director of Security (RAF) at the Ministry of Defence.

On the 20th November, the author and a number of colleagues began an eighteen day detachment on the island of Masirah, situated just off the south east coast of Oman. The deployment was in support of a major NATO exercise known as *'Saif Sareea'* or Swift Sword. The island is about half the size of the Isle of Wight and extremely dusty and barren. The airfield which was being used by the Sultan of Oman's Air Force (SOAF), had ten years before, been a fully operational RAF station, supporting British forces on the mainland, who were assisting the Sultan to fight the internal guerrilla war. However, when the war ended, the RAF pulled out of the region and the SOAF took over the base. During the detachment, everyone involved was accommodated in rows of kahki-coloured tents, which had previously been erected and the scene resembled something from a World War II desert campaign. After quickly settling into their routine, the RAF Police teamed up with a platoon of Royal Military Police and together they carried out a wide assortment of tasks in support of the exercise. In addition, the Joint Police Unit established and maintained a close working liaison with their counterparts from the SOAF Police Section. In the first few days as they explored the base, Flight Sergeant A Rawle, who had been one of the last RAF Police NCOs stationed there before the withdrawal, pointed out various buildings and land-marks, which had been used by the RAF Police. The old RAF Police dog section for instance was still there, as was the old RAF movements control building, complete with a wide selection of RAF squadron crests, including the RAF Police badge, which had been painted on the walls by RAF personnel years before. It was pleasing to see that the current owners had maintained them in good order during the RAF's ten-year absence.

During 1986, Air Dog Brumby one of the first two drug detection dogs to serve with HM Customs & Excise, and handled by former RAF Police NCO, Mr V Jones, retired after a most successful career to become a family pet in the Jones' household. Brumby, during his time with HM Customs & Excise had made 235 drug detections recovering drugs with a street value of over £8 million. In 1979 Brumby had appeared in the 'Personality Parade' at the Crufts Dog Show, and in November 1982, he had attended the 'Pro Dog of the Year Awards' dinner at the *Grosvenor Suite* in London, where he was awarded the gold medal as 'Pro Dog of the Year. After his dog's retirement Mr Jones transferred to VAT duties.

On the 6th March 1987, disaster suddenly struck when the cross channel ferry, the *Herald of Free Enterprise*, capsized as it was leaving the harbour at Zee-brugge. As the ferry system was used extensively by members of the British forces, serving within Europe it was suspected that a large number of Army and RAF personnel and their families had been on board and that a large number of them had perished in the vessel.

During 1987 as the drug culture continued to develop within the United Kingdom, evidence suggested that in order to avoid being detected, some service personnel involved in the abuse of drugs were no longer taking them onto RAF units to use. Instead, it was suspected that they were conducting their illegal activities off base where they had much more freedom and the risk of getting caught was slimmer. Indeed, those caught by the civil police at the time, in possession of what was deemed to be *'user amounts'* would in most cases, be cautioned for the offence and released without charge. The RAF on the other hand took drug abuse amongst its personnel very seriously and offenders if convicted, were imprisoned and discharged from the service. In April, in an effort to overcome the problem of detecting the off base users, the RAF established two drug intelligence teams, one with P&SS (Northern Region) and the other with P&SS (Southern Region). The system of using young but well trained RAF Police NCOs, on covert drug operations, had been developed and used very effectively by the Royal Military Police during the previous few years. Additionally, dogs trained to detect the presence of Cannabis, Heroin, Cocaine and Amphetamine greatly enhanced the search techniques used by the investigators employed with the Drug Abuse Prevention Flights.

On the 14th September, after six long years in existence, the RAF Police detachments to RAF Greenham Common finally ended, when overall responsibility for the security of the establishment was handed over once again to the Ministry of Defence Police. During the six-year period, a considerable number of Provost Officers, RAF Police NCOs and dog handlers from RAF stations all around the United Kingdom and RAF Germany had completed tours of duty on the unestablished task of keeping the anti-nuclear protestors out of the unit. More importantly, they had kept the protesters well away from the Americans who certainly would have used their weapons had the protesters broken into their security site. The whole operation had in the main, been a fairly successful one, which had helped to foster positive relations with the Thames Valley Police, the Ministry of Defence Police and the USAF Security Police throughout.

At the 1987 Annual United Kingdom RAF Police Dog Championship Trials held at RAF Newton, the winning teams included for the first time a member of the United States Air Force Security Police. First place was taken by Corporal Stone and Air Dog Kane, while Corporal Baum and Air Dog Bandit came second, and AIC (USAF) Wilson with Air Dog Sandy from RAF Lakenheath came third.

The next review of dog training came with another survey carried out by a very senior civil servant. Again a *non-animal* expert began looking at the Army and RAF dog training organisations, but he appeared a shrewd and intelligent man who was trying to take a sensible and balanced view, and was very aware of the intense rivalry between the Army and the RAF as he looked at the findings of the previous two reports and other background information. He, like the previous observers, made a number of visits to both training establishments, and again the biggest problem that was raised was what to do with the horses. The Army claimed that the aircraft being operated at Newton and Syerston would cause problems for the horses. Flight Lieutenant Somerville recalled that claim, which had a reasonable element of sense, when he was with the team looking at aspects of horse training at Melton Mowbray; suddenly, and without warning, two rather noisy RAF Tornado jets flew overhead without raising a flicker of interest from the horses. Flight Lieutenant Somerville recalls the civil servant looking at them and smiling, raising the observation that if the horses were not spooked by two fast jets they would hardly have a problem with the Bulldog propeller driven aircraft being operated at Newton and Syerston. Despite a number of good points in favour of both organisations, the days of an independent dog training school for the RAF were rapidly disappearing. Another problem that was starting to raise its head was what was going to be the long-term future of RAF Newton and RAF Syerston. During one of the numerous survey visits, the team were accompanied by a representative from the Defence Lands Agency. While the management of the Dog Training Squadron were waxing lyrical about the wonderful facilities at Newton and Syerston the representative from the Defence Lands Agency was waxing equally lyrical about the closure of Newton in the not too distant future. With that kind of attitude being expressed the Dog Training Squadron argument in favour of moving animal training to Newton and Syerston was seriously compromised. Besides Melton Mowbray or Newton and Syerston being considered as the location for animal training, other locations were suggested and included moving both schools in their entirety to Wiltshire and taking over an old RAF station. It had possibilities, but the costs would have been quite staggering and that idea was quickly set aside. The outcome of all these reports was inevitable though, particularly with the collapse of the *Cold War* and the subsequent economies envisaged throughout the Armed Services; the schools had no real choice but to amalgamate. Eventually, the Army and the RAF had to set aside their differences and come up with a workable scenario for the joint training of dogs.

At RAF Gibraltar on the 14th December, Corporal A Bruce the drug search dog handler, who was serving with RAF P&SS (Gibraltar), was asked by the Gibraltar Customs Service to assist them with searching the voluminous luggage belonging to a Moroccan passenger, who had arrived in the colony on the hydrofoil from Tangier. The officers strongly suspected the passenger of carrying controlled drugs, but had been unable to locate any during their initial search. Corporal Bruce and his dogs responded and after a short time, both dogs indicated that there were drugs concealed inside six pairs of deer antlers, which were mounted onto wooden plinths. In spite of the protests from the owner, the antlers were duly split open and a total of 6.3 kilograms of Pakistani Black Cannabis resin, with a then current street value of £18,000, was recovered and instantly impounded. The RAF Police drug dogs had once again proved their worth and as a result, the Moroccan was subsequently charged, by the Gibraltar authorities, with attempting to smuggle controlled drugs into the colony.

In troubled Northern Ireland during the early 1980's personnel from No 14 Field Intelligence Unit and the Special Air Service were conducting what were described as 'special covert undisclosed operations', the purpose of which was designed to locate arms and ammunition caches hidden by terrorist organisations throughout the Province. The objective of those operations was simply to deprive the terrorist factions of firearms, explosives and ammunition that could be used against the security forces and, or the civilian population. It was in effect, a war of attrition. When such hidden caches were located the weapons were either immediately recovered or, depending on the situation, left untouched but monitored from a secret military observation point nearby. In order to prevent the weapons from being recovered by the security forces it was common practice for the caches and individual weapons to be booby trapped, and therefore caution was always the priority when investigating that type of find. Whenever the terrorists arrived to collect weapons from a 'monitored site', an operation would be mounted to do one of two things. Either they would be challenged in order to detain them for interrogation, or they would be followed in order to gain further intelligence. Whenever such terrorists were challenged they would invariably be armed and would respond by opening fire against the security forces to aid their escape. Initially the 'special covert undisclosed operations' were not particularly effective in producing the required results, after all, looking for a hidden cache of weapons in hostile territory in daylight was hard enough but trying to do it in the dead of night was a near impossible and extremely dangerous task, even for the best trained special forces in the world. At some point, search advisors from the SAS Regiment suggested using dogs to assist them and with the headquarters of P&SS (Northern Ireland) being located across the road from their base they decided to seek expert advice on the matter. Initially, they had spoken to Corporal W Jenkinson, a specialist firearms & explosives (FX) dog handler, who after listening to what the SAS required discussed the matter with the P&SS commander who decided to help. As it turned out, the use of RAF Police FX search dog teams to assist the SAS showed immediate promise. However, working a FX search dog at night provided a number of problems for both the handlers and their dogs. Additionally, the dog handlers were policemen and not fully trained combat soldiers required by the SAS. These were indeed matters that needed to be addressed quickly if the dog teams were to be a professional part of the operation. Indeed, as a way of improving the situation, personnel from the SAS and No 14 Field Intelligence Unit quickly organised an intensive program of fieldcraft and weapon training for all the RAF Police dog handlers detailed to assist them. In addition, the dog handlers began to incorporate night training scenarios into their normal training routine. Initially, Corporal Jenkinson, Corporal P Ford and Corporal R Underwood were assigned to assist with the 'special covert undisclosed operations' and all had varying degrees of success. The type of target area varied; the dog handlers quite often found themselves swimming into a culvert chest deep in water, with their dog either swimming besides them or on their back, in order to clear or confirm a culvert bomb, or they found themselves quietly searching an isolated farm house while the family inside were sound asleep. All operations were conducted on the terrorists' home ground and all were extremely dangerous. As the dog handlers gained valuable experience from their involvement in the operations, the information was duly passed across to the staff at the RAF Police Dog Training Squadron and in particular to Corporal T Steans and Corporal R Irwin, the principle instructors within the FX Search Cell, who used the information to improve training methods. During the mid 1980's, after a successful tour of duty in Northern Ireland, during which over two hundred and eighty documented *special covert undisclosed operations* had been undertaken, Corporal's Jenkinson, Ford and Underwood, were replaced by Corporal's S O'Brien, R Hoare and T Steans who continued to assist the SAS and intelligence units with the important and dangerous work of searching for and recovering hidden weapon caches and terrorist bombs designed to kill, maim and destroy. In fact, Corporal Jenkinson had been later mentioned in dispatches for his outstanding contribution to the *special covert undisclosed operations*. Towards the end of the 1980's Corporal R Newham and Corporal A Frampton were posted onto the strength of P&SS (Northern Ireland) and they continued to provide the same valuable assistance as their predecessors, earning a reputation that the RAF Police could really be proud of.

As 1987 came to an end, so too did the longest close-protection operation ever mounted by the RAF Police. The task was finally concluded, after His Royal Highness Prince Feisal Bin Hussein of Jordan successfully completed his training with the RAF and had qualified as a fighter pilot. The operation had been running since the 1st June 1985, when the prince had first arrived at the RAF College Cranwell, to complete his initial officer and basic flying training. As his training program progressed he moved across the country to RAF Valley on the island of Anglesey and then down to RAF Chivenor near Barnstaple, where he completed his advanced flying training. The team who had been selected for the lengthy operation had been selected from the RAF Police School and various RAF stations around the country and included a number of dog handlers, who provided enhanced security and specialist FX search capabilities during the operation.

On the 7th March 1988, Gibraltar went onto full alert, when three known members of an IRA active service unit, who had been planning to carry out terrorist activities within the colony, were shot dead by members of the Special Air Service, who, acting upon intelligence reports, had been tracking them ever since they set out for the continent. Unfortunately, in retaliation for the shootings, the Provisional IRA stepped up their campaign of terror within Northern Ireland by attacking a mini bus and a coach containing soldiers. In addition, two members of the Royal Signals Regiment who had strayed by mistake into a crowd attending an IRA funeral were overpowered and attacked before being executed by an angry Republican mob. During the early part of 1988, IRA active service units also began a bloody terror campaign in Germany and Holland, by targeting vulnerable British servicemen and their families stationed on the continent. A number of off-duty British servicemen were shot dead in separate 'close quarter assassination' incidents and improvised explosive devices were placed at the Headquarters of the British Army on the Rhine (BAOR) and a number of other army units within Germany.

As the *Cold War* between the East and the West continued to thaw, the co-operation between the British and the Soviet authorities, in the war against the manufacture and importation of illicit drugs, went from strength to strength, as the number of successful customs operations increased. Consequently, a most unusual and prestigious visit took place at the RAF Police School on the 14th September, when the First Deputy Chairman of the Soviet State Customs Board & Council of Ministers; Mr Vitaliy Konstantonovich Boyarov, accompanied by Lieutenant General Pankin of the Soviet Ministry of the Interior, were entertained at the Dog Training Squadron. The visitors had been very impressed by what they had heard about the training being carried out by the Search Dog Cell at the school and had asked, during their week long visit to the United Kingdom, to see it for themselves. After being met by the Station Commander, Group Captain R E Holliday and Wing Commander A V Schofield; the Officer Commanding the RAF Police School, they were given a full briefing and a step-by-step demonstration of the techniques used in the training of the drug detection dogs by the staff in the Search Cell. At the end of the visit, Mr Boyarov, impressed by what he had seen, presented a Soviet State Customs Board Medal to the RAF Police School, which was later displayed within the '*Baldwin Room*' at the RAF Police Museum.

At the 1988 Annual United Kingdom RAF Police Dog Championship Trials the three winning teams were judged to be, Corporal Braddick and Air Dog Sultan, Corporal A Goodenough and Air Dog Sultan, and Corporal Stone with Air dog Kane.

In early December, while President Gorbachev was on route to Washington, to attend an historic summit meeting with President Reagan, he stopped off at RAF Brize Norton near Oxford, for talks with the British Prime Minister; Margaret Thatcher. The subsequent meeting between the two leaders was held in the

Officers' Mess on the unit, while the RAF Police provided the required security measures within the station, and RAF Police dog teams patrolled the perimeter of the domestic site. As a continuing sign of the changing times and a further thawing of the *Cold War*, it was the very first time that a Soviet leader had stepped foot inside a RAF station in the United Kingdom, together with his KGB protection team.

On the 22nd December, people on both sides of the Atlantic Ocean were shocked and horrified, when a PANAM *jumbo jet*, which had taken off on a scheduled flight from London's Heathrow Airport on route to New York, crashed without warning onto the small Scottish village of Lockerbie killing over three hundred people. It later transpired that an improvised terrorist bomb had exploded in a suitcase within the cargo hold minutes before the aircraft broke apart. The disaster devastated the tiny and normally peaceful village and the surrounding area and the wreckage was spread over a very wide area. As the investigation gathered pace Libyan terrorists were suspected of planting the bomb in reprisal for the American bombing of Libya.

On the 20th February 1989, during the early hours of the morning, an armed IRA active service unit placed a bomb against an occupied accommodation block inside Clive Barracks at Tern Hill, in Shropshire. The terrorists were spotted and immediately challenged by a roving guard patrol but because of the arming policy at the time, they were unable to open fire because their magazines containing the ammunition were sealed and not fitted to their rifles. When the terrorists used their own weapons to aid their escape the alarm was raised and the accommodation was cleared just before the bomb exploded. Although nobody was killed in the attack, the event definitely brought about an urgent change in the arming policy for all personnel guarding military installations on the United Kingdom mainland and that included the RAF Police. From that point on, the RAF Police and the RAF guard force started patrolling with magazines containing live ammunition fitted to their weapons and ready, if required, for instant use.

In March, Air Commodore Winch retired as the Provost Marshal, after a rather busy period in office and was immediately succeeded in post by Air Commodore A C P Seymour, who had originally joined the RAF, as a Secretarial Officer, before transferring across to the Provost Branch in 1967. Prior to taking up his appointment as Provost Marshal he had been the Deputy Provost Marshal and Officer Commanding HQ P&SS (UK) at RAF Rudloe Manor.

Since the previous October, the author was serving his second tour of duty in Belize as the Senior NCO in charge of the RAF Police. During his previous tour in 1984/5 he had worked tirelessly to ensure that the dog section, the three handlers and their dogs were maintained and operated in the most efficient manner. Although the kennel compounds for the dogs and the storeroom were adequate, the facilities for the dog handlers such as the office, the dispensary, and the food preparation area were poor and comprised two old military portakabins, which in the hot steamy jungle environment, needed a lot of maintenance to ensure that they simply did not become infested with insects, become overgrown with jungle vegetation or simply rot. Prior to leaving Belize in the Spring of 1985, the author had submitted plans to have a new brick built dog section built to replace the portakabins, however, everything took time in Belize and by the time he returned to the United Kingdom, the work had not started. It was therefore a pleasant surprise when he returned for a second tour four years later to see that work to build the new dog section had begun, even if the pace of progress was agonisingly slow. Incidentally, an X-Ray machine for checking the baggage of passengers boarding RAF aircraft had also been ordered during the authors' first time in Belize and that too was delivered a week before he arrived for his second tour of duty. At the time, the dog section comprised four dog handlers who had recently arrived weeks apart from the United Kingdom; Corporal K Ansell the NCO in charge, Corporal A Goodenough, Corporal N Taffe and Corporal T Jones. The pilfering attacks against the RAF part of Airport Camp were no way as serious as they had been during the authors' first tour, mainly because those responsible for the raids were either in prison or had fled the area. However, that was no reason for complacency and the constant vigilance of the 'roving' dog teams ensured that the RAF sites were secure during the hours of darkness. Eventually, the big day arrived when work to complete the new dog section finished and the section was formally opened for business during a barbeque attended by the RAF Air Commander and invited guests from Airport Camp, including of course, the veterinary surgeon from Belize City. The new facilities included an office, a dispensary, a food preparation area, an isolation kennel and a storeroom, and was a great improvement on the old portakabins that were ceremonially towed away to be destroyed. A short time later, the author and the dog handlers were pleased to receive Flight Sergeant A Hamilton, the PMDI from the United Kingdom, who had been invited to Belize to conduct a formal inspection of the dog section; needless to say, he was impressed with what he saw.

At the 1989 Annual United Kingdom RAF Police Dog Championship Trials held at RAF Newton, Corporal M Dobson and Air Dog Quincey took first prize, while Corporal Edler and Air Dog Raffles came second, and Corporal Cameron and Air Dog King came third.

The year 1989 brought about that great moment in history, which finally signalled to the world, the end of the 'Cold War' between the East and the West. It was brought about by the signing of a peace accord between the American and Russian super-powers to reduce the arms race and with it, their massive stocks of nuclear and conventional weapons. As a further gesture of good will, President Gorbachev announced to the world that he would be making a substantial number of radical changes within the Soviet Union, creating a new policy of openness or 'Perestroika' as it became known. His announcement was followed shortly after by the promised withdrawal of the last Soviet troops from war-ravaged Afghanistan, which had been occupied by the Soviet Union for nine years.

The problem of drug abuse within the Armed forces has always been a worrying issue and as previously mentioned the RAF has always taken effective steps to counter the threat. The relevant British 'Misuse of Drugs' legislation made it an offence to possess, produce or trade in a wide variety of illegal drugs. In early October, the author; newly promoted to Flight Sergeant, took over the Drug Abuse Prevention Flight, at P&SS (Southern Region). He was no stranger to the murky world of drug abuse, having successfully established the first covert P&SS Drug-Intelligence Team at Rudloe Manor a few years before. Accordingly, he quickly settled into his new role and after a meeting with his team introduced a number of operating procedures designed to improve the efficiency and administration of the office. At the time, the Drug Abuse Prevention Flight was controlled by the Drug Abuse Prevention Officer; Flight Lieutenant M Warner, a former RAF Marine Craft Captain. The Investigation Team comprised; Sergeant J M Gordon and Sergeant T Cairns; Corporal J Haggie and Corporal B Bouhgen, while the four-man Drug-Intelligence Team was controlled by Sergeant C Poulter. Finally, Corporal I Todd was the Drug Detection dog handler with his two charges; Air Dog Misty and Air Dog Boss.

As a more relaxed political attitude prevailed in Moscow, the world watched in amazement during October, as the people of East Germany and Czechoslovakia suddenly turned their backs on Communism and demanded their political and democratic freedom. Shortly after, the borders between East and West Germany were opened on the 9th November for the first time since the start of the Cold War and over two million people from the East entered West Germany. That was followed by the dismantling of the Berlin Wall and the dreaded 'Iron Curtain'. In December, both the American and Soviet leaders announced to the world that the Cold War had officially ended and with it, the threat of global nuclear war. As a result, of the announcement, various hard-line regimes within Eastern Europe crumbled as revolution took hold in various forms.

During July 1990, the Iraqi Leader, Saddam Hussein, who was desperate to build up his country's shattered economy after losing the long bloody war with

Iran, made it very clear to the world that he once again wanted to take possession of Kuwait, which he considered to be Iraqi territory. During a powerful speech, he fiercely attacked the tiny state for producing too much oil which had in turn, forced down the overall world prices. Political tension between the two countries quickly mounted and Kuwait placed her meagre military forces on full alert as the threat of military invasion increased.

As the Soviet Union continued to reduce the threat of attack on the West by withdrawing her troops from positions deemed to be intimidating, the British government once again began calling for massive reductions in the United Kingdom's massive defence budget. Consequently on the 25th July, a paper, entitled, 'Options for Change' was presented to parliament, which outlined a number of ways of reducing the country's defences in line with the declining threat to national security. At the time, the authorised establishment of the RAF was 89,000 and the paper called for a reduction in numbers, over a two-year period, to 75,000 personnel.

Iraq invaded Kuwait shortly after midnight on the 2nd August, with a force of 100,000 troops. Kuwait was powerless to thwart the attack and the invaders quickly took control of the entire country, including the valuable oil fields. Although both the invasion and Saddam Hussein were immediately condemned by the international community and the United Nation's Security Council, Iraq continued her occupation and the systematic plunder of Kuwait. In addition, Iraqi troops moved towards the border with Saudi Arabia, who fearing that Iraq was about to invade her territory as well, placed her forces on full alert and invited the Americans and the British in to repel the threat of any impending attack. As a result, 'Operation Granby' and the American, 'Operation Desert Storm', rapidly assembled troops and equipment into the region.

In the Persian Gulf on the 24th February 1991, the Coalition ground offensive to liberate Kuwait began and after only four days, the Iraqi forces were swiftly defeated. As the overall operation was completed in a very short space of time, a huge number of Iraqi prisoners-of-war were suddenly captured by, or surren-dered to, the Coalition forces, making the task of guarding them a massive commitment. To assist in overcoming the problem, RAF Police dog handlers were instantaneously deployed to the prisoner-of-war (POW) compounds at *Mary Hill Transit Camp* to assist. The first few hundred prisoners arrived during the evening of the 28th February, but over the days that followed the number quickly rose to around four thousand prisoners. The RAF Police dog teams were used on a variety of security and containment tasks, providing twenty-four hour coverage at the camp. Apart from being used to patrol the perimeter wire of the enclosures containing the captured Iraqi troops they were also used for escorting prisoners from the Chinook helicopters, which brought them into the camp. The teams worked hard in extremely difficult conditions and it was fairly common for a single dog team to be controlling upwards of four hundred prisoners at a time. On one occasion, the Coldstream Guards Regiment, who was responsible for administration at the camp, issued a supply of sweets and coca-cola to the prisoners. Unfortunately, there was not enough to go around and a riot quickly occurred. Additional dog teams were deployed to the incident and order was quickly restored but not before a few of the more foolhardy prisoners had been bitten by the dogs. A few more incidents of a similar nature occurred over the days that followed and again the speedy intervention of the dog teams quickly brought the situations under control. By the 11th March, all the prisoners had been transferred from the *Mary Hill Transit Camp* over to the camps set up by the United States Army and accordingly, the RAF Police dog teams were stood down from their guarding task.

After a most unpopular directive from the Ministry of Defence, the RAF Police Dog Training Squadron, after much protest to prevent it from happening, finally merged with the Royal Army Veterinary Corps' Army Dog Training School on the 1st April 1991, to form the Joint Service Defence Animal Centre (DAC). The Headquarters of the new formation was located at Melton Mowbray and was commanded by the Officer Commanding Melton Mowbray, Colonel P G H Jepson RAVC. He was assisted by Lieutenant Colonel P A Roffey RAVC and Wing Commander P F Leeds RAF, who was also the Officer Commanding RAF Police School, acting as his deputies. The new unit was divided up into two separate wings. The Army wing, commanded by an Army captain, which looked after the Army's horses and the dogs used to detect firearms and explosives was based at Melton Mowbray, while the RAF Police Dog Training Squadron, re-titled as the Dog Training Wing (Newton) remained at RAF Newton, training the general patrol and drug detection dogs. In addition, the Dog Training Wing (Newton), commanded by Squadron Leader Somerville, continued to train dogs for HM Customs & Excise, the Royal Navy, the Scottish Prison Service and for the American Forces who were stationed within the United Kingdom. The marriage of the two organisations was not without its problems at first, but generally speaking, the people involved made the best of it and simply got on with the job.

During the same month, as a result of the continuing terrorist activity on the United Kingdom mainland, discussions were held at the Ministry of Defence by the Provost Marshal, Air Commodore A C P Seymour, with a view to increasing the internal counter-terrorist measures at a large number of RAF stations around the country. Although the use of patrol dogs was thought to be the most efficient way of providing that deterrent, a substantial increase in the establishment of dog sections at every station would have placed a great deal of pressure on the newly formed Defence Animal Centre, proved to be very expensive and therefore would have been rejected right from the start. As an alternative, a proposal was accepted to trial the use of a small number of specially selected High Profile Counter-Terrorist (HPCT) dogs at three RAF stations over a three-month period. The trial at Shawbury, Cranwell and Uxbridge, was subsequently organised and controlled by the PMDI and started in July 1991. The new concept of using dogs in the HPCT role was quite simple and extremely cost effective to operate. Each station was allocated two trained dogs which were teamed up with qualified RAF Police dog handlers, already established on the strength of the unit, but who were carrying out general police duties. Up until that point, RAF Police NCOs who were employed as dog handlers had been specially established purely for that role and as such, conformed to a special shift pattern that worked alongside those of their colleagues employed on general police duties. However, during the trial period, the NCOs handling the HPCT dogs were incorporated into the normal pattern of shifts, accompanied by their dogs whenever they carried out the regular foot and mobile patrols around the station. The aim of course was to tell the 'outside world' that RAF Police dogs were deployed at those units. At the end of the trial period, the venture was deemed to have been successful and the use of HPCT dogs in that role continued and the scheme was expanded to other RAF stations around the country.

Many veterans associated with the branch were saddened to learn of the death, on the 12th October, of Group Captain A A Newbury OBE, who passed away just a few weeks before his ninetieth birthday. The Group Captain or *Uncle Bert* as he had been affectionately known as in the branch, enlisted into the RAF Police in 1920 and had risen to the rank of warrant officer before being commissioned during the early stages of World War II. In 1947, as the Commanding Officer at the RAF Police School in Staverton, he had done much to ensure that the previously separate general police and dog training elements bonded into a single training school. He had also been instrumental in launching the RAF Police journal *Provost Parade* and for persuading his son in law, Wing Commander McMahon, to design the RAF Police badge and motto. He had been a very popular member of the branch who had a reputation for fairly treating both his officers and his men alike.

At the 1991 Annual RAF Germany dog trials the winning three teams were judged to be, Corporal P Barrass and Air Dog Ricky, Corporal I Whitehall and Air Dog Jasper, and Corporal P Simpson with Air Dog Zeus.

Obstacle training – Climbing down a ladder

RAF Police Dog Team trained to detect the presence of weapons and explosives
being dropped into an operational area somewhere in Northern Ireland 1985

Kennel maids with dogs at the RAF Police Dog Training School RAF Newton 1985

'Stand Still' – An intruder is challenged during continuation training,
carried out on a regular basis - 1986

The RAF Police Security Team tasked with the protection of HRH Prince Feisal of Jordan
in 1987 during his training to become a pilot

RAF Police Dog Teams deployed to guard Iraqi Prisoners-of-War
during the first Gulf War (Iraq) in 1991

Keeping the IRA away - RAF Police Dog handler and his dog
on a counter-terrorist patrol at a RAF unit in the UK

Training Exercise for a RAF Police Dog Team specially trained
to detect the presence of weapons and explosives

6.   1992 – 2004

In former Yugoslavia, violence erupted in numerous Bosnian cities on the 2nd March 1992, following the results of a referendum which had supported total independence for the state of Bosnia. The proposal was rejected by the Orthodox Serbs, who formed a minority of less than one third of the population. However, unlike the Catholic Croats and the Muslim majority, the Serbs were far better organised when it came to military matters and had the support of the Yugoslav National Army in their cause. Despite the outbreak of trouble in the region, Bosnia-Herzegovina quickly gained its independence and was duly recognised by the majority of governments around the world. That did nothing to suffocate the activities of the Serbs, who quickly escalated their violent guerrilla campaign within the region forcing the United Nation's Security Council to condemn the violence which soon developed into a full scale bloody civil war.

At the 1992 Annual RAF Germany dog trials the winning three teams were judged to be, Corporal I Whitehall and Air Dog Jasper, Corporal P Barrass and Air Dog Rickie, and Corporal P Savage with Air Dog Senna.

Sadly, during the year Mr Terry McHaffie, the Chief Training Advisor (Dogs), retired after a long and satisfying career working with RAF Police dogs. With plans to merge the training of military dogs with the Army at Melton Mowbray, the appointment of Chief Training Advisor (Dogs) was not filled. Since the RAF Police took over training dogs in 1944, the post had been filled by three people; Lieutenant Colonel J Y Baldwin, Mr Charles Fricker and finally Mr McHaffie.

On the 1st April 1993, the Royal Air Force and of course, the RAF Police, celebrated their seventy-fifth anniversary in style, both at home and abroad. At the International Air Tattoo at Fairford, the RAF Police Association organised and operated a hospitality suite where a considerable number of veterans from the branch met up with serving members and no doubt exchanged various memories of their past service in various strange places around the world. Acknowledging the work undertaken during its seventy-five years in being, The Chief of Air Staff, Air Chief Marshal Sir Michael Graydon GCB, CBE, ADC, wrote the following note to the Provost Marshal:

'Police work is never easy, but when it involves integration with aircraft operations and their associated support, it places special demands on an individual. The usual contact that the majority of us have with the RAF Police is the corporal, wearing a white hat, smartly performing control of entry duties at the main gate, a function which so often provides the public with its first impression of our service. But that is only the outward show, as the RAF Police are involved in a great many other activities: the greyer areas of counter-intelligence and counter-espionage; criminal investigation and drug abuse prevention and, perhaps of most importance today, the defence of stations against the scourge of terrorism. All of these activities and many more, have provided commanders at all levels, and throughout the seventy-five years of the history of the Royal Air Force, with a firm basis for security and discipline in the hands of a thoroughly professional police force.

I congratulate the RAF Police on the role they have played over the past seventy-five years, and I have no doubt that they will continue to provide the Royal Air Force with outstanding service in the challenging years ahead'.

In September Squadron leader P Somerville took over both dog training wings and uniquely commanded both RAF and Army personnel. The Dog Training School had ceased to exist and was now in a joint training situation with the Army. The Army, because they had the larger requirement, became the dominant partner in the union. As the years went by and the RAF requirement for dogs shrunk, the RAF involvement would weaken further. One of the nearly early casualties of the merger was the disbandment of the RAF kennel-maid trade. RAF kennel-maids did not have the same trade requirements as their counterparts in the Army, and in 1990 a scheme was suggested that the trade be disbanded. Flight Lieutenant Somerville had travelled to Aldershot to argue their case with the head of the RAVC; Brigadier Parker-Bowles, his overall boss at the time. While he was sympathetic to the argument and cancelled the notion at that time to make any changes, sadly, as the years went by, the RAF kennel-maid trade did get disbanded, which according to Flight Lieutenant Somerville, was a sad end to one of the most professional trades it had been his pleasure to work with over the years.

At the 1993 Annual United Kingdom RAF Police Dog Championship Trials held at RAF Newton, the three winning teams were declared as, Corporal N Millman and Air Dog Casper, A/C S Robbins (USAF) and Air Dog Bruno, and Corporal Shepherd with Air Dog Ben.

In November, Air Commodore Seymour retired as the Provost Marshal after an extremely busy period in office. During his appointment, the Warsaw Pact had collapsed, the Berlin Wall had been dismantled and the *Cold War* had ended. With it came the change in defence policy and the government's '*Options for Change*'. Defence cuts, redundancies and 'value for money studies' had closely followed. It had been in 1967, during his first tour as a Provost Officer that Flying Officer Seymour became one of two flight commanders at RAF Akrotiri in Cyprus where he took over responsibility for the RAF Police Dog Section (comprising some fifty personnel), the RAF Police Auxiliaries and the Mounted Section, while Flying Officer P Milner had responsibility for personnel employed within the RAF Police specialist elements and on general police duties. At that time, Cyprus was relatively quiet and British military personnel were able to visit the entire island without restriction. For Flying Officer Seymour, both his work and his off-duty time were tremendously satisfying, and as he settled into his new career he began to challenge elements of RAF operational thinking. For instance, the dog handlers guarding the armed Vulcan aircraft were themselves armed with a dog and a pistol; it was his contention that should an attack be made on the aircraft, and after all, that is why guards were on duty to prevent such an event, the dog would be an excellent weapon but the pistol would be of little use. As a result of presenting his case, the pistols were withdrawn and sub-machine guns were substituted as a better means of defence.

Air Commodore Seymour was succeeded in post on the 29th November, by Air Commodore J L Uprichard CBE, a pilot, who prior to being promoted and taking up his appointment as the Provost Marshal had been the Station Commander at RAF Waddington in Lincolnshire.

On the 6th May 1994 the Channel Tunnel between Folkestone and Calais was officially opened by HM Queen Elizabeth II and President Mitterrand of France.

On the 14th July, as part of the initiative to further reduce the defence budget, the government released another white paper entitled, 'Front Line First'. In doing so, the Defence Secretary, Malcolm Rifkind, announced yet more cuts to the Armed Forces in an effort to reduce the annual defence budget by a further £750 million. The savings of course, signalled the loss of 18,700 jobs within the three military services and the civil service establishment at the Ministry of Defence. The RAF were hit quite seriously and forced to reduce their manpower by a further 7,500, over a two-year period.

During this period, the use of RAF Police dogs was being closely studied once again and proposals were put forward by the Army to have all RAF Police dogs dual handled in a further effort to reduce the overall costs involved. Unfortunately, that was a practice adopted by the Army and it was being fiercely fought off by the RAF, who despite having their limited number of HPCT dogs dual handled, saw the general concept of dual handling as unsuited to the work of their dogs. In addition, further proposals were also put forward to disestablish the RAF Police Dog Demonstration Team and the trade of Kennel Assistant (The title had been changed when a number of men were recruited). Again, the RAF Police were facing difficult decisions and the Dog Demonstration Team quickly began looking for outside sponsorship to offset its running costs. As you can imagine, over that period, with so much uncertainty about and so many studies being conducted, many RAF personnel wondered what the future would hold for them and those serving in the rank and file of the RAF Police, were certainly no exception.

On a glorious afternoon in August 1994, RAF Newton hosted the 37th and final United Kingdom RAF Police Dog Championship Trials to be held before the planned division of the school sent basic police training to RAF Halton and dog training to Melton Mowbray. The historic event was recorded on film by the BBC, who had been invited to the unit to make a presentation for their '*BBC East Midlands Today*' program. In addition to over two thousand members of the general public who turned up to watch the event, the principle guests of the Provost Marshal were Air-Vice Marshal Sir Timothy and Lady Garden who were invited to present the prizes to the winning teams. At the end of an extremely competitive event, the 1994 winners of the trials were declared as Corporal I Dormund and Air Dog Gundo from RAF Kinloss, followed up by Corporal A Bednall and Air Dog Tia from RAF Aldergrove who took second place and Corporal A M Cameron and Air Dog Bruce from RAF Northolt who took third place.

On the 31st August, after twenty-five years of terrorism and bloodshed in Northern Ireland, the IRA agreed to a permanent cease-fire, in order to be accepted into democratic peace talks with the British government on the future of Northern Ireland. Shortly after, as a measure of good will, their action was mirrored by the Loyalist terror groups and in the weeks which followed, the Province witnessed a calm that had not been felt there for a long time. Additionally, the 'National Security Alert State' on military establishments on the mainland was reduced.

RAF Belize, under the command of the Acting Air Commander, Squadron Leader Adams, officially closed down on the 6th September and the last few remaining British military personnel left the garrison a week later. Operational flying in Belize had finally ceased on the 31st July, after providing a valuable service within the Central American enclave for sixteen years. The Harrier jump jet aircraft had been returned home during July 1993 and they had been followed by the Puma helicopters in August 1994. As a consequence, the RAF Police Flight at Airport Camp had been steadily disbanded, leaving Sergeant P R Baker, who had returned for a second tour of duty, and Corporal P Brand, as the last two remaining RAF Police NCOs serving within the region. Of the four RAF Police dogs serving in Belize, two were transferred to units in Germany and the other two were humanely destroyed after being declared too old and unfit for further service. The withdrawal from Belize highlighted just how quickly the RAF presence around the world was shrinking away.

After maintaining a presence in Berlin for almost fifty years, the American, French and British Forces, finally withdrew from the city, on the 7th September, a week after the Russian Forces had withdrawn and returned home to Russia.

Sadly after forty-five years, during which millions of people had been trilled and excited by their spectacular and professional public performances, the RAF Police Dog Demonstration Team, under the final command of Flying Officer T Flett WRAF, was finally disbanded on the 18th September 1994. Although various attempts had been made to save the team by obtaining private sponsorship, the price set to maintain it at £240,000 per year proved unattractive and no one was willing to take on the commitment. The melancholy occasion was marked a month later at RAF Newton with a reunion, attended by both past and serving members of the team. From that point on, it was intended that all future dog displays given at all major public events, such as the Royal Tournament and the major air displays around the country, would be provided by an operational team of both RAF Police and Army dog handlers from the DAC at Melton Mowbray.

Although the facilities at the DAC were very basic in comparison to those left behind at Newton, the RAF Police dog trainers quickly adjusted to their new surroundings and continued to carry out their established task as best they could. From that point on, RAF Police NCOs who volunteered to become dog handlers were instructed to report to the DAC to undergo the basic dog course. The training was divided into three modules; the first being where the student was instructed in the technique of handling and looking after a fully trained patrol dog. Phase two developed the handler in the important art of teasing or baiting a trained and untrained dog to attack and finally, the last part of the course saw the handler teamed up with his of her new partner; the dog. Qualified handlers who were successfully selected to become either a specialist firearms and explosive search handler or a drug search handler, returned to the DAC to undergo a gruelling sixteen-week course to qualify as a firearms search handler or a ten-week course to become a drug search handler. During firearms and explosives search training the student and the dogs were trained in the technique of safely searching for and recovering weapons, ammunition and explosives. Training for the drug search handlers and the dogs followed a similar pattern and on successful completion of the course the dogs were able to detect the presence of Cannabis, Cocaine, Amphetamines and Heroin. On successful completion of training both specialist dog teams were posted onto the establishment of RAF P&SS regions where their services were heavily in demand.

In January 1995 the DAC at Melton Mowbray announced that for the first time efficiency trials would be held throughout the year for all RAF Police HPCT dogs. It was good news for all HPCT dog handlers who greeted it with considerable enthusiasm because they had previously been excluded from the normal Annual United Kingdom RAF Police Dog Championship Trials.

In 1995, after working with RAF Police dogs for forty years Mr C Gilmore, a civilian dog instructor, retired from his post at RAF Newton shortly before the final elements of dog training merged with the Army at Melton Mowbray. In recognition of his long and faithful civil service he was awarded the Imperial Service Medal shortly after he took up retirement. His long association with RAF Police dogs began in 1953 when he joined the RAF Police as a dog handler serving a five year regular engagement.

On the 1st March, the Chief of Air Staff, announced that after forty years of being protected by the RAF Police, the task of providing the security for the nuclear weapons held by the RAF would be taken over completely by the RAF Regiment by the end of the year. The announcement also indicated that the trade of Kennel Assistant was to be disbanded and on top of that, one hundred and fifty members of the branch were invited to take their redundancy. At that point the establishment of the RAF Police stood at 3,076.

The British Army had been conducting security patrols throughout Northern Ireland for over a quarter of a century in support of law and order but on the 24th March, as the cease-fire continued to hold out throughout the Province, it was decided to cease night-time security patrols within Belfast and certain other areas within the Province. Day-time patrols inside Belfast had been curtailed on the 15th January and there had been no adverse effect on the situation.

In April the RAF Police School moved from RAF Newton, which had been ear marked for closure, and after an absence of some fifty-eight years, returned to its first home at RAF Halton in Buckinghamshire. Again, it underwent a name change from RAF Police School to the Provost & Security Training Squadron and moved into Spreckley Hall, a purpose built instructional block that had been built in 1968 to train RAF apprentices. Unfortunately, for the first time, the general police and the dog training elements of the school were permanently parted.

At the first Annual United Kingdom RAF Police Dog Championship Trials to be held at RAF Halton on the 5th August, the three winning teams were, Corporal A Bednall and Air Dog Tia, Corporal A M Cameron and Air Dog Bruce, and Corporal Booth with Air Dog Banjo.

The author had been stationed at RAF Shawbury in Shropshire as the Senior NCO in charge of the RAF Police since February 1994. Upon taking over his new appointment he had inherited two HPCT dogs that were being dual-handled by four RAF Police NCOs. However, because of staff deficiencies resulting from detachments in support of overseas operations such as the Falkland Islands and the Balkans, problems had been experienced for some time in trying to incorporate the dogs into the normal day to day routine. The NCOs handling the dogs were established for general police duties but were also required to use their dogs at the same time. Unfortunately, with the NCOs rotating during their shift between control of entry duties at the main gate, foot patrols with the Station Guard Force and mobile patrols of the unit, there was little opportunity to use the dogs effectively as part of the already over-stretched team. Additionally, the RAF Police NCOs on duty at Shawbury were required to be armed and dressed in No 2 blue grey working uniform and not combat clothing as normally worn by dog handlers. The dog section was situated off the main base and access to it was along a public road. These two factors presented daily problems: Firstly, whenever the dog handlers were able to work their dogs and that was only when they were on foot patrol for an hour, they had to be disarmed prior to leaving the unit to collect their dogs and rearmed when they came back on the unit, procedures that took time. Likewise, the same procedure had to be carried out when they returned their dog to the dog section before moving onto other duties such as the main gate or mobile patrol. Secondly, the uniforms of the dog handlers when walking their dogs became soiled and covered in dog hair so that by the time they rotated duties onto the main gate they looked anything other than smart. If the dog handlers had been taken off the shift to operate independently then the remainder of the NCOs would not have been able to rotate through the different duties or take rest breaks during a twelve hour shift. These points had been highlighted to Command Headquarters for some time but ignored. Things however, came to a head one day in early 1996 when two staff provost officers from Command Headquarters visited the unit to examine ways of further reducing the strength of the already understaffed RAF Police Flight in line with the defence review 'Front Line First'. Despite strong protests, backed up by a wealth of evidence, it was clear that the two officers were intent on reducing the strength of the Flight by three men before they left and even protests from the Station Commander, failed to win them over. As a parting shot, the author brought up the problem of the HPCT dogs and asked that they be removed from the station so that at least the remaining NCOs could take on the extra anticipated work without having to worry about the welfare of the dogs or trying to incorporate them into the working pattern. Surprisingly, the two staff agreed to their removal and within the week both dogs were transferred to RAF Waddington in Lincolnshire. Although the Flight continued to be understaffed at least the removal of the HPCT dogs reduced the complications thereon after.

At the Annual United Kingdom RAF Police Dog Championship Trials held at RAF Halton on the 3rd August, the three winning teams were judged to be,

Corporal A Bass and Air Dog Khan, Corporal A Bird and Air Dog Rexy, and Corporal Moar with Air Dog Sam.

In the Falkland Islands on Wednesday the 13th November, the RAF Police dog handlers from the Joint Service Police & Security Unit, based at Mount Pleasant airfield completed a 'charity dog walk'. The five NCOs and their dogs walked some thirty-seven miles from their base into Stanley in winds that were gusting up to fifty-five knots. Before starting the walk they had collected over £500 from service personnel at Mount Pleasant. Upon arrival at Stanley they were greeted by some of the children from the local school, and their cheque, for the purchase of a new orthopaedic reclining chair, was presented to the Matron at King Edward's Memorial Hospital.

At the stroke of midnight on the 31st June 1997, amidst a tropical monsoon, United Kingdom officials handed the financially successful colony of Hong Kong back over to the Chinese.

At the RAF Cyprus dog trials held at Episkopi on the 9th October 1997, the three winning teams were declared as Corporal P Simpson and Air Dog Max, Corporal S Joyce and Air Dog Jake, and Corporal G Balmer with Air Dog Jarrec.

Unfortunately, following the transfer of dog training to the DAC at Melton Mowbray and the disbandment of the RAF Police Dog Demonstration Team, it seemed that the overall high-profile of RAF Police dogs had dwindled. Indeed, an annual event where the demonstration team were really missed was of course the Royal Tournament, which had been forced to include civilian dog display teams in the program. Although the struggle continued within the branch to re-establish the team, it seemed that the Provost Marshal, for some unexplained reason, was firmly against the idea. Notwithstanding, individual RAF Police dog handlers and sections around the 'RAF world' continued working hard to enhance the skills of their dogs and indeed, a number of those operational handlers regularly came together, often at short notice, and much to the delight of their audiences, to form semi-official display teams at RAF Open Days and other public events. In addition, many of the displays performed by the dog teams invariably supported events designed to raise urgently needed funds for worthwhile charities around the country. As 1997, drew to a close, a television documentary series was filmed at the DAC, during which a number of RAF Police dog trainers, stationed with the agency, gave an extremely good account of themselves as they demonstrated their professional skills when training dogs in the attack and specialist search roles. Soon after, although not unfortunately at the Royal Tournament, RAF Police dogs featured once again at Earls Court in London in order to promote the 'Good Citizen Dog Scheme', an initiative designed to highlight the benefits of owning and caring for pet dogs. Taking part in the initiative were Corporal P Bass and Air Dog Khan from RAF Honington, Corporal S Nicholas and Air Dog Arnie from RAF Lyneham and Flight Sergeant G Mills and Flight Sergeant R Hoare from the PMDI.

By March 1998, the overall strength of the RAF had been reduced to 10,981 officers (10,056 men and 925 women) and 45,083 other ranks (40,991 men and 4,092 women) making a total regular establishment of 56,064. Consequently, the total establishment of the Provost Branch and RAF Police stood at 162 officers and 2,545 other ranks.

During the same month, the government announced that all nuclear weapons held by the RAF, in the form of *WE-177* free fall nuclear bombs, were to be de-commissioned during the year, leaving Britain's nuclear deterrent entirely in the hands of the Royal Navy and her fleet of submarines.

After months of difficult negotiations at the *'All Party Peace Talks'* on the future of Northern Ireland, an historic agreement was finally reached on Good Friday, the 10th April at Stormont Castle. Although terrorist splinter groups on both sides had tried to disrupt the proceedings, the sixty-five page settlement for peace, drafted by the Chairman; US Senator George Mitchell, was duly agreed and signed by Republicans and Unionists. The historic agreement laid the way for a referendum, which was subsequently held on the 20th May asking the people of both Northern Ireland and Eire to back the proposals and support the peace initiative. The turnout to vote on both sides of the border was impressive and when all the votes were counted the results clearly showed that the majority of Irish people in both Northern Ireland and Eire wholeheartedly supported the peace initiative. As such, the splinter terrorist groups opposed to it were acting outside the support of the mass majority in carrying their struggle on.

At the Annual United Kingdom RAF Police Dog Championship Trials held at RAF Halton in August 1998, Corporal I Smith and Air Dog Roma took first place.

In October Air Commodore Uprichard retired from the RAF after completing thirty-three years service. He was succeeded as the twentieth Provost Marshal by Air Commodore R McConnell, BA, a Provost Officer with twenty-three years service, who prior to taking up the appointment had been the Command Provost & Security Officer at Headquarters Strike Command.

During the period from March until the end of May 1999, RAF Bruggen in Germany was heavily committed to *'Operation Engadine'*, itself a component of *'Operation Allied Force'*; the air campaign against the Serbian regime occupying Kosovo and other targets within Serbia itself. Throughout this period the RAF Police, like the rest of the station were on a war footing and therefore operating to maximum capacity. The RAF Police & Security Squadron, assisted by a vastly increased guard force formed from other service personnel from the unit provided additional security measures to all operation sectors within the large station. Although over the years the station had practised *'going to war'* many times, on that occasion it was done under the full glare of the world's media. Indeed, the station motto was *'During Peace-time our Mission is to Train for War'*. Apparently, the media were keen to see the war being fought from the safety of the perimeter fences. Additionally, the station had also seen frequent demonstrations from anti-war protestors who had tried to block the entrances and disrupt movement in and out of the station. However, with the aid of the German civil police the situation had been contained. Although during the days of the *Cold War*, many exercise missions had been launched from the station, it was the first time in years that real time missions had been launched from a RAF station within Germany. On top of all that was happening, the Station Commander and his Station Security Officer were uncertain about the intentions of some of the 26,000 expatriates from the former Republic of Yugoslavia who were living in that part of Germany. Despite tight security around the station and the heavy workload being carried out by all personnel, Corporal S Cobbett of the RAF Police was on patrol with her dog during the evening of the 24th April, when she noticed smoke coming from the back of a large barrack accommodation block. It was just after 10.30pm, when her investigation confirmed that there was a large fire burning within one wing of the H block single storey building. She immediately raised the alarm, called for assistance and began evacuating personnel from within the building. At the time, the majority of the personnel from the Station Fire Section were fully committed waiting for the return of two tanker refuelling aircraft that had aborted a mission to Kosovo due to bad weather. As such, it meant that only one fire tender with a minimum crew was initially sent to deal with fire. However, Corporal Cobbett was quickly joined by other RAF Police NCOs in the form of; Sergeant S Bowen and Corporal's M Keogh, R Morgan and J Churchill. The evacuation of the building was quickly completed with many of those evacuated, wearing only night-clothes. The RAF Police NCOs made a roll call and although four personnel could not be readily accounted for, their whereabouts were confirmed a short time later. While the fire crew battled to control the blaze, a huge crowd appeared to see what was happening. At that point the RAF Police NCOs were forced to push those they had evacuated and the crowd back to a safe location before setting up a cordon around the area. While they were doing so, it was clear that the fire crew were losing their battle to control the fire, which was spreading to the central portion of the building. As the other firemen were still committed to the arrival of the two aircraft, the local part-time civilian fire service was summoned. In the meantime, the senior fire officer was worried that the petrol tanks of vehicles parked against the building might explode if the fire spread much further. After a hasty discussion, Sergeant Bowen, his team and some volunteers agreed to get them moved. When appeals to the car owners failed to produce keys, the vehicles were forcibly entered and pushed away from the danger zone. Although the fire crew maintained a spray of water over the team during that part of the operation, the team were hampered by the thick billowing smoke and as a result one or two personnel needed to be treated later for the effects of smoke inhalation. Shortly after the vehicles had been moved the aircraft landed safely and reinforcements from the fire section arrived at the scene together with the local civilian fire brigade. With the additional resources at the scene the fire was swiftly brought under control and eventually extinguished, but not before half the building had been destroyed by fire and damaged by the water, while the other half had suffered severe smoke damage. Enquiries carried out by the RAF Police at the scene heard from two witnesses that reported hearing two explosions shortly before the fire crew arrived. Given the high security state of the station at the time, sabotage had to be assumed and so the security alert state was increased and measures were swiftly introduced to search the remainder of the station for any evidence of terrorist activity or improvised explosive devices. It was a long and busy night; not only because of the increased security threat but also in finding additional accommodation and clothes for those affected by the fire but by first light the following morning everything had been achieved. No evidence of terrorist activity had been found and all those made homeless had been placed into alternative accommodation, with many going into the 'spare rooms' of homes occupied by service families. During the subsequent investigation into the cause of the fire carried out by investigators from P&SS (Germany), the RAF Germany Senior Fire Officer and a Fire Investigation Officer from the London Fire Brigade were consulted. It seemed that the fire had started in the communal lounge and had been caused when the metal leg of a television table that was placed on an electrical cable, eventually crushed it and caused a short circuit. The two explosions heard by the witness were apparently the windows within the room being blown out as the fire used up all the oxygen in the room. In respect of their actions at the scene of the fire, Sergeant Bowen and Corporal's Keogh, Morgan, Cobbett, and Churchill each later received a Commendation from the Provost Marshal.

On the 29th June, five RAF Police dogs and their handlers from the recently formed RAF Police (Volunteer) Dog Demonstration Team appeared on the 'Good Morning' television program alongside dozens of show business celebrities in order to raise thousands of pounds for charity. The police dogs, all gifts to the

DAC after starting life as unwanted pets, made their appearance during the *'Get up and Give Appeal'*, to demonstrate the skills which had brought them accolades at the Crufts National Dog Show earlier in the year. The live display, which came from the Thames Embankment in London, helped to raise much needed monies for a number of worthy charities which included; Home Start, National Benevolent Fund for the Aged, Mind, The Cystic Fibrosis Trust and the National Eczema Society.

In July, it was announced by the Ministry of Defence, that after the '1999 Royal Tournament', held at Earls Court between 20th July and the 2nd August, the military tattoo would not be held again. The news brought to an end yet another remarkable and highly popular public military event, which fell victim to the seemingly never-ending defence cuts. It was therefore a fitting tribute that the RAF Police (Volunteer) Dog Demonstration Team appeared once again to thrill the crowds at the last ever show. The team under the command of Flight Lieutenant P Fyfe and assisted by Flight Sergeant R Hoare from the PMDI, comprised; Sergeant M Watson and Sergeant P Bass both from RAF Waddington; Corporals P Barass, D Lane, R Heath, N Lyons, K Moar, S Hancock, B Price, S Parker, B Clifton, M Jackman, T Bird and J Hodgson. The Royal Tournament or *Military Skill at Arms Pageant* as it was originally known, had first been presented to the public in London in 1881. It had been an instant success and during its one hundred and eighteen years, representatives from the four arms of the British Forces along with visiting Empire, Commonwealth and foreign troops had demonstrated their skills to an enthusiastic public. In recent years some of the more memorable displays had included; the Royal Naval Field Gun Team, The Royal Marines Band, The Kings Troop Royal Horse Artillery, The Massed Bands of the British Forces, The RAF Queens Colour Squadron, The Royal Signals Motor-cycle Team and of course the RAF Police Dog Demonstration Team, but to name a few. In addition to the show being staged in the arena, the tournament also played host to a plethora of static military displays, information centres and recruiting stands. During a very emotional final show, a number of prominent people and the public were already calling for the tournament to be saved. However, once again it seemed that the cost of staging the event, both in manpower and financial terms, far outweighed its value in presenting the British Forces to not only the British public but to many thousands of foreign visitors each year.

On Saturday the 11th September, the Annual United Kingdom RAF Police Dog Championship Trials took place at RAF Halton. In glorious sunshine a crowd in excess of five hundred spectators watched the six finalists complete for the title of the *'RAF Police United Kingdom Supreme Champion'*. Although the weather was perfect for the crowd the weather conditions called for patience and understanding from the handlers who needed to keep cool-heads under the hot afternoon sun. The judges, Flight Lieutenant R Irwin and Mr G Elliott, had their work cut out to make any major distinction between the teams. However, while they were working out the results the spectators were entertained by the RAF Hawks free fall parachute team and the RAF Halton Area Band. Finally, a decision was reached and the final outcome was a well-deserved win for Corporal R Parker and Air Dog Gizmo from RAF Waddington. Corporal A Burrell and Air Dog Benito from RAF Brize Norton took second place while Corporal S Shepherd and Air Dog Arnie from RAF Lyneham took third place in the competition. The presentations later that afternoon were made by Lady Bagnall and included prizes to RAF Cottesmore for the best maintained RAF Police dog section; RAF Digby for the best maintained HPCT dog section and RAF Kinloss for the most improved dog section. Individual prizes were awarded to Corporal Shepherd and Air Dog Arnie for the best criminal workout and best wind-scent; Corporal Ackers and Air Dog Chunky for the best night workout; Corporal Barrow and Air Dog Bob for the best arena performance and finally, Corporal Moar and Air Dog Sam for being the most meritorious team.

Down in the Falkland Islands on the 20th October, an unusual event occurred when a RAF Police dog named Duke was promoted to the honorary rank of warrant officer. Previous permission had been granted from the PMDI in the United Kingdom for the promotion to take place. Duke was whelped in February 1988 and entered service with the RAF in October 1989. Following successful completion of his training he was 'posted' to the Falkland Islands in February 1990 where he helped to patrol Mount Pleasant Airfield. After nearly six and a half years employed as a working dog, Duke was retired in June 1996 and became the station mascot. In doing so, he was promoted to the honorary rank of sergeant. However, following sterling public relations within local schools and the local home for senior citizens he was promoted to the rank of flight sergeant in early 1998. In addition, Duke had also helped to raise a considerable amount of money for various charitable causes such as the BBC's 'Children in Need, 'Red Nose Day' and the 'Appeal for Wireless' for the Blind'. Being retired, Duke enjoyed five-star accommodation living within the Sergeants' mess, sharing the quarters assigned to the Senior NCO in charge of the dog section.

Throughout the year, the seventeen RAF Police dog handlers employed at RAF Akrotiri in Cyprus had been hard at work raising money for local charities, one of which was the 'Patient Comfort Fund' for the Princess Mary Hospital. Corporal J Dalton, the man behind the project explained that the dog handlers tried to raise as much money as possible for various worthy causes but when they heard that the hospital was in need of better welfare facilities, they took the matter on as their next charity project. The Princess Mary Hospital at RAF Akrotiri provided medical facilities for all British Forces and their families serving on the island of Cyprus. The *'Patient Comfort Fund'* provided amenities that were not issued to the hospital by the military budget such as televisions, flower vases, pictures and children's toys. During the presentation ceremony at the hospital a cheque for £150 was handed over by Corporal Dalton to the nurse in charge of the fund, Flight Lieutenant N Dyson.

At RAF Waddington on the 2nd March 2000, the RAF Police, including the station's dog handlers, mounted a hasty security operation on the base in preparation for the departure to Chile of General Augusto Pinochet. The eighty-four year old general had been arrested in November 1998 at a London hospital following a request from the Spanish authorities for his extradition to face charges of murder, torture and kidnapping arising from his term as the Chilean leader when any opposition was ruthlessly crushed. During the intervening sixteen months a complicated legal battle had been waged in an effort to challenge the extradition and during that period the general had suffered a stroke and his health had deteriorated to a point where he was deemed unfit to stand trial. Accordingly, the Home Secretary, Jack Straw, allowed him to leave the United Kingdom to return home. Originally, it had been planned that he would leave RAF Brize Norton in a Chilean Air Force aircraft. However, in the final hours before his departure, the media and hostile pressure groups besieged the Oxfordshire base and as a security precaution his aircraft was transferred to RAF Waddington near Lincoln where it took off without interference.

Between the 7th and 8th September, a team from the DAC at Melton Mowbray completed what is believed to be the longest triathlon in England, hence the title of their conquest *'The Ultimate English Triathlon'*. The team comprised two members of the RAF Police; Squadron Leader A Walker and Sergeant D Blundell and four members of the Royal Army Veterinary Corps; Major M Sheriff, Sergeant J Rowlinson, Private J Norwood and Corporal S Todd. The team started their gruelling event just before 0600 hours on the 7th September and completed it shortly after 0600 hours the following morning. First, the team swam across Lake Windermere; England's longest lake measuring 10.5 miles, in five hours thirty-eight minutes. Secondly, they ran to Scafell Pike; England's highest mountain and a twenty-two mile round trip, in five hours and thirty-three minutes. Finally, the team mounted their bicycles and rode to the DAC in Melton Mowbray, a distance of one hundred and ninety-five miles in thirteen hours and thirteen minutes. The six personnel formed three teams for the event and each team was responsible for covering a third of the event. At the time, the weather conditions in the Lake District were described as poor and complications were encountered during the swim when it poured down with rain and then poor visibility on the mountain slowed down the pace of the team. However, the challenge was successfully completed and of course the event raised considerable funds for a charity adopted by the DAC.

The Final phase of the Provost Marshal's United Kingdom Dog Efficiency Competition took place at RAF Halton on the 9th September. Every year the PMDI conduct an inter-station efficiency inspection at all RAF Police dog sections throughout the United Kingdom to identify the very best operational dog teams. The final phase of the exercise is a week-long elimination process to highlight the best six dog teams that will take part in the Annual United Kingdom RAF Police Dog Championship Trials at Halton. After a tiring day of putting their best into the final phase of the competition, the winner of the six teams was declared to be Corporal Devlin and Air Dog Sabre from RAF Honington, while the Inter-station Efficiency Award went to RAF Conningsby and the award of Most Improved Section went to RAF Lossiemouth. The principle guest, Air-Vice Marshal N Sudborough from Headquarters Strike Command, presented the prizes to the winners. Finally, to round the day off, the public audience was treated to a display by the Hawks RAF free fall sport parachute team.

At RAF High Wycombe on the 23rd September, the RAF Police Flight hosted the second 'Annual Pet Dog Efficiency Competition' on the sports field at No1 Site, in aid of the charity, 'Hearing Dogs for Deaf People'. The event started just after lunch and comprised nine teams of dogs and owners of all shapes and sizes. Corporal I Short had devised the successful event the previous year but that year he had organised it into three phases; obedience, obstacles and the long stay. Phase one involved on or off the lead obedience, followed by what was described as a frontal recall and a free exercise. The latter was left to the owners' imagination and on the day, produced tricks ranging from 'giving a paw' to Sergeant A Bednell's German Shepherd dog retrieving a ball from a bucket of water. Phase two was the obstacle phase and comprised a three-foot high jump, a short jump, long jump, plank walk, barrel jump and a window jump. The aim of that phase was to complete the course in the fastest time with points being deducted for owners rather than pets failing to negotiate any obstacles. The most entertaining individual of that phase was Corporal Willis who completed the whole course while his 'borrowed' dog, Stanley, ran around the crowd looking for his real owner. The third phase involved having the dog stay well away from its owner for some time until called forward. The event, judged by Flight Sergeant C Poole, Corporal I Bulloch and Corporal J Blandford, was won by Sergeant Bednell and Tess, with the 'Most Entertaining Trophy' being awarded to Mrs Paula Gullinery and Jake, a six-month old German Shepherd dog. The other teams were Sergeant D Hammond and her Labrador Brandy; Corporal Willis and Stanley, a Staffordshire bull terrier crossbreed; Mrs Jocelyne Tack and her *Hearing Dog for Deaf People*, Bruno; Mrs Karen Bulloch and Collie cross Domino; Corporal J Baird and Collie cross Sparky; Senior Aircraftswoman T Cussell and retired drug detection dog Pepper, and finally Mrs Claire Blandford and Poppy.

On the 29th September, Air Commodore McConnell took up a new appointment at the Ministry of Defence and was replaced as Provost Marshal by Air Commodore C R Morgan RAF, a Provost Officer who, prior to being promoted and taking up his new appointment as the twenty-seventh Provost Marshal, had been the Deputy Provost Marshal and the Officer Commanding HQ P&SS.

At RAF Benson in Oxfordshire on the 9th March 2001, a small handover ceremony marked the entry into service of the RAF's latest support helicopter, the Merlin HC3, operated by a reformed No 28 Squadron. The Merlin was earmarked to complement the hard-working Chinook and Puma helicopters based at RAF Odiham, RAF Benson and RAF Aldergrove in Northern Ireland. So important was the deployment of the Merlin that a RAF Police dog section was specially established at the unit to guard the new asset. One of the initial members of the new section was Corporal(W) A M Barnsdale, who had joined the RAF the year before. Her late grandfather, Corporal G Collick had served with the RAF Police during and just after World War II, and had been stationed for most of that time out in Bangalore in India, where for much of the time he was employed as a police motorcyclist. Prior to being posted into RAF Benson, Corporal Barnsdale had served as a *part-time* HPCT dog handler at RAF Henlow in Bedfordshire, but had yearned to be employed full-time on dog handling duties, hence the move to RAF Benson to work with a fully trained patrol dog.

Three years after the signing of the *'Good Friday Agreement'* in Northern Ireland, peace within the Province seemed in deadlock. Although the IRA declared that it was still committed to a permanent peace, it nevertheless still refused to hand in their weapons.

Corporal S Reynolds and Air Dog Zak from RAF Kinloss scooped the top prize in the Annual United Kingdom RAF Police Dog Championship Trials held at RAF Halton on Saturday the 8th September 2001. The event, which was sponsored by Iams UK Ltd Eukanuba, was contested by the best RAF Police dog teams within the United Kingdom. Twelve competitors battled it out over seven days in exercises covering all aspects of police dog handling. On the final day, they took part in the Agility and Command Competition and criminal work-out phases. Corporal Reynolds and Air Dog Zak, who had only been together for seven months before the competition were crowned overall champions for 2001.

Close behind them came Corporal B Milne and Air Dog Ben from RAF Lossiemouth, who won second place. Finally, Corporal Rae and Air Dog Max, also from RAF Kinloss, won the Agility and Command Trophy.

In America during the morning of the 11th September 2001, Islamic terrorists, thought to be under the control of Osama Bin Laden based in Afghanistan, launched a truly horrific attack in New York and Washington DC, leaving several thousand people dead and many more injured and traumatised. Prior to the attack, four American commercial Boeing airliners had been hi-jacked and two were flown to New York where they were crashed into the twin towers of the World Trade Centre in Manhattan, which eventually collapsed. The two other aircraft had been ordered to attack Washington DC. However, whilst on route, one of them crashed in Shanksville, Pennsylvania, after passengers tried to tackle the hijackers. The other aircraft, however, continued its flight and shortly after the New York attack, crashed into the Pentagon building. It was without doubt the worst suicide attack ever launched by any terrorist organisation and left the world shocked by what had happened.

In Gibraltar on Saturday the 15th September, the RAF Association launched its annual 'Wings Appeal' collection to raise money for a number of charities within the colony. In order to help raise money for the appeal, members of the Joint Provost & Security Unit Dog Section decided to undertake a sponsored dog walk from the top of the famous rock down into the Piazza in the town below. In addition, authority was granted for members of the section to give a police dog demonstration to members of the public who had gathered in the Piazza to watch the event. Some of the RAF Police personnel who took part in the walk and the public display included; Corporal N Street, Corporal P Tyrer and Corporal(W) H Murphy. In all, at the end of the day £2,900 was raised by the section, which was later distributed to the RAFA Wings Appeal and to the St Bernadette Occupational Day Centre which provided therapy for mentally and physically handicapped people.

American and British forces commenced 'Operation Enduring Freedom' on the 7th October, and launched massive raids against Al Qaida terrorist and Taliban targets within Afghanistan. During the initial stages of the strike, cruise missiles, launched from British submarines were sent into what was described by American President George W Bush, as the 'War against Terrorism'.

The Northern Area Voluntary RAF Police Dog Display Team raised just over £1,200 for charity and covered over 1,500 miles travelling to various venues around Scotland during the 2001 Summer dog display season. The money raised was divided between the Moray McMillan Hospice Appeal and the RAF Association. Being the only RAF display team of any type based in Scotland, the

Northern Area Voluntary RAF Police Dog Display Team continued to be popular and in huge demand.

In January 2002 as part of the *'Provost 2000 Strategy'*, the Provost Marshal announced major changes to the future role of the RAF Police, in which he envisaged the police trade concentrating more on policing and specialist security duties rather than routine guarding commitments. The policy changes, agreed by the Air Force Board, meant that routine armed guarding of RAF units would be carried out by all RAF personnel up to the rank of corporal, with the newly developed Military Provost Guard Service (MPGS) taking over many of the routine guarding duties that had for many years been performed by RAF Police NCOs. It was further announced that over the following two years, the establishment of the RAF Police trade would be reduced to what was described as *'crisis establishment levels'* using natural wastage and reduced recruiting. The Provost Marshal further stated that there were no plans to make serving personnel redundant and he stated that no individual would normally be required to undertake station guard force duties for more than seven days a year while the security alert state remained normal. Since the early 1960's, the majority of RAF Police NCOs serving on stations, rather than with P&SS, had been largely over-trained as RAF Police NCOs, whilst being mis-employed as extremely smart looking security guards at the RAF stations on which they served. The recently formed MPGS which will take on many of the routine guarding commitments falls within the Provost Branch of the Army Adjutant Generals' Corps. The aim of the MPGS is to rationalise armed guarding arrangements at Defence establishments. They are responsible for maintaining the security of those sites and are expected to carry out the full range of security duties to the highest professional standards. MPGS duties are varied and include controlling entry and exit to sites, operating control rooms and guardrooms to ensure that all visitors are properly identified and dealt with correctly and efficiently. They are expected to carry out routine patrols of the site perimeter and take any action necessary to maintain the security of the site. All MPGS soldiers are trained to a high standard at the Adjutant Generals' Corps Training Centre, Worthy Down in Winchester, where regardless of their background, they all receive the knowledge and skills they need to be able to operate effectively as part of a small but very important team, respected by their military and civilian counterparts. The security element of the week-long initial training course provides MPGS soldiers with instructions regarding powers of arrest, powers of search, the use of force, patrolling techniques, incident handling and accounting for security equipment. Additionally, the recruits are taught how to operate within the control room, how to process telephone calls as well as receiving instruction on the importance of maintaining notebooks, occurrence reports and security registers. Depending upon the site requirements, there are opportunities for suitable MPGS soldiers to train as dog handlers at the in DAC Melton Mowbray.

On the 8th February, the British Defence Secretary, Mr Geoffery Hoon, stated that the British Armed forces were stretched to the limit and urgently needed more resources if they were to engage more fully in world-wide military operations. He went on to say that the forces were operating at the limit of their capabilities and it was important that it was recognised that there was a limit to what they could achieve. While it was vitally important to respond to catastrophic humanitarian problems, there was only so much that a country the size of Britain could manage with limited resources. He added that if Britain was going to engage more fully in the world then obviously it would need the resources to achieve that that goal.

It was mainly thanks to the recently introduced 'RAF Pets' Passport Scheme', that Air Dogs Oscar and Ferdie were enjoying international success in bringing to justice drug offenders from as far away as the Falkland Islands. The scheme meant that Corporal(W) V Lyons, working with her two dogs; Oscar, a German short haired pointer, and Ferdie, an English Springer spaniel, could deploy for the first time in 2002 to the South Atlantic to pursue their human quarry and return without the dogs having to undergo six months quarantine. Following a gruelling eighteen-hour, 8,000-mile military flight both dogs were soon on duty at military sites, as well as assisting local police, customs and immigration officials with searches of civilians. Flights in a Sea King helicopter to remote settlements, a trip in a motor launch to cruise ships outside Stanley's harbour, and scaling a dirty rope ladder up to the deck of a Spanish trawler, ensured that their work was far from the normal routine that Corporal Lyons and her four-legged colleagues were used to in the United Kingdom. Each dog was a specialist in its own right; Oscar detects drugs in clothing and baggage, while Ferdie is trained to search premises. Following their successful deployment, plans were in hand to use the team to conduct similar operations at other overseas locations that had, up until the introduction of the scheme, been free from the threat of drug detection dogs suddenly turning up to conduct searches for illegal drugs.

The British Defence Secretary announced details of 'Operation Veritas' on the 18th March, which entailed dispatching a Commando Battle Group to work with American, Canadian and Coalition forces from seventeen other countries carrying out operations against remaining pockets of Al Qaida and Taliban resistance in Afghanistan. In addition, he announced that the International Security Assistance Force (ISAF) would be deployed to assist the new Afghan Interim Authority in providing security and stability within the capital of Kabul.

During the year, at the age of nine, Air Dog JB, a jet black German Shepherd dog, hence the initials JB, serving at RAF Lossiemouth and handled by Corporal B Marshall, was retired from operational service to become the new pet in the Marshall household. He had originally been donated to the RAF by the Battersea Dogs Home in 1994, and during his service had attained second place in the Annual United Kingdom RAF Police Dog Championship Trials of 2000. However, during the last years of his service Air Dog JB had featured a number of times in the limelight as the station's official mascot. He appeared on live national television in November 2000, when he performed on the BBC program, 'Children in Need Appeal'. He was also introduced to HRH Prince Michael of Kent during a Royal visit to the station. In his capacity as the Patron of the Battersea Dogs Home, the Prince was delighted to see that one of the refuge's former dogs had made such a successful transition.

During the summer, the American President, George W Bush, had called for world support in helping him to eliminate the Iraqi leader Saddam Hussein, who he warned was manufacturing weapons of mass destruction including a possible nuclear weapon. It was, he said, clear that the Iraqi leader posed a very real threat to world security and millions of lives could be at stake if positive and urgent action was not taken to remove Saddam Hussein and his regime from power and destroy their arsenal.

Following studies designed to produce the best trained multi-use dogs and handlers working within the British Armed Forces, the DAC issued a statement during the year to explain to senior military officers just what they could expect from the Service Police Dog (SPD). The brief started off by explaining that the SPD was not a 'super-dog' designed to solve every unit's policing problems, but was a multi-functional police dog trained to aid crime reduction and crime prevention. Indeed, the SPD was described as a highly trained specialist animal to be placed alongside those dogs trained to detect drugs, explosives and weapons and as such, was not to be employed merely as a patrol dog to be used on general security duties or static guarding.

As a tracker and under favourable conditions, the SPD could be used to follow the scent of a person for up to three miles and three hours after that person had left the scene. In doing so, the handler would introduce the dog to the area where the person was last seen or known to be and the dog would pick up on the freshest human scent. In searching, the SPD has two capabilities; property location and person location. In respect of locating property, the handler, using the wind to his favour, uses his dog to search a defined area to locate property that has been discarded or indeed hidden. In doing so, the dog will indicate to the handler the scent of any property foreign to the area being searched. Although the SPD could under those circumstances indicate the presence of drugs, weapons or explosives that is only because they are classified as *'foreign'* and not because the dog has been specially trained to detect them. As SPD's are trained to retrieve located items, it remains important that they are not used specifically to look for explosives or drugs, and under such circumstances the assistance of specialist dog teams should be sought. In respect of locating people, the dog will search, unleashed, any building or outside area to locate and indicate the presence of anyone in hiding. As they have been trained not to bite under those conditions the SPD may be used to search for a lost child or an injured person. Should criminal offenders become aggressive towards the handler then the SPD will react to protect the handler.

Although the SPD may be used to apprehend criminal offenders in the same way as patrol dogs, they have many additional safety features trained into them in order to keep the handler out of court. These features include; the dog stopping without command when released to apprehend an escaping offender and the offender surrenders. Under such circumstances the dog will sit in front of the stationary offender or rotate around him to *contain* him until the handler arrives. If the offender continues to flee or becomes aggressive then the dog will resume his attack. Should the handler release his dog to apprehend a fleeing person and then realises that he has made a mistake then the dog has been trained upon command from the handler to either lie down or return to him; the important part is that the dog breaks off from the chase. The same command can be used if for some reason the dog decides to start a chase. The SPD may also be used effectively to control a crowd or to separate a fighting mob. In such a scenario the dog is allowed to work on a long leash and will, whilst working, bark aggressively at the crowd to gain their attention. Should the crowd fail to disperse or continue to be aggressive then the dog will bite them. Finally, the efficiency of all SPD's in service with the RAF will be assessed each year by the PMDI to remain operational and licensed for use.

At RAF Lossiemouth in Scotland Air Dog Ben, handled by Corporal Pratt, was given hero status when he helped to save the life of a local civilian dog that had ingested rat poison. On the 10th September, Sergeant P Barrass the Senior NCO in charge of the RAF Police dog section, had answered an emergency call from his local veterinary surgeon, Mr J Donald, who urgently needed canine blood to save the life of a three-year-old working Border Collie owned by a local farmer. Seven-year-old Ben was chosen and after being sedated, 300ml of blood was drawn from his jugular vein and transfused straight into 'Mac' the dying patient, who responded so well that he went home the next day and continued to make a full recovery. Just twenty-four hours later his blood brother and saviour, Ben, described by his handler as a totally reliable and wonderful animal, was back on duty and seemed none the worse from his life saving ordeal. After a few more days, Mac, having made a full recovery, was also back at work on the farm at Nairn, near RAF Lossiemouth. The DAC had acquired Ben some years before from the Battersea Dogs Home, where he could easily have found himself on death row if he had remained unwanted. Although it was reported in the local press that Air Dog Ben had made military history in becoming the first canine blood donor in the RAF, that was not in fact correct because in 1964, a similar case occurred at the dog section at RAF Khomasker in Aden, which at the time was under the control of Sergeant B Darnell. It occurred when the blood count of Air Dog Barron, handled by Corporal N Mason, was found to be dangerously low and under the direction of veterinary surgeon, M R Sadic Ali, he was given a blood transfusion directly into his spleen from another RAF Police dog, Air Dog Jessie, handled at the time by Corporal R W Cobham.

On Saturday the 11th September, RAF Halton again played host to the Annual United Kingdom's RAF Police Dog Championship Trials. On what turned out to be a warm sunny afternoon, Corporal Morgan and Air Dog Sam from RAF Brize Norton were declared Supreme Champions and top RAF Police Dog Team for 2002. At the conclusion of the prize ceremony the assembled crowd was treated to a fly past by a Lancaster bomber and a spitfire from the RAF Battle of Britain Memorial Flight.

On the 1st February 2003, the American space shuttle *Columbia* exploded about ninety kilometres over central Texas as it re-entered the earth's atmosphere, killing all seven members of the crew. The shuttle was returning to earth after a successful sixteen-day mission in space carrying out experiments and re-supplying the International Space Station. Sadly, it was the second such tragedy involving a shuttle; the last being on the 28th January 1986, when *Challenger* exploded shortly after lift-off from Cape Canaveral, killing the entire crew of seven.

At *Harrods*, the Knightsbridge department store on Saturday, the 8th February, the RAF Police went on a recruiting drive with a difference, hoping to attract not men and women into the Service, but more dogs. It seemed that while there was no shortage of dog handlers volunteering to join up, the services were once again experiencing great difficulty in 'recruiting' suitable dogs. Although the DAC found many of its new 'recruits' from individual public donations and the Battersea Dogs' Home, ensuring that the formerly abused and unwanted animals selected, went on to lead a useful role within the services, the supply was not meeting the demands. During the event, four service police dogs and their handlers spent the day in the store's pet section meeting shoppers and telling them all about the canine career opportunities on offer to donated pets. In doing so, the team of four hoped to recruit German Shepherd dog types to train as patrol dogs, and gun dog breeds to be trained to detect arms, explosives and drugs.

On the 25th February, a group of fifteen children from Belarus visited RAF Lyneham as part of a four-week 'respite' holiday. The children's visit to Wiltshire was sponsored by the Mid Wiltshire (Devizes) Link of the Chernobyl Children's Life Line. The charity provided respite care for children aged between eleven and twelve from Belarus, who following the Chernobyl nuclear power station disaster, were constantly exposed to the dangers of radiation. The time that the children spend in Wiltshire in a clean environment, enhanced their immune system, reduced the level of radiation in their bodies, and gave them hope for the future. Their visit began with a trip to see the RAF Police dogs in action. They were able to see a police dog in pursuit of a simulated intruder and afterwards they watched the dogs demonstrating their skills of obedience and agility. The visit to the dog section was followed by a visit to the Fire Section and a look around one of the new C130J Hercules transport aircraft stationed at the unit. At the end of the successful visit all the children left the RAF base with huge smiles on their faces that said it all.

As a continuing theme, the staff of the RAF Police dog section at RAF Cottesmore saw themselves committed to a number of charity projects within their local area. The previous year RAF Cottesmore had hosted the Provost Marshal's Central Region dog trials and dog teams from the unit had been awarded the first and second prize. The overall winners had been Corporal P Harwood and two year old Air Dog Buster who had been teamed together for five months, and Corporal K Wilson and Air Dog Harley who had clinched the second place. The annual regional dog trials are designed to encourage handlers to aim for the highest operational standards and they are assessed on their ability to conduct a night wind-scent patrol, detect and of course apprehend intruders. Additionally, they are assessed in the arena for obedience, distance control, speak on command, article retrieval, the stay exercise and finally a series of agility exercises. Every dimension of the dogs' working life is put to the test with the winning teams been chosen to compete in the Annual United Kingdom Dog Championship Trials held at RAF Halton. For a number of years the section had been providing a 'boarding kennel' service to the dogs of all service personnel stationed at the unit and the larger portion of the modest charges made from the facility had been donated to charitable causes. One of the charities supported in 2003 was the *'Sue Ryder Care Centre and Hospice'*, situated at Thorpe Hall in Peterborough. The charity had been established in 1953, to help people with life limiting illnesses and to improving the quality of life they had left. In 2003 the charity had over four hundred shops and eighteen care centres operating throughout the country. Thorpe Hall had twenty-two beds offering specialist 'in-patient' care for the terminally ill as well as operating a day care centre with special facilities for another sixty patients per week who were suffering from neurological illnesses such as Parkinson's Disease and Multiple Sclerosis. As part of their charitable work, Corporal's M Pratt, D McDonagh and C Hebden, together with their police dogs; Sam, Buster and Harley visited the hospice to greet members of the staff and the patients, but they also found time during their visit to present a cheque to the hospice for £250; the sum raised by the RAF Police dog section during the year for the centre and hospice. The first port of call for the three RAF Police NCOs and their dogs was to the Day Care Centre where the patients were given the chance to meet the team, the dogs and to ask various questions about the work of the RAF Police dog. After a busy session the team moved into the wards to meet some of the residential patients with whom they chatted and answered many more questions concerning their work and the training of the dogs. Although the patients were very ill the visit certainly managed to cheer them up and one patient even managed to play a game of 'fetch' with Air Dog Sam for a while. After spending just over an hour within the wards the team moved outside into the extensive gardens of Thorpe Hall in order to present the cheque on behalf of everyone at the RAF Cottesmore RAF Police dog section to Miss Judith Jacklin, the centre's corporate fund raiser.

On the 20th March American and British forces launched a number of air strikes on targets around Baghdad and in the south of the country to prepare for a full stage military invasion of Iraq to oust Saddam Hussein and destroy his weapons of mass destruction. In particular, on the 21st March, strikes were launched on targets where intelligence sources thought that high-ranking Iraqi officials, including Saddam Hussein, were holding a briefing. Although the target areas were extensively damaged, it seemed that Saddam Hussein had survived.

Continuing their charity work, the RAF Police dog section at RAF Cottesmore had for many years been making donations to, and helping out at the 'Leicester Animal Aid', a pet rescue centre at Huncote that had been founded by Dorothea Farndon in 1956. During their association with the centre, RAF Police dog handlers had helped to provide kennels, a free-run compound and other essential equipment. Additionally, the handlers had also helped to construct new facilities and in some cases demolish others that were no longer required. On the 8th June Corporal's M Pratt, P Compton and D McDonagh together with their dogs; Sam, Igor and Buster made their way to the Huncote centre to participate in their 'Open Day'. Their first duty of the day saw them assisting local radio presenter Dale Neil from *Radio Leicester* in opening the new 'Intake Block', a facility that provided twenty indoor kennels with under floor heating, a food preparation area and a veterinary dispensary. Afterwards, Corporal Pratt and Air Dog Sam entertained the assembled crowd to a display of obedience and agility and that was followed by Corporal's McDonagh and Compton, playing the part of the criminal, and Air Dog Buster showing the spectators just how effective the RAF Police dog teams were in apprehending any would-be criminal. At the end of the display and a very active day out, the three RAF Police NCOs were able to present dog food, toys and equipment to the value of £350 to the centre.

On the 19th April, after securing the Baghdad International Airport to the west of the capital, American forces entered Baghdad and faced only light opposition. In the main, the population of the city came out onto the streets to welcome the Americans and the liberation after years of oppression under the *'Saddam Regime'*. During the hours that followed, the population, confident that Saddam Hussein and his henchmen were no longer a threat, started to demolish and deface the statues and posters of their former leader and began looting former government buildings. Although pockets of resistance continued to be encountered around the city, the American moved in quickly to eliminate them before making plans to move further north to liberate other key towns. By the end of April, Coalition forces were established in Iraq and began the process of trying to restore order and government. While British forces were mainly deployed in Basra and around the south, the Americans were deployed in Baghdad and throughout the rest of the country. Although it was not certain whether Saddam Hussein and his top aides had escaped or had been killed a number of other former people on the American *'wanted list'* had been captured. In addition, the search for the weapons of mass destruction, allegedly held by Saddam Hussein continued throughout the country.

On the 13th August, four members of the RAF Police based at the DAC Melton Mowbray were presented with medals by the Commandant, Colonel D A McDonald RAVC. While Corporal A Reynolds and Corporal T Penman were awarded RAF Long Service & Good Conduct Medals, Corporal M Thompson and Corporal M Moscrop received the Air Operations Iraq Medal for their recent service in Kuwait. At the time, although dog training was firmly under the control of the Royal Army Veterinary Corps, there were still twenty-eight members of the RAF Police based at the DAC, working in every department of the Canine Division. The three senior officers; Squadron Leader A Schollar, his deputy, Flight Lieutenant D Pascoe and Warrant Officer K Dowers were employed within the unit headquarters, while Flight Sergeant G Mills held the post of Senior NCO in charge of Specialist Training. Sergeant O Lloyd held the post of

Senior NCO in charge of training Drug Detection Search (DDS) Dogs, Sergeant P Penman held the post of Senior NCO in charge of training the Armament & Explosives Search (AES) dogs, Sergeant K Moar held the post of Senior NCO in charge of the QPD2 Training Cell and, Sergeant P Barrass held the post of Senior NCO in charge of the Dog Procurement Cell. The remainder of the junior NCOs were employed on various aspects of training dogs and dog handlers at the DAC. The newly designed QPD2 (Qualified Police Dog Handler 2) course, originally set up by Sergeant D Brooks and Corporal Moscrop, was intended to produce and maintain a pool of high quality and experienced dog trainers, and in doing so, the course also produced highly trained patrol dogs, which invariably ended up serving with the RAF Police. The intensive six-week course was designed to enhance the students' knowledge of dog handling and training techniques and in doing so, each student was required to train two untrained dogs to the basic pass-out standard demanded of a patrol dog. The pressure started on the very first day of the course when each student was required to take and pass a theory examination covering basic dog handling duties and the role of a Practical Training Assistant (*The criminal*). If the students successfully passed the initial test then they remained with the course but if they failed they were returned to their unit. Those that remained however, were required to take and pass further theory progress tests that were set each week by their training supervisors. The first NCOs to successfully pass the QPD2 course were; Corporal M Berry, Corporal N Ward, Corporal C Jones and Corporal N Heron.

On Saturday 6th September, RAF Halton was again the venue for the Annual United Kingdom RAF Police Dog Championship Trials. On what turned out to be an afternoon of sun and heavy showers, Corporal S Reynolds and Air Dog Darren from RAF Lossiemouth were declared, Supreme Champions and top RAF Police Dog Team for 2003, by the judges, Warrant Officer J Day and Flight Sergeant K Philipson. In the 2001 competition, Corporal S Reynolds, then serving at RAF Kinloss, and Air Dog Zak had clinched the championship but sadly Zak died a few months later. Unfortunately during the prize ceremony the weather suddenly changed and it poured down with rain sending the assembled crowd of spectators running in every direction in search of shelter.

Sadly, in November, former Corporal Robert Mackaye Bruce, who had served in the RAF Police as a dog handler between 1950 and 1955 and then had been a civilian instructor for a few more years at the RAF Police Dog Training School, passed away in hospital after being ill for many months, and was cremated on the 13th November at the Horsham St Faith Crematorium. At the time of his death he was a member of the RAF Police Association, and his comrades at the Norfolk Branch of the RAFPA decided to ensure that his association with the

RAF would not go unnoticed. Consequently, as the funeral cortege arrived at the crematorium there was a dramatic *'fly past'* by two USAF F15 fighter aircraft from RAF Lakenheath. Under the guidance of Sergeant G Owen, the coffin was then taken into the crematorium by a RAF Police bearer party comprising Corporal's Kinzel, Wilson, Thomas, Smith and Bunyan, all volunteers from RAF Honington. As the coffin was taken into the crematorium it passed the RAF Police guard of honour comprising Corporal Hutchinson and Air Dog Wolf, assisted by Corporal's Hargest and Dickson from the RAF Police dog section at RAF Marham. During the service the lesson, Psalm 103, was read by Norfolk Branch RAF Police Association Vice-Chairman Doug Stott, suitably dressed in Scottish national dress, and letters were read out from various dog trainers and friends who had known. After the service as the cortege left to view the floral tributes, a Jaguar aircraft from RAF Coltishall, piloted by Squadron Leader I Smith, flew over and went into reheat, and flew straight up into the clouds. In short, Robert Mackaye Bruce, described by those who knew him as an *'extremely nice man'*, and someone who could apparently trace his lineage back to that other famous *'Robert Bruce'*, was given quite a send off.

Commemorations around the world on the 17th December, marked the first century of flight by fixed wing aircraft. Exactly one hundred years before in America, two brothers, Wilbur and Orville Wright, made a successful flight in a *'heavier than air'* flying machine called the *Kitty Hawk*.

At the beginning of 2004 the most distant RAF Police dog section in the *'RAF world'* was still located at Mount Pleasant Airfield on the bleak and windswept Falkland Islands some 8,000 miles away from the United Kingdom. At the time, the fourteen man section, located on that isolated outpost in the South Atlantic Ocean, was under the tight control of Sergeant R May, assisted by Corporal S Coopey. The dog handlers, like almost everyone else serving on the islands, served a four-month detached tour of duty away from their home unit, and for those who were married the tour was *'unaccompanied'*. Given the islands close proximity to Antarctica the weather each day could be foul; even during the summer months on the Falkland Islands all four seasons could be experienced in any given day. As such, the weather conditions that the dog handlers have to cope with whilst training and working can be fairly rough. Of the thirteen German Shepherd dogs on strength, one is a Service Police Dog (SPD), trained to search, track and deal with a number of special problems, while the others are security patrol dogs. The role of the RAF Police dog section at Mount Pleasant was to; conduct security patrols of the airfield and its operational assets, provide a specialist dog team to assist with searching, tracking and public order, and, provide assistance to the British Force Commander during times of conflict. In

October, Corporal A Ackers and his two drug detection search dogs; Luther and Mel, visited the islands for a month and carried out a significant number of drug detection searches. In November, members of the section together with their dogs organised a special dog demonstration for the residents of Stanley, located some thirty-five miles away from the base. The display of what the dogs were capable of doing was a huge success and certainly helped to develop public relations on the islands. Soon after, Corporal A Garnett and Air Dog Tyson a SPD, were called to assist at an incident that had developed in one of the many bars on the unit at Mount Pleasant. Although the RAF Police managed to calm the situation fairly quickly, one drunken individual decided not to do as instructed and lunged at Corporal Garnett and Tyson. Not surprisingly, Tyson reacted to defend his handler and in doing so bit the assailant. At the time, the other members of the dog section included; Corporal's C MacGinley, P King, S Thorpe, M Miles, L Armstrong, P M D Flint, T Blandford, C Cullen, P Taylor, N Furniss, and L Farmer.

In February Air Commodore C R Morgan retired as Provost Marshal and was succeeded in post by Air Commodore P J Drissell MA BSc, a RAF Regiment officer, who prior to taking up his post on promotion had been the Deputy Director Defence Resources and Plans at the Ministry of Defence.

On the 11th March, *Al Qaida* terrorists were believed to have been responsible for detonating bombs on three packed commuter trains in Madrid, which killed over two hundred people and injured more that one thousand two hundred and fifty. The month of March 2004 also marked sixty remarkable years of the RAF Police working with dogs, when as an organisation they had sent the first RAF Police NCOs to be trained as dog handlers whilst negotiations were ongoing to take over the Ministry of Aircraft Production Guard Dog School at Woodfold in Gloucester in the closing days of World War II.

In April, Air Commodore Drissell issued his first Provost Marshal's bulletin to all personnel within the RAF Police branch. One of the key areas he mentioned was of improving the public relations image of the branch, and accordingly went on to say:

'Improved corporate communications will be a key element of my strategy for the coming year. I will be appointing a flight lieutenant to develop a RAF Police corporate communications organisation strategy. The aim will be to cover both internal and external public relations. In the coming year I would wish to see much greater coverage of RAF Police activities in the service media and beyond. I also wish to develop opportunities to improve general awareness of the RAF Police organisation and its considerable achievements, which have gone unsung for far too long. This will require the active involvement of everyone in the RAF

Police if we are to succeed. I will be looking for units and individuals to send us interesting articles and photographs that the media will want to publish. This will require effort and imagination; I see far too many 'team' photographs and too few 'action' photographs that truly capture the imagination. Most would agree that the loss of the RAF Police Dog Demonstration Team through a cost-cutting exercise some years ago deprived us of an excellent public relations tool. Since we lost the permanent team, we have continued dog demonstrations on a part-time voluntary basis. The volunteers have done an outstanding job and I have been immensely impressed by the commitment they have shown, and no less in the tremendous support they have received from station colleagues in providing the essential shift cover to allow the teams to perform. But I feel we could, as a branch, do much more and I wish to improve the profile of the RAF Police dog demonstration teams. I want the teams to be better supported. To that end, I will be looking for a volunteer of wing commander or squadron leader rank, and a deputy, to chair a committee on my behalf to investigate ways of improving the resources and the support given to the dog demonstration teams. They in turn, will be looking for committee members of all ranks. I want to pursue all options to improve support to the teams, including sponsorship, to produce the best possible team that we can'.

The RAF was out in strength at Cornwall's biggest annual public event held at the Royal Cornwall Showground in Wadebridge between the 10th and the 12th June. Visitors to the show saw the RAF in the air, on the ground, at work and at play. The Central Band of the RAF performed each day with thirty five first-class musicians who played extremely well and treated the spectators to a spectacular marching display. On the first day of the show, the *RAF Falcons* parachute display team dropped in to the main arena, but no sooner had they landed when they were whisked off to RAF St Mawgan to board a Hercules C130 aircraft for their next drop into Guernsey. One of the highlights staged in the main arena, which thrilled the spectators was a Volunteer RAF Police Dog Demonstration Team from RAF St Mawgan. Essentially, the display was all about teamwork, trust and understanding between the dog and its handler, and while the underlying task is a serious one, the dogs loved performing before the crowd. During the display the dogs were seen jumping through hoops, negotiating tricky terrain, walking over see-saws and demonstrating their obedience. After the display the specta-tors got the rare chance to get up close to meet the dogs and their handlers.

Also on the 12th June, another Volunteer RAF Police Dog Demonstration Team performed a display for the public at HMS Collingwood, a naval shore establishment located not far from Portsmouth, during the annual 'Naval Field Gun Display Competition'. With the exception of the demonstration team formed by kennel-maids at RAF Debden, in the fifty-eight year history of the RAF Police using dogs for public displays the dog handlers had always been predominantly male, however, appearing at that event was the first 'all female' RAF Police Dog Demonstration Team, comprising five RAF Police NCOs and dogs from RAF Brize Norton and RAF Waddington. The team led by Corporal Lisa Keetley, marched onto a sunny showground at 2.30pm and were immediately met with a huge round of applause from the large crowd that had gathered to see them. During the virtually faultless thirty-minute display every member of the team showed excellent control over their dogs, an achievement that was made all the more difficult by the constant gunfire coming from the field gun competition being staged just two hundred metres away, and the crowd loved them. The other members of the team taking part were Corporal Helen Murphy, Corporal Melanie Miles, Corporal Julie Crole and Corporal Rebecca Pithouse. During the late 1960s a number of experienced RAF Kennel maids at Debden were given permission to form their very own dog demonstration team, which was success-fully used to thrill and entertain the crowds attending summer fetes, galas and charity events that were organised within the local area.

On 21st July The Secretary of State for Defence, Geoffrey Hoon, published a document entitled, 'Delivering Security in a Changing World: Future Capabilities', which described the planned transformation of the British Armed Forces in line with the policy requirements set out in the defence white paper of December 2003. The Government's 'Strategic Defence Review' of 1998 had set out new priorities for Defence and the Armed Forces and had launched a period of further change in force structures, weapons systems and manpower require-ments. However, since that time there had been major developments in the security challenges facing the British forces and their allies and their ability to adapt to change had increasingly dominated the way ministers and military commanders were planning for the future. From the announcement made by the Defence Secretary it was clear that within a few years the RAF would be a much smaller force but one which he felt confident would still be capable of deploying a larger expeditionary force than that used during Operation TELIC, the second Gulf War. As such, it was planned to reduce the trained strength of the RAF from the current level of around 48,500 to 41,000 by the 1st April 2008.

After another year of hard work and planning the Annual United Kingdom RAF Police Dog Championship Trials took place at RAF Halton on Saturday the 4th September. Air Commodore Drissell had taken a personal interest in the dog trials; his first as Provost Marshal, and as such, he had made sure that everything that could be done to make the day a success was in fact carried out. As with every trials competition, the final event was the end of a very long and intricate process to identify the very best. On Monday the 30th August; a bank holiday to most other people, the twelve best dog teams from around the country were invited to RAF Halton to begin the week-long series of tests and assessments which made up the competition. After completing his four year tour of duty with the DAC, Warrant Officer K C Dowers made his way to Halton to assist the two PMDIs; Flight Sergeant K Braddick and Flight Sergeant D Nellist, to assess the teams as they were put through a gruelling series of tests. The process began on Monday afternoon when Warrant Officer Dowers and Flight Sergeant Nellist carried out a full inspection of the assembled dog teams and their equipment. A great deal of work had been done by the competitors in preparing immaculate uniforms and boots. Likewise, their dog equipment had been cleaned, treated and waxed and the dogs themselves were clean and well groomed. After the inspection, each dog handler was questioned on their dogs record of service; the responses were excellent and very few points were deducted.

On Monday evening, the first night phase began and competitors 1 – 6 travelled to RAF Benson with Warrant Officers Dowers, while competitors 7 – 12 went to RAF Bicester with Flight Sergeant Nellist. At Benson, Warrant Officer Dowers hid inside a very large and dark hangar used to store equipment and each dog team was given fifteen minutes to search the hangar, find the man, and deal with him in accordance with the current rules of engagement. Only one team failed in that test, but all the dogs worked feverishly and determinedly to flush out the intruder. Over at Bicester meanwhile, Flight Sergeant Nellist and two PTAs hid themselves in a large open area filled with equipment, and complicated by a great many bushes and undulating ground.

Each dog team was given twenty minutes to search the area in the dark for the armed intruders and deal with the aggressive situation in accordance with the current rules of engagement. At the end of the evening, Flight Sergeant Nellist reported that all the teams worked well with only two failing to complete the test in the allotted time. On Tuesday afternoon all the competitors were tested on the 'Send Away' exercise, which is a demonstration of control and involves the handler sending his dog away to a particular area; a test most handlers on the day achieved successfully. Later that evening all the competitors were tested on the 'Long Stay' exercise, which saw all twelve dogs sitting quite contentedly off the lead waiting for their handlers, who were out of sight for five minutes, to return. The rest of the night was then spent completing the second phase of night tests with competitors 1 – 6 going off to RAF Bicester with Flight Sergeant Nellist and competitors 7 – 12 going off to Benson with Warrant Officer Dowers to complete same tests mentioned during the first phase. Again, all teams worked extremely hard but one team failed to find Warrant Officer Dowers in the hangar in the time allotted and two teams at Bicester failed to finish their exercise in time. After a few hours sleep, all the competitors were taken on Wednesday morning to the airfield at RAF Weston-on-the-Green for the wind-scenting test. An area approximately 250 square metres complete with thick undergrowth, bushes, trees and very uneven ground was used to hide the two PTA criminals, one in possession of a hidden weapon. Following a briefing, each competitor had to explain to Warrant Officer Dowers why and how they would be searching the area, and how their dog would react to a wind borne scent. Using the wind, each team in turn then set about executing their task.

During this phase, Warrant Officer Dowers, an experienced dog handler and trainer with many years service, was amazed by the wind, which changed direction so many times in such short periods, making the task of the competitors extremely challenging. Indeed, one of the teams actually changed his patrol technique four times to achieve his goal. Even though the changing wind direction complicated the test, all the competitors actually coped extremely well with the situation and professional and determined work culminated with all the teams arresting both intruders. With the night work completed, the competitors took advantage on Wednesday evening to relax in the RAF Police Club at RAF Halton, where no doubt the previous three days of tests were analysed in some detail. Thursday was 'Arena Day' the phase where each team was tested on obedience, distance control, speak or retrieve, obstacle course and finally, the criminal work tests. Each phase of the tests was exacting and points were deducted for simple errors such as wide turns, excessive commands, extra bites from over-keen dogs and lack of determination but to name a few. At the end of a very intensive day, Warrant Officer Dowers was able to tally up all the score points, after which he was able to inform the competitors who would fight it out on the final day of the competition to become the RAF Police Champion Dog Team for 2004. Activity on Friday was restricted to final arena preparation and rehearsals for the march-on of all teams for the prize giving ceremony.

The dog trials are steeped in history and just participating in them is reward enough for many dog handlers. Getting through to the final day however, extends that reward into a combination of apprehension and excitement, and winning the event is indeed something very special. The RAF Police dog handler is without doubt one of only a few RAF personnel who can look forward to pitting his or her skills against fellow professionals in open competition, so the long lonely and often cold nights on duty can be dealt with by realising that better may follow with a lot of hard work and determination. On Saturday morning the weather as it had been all week was glorious. The competitors were introduced to the Provost Marshal who, whilst chatting informally, presented each dog handler with a framed Competitors Certificate. Shortly after 2pm and the playing of the National Anthem, the competition, in front of over five hundred spectators, began with Flight Sergeant Braddick marching into the arena with Sergeant K Moar the Arena Steward. Warrant Officer Dowers was joined by Squadron Lear K Prescott, a former RAF Police dog trainer of some repute, and together prepared to judge what they witnessed before them in the arena. First on the program was the Control and Agility Competition and Corporal Hebden and Air Dog Harley, the first team to enter the arena performed high quality heelwork and distance control tests. Harley speaks on command, but came a little unstuck on the combination obstacles and appeared a little jaded in the heat of the afternoon sun. Nonetheless, the team from RAF Cottesmore set a good standard. Next came Corporal S Reynolds and Air Dog Darren from RAF Lossiemouth, followed by Corporal Radcliffe and Air Dog Prince from RAF Waddington, who again presented a good overall performance.

After a short break to prepare the arena for the main competition and the culmination of the week's work, the criminal work-out commenced. First into the arena was Corporal Hitchen and Air Dog Taz who performed very well showing determination and good teamwork in dealing with hostile adversaries. Next came Corporal Curren and Air Dog Deefer. Deefer was exceptionally keen and took considerable effort to control but Corporal Curren being an experienced handler triumphed and the team gave a very good account of themselves. Corporal Reynolds and Air Dog Darren then entered the arena. The reigning champion had lost points throughout the week due to a night-work mishap but their performance in the arena compensated for that and they gave a very good performance. Corporal Crole and Air Dog Taz then gave a solid demonstration of teamwork and procedural accuracy. Corporal Hebden and Air Dog Harley then completed the afternoon's competition. At that point another break was taken and while the arena was prepared for the RAF Police (Volunteer) Dog Demonstration Team, the spectators were entertained by the Amersham Voluntary Band.

After the break, the Dog Demonstration Team under the control of Sergeant Anderson, then worked their normal magic with precise movement and well-rehearsed routines which trilled the audience. Towards the end of the afternoon the competitors marched back into the arena for the awards ceremony and the Provost Marshal gave a short address to the assembled audience and the Principle guest, Mr I C F Andrews the 2nd Permanent Under-Secretary of Defence, before presenting the prizes. For the first time in forty-seven years, the title of RAF Police United Kingdom Champion was awarded to a female and furthermore female dog handlers dominated the 2004 trials in all but two positions. At the end of a very tough competition the United Kingdom Champion was declared as Corporal(W) C Hebden and Air Dog Harley from RAF Cottesmore, while second place was awarded to Corporal(W) J Crole and Air Dog Taz from RAF Brize Norton, and third place was awarded to Corporal S Reynolds and Air Dog Darren from RAF Lossiemouth. In the 'specialist' section of the competition Corporal(W) V Lyons and Air Dog Oscar from P&SS (Northern Region) were declared as the Drug Search Dog Efficiency Winners, while Corporal A Kyte and Air Dog Charlie from Gibraltar were declared as the Armaments and Explosives Search Dog Efficiency Winners. Corporal Ratcliffe and Air Dog Prince from RAF Waddington were declared the winners of the Agility and Control Competition and the best night-work team. Corporal Brown and Air Dog George from RAF Lyneham were declared as the best wind-scenting team and Corporal Strange and Air Dog Jess from RAF Cottesmore were declared the best turned out team. At the end of a very competitive and exciting day, the Provost Marshal stated that for him personally the one thing he had witnessed throughout was the sheer pride and professionalism shown by all the competitors and those supporting the event. The annual dog trials, he said showed the RAF Police at their absolute best and it made him extremely proud to be a part of the organisation. Incidentally, the Champion, Air Dog Harley was originally rescued by the RAF Police from the Battersea Dogs Home in London.

Following on from the Provost Marshal's desire to increase the profile of the RAF Police, selection for the newly structured official RAF Police Dog Demonstration Team (DDT), under the command of Flight Lieutenant T Mayes, took place at RAF Waddington on the 28th and 29th September. As expected, the selection process attracted a considerable amount of interest, with over twenty dog handlers from six units attending. In addition, at least ten other dog handlers expressed their desire to attend but, unfortunately had other service commitments over the period. All those who attended demonstrated considerable professionalism and enthusiasm throughout the selection process, which included interviews and practical dog work, together with affirmed commitment, therefore it was decided that the best way forward was to form a squad. The squad would form the foundation from which it was planned to select individuals for various commitments in 2005, which hopefully would include; Crufts and the Edinburgh Tattoo. The squad would be made up from those attending the selection, those who were unable to attend and any future volunteers. Notwithstanding that, the final team would undoubtedly be selected for events from those who mostly demonstrate their commitment to delivering a professional and polished performance. Unlike the original DDT, the new squad would be made up from operational dog handlers and because they would be dispersed throughout the United Kingdom, four units were identified, which will become centres of excellence from which future training will be co-ordinated. The RAF units concerned are; Brize Norton (Oxfordshire), Waddington (Lincolnshire), Lossiemouth (Scotland) and Aldergrove (Northern Ireland). The DDT manager; Sergeant G Anderson, had been tasked to standardise the training so as to ensure that all of those units would be working in unison.

Supreme Champion – Winner of the UK RAF Police Working Dog Trials Competition in 2001.

Cpl Anna Barnsdale and Air dog Baz; one of many young women
joining the RAF Police to become dog handlers – 2001

A Criminal workout during the 2002 UK RAF Police Working Dog Trials Competition

RAF Police Dog Demonstration Team shortly before being axed in Defence cuts

Each year RAF Police Dog handlers at home and abroad raise a considerable amount of money for a wide array of charitable projects

This is a sight you really do not want to be confronted with!

All Female RAF Police (Volunteer) Dog Demonstration Team – 2004

Cartoon – Recruiting RAF Police dogs.

7. The Lighter Side of Dog Handling

After all the serious aspects of handling RAF Police dogs, I thought that to finish off this remarkable history I would include here a few humorous stories concerning RAF Police dogs and their handlers, or indeed, in some cases their victims. Although this is only a small collection, each and every RAF Police dog handler, and there have been many, can relate a small book in itself, of some of the funnier moments connected with that part of the RAF Police Branch. Some of the names in these stories have been changed to protect the innocent and so as not to cause anyone concerned undue embarrassment. The individual stories are credited with the names of the author.

A RIGHT DOGS DINNER by Stephen R Davies

At a RAF Wyton in Cambridgeshire in 1975 Corporal Davies was teamed up on shift with a senior corporal called 'Ivor'. Ivor wasn't particularly a dog lover but the duty RAF Police patrol was required to check the dog handlers periodically to make sure they were alright. Now, Ivor as the senior patrolman, would always insist on driving the car while Davies was relegated to the passenger seat to man the radio. During the course of the patrol Ivor would drive up to each dog handler in turn, stop the car and lower his window to speak to them. The dog handlers would always stand slightly back from the car, for fear of the dog jumping up and scratching the paintwork on the vehicle. Ivor would then do one of two things; produce and eat his sandwiches, or light up a cigar and blow smoke at the dog. He seemed to take great delight in both these activities, which of course upset the dogs and their handlers. Some time later, Ivor went on annual leave and Davies was entrusted with the vehicle and the patrol. However, on the first night of Ivor's return, he was relegated back to the passengers seat. Off they went on patrol and Mick was one of the dog handlers on duty that particular evening. They approached Mick's designated patrol area and Ivor wound down his window to speak to him, and at the same time, he reached for his sandwich box. He slowly opened the lid and took out a juicy looking salmon sandwich, which he started to eat in a teasing manner. As usual, the dog started to get upset. Ivor smiled, and at that precise moment, a command was issued to the Alsatian dog, and about 89 lbs of hairy beast came rushing into the car, through the open window. Ivor screamed and his sandwiches went everywhere, closely followed by the dog, who quickly gobbled them all up. Davies almost died on the spot with laughter and could only open his door to fall out of the car. The dog followed him and in an instant was back at his master's side, licking his jowls and looking extremely pleased with himself. It took a little while longer however, for Ivor to recover his composure. In the end, Davies was forced to confess that while Ivor had been on leave, he and Mick had worked really hard training the dog to jump into the car through the open window. Ivor, as you can imagine, was not amused, but he didn't tease another police dog after that! Mind you, Davies was constantly reminded about just how expensive salmon was to buy.

AIRBOURNE STUNTS by Stuart McArdle

Stuart was one of the dog handlers on duty late one night at RAF Luqa in Malta when he heard a frantic scream for help coming from the end of the runway. Together with his dog he made his way carefully along the 'active' runway towards the source of the noise and was stunned by the sight before him. A dog handler, a new arrival to the unit, was standing underneath his German Shepherd dog, which was suspended in the air above him. It seemed that the handler had been patrolling the area and had stopped at the end of the runway for a rest and to watch the aircraft coming in to land. Before sitting down on the grass, he had fastened the end of the dog's lead to a pole that was protruding from a metal case and lying parallel to the ground. After a few minutes he heard a ringing sound coming from the box and the pole that was parallel to the ground was suddenly catapulted into the upright position taking his dog with it to a height of about eight feet. The extremely startled dog was left dangling by his lead and collar and all the equally startled handler could do was to get up under the dog to support its weight and prevent it from being choked to death. What the handler had not realised was that the pole to which he had fastened his dog's lead was part of the 'Aircraft Arrester Barrier' (a larger and stronger version of a table tennis net) which was automatically raised when an aircraft landed in order to stop it careering off the runway should its brakes fail. After a few tense minutes the aircraft landed safely, the barrier was lowered again and the dog was quickly unfastened. Although the dog was confused he was unharmed and showed no long-term effects, the handler, on the other hand, was the brunt of many jokes for years afterwards.

TIME FOR WALKIES by Stephen R Davies

Corporal Ade Palmer arrived at RAF Wyton during the baking hot summer of 1975 together with his police dog, Air dog Mick. Both were new to the service, Mick was a recently acquired gift dog, and Ade had just completed his basic police course and the training to become a dog handler. After being at Wyton for a few days, Ade decided to exercise his dog and at the same time explore the local area around the base. It was a particularly hot day when they left the dog section in mid morning, intending to find their way down to a path by the nearby river that would take them through some pretty villages towards Huntingdon. As the hours passed and the temperatures continued to soar, a number of Ade's colleagues began to get worried that he and his dog may have got lost or that something worse had happened. It was pretty hot out there and Ade had not taken any water with him on the walk. Although Mick possessed a good temperament, technically, Ade should not have taken him beyond the bounds of the RAF base. Another hour passed and the search party sent out to look for them returned with no news. At that point it was decided that if they had not reappeared in another fifteen minutes then the boss would have to be told and a full search mounted to find them. With literally minutes to spare, a taxi approached the main gate to the base and there in the front passenger seat was Ade, well in fact, it could have been anybody really, because Air dog Mick, a huge beast, was sitting on his lap looking out towards us. As the pair baled out of the vehicle and Ade paid the fare, we gathered around to find out what had happened. It seemed that they had gone much further than expected and when Ade, and his dog, found themselves too tired to walk back, Ade hailed a taxi and after showing the driver his warrant card, persuaded him to take them back to Wyton. After that, Ade didn't take his dog for another walk beyond the boundary of the base.

THE WHEEL BEARINGS by Stewart McArdle

There was a Vulcan pilot stationed at RAF Waddington in Lincolnshire in the early 1960s who seemed to take great delight in being particularly obnoxious to the RAF Police NCOs who were guarding the armed Vulcan bombers that were on standby 24 hours a day to be launched within 10 minutes if required. Anyway, after just one more incident with that particular pilot, two of the RAF Police dog handlers decided to 'get their own back' on the officer, who owned and drove a mini, which he parked close to the dispersal site. Seeing that no-one was about, the two dog handlers placed some pebbles inside the front hub-caps of his car. Later that evening as the pilot started to drive off he heard a terrible noise coming from his front wheels and quickly stopped to investigate. At that point, one of the dog handlers approached and politely enquired what was wrong. The pilot explained the situation and the dog handler confidently identified the problem as broken wheel bearings. Just as the officer was about to curse, the dog handler explained that by chance one of his colleagues was a former mechanic and that if the officer was to leave his car at the dog section then he would get him to look at it later that night. The officer was elated and readily agreed and was for once quite pleasant. He duly left the car at the dog section and got a colleague to give him a lift home. After he had left the two dog handlers 're-paired' the car by simply removing the pebbles. The following evening, the 'not too intelligent' pilot arrived at the dog section and was delighted to hear that his car had been mended. He duly handed over £20 to the two dog handlers and drove off. As a result of his kind gesture the dog handlers and some of the station policemen who had been given a 'hard time' by the officer, held a party using the money to purchase the beers. During the evening the pilot was toasted many times for his kind gesture. Funnily enough, after that, the pilot didn't seem to be quite as obnoxious to the RAF Police, who after all, were there to guard him, his aircraft and his crew.

'PRINCE VERSES JUSTIN' by Stewart McArdle

At RAF Finningley during HM Queen Elizabeth's Silver Jubilee in 1977, the RAF Police Dog Training School established and manned a display stand, and Corporal S McArdle, accompanied by his dog, Justin the reigning RAF Champion, was detailed to supervise it and to accommodate enquiries from the general public, especially if those enquiries concerned the donation of suitable breeds for RAF service. Some time later two youths came running up to the stand and started shouting and teasing Justin, who despite being the reigning RAF Champion had a very nasty temperament when teased. Accordingly, Corporal McArdle politely but firmly advised them to clear off before they got bitten. At that point a group captain appeared from nowhere and started to reprimand Corporal McArdle. It transpired that the two trouble makers were no less than the royal princes, Andrew and Edward. A little later the matter was brought to the attention of the officer commanding the dog school and again Corporal McArdle was hauled over the coals. In hindsight, perhaps the reprimands may have been worth it if Corporal McArdle had said nothing and had merely let Justin handle the matter by himself.

DOG BITES by Stephen R Davies

At another RAF station in 1976 there was a particularly well trained but friendly dog by the name of Prince. He was the pride and joy of his handler, Paul. Prince was an excellent attack dog who could be trusted to tackle any would-be criminal who got in his way. Anyway, when I say that Prince was very friendly, well he was to almost everyone except to Pete, a fellow RAF Police NCO. For some reason Prince just didn't like Pete and whenever he tried to make friends with him, the dog just turned into a snarling monster. Perhaps it was Pete's red hair that did it, who knows! Anyway, one evening I was on duty as the mobile patrolman and was busy doing my rounds, checking the windows and doors of sections that had closed down for the night. It was a very quiet evening and it hadn't long gone dark. Suddenly my police radio crackled into life and the guardroom staff summoned me with some urgency. I responded and was informed that one of my colleagues, who was on duty in a security post on the airfield had been badly bitten by a stray dog and required immediate assistance. Without further delay, I ran back to my vehicle, started it up and drove quickly to the location concerned. Arriving there a few minutes later I was confronted by Pete who was holding his right arm tightly and there was quite a lot of blood gushing out of it. I quickly tried to stop the bleeding but I wasn't having much success. I asked Pete what had happened and he told me that he had seen a stray dog running around on the airfield. He had called it over and when he had tried to get hold of it, the dog suddenly went wild and bit his arm. Anyway, as I was putting Pete into the car who turned up at the scene, but Paul with Prince, who incidentally seemed quite calm considering that Pete was close by! I must admit, at the time I didn't give it a second thought really. Shortly after, we arrived at the Station Medical Centre and Pete was soon stitched up, jabbed up and out of danger. As serious as the wound was, Pete was quite lucky really, because the dog hadn't punctured the main artery. Anyway, he was back on duty again a few days later and showed no ill effects. Mind you, we never did find the stray dog and although we all suspected Prince, Pete continued to stick with his original story. It's funny though Prince seemed to have that contented look on his face, from that moment on, as if some old score had been truly settled!

It seemed quite ironic at the time but a few days after that incident occurred I was on evening duty again, when I was informed that another one of the dog handlers had been bitten and required assistance. 'Not two in a row', I remembered saying, 'Just think of the paperwork involved'! Anyway, off I went again, trying to steer the car and pull medical pads out of the first aid kit as I drove along. A few minutes later, I arrived at one of the aircraft dispersal areas and quickly spotted the dog handler, 'Freebie', standing there holding his left hand which had blood streaming from it. His dog, Shep, was sitting obediently at his masters' feet, looking up at him in a confused way. Well, the dog seemed calm enough and I asked Freebie if it was alright to approach. Freebie beckoned me forward and I approached him with the first aid kit at the ready. I asked him what had happened and somewhat embarrassed, he told me that his dog had found something, which he had started to chew. Freebie had gone over to the dog to investigate and saw that Shep was holding a squirrel in its jaws. Freebie immediately told the dog to leave it and had pulled the frightened furry animal from the dog's jaws. As a gesture of gratitude, the squirrel had bitten Freebie on the finger before running off, apparently none the worse for his ordeal. Well, I couldn't control my emotions any longer and burst into laughter. It was then that I understood why Shep had been looking at his master in such a confused way!

NAGASAKI DAY by Stephen R Davies

My arrival at Greenham Common on the 9th August 1984, coincided with the women's peace camp's celebration of Nagasaki Day and the peace women, bolstered by reinforcements from around the country, were determined to cause as much disruption as possible. I went out on patrol with one of our young provost officers called Mark. We hadn't been out very long, when we were called to assist with a demonstration that was blocking the main gate. When we arrived a few minutes later we were confronted by lots of ladies lying down in the road, blocking all access to the unit. What made the situation worse was the fact that they were all completely naked and smeared in their own excrement. As you can imagine, both the MoD and Thames Valley Police were reluctant to handle them in any way. We were told that a 'special squad' of policemen had been called forward to remove them so we sat and waited. After a while, the squad, donning protective clothing, arrived and one by one, the women were lifted and placed into a RAF coach that was parked just inside the unit. The idea being that we would escort it, when full, onto the airfield, where the women would be transferred to waiting, windowless police vans. After a while, all the women were loaded on board and a convoy of police vehicles escorted the coach onto the airfield. As soon as we arrived, the coach pulled onto an empty aircraft dispersal area and the police vehicles were positioned around it to form a cordon. The civil police vans pulled up near by and the senior police officer signalled for transfer to begin. However, as the rear doors to the coach opened, the first woman out was carrying a large clear plastic bag. The bag seemed to have been used as a toilet during the journey and was quite full. It all happened so quickly, but she started to swing the bag around above her head and then hurled it. Everyone took immediate cover. Well, everyone except Colin, one of our dog handlers, who had been using his radio at that precise moment. Unfortunately, he took the full force of the attack and was covered from head to toe in the evil smelling contents of the sack. The women exploded into a loud roar of laughter as our colleague stood stunned and soiled. As you can imagine, when we came to leave nobody wanted Colin to ride in their vehicle.

THE HAMMOCK by Stewart McArdle

One evening at RAF Laarbruch sometime during the summer of 1972, Corporal McArdle who was on duty as one of the dog handlers came across a large piece of canvas whilst on patrol and after meeting up with three other RAF Police dog handlers, decided to construct a hammock on the edge of the pine woods overlooking the large aircraft dispersal area that he and the other three dog handlers were responsible for patrolling. Now, everyone knows that to make a really good hammock the ends need to be spread out for it to hang properly. However, as it was time for Corporal McArdle to go into the security control room for his meal break, he merely tied each end of the canvas to adjacent trees without spreading the ends and told the others not to touch it until he returned. Now, it seemed that one of the other dog handlers was just a little too keen to try out the new hammock and had climbed into it. Unfortunately, the weight of his body once in it had caused the canvas to close up on him trapping him by the neck for almost an hour before Corporal McArdle returned. In fact he was actually 'trapped' for a little longer, while everyone else who was on duty that night got called to the area to witness the spectacle.

THE GHOSTLY HAND by Stephen R Davies

On one RAF station on which I served we had a dog handler who believe it or not, didn't like the dark. That was just a bit strange because the dog handlers mainly worked night shifts. One night he was sent out to patrol the bomb dump; a large area some distance from the main camp area. It wasn't very long before a call for assistance came from that particular area. Apparently, something very strange had been seen floating in one of the emergency water supply reservoirs. When over the radio he was pressed for further details of what he had actually been seen, our poor dog handler, was forced to say that he had spotted what looked like a floating ghostly hand, bobbing up and down in the water. From the tone in his voice, he had obviously been startled by his discovery. We made our way over to the area concerned and found him standing under the sanctuary of an illuminated street lamp. We persuaded him to take us back to the area concerned so that he could show us what he had seen. He was reluctant to do so initially, but had no other choice. When we arrived at the reservoir, there was indeed a hand bopping up and down in the water and it indeed it was glowing like a phantom from the deep, reaching up as if to catch hold of anyone unfortunate enough to be passing by. My colleague and I started to laugh and the dog handler immediately realised that he had been the subject of a rather gruesome practical joke. To make the hand was quite easy really. We had used a 'light tube'

---

that was an emergency source of light used in survival kits. There was a non-toxic chemical contained inside a clear plastic tube, together with a small glass phial containing another chemical. To obtain the glowing light effect the plastic tube was bent in order to break the inner glass phial, which as a result mixed the two chemicals together and made the whole tube glow quite brightly. The light could last for several hours and be seen from quite a distance. We had used a surgical glove and then poured the glowing liquid into it for effect. We then inflated the glove slightly, tied it at the wrist and placed a small weight there to make it bop up and down in the water. It certainly achieved the desired effect that night that's for sure.

THE MASK by Stephen R Davies

During the late 1970's there were some rubber face masks on sale in joke shops. Now, one of those masks looked remarkably like the features of our own Irish Flight Sergeant, Murphy. As soon as I saw the mask, I couldn't believe just how incredible the resemblance was. An idea began to form and so I bought one of them. I took it back to the unit and gave it a slight haircut and then tried it on whilst wearing my beret. It was incredible really. I went to show two colleagues, Billy and Tony and they too thought it was fantastic. That night, I took the mask on duty with me, and as luck had it, I teamed up with Tony on mobile patrol. We set off and our first port of call was to visit all the dog handlers that were on duty at various points around the airfield. As we approached our first target, I put the mask on and replaced my beret. Tony brought the Landrover to a halt and shouted across to the dog handler, telling him that the Flight Sergeant wanted a chat. The dog handler approached to within a safe distance and I took over. From where he was standing it was obvious that the disguise was working. In my best Irish accent, I asked him if everything was okay and he replied that it was and then I asked how his dog was. Again, he replied that it was okay. The deception was obviously working very well and we decided to move on in order to try it out elsewhere. I bid the dog handler a good night and we drove off giggling at the success of our latest joke. We visited all the dog handlers that night, and everyone really thought that I was Murphy. I couldn't quite believe just how successful the prank had been but the best part came later into the shift. As usual, the Flight Sergeant decided to go out and visit his troops on their areas of responsibility and that included all the dog handlers. Well, nothing unusual happened until he was about half way through his rounds. A young dog handler who hadn't been at the unit long innocently remarked that it was unusual to see him twice in one shift. As you can imagine, Murphy was somewhat confused with the remark.

However, instead of investigating further there and then, he returned to the operations room, still looking confused, to ask one of the controllers if he had been out earlier in the night. As Tony and I were in having a tea break at that particular moment we almost died laughing and had to quickly leave again. Because the prank had proved so successful, we played it out a few more times over the following months until the Flight Sergeant finally worked out what was happening. Luckily, he managed to see the funny side of it in the end.

THE SHOOTING CLUB by Michael O'Neill

They were in a state of shock! After countless years of mind numbing security duties, the unit had become declassified in the security sense. The bomber aircraft that the RAF Police had guarded so meticulously and efficiently were pensioned off and their deadly weapons were returned to the United States Air Force. From that point on the unit was officially on a 'Care and Maintenance' footing. Overnight the RAF Police section shrunk from 120 to roughly 25 personnel. However, the administrators of the unit still required airfield patrols to be conducted and the 3 dog handlers were required to patrol the now empty 'bomb dump' and airfield as normal. The station adjutant, who overnight became the commanding officer, thought it would be a jolly good idea to form a shooting club, using the redundant airfield as a sort of private estate. There was always plenty of 'game' about and always had been. The idea seemed extremely viable and so the RAF Police dog handlers were detailed to be the 'gamekeepers' in this exciting new venture and pre-selected parts of the airfield were fed with corn to encourage the 'game' into those areas. The adjutant stipulated that members of his new club would meet on Saturdays for their newly found 'sport'. However, the RAF Police dog handlers' 'big game shooting club', met on the midnight shift, Mondays through to Friday. The method they used was slightly more direct and not unlike being on safari. While one man drove the Landrover around the airfield, his partner would stand up through an opening in the canvas roof and would take the game with his shotgun as it was stunned by the glare of the headlights on full beam. Hares, rabbits, partridge, and pheasants were easy prey and a local butcher paid fair prices for the haul so the midnight safaris were financially rewarding as well. The adjutant and the rest of the unit shooting club, however, could never really understand the shortage of game when they met on Saturdays!

LOFTY REACTS by Stewart McArdle

It was at a RAF base in Suffolk in 1978, and Sergeant S McArdle was the duty sergeant in charge of the RAF Police shift that were tasked with security at one of Britain's nuclear weapon storage sites. The job was pretty mind bending at the best of times and it fell to the sergeant in charge to keep his men alert and cheerful. Accordingly, from time to time a number of practical jokes were played on certain NCOs, especially new men posted into the unit, which was one way of keeping morale high and attitudes focused. It was also standard practice for the sergeant to initiate a number of 'no notice' security exercises throughout the course of the shift to test the reactions of his men to various incidents. On one occasion, a recently graduated dog handler named 'Lofty', on account of him being six foot seven inches tall, was the victim of the latest prank. It seemed that he had not yet made the adjustment to working night shifts and was prone, when inside taking his breaks, to falling asleep in a chair. It was while he was fast asleep that Sergeant McArdle initiated his 'no notice' exercise. At a given alert signal, every NCO had a defensive position to take up and man as quickly as possible, regardless of where he was in the site or what he was doing. The signal was initiated and everyman reacted as if their very life depended upon it, which in a real security situation it might. Lofty of course, was rudely awoken, leapt out of the chair and was out of the door with lino floor tiles stuck to the soles of his boots; it seems that some prankster had super-glued his boots to the floor as he slept! To his credit though, the fact that his boots had been glued didn't stop him from reacting and he made quite a comical sight as he literally pulled up the tiles and continued to his designated position 'bandy-legged' as if he was wearing snowshoes.

THE NOISE TEST by Jim Henry

During his assessments of potential gift dogs to the RAF, Corporal Henry was required to test the dog's reaction to noise by simulating gunfire. In the later days of his time with the dog collection unit he was issued with a starting pistol, which was ideal for the test. However, he had to be careful where the test was carried out because the noise of a pistol being fired in a closed in space could easily alarm the neighbours never mind the dog. In the early days however, the dog collectors used a homemade cardboard device that was basically a triangle shaped piece of card with a brown paper insert. To make a sharp cracking sound, similar to a gun shot the device had to be swung in a downward motion very quickly. The idea came from a once a sought after gift in a popular children's comic. Unfortunately, it could be extremely embarrassing if for some reason the card was damp; the result would be a rather dull plop. On one occasion Corporal's Henry and Scorer were in Middlesborough inspecting a dog. After the usual questions with the middle aged lady owner of the dog, the two NCOs asked her to fetch the dog outside into her garden so that they could get a better look at it. All was going well but when it came to conducting the noise test they discovered that the 'clapper board' as it was known, was damp and totally useless. Not to be outdone by the setback, Corporal Scorer stated that he could still carry out the test. He instructed the lady to go down to the bottom of her garden with her dog and wait until he instructed her to slowly walk back up the garden path towards the house. The lady did as she was instructed and on Corporal Scorer's command she and the dog walked back up towards the house. At that point, the two NCOs had positioned themselves behind the garden shed, which the lady had to walk past on her way up to the house. Corporal Scorer's idea for the noise test was to make use of two galvanised dustbin lids, which he had picked up ready for when the lady and her dog came past. Of course, she was totally unaware of what the test comprised and as she and the dog approached Corporal Scorer suddenly leapt out in front of them, swung both lids together and made one hell of a bang. The noise was so loud and so sudden that even Corporal Henry jumped out of his skin and he knew what was happening. Hardly surprising, the lady screamed and staggered back against the shed, dropping the dog's lead and the last they saw of the dog was him leaping over the neighbours fence followed by the next fence until he was out in the street. It took a little while for the lady to recover her composure and a lot of effort from the two NCOs to control their laughter. After a while the dog was returned to the house by a young boy, but was subsequently rejected by Corporal Scorer for being noise shy.

'FIRST AID' by Stewart McArdle

It was during late 1966 and the RAF Police Dog Demonstration Team were giving the half time entertainment during a first division match football match. At the time, the sergeant in charge of the team was a bit of a worrier, especially when things were not going smoothly. So you can imagine just how upset he was when he learned that one of the dog handlers had left his white ankle gaiters at home. The sergeant was even more concerned that day because the officer commanding the dog school was attending the match as a guest of the management. At the time, Corporal S McArdle was a member of the team and it was him who came up with the bright idea of using four inch white bandages from the first aid box. The sergeant, seeing a way around the problem, readily agreed and soon after Corporal McArdle wrapped the bandages around his colleagues' ankles. When he had finished the effect was quite good and given the distance between the pitch and the stands nobody would know the difference. At the appropriate time the team marched smartly onto the pitch and began their demonstration. Everything was going fine until the bandages started to come undone as the dog handler wearing them ran up and down the line of obstacles. Things then degenerated as the NCO got all tangled up and tripped over the streaming bandages. Of course, that was it, the rest of the team burst into laughter and their uncontrollable laughter brought the display swiftly to a halt. Both the sergeant and the commanding officer were not at all pleased that afternoon and as a result the team spent much of that weekend painting lots of display equipment.

MAN'S BEST FRIEND by Barrie Dove

There has always been a friendly rivalry between RAF Police 'station cops' and 'dog handlers' in one form or another. It's also true that dog handlers never miss an opportunity to show off the skills and intelligence of their four legged friends – and so the tail begins …. pardon the pun!

During my second tour of duty as a dog handler in Norfolk I teamed up with a grand old pooch called 'Lucky Jim'. He had already served for several years and was willing and able to perform a variety of tricks. It was customary for dog handlers to take their break in the guardroom, where the dogs were confined in a room at the back with a bowl of water and the odd sausage etc. On one occasion the duty station cop mentioned that earlier in the evening a mouse had appeared in the guardroom, searched around for a while and then disappeared again. He then proposed setting a trap for the mouse by propping up a waste bin with a pencil on a string and placing a piece of cheese under the bin as bait, and added that Lucky Jim would not be quick enough to catch the trapped mouse once the bin was lifted up. The challenge was accepted and the trap was set up. Sure enough after a few minutes, the mouse reappeared and headed straight for the bait. At that moment the pencil was pulled clear trapping the mouse within. Lucky Jim was brought into the guardroom and shown the bin and told to watch it. All the signs were there, ears erect and pointing forward – total concentration! As the bin was lifted clear the command 'get him' was issued, whereupon Lucky Jim dived forward and gobbled up the cheese as he watched the mouse dart away back into his hole. The station cop of course almost fell off his chair laughing. However, I quickly recovered and said 'How's that then for intelligence, Lucky Jim knew instinctively that the cheese was more nutritious than a mouse'. On reflection, perhaps the title of this story should have been 'Mouse's Best friend'.

HAVE DOG ... WILL TRAVEL by Jim Henry

Travelling by train with a RAF Police dog was made more difficult when you had to cross London to reach Liverpool Street station for the onward journey to Audley End, the local rail station for RAF Debden, which was then the RAF Police Dog Training School. It could be a daunting experience for a dog having to be escorted through the London Underground, however, most seemed to cope well with the experience. Officially, under such circumstances, RAF Police dog handlers could request transport to cross London by telephoning RAF Movements who would despatch a vehicle to convey the handler and his dog to Liverpool Street. However, there was always a delay so Corporal Jim Henry generally never bothered them and made the journey under his own stream.

However, his method backfired on him on one such occasion when he arrived at the Underground station to find that the lifts were out of order. Under the circumstances there was nothing he could do but use the nearby escalator. Of courses, the safety regulations in force called for all animals to be carried by their owners. Although Jim's dog was quite willing to get on and off the tube trains, being carried up the escalator proved to be another matter. Additionally, Jim was more than a little concerned about having to step onto the escalator carrying his 85lb friend.

For a moment he considered going back and calling for assistance from the RAF Movements Unit but then dismissed the idea, picked up his dog and stepped onto the moving staircase. The dog seemed to be handling the situation well until they were about half way up and then he decided that the escalator wasn't for him. For the rest of the journey, which seemed a whole lot longer than it really was, he and the dog wrestled each other in the confusion. Not surprisingly, other travellers going up the escalator gave the pair a very wide berth, while those travelling down on the opposite side were entertained by the sight of a uniformed RAF Police NCO trying to prevent his squirming dog from trying to rip Jim's left ear off. It certainly provided the travellers with something a little more exciting than having to read the boring publicity posters on the walls as they passed. Eventually, the pair made it to the top without serious incident and after dusting himself off, Corporal Henry and his dog continued on their way as if nothing whatsoever had happened.

THE BANK RUN by Pip Waller

Corporal Waller and his dog Tarzan where stationed at RAF Finningley in 1961. It was a regular occurrence for the RAF Police to be called upon to act as escorts for the unit accounts officer when he made his weekly trip out to the bank in

Doncaster to collect the unit payroll. So, on this particular occasion, Corporal Waller and his dog were detailed to assist and because they were going into town it meant that Tarzan was given a good grooming beforehand while Corporal Waller put on his best uniform. Before they left the unit, the accounts officer, briefed the driver and the escorts on the nature of the duty, the security implications should they be attacked, and the fact that being out in the 'public eye' they were to remain smart and professional at all times. Shortly after, they boarded the vehicles and set off for Doncaster. As they drew up outside the bank, the accounts officer and the escorts carried out a visual check to ensure that there was no threat lurking and once satisfied, they left the vehicle and assembled on the pavement. At that point the accounts officer carefully checked his cap and his tie, and quickly brushed down his uniform with his hand before giving the order to enter the bank. Corporal Waller had been briefed to lead the way with his dog and as he did so the rest followed closely behind. It was just as they were entering the bank that poor old Tarzan had a desperate need to evacuate his bowels and did so, on the large rug at the entrance. Unfortunately, the accounts officer whose attention was no doubt elsewhere failed to notice in time and promptly walked into the mess. The smell inside the bank, the confusion at the entrance, and the embarrassment of the accounts officer said it all. Needless to say that Corporal Waller and Air dog Tarzan were never detailed for the 'bank run' ever again.

DON'T CRY MA'AM by Stewart McArdle

The RAF Police Dog Demonstration Team were always a firm favourite with the public every year at the Military Tattoo held at Earls Court. In 1964 Corporal S McArdle was on the team and he recalls how the dogs' kennels that year were positioned directly under the stables in the basement. As a consequence of urine from the horses seeping through the wooden floor from above, the dog handlers were regularly having to clean out the kennels. Half way through their stay, the sergeant in charge informed the team that HM the Queen and the Duke of Edinburgh were due to visit the following evening and that he wanted the place cleaned, disinfected and brought up to 'inspection standard'. The RAF had brought in hundreds of gallons of 'Racasan' for use in the chemical toilets and the dog handlers had been using it as a disinfectant. Unfortunately, the use of undiluted Racasan in a confined space had the effect of clearing ones sinuses and making ones eyes water rather badly. So, prior to the Royal visit the handlers gave the kennels a good going over using a considerable amount of undiluted Racasan. When the Queen and Prince Phillip duly arrived it was obvious that too much of the chemical had been used because their eyes were streaming and the

Duke was definitely not a happy man. In addition, it seemed that the sergeant in charge of the team was about to have a stroke.

SO WHAT KEPT YOU THEN? by Stewart McArdle

Corporal S McArdle was serving as a dog handler at RAF Luqa on the island of Malta in 1967. One night shift he walked up onto the airfield with his dog to take over duty from the evening shift dog handler. However, when he arrived at the aircraft dispersal area there was no sign of the man he was about to relieve. He tried to contact him by radio but there was no reply. He searched everywhere but there was no trace of him and by 0030hrs Corporal McArdle was beginning to get worried that something serious may have happened to him. He enlisted some assistance in making another search of the area but neither the dog handler or his dog could be found. After a hectic forty minutes or so, Corporal McArdle sat down on an engine crate to have a drink of water when he had the fright of his life as an eerie groan emanated from the crate. When he finally stopped running, he thought he had better go back to investigate. When he returned to the crate and lifted the lid, the evening shift dog handler, who was laid out like a corpse with his dog lying along side him, simply asked, "So what kept you then".

WHEN RANK AND COMMON SENSE FAIL TO AGREE by Terry Langford

In 1952, the naval shore establishment HMS Grange Fort, in Gosport had a small number of RAF personnel working on the unit, two of whom were RAF Police dog handlers. One of them, Acting Corporal Terry Langford was a National Serviceman and the unit on which he served was close to his home and considered something of a 'cushy' posting. All was well in the world until a naval lieutenant commander approached Terry one day and told him that he had arranged for some senior naval officers to view a demonstration of what the RAF Police dogs could do. The officer was convinced that the deployment of dogs was useful in maintaining security and acting as a deterrent to thieves and anyone else intent on mischief. He was of the opinion that the Royal Navy should have its own patrol dogs and the planned demonstration was apparently his first step in convincing his superiors that dogs were an efficient and cost effective way of providing that service. As such, he instructed Terry to attend with his colleague and their dogs the following day at 1400 hours where they would give the high-ranking visitors a demonstration of tracking. While it all seemed a good idea, Terry attempted to point out to the officer that their dogs were not trackers but were patrol dogs trained to pick up the scent of an intruder in the wind. He further attempted to advise the officer that if he spoke to the commanding officer at the RAF Police Dog Training School and explained what he wanted then they would probably send down a fully trained handler and tracker dog to carry out the demonstration. His well intentioned advice however, was not what the officer wanted to hear and Terry was curtly informed to be ready for the demonstration as ordered. The following afternoon, a large number of very senior naval officers were assembled in an area where they could watch the demonstration close-up and shortly after, the two dog handlers brought their dogs out. At that point a motorcyclist duly arrived towing a dummy and set off into the distance dragging the dummy behind it; the senior officers looked on with great interest. After a suitable delay to allow the dust to settle the order was given to 'track'. Well, Terry set off first, in the direction that the motorcycle had taken, pulling his dog who thought it was playtime. No matter what Terry tried to do he just simply could not get his dog to do something that after all he had not been trained to do. It was a disaster. The other dog handler was given the same instruction and of course it all ended with the same farcical outcome. The lieutenant commander was not a happy man as all eyes turned towards him and he could do nothing to turn the situation around. The senior officers, far from being impressed, started to drift away muttering about the demonstration being a complete waste of their time, while the extremely embarrassed lieutenant commander tried desperately to retrieve something of his professional reputation that was fast disappearing. Years after, Terry firmly believes that the disastrous demonstration that afternoon was probably the single factor that put the Royal Navy right off establishing its own patrol dog section. As for the lieutenant commander, well, Terry has no idea if he was ever promoted.

BEWARE OF LOW FLYING AIRCRAFT by Gordon Smith

In 1958 Acting Corporal Gordon Smith and Air dog Ranee had just started their shift one evening at RAF Aldergrove and were walking around the perimeter track, heading for their patrol area, when a Shackleton aircraft came in to land, touched down, and then quickly took off again, roaring over the startled dog handler and his dog.

"Gee, thought Corporal Smith, that's exciting", and naturally assumed that the aircraft was practicing 'circuits and bumps' (landing and taking off again). However, at the end of his shift Corporal Smith was ordered to report to the Orderly Officer who gave him a right dressing down for apparently ignoring the 'red light' which in turn caused the Shackleton to abort its landing. Unfortunately, no one had ever told him about red lights on the airfield and he hadn't actually seen a red light anyway.

WOLF by Madge Joseph (nee Chapman)

At Netheravon in the early 1960s one of the dogs at the RAF Police Depot was called Wolf and he was the pride and joy of a bashful young trainee dog handler called 'Mac'. This particular dog had a very unusual party piece. He absolutely adored being groomed, so much so that he used to ejaculate during the process – much to the acute embarrassment of the handler. The kennel maids at the Depot, however, thought it was hilarious and used to take great pleasure in watching this phenomenon and 'taking the micky' out of poor Mac each day. In fact, word used to go around the kennels like wildfire that Mac was about to groom Wolf. It was apparently one of the highlights of the day!

A BRILLIANT SHINE by Madge Joseph (nee Chapman)

At Netheravon in the early 1960s the trainee dog handlers at the RAF Depot suddenly started to ask the WRAF kennel maids for their 'RAF issue' sanitary towels, which apparently were brilliant for cleaning the windows in preparation for the weekly inspections, during the period leading up to the 'annual formal inspection' of the station by the Air Officer Commanding.

At the time of course, the station Supply Officer and his staff had no idea why the WRAF were suddenly going through so many, and being men, were no doubt to embarrassed to ask. I suppose had they plucked up enough courage to ask, the reply they would have received from the kennel maids may well have been something like: "Don't worry, it's just a difficult period we are going through at the moment". Apparently, they were also brilliant for cleaning shoes!

BLOT ON THE LANDSCAPE by Stewart McArdle

Sergeant Stewart McArdle was serving at RAF Marham in early 1983 and he and his team were working really hard to prepare the section for a formal visit by Mr Terry McHaffie the Chief Training Advisor (Dogs) and Flight Sergeant John Watts, the Provost Marshal's Dog Inspector. It was such a high-profile visit that Sergeant McArdle, a man with very high standards, ensured that everything was scrubbed from top to bottom; the kennels, the compounds, the dispensary, the offices … and everything else. After a hard week's work the place was gleaming and in perfect condition.

Although Flight Sergeant Watts was an old friend of Sergeant McArdle from their days together on the Dog Demonstration Team, Sergeant McArdle's pride would not let that compromise presenting an immaculate section for inspection. On the other hand, Flight Sergeant Watts knew just how seriously Sergeant McArdle took his duties as the senior NCO in charge of the dog section.

The day arrived and Mr McHaffie and Flight Sergeant Watts went off to inspect the section. All the handlers had taken their dogs out while the inspection was being carried out. Suddenly there was a shout from Flight Sergeant Watts.

"Sergeant McArdle... what is *that*?" He pointed into a compound where, in the middle, was a great pile of dog excrement.

Flight Sergeant Watts knew what Sergeant McArdle's reaction would be and he was right. He 'blew his top' and went off to find the handler who had failed to notice the mess before the inspection. Eventually, when Sergeant McArdle had cooled down, he returned but as he walked round the corner of the kennels he saw Watts and McHaffie doubled up laughing and holding a plastic pile of dog excrement, purchased from a joke shop.

Although Sergeant McArdle saw the funny side of the joke he did manage to get his own back a little later on when serving in troubled Northern Ireland. Sergeant McArdle was stationed at RAF Aldergrove outside Belfast when Flight Sergeant Watts arrived from the UK to carry out an inspection of RAF Bishops Court. Sergeant McArdle was detailed to meet him at the airport and take him in a van to Bishops Court further north. As soon as Watts entered the van McArdle asked him if he had collected his weapon and flak-jacket from the armoury.

"No," replied Watts.

"Okay," said McArdle, "In that case for your own safety you will have to stay on the floor of the van until we get to Bishops Court".

It was nonsense, of course, but knowing no differently, Watts complied with the request and remained 'glued' to the floor, missing the scenery, as McArdle struggled to control his laughter during the journey.

Oh, revenge is sweet!

Looking to the Future

Now well into the 21st Century, the global commitment of the British Armed Forces in support of United Nations, NATO and European Union operations continues to place heavy demands on all personnel serving within the RAF, irrespective of whether they fly or operate from the ground; the common factor is that they are all in the service to support airborne operations. Ongoing major defence reviews and studies are currently reshaping the British Armed Forces, including the RAF, and the downsizing of the RAF Police will produce a smaller but more professional force in due course; a force able to concentrate on providing fully trained personnel to look after major security and police issues.

The future employment of dogs and the role of RAF Police dog handlers are also being examined in what has been deemed a *'cradle to grave'* study by the Provost Marshal and his team of experts. Additionally, the expansion of the Military Provost Guard Service and the future use of security patrol dogs by that force on defence establishments, including RAF stations, may well take over the bulk of general dog work, leaving the RAF Police and their counterparts, the Royal Military Police, to employ dogs purely for specialised police duties and searching for arms and drugs in a manner employed by the civil police forces. RAF Police support to the force protection of a deployed Air Force during operations and conflict is now standard, but the current use of RAF Police dogs has not yet caught up with that concept and again is currently under review.

During the past sixty years the RAF Police can be proud of some incredible achievements in the training and deployment of their dog teams, and have, during that relatively short time, earned a well-respected reputation around the world. Additionally, many former RAF Police dog handlers and trainers have taken the skills and experiences gained during their service careers into other organisations at home and abroad, such as the civil police, the prison service, customs & excise, animal welfare services, registered charities and the private security industry. Others have gone into business on their own as consultants or have established their own breeding kennels to provide highly-trained dogs to the public, law enforcement agencies, the military, registered charities and private security organisations both at home and abroad. Indeed, if Lieutenant Colonel Baldwin and his original team of trainers were still alive today, I feel sure that they would be delighted and most impressed with the progress made by the Royal Air Force Police and its dogs in such a short time span.

~ THE END ~

But the story continues... so if you were a RAF Police dog-handler or a kennel-maid and you have a story to tell me about RAF Police dogs, then I would be delighted to hear from you. My e-mail address is: steveguida@hotmail.com